Advanced C Programming
for Displays

Advanced C Programming
for Displays

*Character Displays, Windows,
and Keyboards for the UNIX and MS–DOS
Operating Systems*

Marc J. Rochkind

*Advanced Programming Institute, Ltd.
Louisville, Colorado*

Prentice Hall, *Englewood Cliffs, New Jersey   07632*

Library of Congress Cataloging-in-Publication Data

ROCHKIND, MARC J.
  Advanced C Programming for Displays

  Bibliography: p. 319
  1. C (Computer program language) 2. UNIX
(operating system) 3. MS–DOS (Computer operating system)
I. Title.
QA76.73.C15R63 1988   005.4'3   87–18671
ISBN 0–13–010240–7

Cover design: *Lundgren Graphics, Ltd.*
Manufacturing buyer: *Paula Benevento*
Indexer: *Barbara Palumbo*

©1988 by Prentice-Hall, Inc.
A Division of Simon & Schuster
Englewood Cliffs, New Jersey, 07632

UNIX® is a registered trademark of AT & T.
MS–DOS is a trademark of Microsoft.

Prentice Hall Software Series
Brian W. Kernighan, Advisor

Printed in the United States of America

10 9 8 7 6

ISBN 0-13-010240-7 025

PRENTICE-HALL INTERNATIONAL (UK) LIMITED, *London*
PRENTICE-HALL OF AUSTRALIA PTY. LIMITED, *Sydney*
PRENTICE-HALL CANADA INC., *Toronto*
PRENTICE-HALL HISPANOAMERICANA, S.A., *Mexico*
PRENTICE-HALL OF INDIA PRIVATE LIMITED, *New Delhi*
PRENTICE-HALL OF JAPAN, INC., *Tokyo*
SIMON & SCHUSTER ASIA PTE. LTD., *Singapore*
EDITORA PRENTICE-HALL DO BRASIL, LTDA., *Rio de Janeiro*

For Dad and Lea

Contents

Preface

My purpose in writing this book is to help you design C programs that interact with a user via character displays and keyboards. These ubiquitous devices are typified by alphanumeric ASCII time-sharing terminals and by personal computers with integrated screens. It's not hard to program for these; I expect that most readers have already done so, many times. But it is hard to program for them in ways that are modular, portable, and, especially, *fast*.

The techniques and algorithms I've included are the best available for two widely used programming environments: UNIX, in all its versions (AT&T, Xenix, Berkeley), and MS–DOS, for IBM PC–type computers. There's detailed information about both the Curses and Termcap packages on UNIX, and some guidelines to help you decide which to use in different situations. The IBM PC has an extremely fast screen, and I've included all the information you need to use it to its full potential. In 1982, I programmed one of the first IBM PC windowing products, the EDIX screen editor, which is known for its display speed. I've learned a lot since then—the screen editor developed in this book is even faster than EDIX!

This book is organized around layers of abstraction, and, hence, it is best read sequentially, from the beginning, although you can skip most implementation details the first time through. The development goes bottom-up, starting with the abstract objects that can be displayed—*characters*—and their *attributes*. Then the *physical screen*, a matrix of characters, is introduced, with a common interface that has five separate implementations behind it: direct terminal escape sequences, Termcap, Curses, the IBM PC Basic I/O System, and IBM PC memory-mapped video. The physical keyboard comes next, and then a *virtual keyboard* that can be customized for any and all function keys. The next level is *windows*, which allow a single physical screen to be broken up into several smaller, possibly overlapped, rectangular regions. Finally, *virtual screens* are introduced to allow the text behind a window to be of any size at all, even bigger than the physical screen, and to automate scrolling. Tying everything together is a screen editor, which is first programmed to use the physical screen. It's reworked to use windows, and, again, to use virtual screens.

The code for everything is shown in this book, in its entirety, including the lowest-level assembly language programs that deal directly with the IBM PC hardware. I thought about just including the highlights and leaving the details as exercises, but I decided that, since I prefer to read through programs that are complete, perhaps you will, too. After all, the part I consider too mundane to include may be just the part that you want to see. But this doesn't mean that you should feel obligated to read all of the code—there's nearly nine thousand lines of it! You'll probably want to check out a few things that I emphasize in the main text and refer to other parts of the code as your interests dictate. I encourage you to get the programs running on your local system. Any version of UNIX, or any IBM PC–compatible computer, will do. Appendix C tells where you can get the programs in computer-readable form.

I've assumed that you already know C to the extent that you've written a few non-trivial programs in it. If you're rusty, you'll want to keep your favorite C book nearby. You should also know something about the operating system under which you'll be working, either UNIX or MS–DOS. If you've programmed in C in that environment, that's good enough. You don't have to know anything at all about displays and keyboards.

This book can be taken in different ways by readers with different perspectives and goals. For UNIX programmers, it's a book about how to use Termcap and Curses, and how to issue system calls that control and access the keyboard. For IBM PC programmers, it's a book about how to program at the BIOS and display-memory levels, including the difficulties in handling color monitors. For students of C, it's a book about modular programming that contains real, industrial-grade programs, not toy programs made up for a textbook. For readers who want to learn about windows, it's a book that compares different approaches to such systems and gives implementation details on one. Finally, for readers who want some real-world display and keyboard code, it's not a book at all—it's a software package!

I knew when I began this book that its focus on characters, rather than graphics, would raise some eyebrows. My friends kept asking me how my *graphics* book was coming along; I think they doubted there was enough material on characters to even fill a book. Certainly graphics—especially with windows, mice, and so on—are the "in" thing. But I had my reasons for sticking with characters:

1. For low-cost terminals and computers, character displays are much faster than graphics displays, as Chap. 1 will make clear. I've found that I can design a *better* user interface with characters, because I'm free to use multiple windows, help screens, multi-line error messages, drop-down menus, and four-directional scrolling—all without slowing down the user. Graphical displays are sexy-looking, but their sluggishness on any but the fastest computers hampers their usability.

2. Most business systems use terminals connected to a multi-user computer. It's impractical to do graphics on these because the transmission rate isn't nearly fast enough and graphics terminals probably would cost too much. Programs that use only characters are therefore much more portable and, hence, of more commercial value. Unfortunately, from what I've seen, some of this commercial value is lost because the user interfaces on many business systems are abysmal. Perhaps their designers thought you needed a graphics display to do better. I don't believe it, and I hope the techniques presented in this book will give programmers the means to do much better with the equipment they already have.

3. Because character displays are easier to understand, the programs in this book are more readable than they would be if they used graphics. (I'm assuming they would still be *real* programs, not toy ones.) I can show you how windows work, for example, with actual, runnable code. In explaining the algorithms, I've included comments about alternative graphics approaches, so you'll gain insight about graphics displays, too.

4. Finally, nearly every programmer has access to a computer with a character display, so you can try out the programs, and perhaps enhance them, if you want to. No special equipment or software is required. This book can therefore be used as a supplemental text for a course on C programming, operating systems, or user interface design, provided students can use UNIX terminals or PCs for homework assignments.

Several software vendors contributed packages that helped me write this book. The most direct help was provided by the Santa Cruz Operation, whose excellent Xenix System V for the IBM AT was used to debug the programs under UNIX, and by Digital Research, whose GEM Draw was used to make several of the illustrations. GEM was also my first day-in, day-out exposure to a graphics windowing environment and my first opportunity to see if my racquetball skills would help any with a mouse (they didn't, but Space Invaders sure did). Computer time was provided by the University of Colorado Computer Science Department, to check out the code under Berkeley UNIX on a VAX, and by Carl Brandauer of Daemon Associates, for System V on a 3B2. Thanks also go to Blaise Computing for their Asynch Manager, to Metagraphics for their MetaWINDOW library, to Microsoft for Windows, and to Quarterdeck for Desq. These products all contributed to my education in graphics, windows, and the implementation of terminals.

I'd like to thank Jeff Haemer, Augie Hansen, Greg Hidley, Brian Kernighan, and Carol Meier, who reviewed drafts of this book. Augie also contributed the code for the IBM color display (Appendix B). Ken Arnold, the inventor of Curses, graciously took time over lunch one day to explain a few of its mysteries to me.

Finally, I'd like to thank Pat Henry, my editor at Prentice Hall. She's a pleasure to work with, and not only because she never once bugged me about taking twice as long as I was supposed to.

Marc J. Rochkind

Advanced C Programming
for Displays

CHAPTER 1

Basic Concepts

1.1. A Quick Look at Computer Graphics

Computer graphics is, according to [New79], the "creation and manipulation of pictures with the aid of a computer." This definition is certainly general enough, since everything visual coming out of a computer, even text, can be considered to be a "picture." And any input—whatever its form—that affects that output would be included, too. We can narrow the definition by including the adjective *interactive*. This means that there is a human user who is viewing the pictures while they're being produced, and that the user has control over them. By contrast, *passive* computer graphics would apply to output from a plotter, or to computer-generated films. The user watches the output, but can affect it only after the show is over.

The term interactive suggests some additional attributes of the interface between user and computer: The participation of the user is so frequent that there appears to be a conversation going on. Indeed, this conversation, rather than the manipulation of the pictures, may be the entire point, as in the use of icons to copy files. The graphical output must be generated so fast that it can keep up with the running program; a chess game should seem like the real thing, not like postal chess. Finally, a relatively small display area—less than a square yard, say—should be continuously reused and selectively updated. Graphics produced on a scroll of paper, no matter how quickly, does not qualify as interactive.

Conventionally, interactive computer graphics takes place while the user is sitting in front of a rectangular display that the computer can update in fractions of a second. The user types on a keyboard and manipulates some sort of pointing device, frequently a little box with a rolling ball under it called a *mouse* (its connecting wire is its tail). Lots of other arrangements are possible, ranging from scoreboards in stadiums to three-dimensional movie screens that surround the user, but the conventional one will serve our needs in this book.

Many interactive graphics displays can draw any shape at all, including text characters arranged into a rectangular matrix, with each character having the same height and width (that is, no proportional spacing). When this is all we can do on the display, or all we care to do, we refer to it as a *character display*. Another widely used term is *alphanumeric* display.

The only input device dealt with in this book is the keyboard, so the branch of computer graphics that we're concerned with is described by the phrase *interactive character displays and keyboards*. This is a tiny corner of computer graphics, but, for the overwhelming majority of computer users, that's the only corner they ever experience. Probably over 95 percent of computer applications are character-based and take all of their input from the keyboard. The rest of the computer graphics field is growing explosively today, as hardware gets better and cheaper and software gets more competitive and ambitious, but characters and keyboards will dominate for a long time.

We'll call the equipment with which the user physically interacts, consisting of a display and one or more input devices, a *workstation*. We'll use this term to refer to all such setups, not just those that have large graphics displays and powerful CPUs. We could use the word *terminal* instead, but that implies a connection to the main CPU over a communication line. We want a term that also includes displays and input devices that are integrated into the rest of the computer, as on a typical personal computer.

These days, whether a workstation displays characters only or more general graphics as well, depends mostly on how it is used, not on its inherent design. The hardware inside a typical character terminal, for example, can easily handle arbitrary graphics. It's just that the terminal's CPU isn't programmed to handle graphics. To be sure, if it were, other hardware changes might have to be made also, such as adding more memory or speeding up the CPU, but the basic design would remain. Another example illustrating the difficulty of tagging a display as *character* or *graphics* is the IBM PC, which can be either, depending on which mode the display software selects. One more example would be the Apple Macintosh, clearly a graphics computer, running a communications program that makes it a character-based VT−100 terminal. Thinking of it as having a graphics display when it's behaving like this isn't useful at all.

So we should keep in mind that characters are just a stereotyped usage of graphics, not a different technology altogether. Well, then, why write programs that work only with characters? Why not make everything graphics? Here are three reasons:

1. Character-based programs are much simpler than graphics programs because they deal with fewer types of objects (letters, numbers, punctuation marks), which are all of the same size and which can be positioned in a limited number of ways (anywhere on a 25-by-80 grid, say).

2. Character-based programs use less memory and can update the display faster because much less data has to be sent to the display. For example, a 25-by-80 character display can be completely filled by outputting 2000 bytes. To fill the same area with a graphics image might take over 30,000 bytes.[1] Because response time has a great influence on the ease of use of an interactive program, it often turns out that a character-based design is more usable. Graphics interfaces may *look* easy to use, but they're often too sluggish. Another unexpected tradeoff concerns color: On many IBM PC displays, color can be shown only in character mode—high-resolution graphics mode is black and white only.

3. Since practically all interactive displays can display characters, but relatively few can display graphics, a character-based program can be used everywhere. This universality benefits both users and vendors.

We'll try not to draw a gratuitous distinction between characters and graphics in the rest of this introductory chapter, but the remainder of this book deals only with characters.

1.2. A Concrete View of Workstation Hardware

This section reviews hardware for interactive workstations at a fairly low level, from the standpoint of the hardware itself. Naturally, properties of the hardware strongly influence how it is manipulated from programs. But such a low-level view is too confusing to be an effective basis for programming. For example, at the hardware level, CRT and LCD displays are quite different, but the fact that one uses a cathode ray and one uses liquid crystals is completely irrelevant to the programmer. What may be relevant is their comparative sizes, resolutions, speeds, and ability to display colors. In Sec.

---

[1]My bit-mapped IBM PC display is 350 pixels high and 720 pixels across. When it's in character mode, each character occupies a box 14 pixels high and 9 pixels wide. To fill it in graphics mode takes 252,000 bits, or 31,500 bytes.

1.3, we'll view hardware from this more abstract perspective. There's an excellent, up-to-date summary of graphics hardware in [Hea86], on which much of what follows is based. Another recommended reference is [Art85].

1.2.1. Output Devices

An output device for interactive graphics consists of a screen, a controller that drives it, memory in which to store the current image, and an interface to the rest of the computer system. We'll discuss each of these four components separately.

The most common screen in use today is a *cathode ray tube*, better known by its initials, CRT. The inside of the glass at the front of the picture tube is coated with phosphor. When a beam of electrons hits a spot on the screen, that phosphor glows, but not for very long. The beam has to strike the spot often—say, thirty times a second—to keep it glowing. This is called *refreshing* the display. If it isn't refreshed often enough, the display flickers. At a given refresh rate, some kinds of phosphor flicker more than others, depending on their *persistence*. Screens intended primarily for characters have long-persistence phosphors, while screens intended for animation (such as TV sets) have short-persistence phosphors.

Since there's only one beam, it has to move around to cover the entire screen. In a *raster-scan* display, the most common type by far, the screen is organized into rows of points, called a *raster*. A picture is made up of points, so each is a picture element or *pixel*. The beam travels across a row (turning on and off as it goes), then to the next row, and so on until, after the last row, it goes back to the top. To get from one row to another, the beam is turned off and returned to the left edge of the screen, like the carriage return of a typewriter. This is called *horizontal retrace*. Going from the last row back to the top is called *vertical retrace*. Because the CRT's controller is idle, the retrace periods provide opportunities for the display's memory to be accessed by a CPU without interference. We'll exploit this when we program for the IBM PC in Sec. 3.7.

The number of points, or, more precisely, the number of points per linear unit, is called the *resolution*. Low resolution rasters have about 200 pixels vertically and 160 pixels across; high resolution rasters have 1000 or more pixels in each direction. This is a range of 32,000 to 1,000,000 total pixels. For inexpensive personal computers, some typical displays are 350-by-640 (224,000 total) for the IBM PC, and 342-by-512 (175,104) for the Apple Macintosh.

A high resolution display might have about 80 to 100 pixels per inch, depending on the total number of pixels and the physical dimensions of the screen. This may look pretty good, but it's lousy by printing standards, being comparable to a cheap draft-quality dot-matrix printer. A laser printer usually has 300 dots per inch, and a typesetter 1000 or more. The resolution is often higher across than down, so the *aspect ratio* is greater than one. You have to take this into account when drawing; if you don't, circles and squares will be elongated.

To lower the cost of a high-resolution display, it can be scanned at half the normal refresh rate by visiting only every other row on each refresh. This is called *interlacing.*   Unfortunately, this often causes noticeable flicker. Sometimes a so-called high-resolution display has to be operated at a lower resolution in order to avoid interlacing flicker.

Besides raster scanning, the other way to cover the whole screen with only one beam is to move it only to the parts to be lit up (like a pen plotter). This is a *random-scan* display. Because it's best suited for drawing lines, it's also called a *vector* display. Random-scan displays are rarely, if ever, used in modern workstations because raster-scan displays are more general, entirely satisfactory, and cheaper since so many of them are manufactured.

Different types of phosphor glow in different colors. A color screen has dots of red, green, and blue phosphor at each pixel location. There is an electron gun for each color, and a *shadow mask* to help direct the guns to the right dots. The intensity of each gun can be varied, so that the amount of red, green, and blue can be controlled, in order to provide for lots of different colors. At least two bits are needed to describe each pixel on a color CRT, and typically three or four are used. So color requires more memory and more processing.

Other attributes can be controlled by manipulating the electron beam alone; they don't require special phosphors. A pixel will blink if the gun is turned off and on at regular intervals. A pixel's intensity can be varied by adjusting the intensity of the beam. Given a picture made of a group of pixels, such as a character, it can be displayed with white and black reversed (*inverse video*) by inverting the on/off state of its pixels.

An alternative way to keep a phosphor-coated screen glowing, instead of refreshing it repeatedly with a beam of electrons, is to line it with a grid that can hold a charge. The picture is drawn—just once—on this grid with an electron gun, and the grid then controls a second, continuous "flood" stream of electrons that excites the phosphor only where the picture was drawn. This is called a *direct-view storage tube*, or DVST. It can hold a huge, complicated picture without any flicker at all. A DVST can't display color, although that probably is not technically impossible. But its biggest disadvantage is that it can't be selectively erased—the whole screen has to be cleared at once (like an Etch-A-Sketch toy). This disqualifies it as a display for *interactive* graphics in the sense that we have been using the term. DVSTs are random-scanned, not raster-scanned.

Technologies other than CRTs, but which have similar properties, are used in special situations. A *plasma panel* is flat and rugged, so it's ideal for portable computers provided that enough power is available. When it isn't, a *liquid-crystal* display (LCD) is sometimes used, but there has to be lots of ambient light or else the display is almost impossible to read.[2] This problem is alleviated by backlighting the display, but that takes additional power.

Because a refresh CRT has to be refreshed so often, it's impractical to operate the electron beam directly from the application CPU. Instead, this is done by a specialized *controller*. Physically, the controller may be in the same box as the main CPU (as in the IBM PC), or in the same box as the screen (as in a terminal).

A controller may be extremely simple, with just enough smarts to aim the electron gun and turn it on and off at the right times, or it may be a powerful computer in its own right, with its own microprocessor and memory. In fact, it's best to consider the main CPU and the display controller to be two components of a distributed processing system.

Simple controllers can display pixels only, fixed-size characters only, or both. Complex controllers can also draw geometrical shapes, such as circles and lines, and some can display characters in various fonts and sizes. Some implement the Computer Graphics Interface (CGI), a soon-to-be ANSI standard [CGI85]. Some provide a windowing system. Some provide for fill-in-the-blanks forms. The idea is to offload the main CPU by connecting it to a more specialized CPU.

The controller keeps the data it is displaying in local memory to avoid interfering with the application CPU. If the organization of this memory resembles the raster, it is called a *frame buffer*. In a fancier controller, one dealing in higher-level objects, the memory may be organized into a *display list*. This can have whatever structure the controller's programmers dream up, but it does have to provide for flexible modification and rapid access. A controller might have both a display list and a frame buffer.

The application CPU has to communicate with the controller. In a terminal, each is connected to a *communications port*, and they communicate over a hard-wired line, across a network, or with modems and dial-up lines. Lots of different communications protocols can be used: RS–232C, SDLC, X.25, and so on.

The biggest disadvantage of a terminal is that it takes too long to fill the screen, which severely limits the user-interface design techniques that can be used. Drop-down menus and pop-up dialog boxes may be impractical. Sideways scrolling—essential for spreadsheets—may be effectively impossible. It's better to connect the display and the main CPU more intimately. In a personal computer, this is most often done by having them share the frame buffer. Whatever the application writes there is almost instantaneously displayed. Clearly, in this case the organization of the frame buffer must be

---

[2]I wrote a few chapters of this book on a battery-powered "laptop" computer with a 25-by-80 character LCD screen. I solved the lighting problem by working on a picnic table in a mountain park.

known to the application. Typically it's either a matrix of characters and attributes, or a bitmap.

Let's quickly describe the two display systems covered by this book: the IBM PC displays and typical ASCII terminals.

IBM offers several display options for the PC, and other vendors offer even more. Each has the ability to display text (25 rows by 80 columns), and most can display graphics, in varying resolutions. These are the most common arrangements:

1. *IBM Monochrome Display Adapter (MDA).* This displays black and white characters only—no graphics at all. Characters are drawn in a generous 9-by-14 box, and they're exceptionally clear. All eight bits of a byte are used, so 256 characters can be drawn. Besides the ASCII characters, there are foreign characters, line-drawing characters, mathematical characters, and, well, weird characters (known as *dingbats*) such as smiling faces and musical notes. Every character is associated with an attribute byte. Attributes may be blinking, bold (intense), inverse, underlined, or normal, separately or in combination. The other bits of the byte are wasted, but this is because the same memory layout is used for color. The display controller and the main CPU share the frame buffer (it's *memory-mapped*); each can access it at any time, with no interference. The display operates at about 112,000 baud, nearly 100 times faster than a typical 1200-baud dial-up terminal. You have to operate the controller with a particular kind of display commonly called a TTL display.

2. *IBM Color/Graphics Adapter (CGA).* In character mode, this is like the monochrome adapter: It uses the same storage layout, is memory-mapped, displays the same characters, and supports the same attributes except for underlining. That bit and other bits in the attribute byte are used to display colors. There are sixteen foreground colors and eight background colors. In graphics mode, there is a choice of resolutions: 200 pixels high by 320 wide or 640 wide. At the lower resolution, a pixel may be one of four colors; at the higher, the display is black and white.

   In character mode or high-resolution graphics mode, the main CPU and the display controller can't access the frame buffer at the same time, so the CPU has to stay away except during retrace intervals. This hassle is discussed in detail in Sec. 3.7.1.

   You can hook a variety of monitors to the controller, ranging from a TV set to an RGB monitor (so called because its guns respond directly to the red, green, and blue signals generated by the controller). The monitor may not even be in color; it may show only shades of gray. It's not possible for a program to determine what kind of monitor is attached—it has to ask the user, or display colors (or shades) that will always be OK. Few IBM PC application programs deal with this problem well.

When an LCD display is used in an IBM-compatible computer it usually emulates the Color Graphics Adapter, but it can show only black and white—not even shades of gray. Some applications' output, which looks splendid in color, can't even be seen on an LCD.

3. *IBM Enhanced Graphics Adapter (EGA).* This can emulate the other two adapters (MDA and CGA), with the bonus that the CPU can access the frame buffer without interference. It also offers some additional graphics modes. One of these allows graphics on the same display that the monochrome adapter uses (350-by-640 pixels). The others are for color only (200-by-320 or 640, with sixteen colors, and 350-by-640 with sixty-four colors). For color, the EGA uses a special monitor—the standard RGB monitor used with the Color/Graphics Adapter won't work.

4. *Hercules Graphics Adapter (HGA).* Like the EGA, this does graphics on the IBM monochrome monitor, but at a higher resolution, 348-by-720. The HGA also displays text identically to the Monochrome Display Adapter. It can't show color at all, and it can't drive any other types of monitors.

If this list isn't confusing enough, you can look up the other combinations that we haven't listed. At least a half-dozen other controllers are in widespread use, including new 480-by-640 controllers that IBM introduced in 1987. Fortunately, there's much less confusion with characters than with graphics. All of the adapters can display the same characters, and all are 25-by-80.

A typical time-sharing terminal has a 24 or 25 row by 80 column character display and a keyboard. The display can handle at least the ASCII character set, and sometimes non-standard foreign or line-drawing characters, too. It is connected to the application CPU via a hard-wired or dial-up line, operating in *full-duplex*, which means that it can receive and send simultaneously. A character or group of characters is sent from the keyboard as soon as it's typed, without waiting for a line or page to be completed. Usually, each typed character is processed by the host operating system or application program, and a response is displayed before or while the next character is typed. Although the processing load on the communication system and the CPU is heavy, the resulting flexibility is worthwhile.

Only a few display operations are standardized by the ASCII character set: carriage return, line feed, backspace, horizontal tab, and a few others. To allow additional operations, such as scrolling, clearing, moving the cursor, and so on, *escape sequences* can be sent to the terminal. These start with the escape character, to distinguish them from ordinary character sequences. What follows the escape varies from terminal to terminal, making it difficult to program display applications that can be used on different models. An excellent solution to this Tower of Babel is provided by UNIX's Termcap system (developed at the University of California at Berkeley), which is described in detail in Sec. 3.4. There is an ANSI standard for escape sequences, but even those manufacturers who follow it implement features that go beyond the standard, for which they make up their own sequences. So, in effect, it counts as just one additional terminal type to worry about.

Another common terminal design is typified by the IBM 3270 class of terminals. These use IBM's EBCDIC character set, not ASCII. They are designed primarily for forms applications; text editing can be done by treating each line as a field. The application downloads a *mask* which establishes data entry fields on the screen. The user can type only into these fields and use only characters of the appropriate category (letters, digits, and so on). Mistakes can be corrected by moving around on the screen, using local processing only. When the form is complete, the user presses the *enter* key; the data is collected from the fields, arranged into a message, and sent to the application CPU. There are also ASCII terminals that constrain typing to fields in a form, and which allow local editing before anything is transmitted.

Almost all terminals operate at slow (by PC standards) communication speeds, ranging from thirty to 960 characters a second. This speed must be taken into account when designing applications that will run on such terminals. Frequently, attempts to provide a good human interface by displaying menus, dialog boxes, windows, and so forth, just end up irritating the user. This is one reason why steady users of time-sharing systems prefer command-driven interfaces. In Chapter 3, we'll see how the speed of terminals complicates the interface to them, and we'll explore some programming tricks that can help a little.

Graphics terminals, or character terminals with graphics options, also exist. It isn't practical to send bitmaps to a graphics terminal because it takes too long. For example, at 960 bytes per second, it would take about thirty seconds to fill the screen of a 350-by-720 pixel display. A better approach is to interface with the terminal at a higher level using, say, the Computer Graphics Interface. This allows the application to send lines, polygons, circles, text, and other relatively large objects, rather than just bits. Even better, install a microprocessor and some memory in the terminal so it can do most of the graphics processing locally. Applications that are primarily graphics, such as computer aided design (CAD), can run almost entirely in the terminal. But then it's no longer a terminal—it's a diskless personal computer.

We're only concerned with character terminals in this book, and only with the full-duplex, ASCII, character-at-a-time variety.

1.2.2. Input Devices

Most interactive input devices allow you to either push a button or point at
something, either on the screen or on a document next to the workstation.
The obvious button-pushing device is the keyboard, which typically has about
eighty-five buttons and even more combinations of buttons. There are also
one or more buttons on a mouse. Voice input is like button input, too,
because it's used to input either text or commands. Pointing devices are
much more varied; they include mice, joysticks, trackballs, light pens,
graphics tablets, touch-sensitive screens, and even gadgets that you put on
your forehead and aim like a miner's lamp.

Almost all keyboards have most of their buttons laid out in a standard
typewriter-like arrangement usually referred to as QWERTY, although
alphabetic and Dvorak layouts are sometimes used. For entering text, the
layout of these keys doesn't affect the application, any more than, say, the
color of the keyboard does. However, when control-key combinations are
used to simulate function keys, the assignment of keys to functions may be
sensible only with a particular layout. For example, sometimes Control–E,
Control–X, Control–S, and Control–D are used for cursor keys because they
form a diamond pattern on a QWERTY keyboard.

Aside from its typewriter-like part, nearly all keyboards have additional
keys for cursor movement (typically labeled with arrows), editing (such as
Insert, Delete), and generic functions (such as F1, Attention). Because few of
these keys are included in the ASCII standard, and because there are so
many combinations, it isn't possible to handle them all in a 7-bit character
code. Some keyboards use a full eight bits for function keys (giving an
additional 127 codes), but this may make communication difficult because the
high-order bit is frequently tampered with by operating system device
drivers, modems, communication processors, or networks. So it's more
common for a function key to transmit an escape sequence. The application
program then has to deal with the fact that a single keystroke may generate
an arbitrary number of input characters.

There is no standardization whatsoever among keyboards when it comes
to function keys. Consequently, it's hard to design a good user interface that
exploits these nicely labeled keys and, at the same time, is reasonably
portable across keyboards. We'll give a neat solution to this problem in
Chapter 4. An even worse problem, to which we won't give a solution, is that
user manuals and help screens are hard to write when the keys on the
keyboard can vary from user to user. Two approaches are commonly used:
Either refer to keys generically (such as "the [Home] key") and assume the
user has memorized the bindings of the generic names, or forget about everything except ASCII keys. That is, use Control–E whether the terminal has
an up-arrow key or not.

Pointing devices, such as mice, are normally thought of as graphics devices, but they can be used with character displays, too. They are normally linked to a cursor on the screen. This allows the device to be positioned accurately by watching the cursor, instead of going by the physical movement of the device. The CPU can sense the position of the cursor, in terms of row and column coordinates, and what buttons are currently down, if the device has buttons also. Since the cursor always has some position, the application program would waste time sampling it continuously, so usually there's a device driver that monitors the device and provides input only when it's requested. Terminals rarely have pointing devices, although there's no technical reason why. It's probably because existing time-sharing applications seldom use such things as mice, so there's little demand for a pointing device on the part of buyers.

We won't treat pointing devices at all in this book, even though they are widely used with character-based applications, primarily because there just isn't room. What pointing we need to do, such as in the text editor in Chapter 5, we'll do with pushes of the cursor buttons.

1.3. An Abstract View of Workstation Hardware

It's interesting, and perhaps fun, to talk about workstation hardware, but that degree of detail only distracts and confuses when it comes to programming. For programming we need a view that's less concerned with physical properties. We don't usually care *where* a function is performed—in the controller, in the operating system, in a subroutine package—but, rather, what interface is provided. It matters to programmers that a display acts like an array of 8-bit characters, rather than 1-bit pixels, but it seldom matters how the characters are formed from pixels, or whether the character shapes are in ROM or RAM memory. A suitably abstract view leads to more than just portability and maintainability—it leads to sanity.

An abstract display can show a collection of visual *objects*, each at a specified *location* and each with an associated set of *attributes* such as intensity, color, and so on. For the displays we're most concerned with, location is always specified in terms of a rectangular coordinate system, so that each point is specified by a row and column number. Row numbers start at zero at the top of the display and increase downward; columns start at zero at the left and increase rightward. The number of rows and columns determines the number of locations that can be specified for objects, that is, the resolution.

Now we can distinguish between graphics and character displays solely in terms of the objects that can be displayed. For maximum flexibility, an object is a single pixel. Such a display is called a *bitmap* display, but bear in mind that a pixel may require several bits to describe if it can have more attributes than mere existence or nonexistence. As all other objects are made of pixels, this type of display is a superset of the other types. The problem is that so many pixels make the description of the object unwieldy: time-consuming to compute and transform and time-consuming to transmit from the application CPU to the display controller.

If we're willing to trade off flexibility for compactness, we can choose more interesting objects. Because many elements of pictures are—or could be—lines, circles, polygons, and other easily specified geometrical forms, a display that can handle these types of objects can be much easier and faster to deal with. For example, a circle can be described by three integers, two for the center, and one for the radius, for a total of forty-eight bits. A bitmap specification for the same circle may require a thousand bits.

If standard geometrical shapes aren't suitable, the display controller can be designed to take more varied shapes such as electrical resistors, office chairs, eyebrows, spaceships, or whatever. These can be downloaded as bitmaps at the start of processing or stored permanently in the controller. Then they can be referenced as graphical objects via a system of component identification numbers. The controller might be able to enlarge a stored object, rotate it, color it, and so forth.

A character display restricts objects to a set of predefined character shapes, which are either built-in and unchangeable or downloaded as bitmaps when the display is initialized. The most common example of this is a display with 256 possible characters, so that a byte is sufficient to specify one of them. But two or more bytes may be used, in, for example, a display for Chinese characters. A further restriction is that characters can't go just anywhere, but only in designated cells, which are arranged in a rectangular array. A cell may be 8 pixels square, or 7-by-9, or 9-by-14, or whatever the designers prefer, but this needn't affect the programming of the display if rows and columns are interpreted as character positions instead of pixel positions. We therefore refer to a character display as, for example, 25-by-80 characters, not 200-by-640 pixels. This abstraction allows our programs to work right no matter how the characters are drawn.

Rather than give the location of every object, it's faster for an applica-tion program to just specify the location for the first object of a group, with the understanding that the objects will be displayed next to each other. Furthermore, the object at the end of one row is considered to be next to the first object on the next row. Thus, an entire screenful of objects can be specified by simply providing a long array of object identifiers, without any specific row and column numbers at all. This is the case when the connection to the display is via a shared frame buffer. When the connection is via a communication line (that is, the display is a terminal), it's more common to specify a row and column number for every object, or at least for every group of adjacent objects that are transmitted together.

It's a good idea to hide the physical nature of the connection between the application and the display so that the application doesn't know whether it uses shared memory, direct memory access (DMA), a network, a hard-wired line, or a dial-up port. Indeed, the installer may make this decision later, long after the application is programmed. The best abstraction to use, particularly from a C program, is a simple function call, that looks something like this:

```
displayobjects(row, column, objectcount, objectlist, attributelist)
int row, column, objectcount;
OBJECT *objectlist;
ATTRIBUTE *attribute;
```

The variables **objectlist** and **attributelist** are arrays of abstract types, the definition of which is left to your imagination. This function call could be used to display any objects at all, whether pixels, characters, or chess pieces. You'll see a resemblance between this model function and the functions **PSwrite, Wwrite,** and **VSwrite** that we'll introduce later in this book.

Even at this abstract level, a programmer needs to know about a few more properties of the display. How long does it take to display something? This will have a major effect on the design of the user interface. How readable are the objects? This may affect whether the user can, say, proof-read a document on the screen or whether it has to be printed. How many objects can be displayed? The size of the display is of obvious importance. Whatever properties are relevant, they should be stated in abstract terms, so the programmer is not forced to deal with low-level properties like electron-gun retrace intervals, LCD contrast, character-cell size, and so on.

On the input side, another set of abstractions can help shield programmers from confusing details. Each press of a key on a keyboard generates a keystroke, identified by an integer key code. Key codes less than 128 correspond to ASCII codes, which are already sufficiently understood and standardized to be used directly in programs. Codes above 128 are assigned to abstract function keys, using a scheme like this:

```
Cursor up       301
Cursor down     302
Insert          312
    . . .
```

Now, the program can be written to receive a sequence of key codes, and the issue of mapping them to an actual keyboard can be dealt with separately. This *virtual keyboard* is the subject of Chapter 4.

There are other input devices besides keyboards, of course. The Graphical Kernel System [Hop83] defines a nice set of abstractions that seems to cover the spectrum:

Locator   Inputs a position; for example, a mouse moving a cursor.

Pick   Identifies a displayed object; for example, clicking a mouse button
                 while the cursor is on an icon.

Choice   Selects from a set of alternatives; for example, choosing a menu
                 item with the space bar and the return key.

Valuator   Inputs a value; for example, turning a dial.

String   Inputs a line of text; for example, typing on a keyboard.

Stroke   Inputs a sequence of coordinates; for example, drawing on a
                 tablet.

These abstractions allow a huge variety of input devices to be used to their
fullest without cluttering up the program with too many irrelevant details
about any particular device.

   When a pointing device, such as a mouse, is used along with the
keyboard, it can be assigned key codes, too. Perhaps numbers above 1000
would be taken as coordinate values. The problem with this scheme is that
there's no way to specify when the pointer should input a pair of coordinates.
One way is for it to input something only when one of its buttons is pressed
or released (if it has buttons), but that's not sufficient in all cases. A
reasonable arrangement is for the button action to be input as a key code,
and for the program to obtain the coordinates via a separate function call
that can be invoked as often as needed.

   Rather than sticking with just integer key codes, a more general scheme
would replace the keyboard abstraction with an event queue. Now a
keystroke is just one type of input event. (The flexibility of mapping abstract
codes to keyboards would remain.) Other events might be mouse button
actions, mouse movements, window boundary crossings, floppy disk inser-
tions or ejections, time-of-day changes, arrival of interprocess messages, and
so on. Indeed, with an event queue, the application program might be organized like this:

```
while (have_events()) {
    get_event();
    process_event();
}
```

   A clever choice of event types can allow a program to be relatively
independent of the input devices. It may be practical, for example, for the
program to be independent of whether a mouse or cursor keys are used to
point to locations on the screen.

   Because we're concerned only with keyboards in this book, we'll use just
the abstract key code model for input. We won't use an event queue.

We've been focusing on the *physical display*, of which there's only one per workstation, and the objects that can be displayed on it.   Instead of outputting to the physical display, the application can instead output to one of a group of abstractions called *windows*. A window is rectangular, like a physical display, and it can show the same objects.   However, it can be smaller than the physical display, its size can change dynamically, there can be as many windows as the application needs, and they can freely overlap one another.   A window being written to, then, may be partly or entirely obscured, but the application doesn't have to be concerned with that.   When an obscured area is uncovered, the application will be told (via a function call or event) to fix it up, which it must be prepared to do at any time.   An even higher level abstraction is the *virtual screen*. Unlike a window, it can be any size at all, even bigger than the physical screen, and the application never has to repair damaged areas when an overlapped section is uncovered—this is handled automatically. Fig. 1-1 shows the relationship between physical screens, windows, and virtual screens.

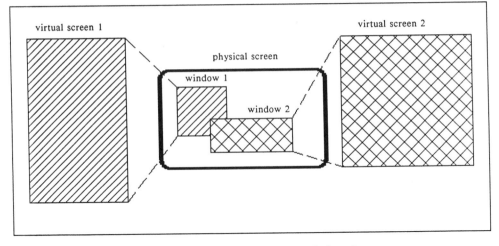

Fig. 1-1. Physical screen, windows, and virtual screens.

The terms window and virtual screen are used differently by different authors, and sometimes other terms are used that mean almost the same thing. What we call a virtual screen is sometimes called a window, and what we call a window may be called a *viewport*. In GKS terminology, a viewport is a region of the physical screen that is referenced by device coordinates (window, to us), and a window is the corresponding rectangle of the entire problem area (virtual screen, to us), referenced by *world* coordinates.   In [Pik83], Rob Pike coins the term *layer* to refer to a window that can be written to asynchronously, without regard to whether it is fully visible. Like a virtual screen, a layer is updated automatically when an obscured part becomes visible, but, unlike a virtual screen, a layer can be no bigger than the physical screen.

Our physical screens, windows, and virtual screens can display characters only, but our definitions of the terms would be the same even if they could display graphics. We were careful to speak in terms of abstract objects, not of characters.

1.4. User Interface Management Systems

The abstraction of virtual screens has removed us considerably from electronic beams scanning phosphor-coated glass. That's as far as this book goes, but that's hardly the limit. There's a lot of commonality in the way windows, virtual screens, and logical input devices are used in typical applications to implement the user interface. Rather than program this each time an application is developed, it's more efficient to interpose an additional layer of abstractions called a *user interface toolkit* or *user interface management system* (UIMS). This layer implements a collection of general-purpose tools that handle common mechanisms such as:

1. *Menus.* These allow the user to issue commands by choosing from a list instead of typing commands from memory. Types of menus in widespread use are drop-down or pull-down menus that descend from a menu bar at the top of the screen or window, pop-up menus that appear at the cursor, and horizontal menus that appear in one or two rows at the top or bottom of the screen.

2. *In-line editing.* An editing tool handles common typing tasks that may involve input and correction of text, such as entering data in a field of a form or specifying a file name. If it's sufficiently flexible, it could also be used as a component of a text editor or word processor.

3. *Prompts.* A prompting tool displays a sentence or so of instructions to the user and then requests textual input, using the editing tool. Usually a prompt box appears on the screen and then disappears again when the input is complete or when the activity has been canceled. A simple form of prompting is a yes-or-no question, such as, "File exists– OK to overwrite?"

4. *Alerts.* An alert tool displays a message to the user, usually in a pop-up box. To ensure that the message won't be ignored, the user must hit a key or click with the mouse on an OK icon to make the box go away.

5. *Controls.* A control tool allows the user to specify options by using a variety of mechanisms such as sliding pointers, dials, check lists, and so on. Typical uses would be to select page layout characteristics for printing or to choose modem options for a communications program.

6. *Help.* A help system gives the user online access to reference material that has been organized specifically for use during the running of the program. It should be integrated with the rest of the UIMS tools so that requests for help are handled automatically. The application designers still have to write the help text, of course.

7. *Printing.* A printing tool supervises all printing activity, whether from word processors, report generators, or drawing programs. Ideally, print jobs can be queued for printing in the background, so the user can continue working.

Establishing a UIMS to perform these tasks has several benefits: It saves development effort and, if shared subroutines can be used, it saves space, too. It helps promote a uniform human interface across applications (the Macintosh is the best example of this). It allows designers to build their human interface out of piece parts whose usability has already been established, thus lessening the chance that major redesign will be required as a result of user testing. It allows the user interface to be fine-tuned—perhaps even translated into foreign languages—without having to modify the application.

UIMSs are currently a hot research topic, principally because of two fairly recent developments. First, more and more people who aren't computing professionals are using computers, and the training, productivity, and job satisfaction of these people has become a major social and economic issue. Second, inexpensive but powerful workstations are available today, so that CPU cycles are no longer too precious to be devoted to the user.

Outstanding commercial UIMSs are already in common use, most of them based on research that took place in the 1970s. Many of these systems are available for popular microcomputers. Examples are Apple's Macintosh User Interface Toolbox; Microsoft's Windows and IBM's TopView, for IBM PC-type computers; and Digital Research's Graphics Environment Manager (GEM) for IBM PCs and the Atari ST.[3] UIMSs for UNIX include Andrew from Carnegie-Mellon University, and X from MIT, both of which are portable across CPUs and display hardware. Proprietary systems are offered by just about every vendor of graphics workstations, such as Apollo, AT&T, Digital Equipment, Hewlett-Packard, IBM, Sun Microsystems, and, let's not forget, Xerox, who pioneered the UIMS idea.

No two research or commercial UIMSs have the same programming interface. This certainly is not because the people who designed them felt that they should be different—of all people, they clearly know better. The field is just too new. A good, fast, small UIMS, like that in the Macintosh, is

---

[3]I have developed a UIMS, based on the software presented in this book, that works with any UNIX terminal or IBM PC-type computer. Write to the address given in Appendix C for further information.

a magnificent technical achievement, and we're awestruck at the brilliance of its designers because we feel that what they did was terribly difficult. As long as each new UIMS seems like a breakthrough, compatibility will seem inappropriate. This is reminiscent of the state of compiler writing in the 1960s, when a new compiler was cause for wonderment and each group of compiler writers invented their own methods. As UIMS concepts and techniques mature, we can hope that a set of common tools and programming interfaces will emerge. Perhaps this will be stimulated by the invention of a simple, powerful, portable, overwhelmingly popular system that kills off the competition—like what happened in operating systems when UNIX came along. So far, no existing UIMS is even close to such widespread acceptance. This is as it should be, because we need innovation more than conformity right now.

1.5. Summary

We began this chapter with a quick review of computer graphics, but then focused in on *interactive character displays* and *keyboards*, the subjects of this book. At the lowest level of abstraction, we introduced the concepts of *objects* with *attributes*, displayed at *locations* in a rectangular array. For our purposes, the objects are characters and the locations are character positions. There are usually 24 or 25 rows and 80 columns of characters.

Because keyboards vary so much, we also introduced a *virtual keyboard* that transmits the same key codes regardless of the peculiarities of the actual keyboard.

Applications can be designed to write to the *physical screen*, which is the same size as the actual display. Or, an application can write to a *window*, which is a rectangular area within the physical screen. Windows can overlap, but the application programmer need not worry about this because clipping is performed automatically. However, the application must be prepared to repair damaged parts of the window when they are uncovered. It's even easier for an application to write to a *virtual screen*, for it can be bigger than the physical screen and the application programmer need not even worry about repairing damage, as that's handled automatically.

The remainder of this book is organized around the abstractions discussed in this chapter:

Chapter 2: objects and attributes
Chapter 3: physical screen
Chapter 4: virtual keyboard
Chapter 6: windows
Chapter 7: virtual screens

Chapter 5 presents a screen editor designed to use the physical screen and virtual keyboard. We'll modify it in Chapter 6 to use windows, and again in Chapter 7 to use virtual screens.

CHAPTER 2

Terminology and Programming Environment

2.1. Introduction

In this chapter, we'll first introduce basic terms that will be used throughout this book, including *character*, *attribute*, *cell*, and *rectangle*. Next, we'll define four operating system environments in which the programs in this book will run: MS–DOS on the IBM Personal Computer, AT&T UNIX Systems III and V, Microsoft Xenix, and Berkeley 4BSD.[1] Finally, we'll show some low-level utility functions that help establish a uniform programming interface to these four disparate environments.

2.2. Characters

Characters are represented inside a computer by an 8-bit code occupying one byte of memory. (On a computer with a 36-bit or 60-bit word, a character might occupy nine or ten bits.) There are 256 codes, ranging from 0 through 255. The first 128 of these (the rightmost seven bits) are defined by the American National Standard Code for Information Interchange, better known by its abbreviation, ASCII (pronounced "askey").

ASCII codes from 32 through 126 (space through tilde) are displayable and printable characters, and we will assume that all displays of concern to

---

[1]The term 4BSD stands for 4.2BSD and 4.3BSD.

us in this book can display them. Codes from 0 through 31 and 127 aren't
actual characters at all but are control codes. Many of these are supposed to
cause some action when sent to a display or a printer; examples are
backspace and carriage return. Other control codes are used to delimit data
(such as a record separator), but the ASCII standard doesn't say how these
codes are to be used, only what their names are.

For most of this book, we won't use ASCII control characters to control
the display. Instead, control functions will be performed by calling C
functions. We'll use ASCII control characters only when we implement the
physical screen functions for a terminal.

Some displays, notably those for the IBM PC, can display more characters than just the ninety-five ASCII displayable characters. These so-called
extended ASCII characters include characters for line drawing, mathematics,
and foreign languages. The line-drawing characters are particularly
important to many application designers. They are important to us, too,
because we'll be using them for window frames. However, their use hinders
portability of applications to other displays because these line-drawing
characters are not standardized and not always available on the display
device and because many communication systems won't transmit a full eight
bits per character (the eighth bit may be used for parity).

To alleviate this situation a little, we'll define symbolic constants for
several commonly used line-drawing characters. Each physical screen
implementation must then map these codes to whatever the display can
handle. For example, the corner characters might be mapped to plus signs
(+). The lines may not look as nice as those on the IBM PC, but they'll at
least be recognizable. We won't even try to handle the other symbols
(mathematical, foreign language, and so on).

The line-drawing symbolic constants are shown in Fig. 2–1. They are
defined in a C header file named **display.h**:

```
#define C_UL      218        /* upper left */
#define C_UR      191        /* upper right */
#define C_LL      192        /* lower left */
#define C_LR      217        /* lower right */
#define C_XD      194        /* T-intersection down */
#define C_XU      193        /* T-intersection up */
#define C_XR      195        /* T-intersection right */
#define C_XL      180        /* T-intersection left */
#define C_XX      197        /* 4-way intersection */
#define C_H       196        /* horizontal line */
#define C_V       179        /* vertical line */
#define C_ULD     201        /* next group similar, but double */
#define C_URD     187
#define C_LLD     200
#define C_LRD     188
#define C_XDD     203
#define C_XUD     202
#define C_XRD     204
#define C_XLD     185
#define C_XXD     206
#define C_HD      205
#define C_VD      186
#define C_HATCH   176        /* hatching */
#define C_SPACE   255        /* alternate space */
```

It makes no difference what the actual numbers are, as long as they are unique and greater than 127, since the physical screen implementations will map them to characters appropriate for each display. But by choosing them to correspond to the IBM PC character set, we eliminate the need to map them when the actual display is in fact attached to an IBM PC.

The hatching character (**C_HATCH**) is used to fill in large areas. The space character (**C_SPACE**) is equivalent to the ASCII space character in that its screen appearance (or lack of appearance) is the same. It's available in case an application needs to represent some spaces differently from others. A text editor might use it for spaces that have been added to justify a line of text, in order to indicate that such spaces were not typed by the user.

┌	C_UL		╓	C_ULD
┐	C_UR		╖	C_URD
└	C_LL		╙	C_LLD
┘	C_LR		╜	C_LRD
┬	C_XD		╥	C_XDD
┴	C_XU		╨	C_XUD
├	C_XR		╟	C_XRD
┤	C_XL		╢	C_XLD
┼	C_XX		╫	C_XXD
─	C_H		═	C_HD
│	C_V		║	C_VD
▓	C_HATCH			C_SPACE

Fig. 2-1. Screen showing line-drawing characters and their associated symbolic constants.

To show how these constants might be used, here's a short program that displays the screen shown in Fig. 2-2. In Chapter 6 we'll use a similar technique to draw frames around windows.

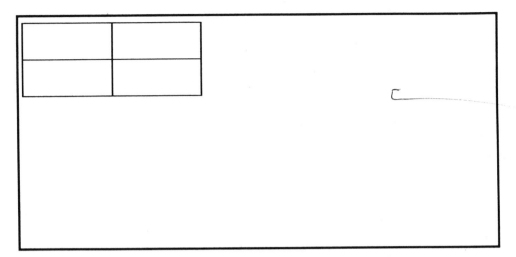

Fig. 2−2. Screen showing output from the line-drawing program.

```
#include "display.h"

#define HEIGHT       9
#define HALF_HEIGHT 5
#define WIDTH       31
#define HALF_WIDTH  16

/*--------------------------------------------------------------------
    Draw some boxes.
--------------------------------------------------------------------*/
void main()
{
    int r, c;

    /* top row */
    putchar(C_UL);
    for (c = 2; c < HALF_WIDTH; c++)
        putchar(C_H);
    putchar(C_XD);
    for (c = HALF_WIDTH + 1; c < WIDTH; c++)
        putchar(C_H);
    putchar(C_UR);
    putchar('\n');
    /* upper half */
    for (r = 2; r < HALF_HEIGHT; r++) {
        putchar(C_V);
        for (c = 2; c < HALF_WIDTH; c++)
            putchar(' ');
        putchar(C_V);
        for (c = HALF_WIDTH + 1; c < WIDTH; c++)
            putchar(' ');
        putchar(C_V);
        putchar('\n');
    }
```

```
/* middle row */
putchar(C_XR);
for (c = 2; c < HALF_WIDTH; c++)
    putchar(C_H);
putchar(C_XX);
for (c = HALF_WIDTH + 1; c < WIDTH; c++)
    putchar(C_H);
putchar(C_XL);
putchar('\n');
/* lower half */
for (r = 2; r < HALF_HEIGHT; r++) {
    putchar(C_V);
    for (c = 2; c < HALF_WIDTH; c++)
        putchar(' ');
    putchar(C_V);
    for (c = HALF_WIDTH + 1; c < WIDTH; c++)
        putchar(' ');
    putchar(C_V);
    putchar('\n');
}
/* bottom row */
putchar(C_LL);
for (c = 2; c < HALF_WIDTH; c++)
    putchar(C_H);
putchar(C_XU);
for (c = HALF_WIDTH + 1; c < WIDTH; c++)
    putchar(C_H);
putchar(C_LR);
putchar('\n');
exit(0);
}
```

Because standard C output functions (such as **putchar**) are used to output the characters, this program will work only on computers equipped with a display that includes these characters as part of its native character set. The IBM PC is suitable, of course, but few computers running UNIX are. To achieve portability across displays, you can't output these line drawing characters directly; you must use the functions that are part of the physical screen, window, or virtual screen modules. We'll get to those functions later in this book.

2.3. Attributes

Possible character attributes are inverse (black-on-white instead of white-on-black), blinking, underlined, intense (bold), and normal. Sometimes these can be combined (blinking and underlined), but we'll only use them separately. Symbolic constants to represent the attributes are also defined in **display.h**:

```
#define A_NORM      0x07        /* normal */
#define A_INVERSE   0x70        /* inverse */
#define A_INTENSE   0x0F        /* intense */
#define A_BLINK     0x87        /* blink */
#define A_UNDER     0x01        /* underline */
```

Again, the actual numbers don't matter, so we've chosen the codes used by the IBM PC display. The important thing is that they're unique.

Few terminals support all attributes, although most support at least normal and inverse. Physical screen implementations will usually map all non-normal attributes to inverse. To ensure that the design of an application is portable, you should avoid using blinking, underlined, or intense.

The definitions of attributes could be extended to support colors, but we won't do so because colors are even less portable than monochrome attributes. (Have you seen many color ASCII character terminals?) If you are concerned only with the IBM PC, and you have a color monitor, you'll discover that the programs in this book will work fine with attributes set to the bit patterns for the various colors available.

We can't show a simple program to illustrate the use of attributes, as we did in the previous section, since attributes aren't handled by standard C functions like **putchar**. However, all of the physical screen, window, and virtual screen display functions that we'll present later allow an attribute to be specified whenever characters are displayed. We'll defer an example until then.

2.4. Character Cells and Display Buffers

Physical screens, windows, and virtual screens consist of a rectangular arrangement of characters, each of which has an attribute. We can represent each character position by a data structure called a *cell*, defined in **display.h** like this:

```
typedef struct s_cell {
    char chr;                   /* character */
    char att;                   /* attribute */
} CELL;
```

The **chr** member can hold any 8-bit code, but the display functions in this book support only the ninety-five displayable ASCII characters (32 through 126) plus the line-drawing characters defined in Sec. 2.2. Other codes, especially those below 32, should not be used because they might cause the display device to behave erratically. The **att** member can hold any of the five attributes defined in Sec. 2.3.

Whenever a display buffer is needed (to represent, say, a virtual screen), a two-dimensional array of **CELL** structures can be used:

```
#define ROWS 24
#define COLS 80

CELL dspbuf[ROWS][COLS];
```

Throughout this book, rows and columns are always numbered starting with zero. For example, on a 24-row display, the row numbers range from 0 through 23. Row numbers increase as you go down, and column numbers increase as you go right, so row 0, column 0 is at the upper left.

The C language does not define which member of the **CELL** structure comes first in memory, and it would be unwise to program in a way such that the order matters. But because the IBM PC physical screen implementations run only on CPUs like the Intel 8086 (including the 8088, the 80286, and the 80386), there's no loss in portability if those particular modules assume that the order of members corresponds to the layout of display memory in the IBM PC. This assumption allows the **CELL** structure to be used to represent actual display memory (the frame buffer) as well as buffers in the application's own address space. Then a buffer can be copied to display memory without rearranging the order of characters and attributes, which would take too much time. For the other physical screen implementations, the order makes no difference because actual display memory is inaccessible. The IBM PC ordering is as good as any.

2.5. Additional Definitions

The header **display.h** also includes definitions not especially related to character displays but which are useful throughout this book.

A **BOOLEAN** type-definition is handy for flag variables and for values of functions:

```
typedef int BOOLEAN;
#define FALSE    0
#define TRUE     1
```

Next are macros to calculate the minimum and maximum of two expressions:

```
#define MIN(x, y) ((x) < (y) ? (x) : (y))
#define MAX(x, y) ((x) > (y) ? (x) : (y))
```

Note that **x** or **y** will be evaluated twice. These macros (in fact, most macros) shouldn't be called with arguments that have side effects, as in this example:

```
k = MIN(i++, j++);
```

Here, either **i** or **j** will be incremented twice, which is almost certainly wrong.

We could have made **MIN** and **MAX** functions instead. In fact, most macros with parameters can be coded as functions. The trade-off is that macros generate a copy of the code for each invocation, while functions take time to call. We generally use macros only for very short sequences of code, usually less than a line, and only if we think the macro will be called frequently. Functions defined on the fly, during top-down refinement of the program, stay as functions even if they contain only a line of code.

Four directional constants are used by functions that move text around on the screen:

```
#define DIR_UP      0
#define DIR_DOWN    1
#define DIR_LEFT    2
#define DIR_RIGHT   3
```

Finally, since **display.h** will be included by every source file, we'll put four more includes there to save some typing:

```
#include <stdio.h>
#include <ctype.h>
#include "port.h"
#include "dsputil.h"
```

The files **stdio.h** and **ctype.h** are part of the Standard I/O Library that we assume is present in all environments in which the display software will run. The files **port.h** and **dsputil.h** go with corresponding C source files that we'll introduce later in this chapter.

2.6. Rectangles

Several display functions operate on a rectangle of cells. The dimensions of a rectangle are stated in terms of the row and column of the upper left and lower right corners. These four numbers are arranged in a **RECT** structure, defined in **display.h**:

```
typedef struct s_rect {
    short r1, c1;                /* upper left corner */
    short r2, c2;                /* lower right corner */
} RECT;
```

Four macros are defined to calculate the width and height of a **RECT**, in order to assign four coordinate numbers to a **RECT** and to copy one **RECT** to another. The copy operation is needed because not all C compilers support structure assignment.

```
#define RWIDTH(a) ((a)->c2 - (a)->c1 + 1)
#define RHEIGHT(a) ((a)->r2 - (a)->r1 + 1)
#define RASG(a, row1, col1, row2, col2) ((a)->r1 = row1, (a)->c1 = col1,\
  (a)->r2 = row2, (a)->c2 = col2)
#define RCPY(dst, src) ((dst)->r1 = (src)->r1, (dst)->c1 = (src)->c1,\
  (dst)->r2 = (src)->r2, (dst)->c2 = (src)->c2)
```

This program fragment shows how these macros are used:

```
RECT rect1, rect2;

RASG(&rect1, 10, 15, 20, 75);
RCPY(&rect2, &rect1);
printf("width = %d; height = %d\n", RWIDTH(&rect2), RHEIGHT(&rect2));
```

The output was:

```
width = 61; height = 11
```

Note that these rectangle operations operate only on the *coordinates* of the rectangle's boundary, not on the characters and attributes themselves.

It's sometimes necessary to find the intersection of a given rectangle with another rectangle whose upper left corner is at (0, 0). The cross-hatched region in Fig. 2–3 shows the intersection of an arbitrary rectangle A with a rectangle B that extends from (0, 0) to (**maxrow, maxcol**). We might take such an intersection when filling a rectangle on the physical screen. It's convenient to let the caller specify any rectangle at all, even if it goes beyond

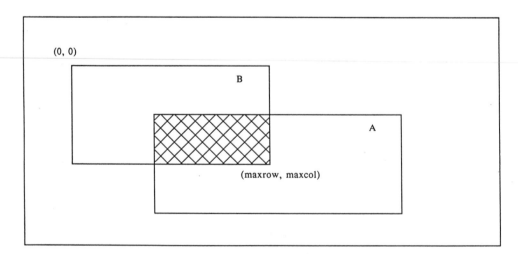

Fig. 2–3. Intersection of rectangles A and B.

the boundaries of the screen. The physical screen fill function would only fill
the intersection of the specified rectangle with a rectangle extending from (0,
0) to, say, (23, 79).

The function **intersect** in **dsputil.c** intersects the source rectangle
pointed to by **srcp** with the rectangle extending from (0, 0) to (**maxrow,
maxcol**). The resulting rectangle is returned through **dstp**. The function
returns **FALSE** or **TRUE** depending on whether the intersection is empty.

```
/*-------------------------------------------------------------------
    intersect - intersection between 2 rectangles
    RETURN: Is intersection non-empty?
-------------------------------------------------------------*/
BOOLEAN intersect(srcp, maxrow, maxcol, dstp)
RECT *srcp;                             /* source rectangle */
int maxrow;                             /* max row of clipping rectangle */
int maxcol;                             /* max column of clipping rectangle */
RECT *dstp;                             /* destination rectangle */
{
    dstp->rl = MAX(0, srcp->rl);
    dstp->cl = MAX(0, srcp->cl);
    dstp->r2 = MIN(maxrow, srcp->r2);
    dstp->c2 = MIN(maxcol, srcp->c2);
    return((BOOLEAN)(dstp->rl <= dstp->r2 && dstp->cl <= dstp->c2));
}
```

Since we know that a display function will clip an argument rectangle to
a boundary that makes sense, it's often convenient to call it with a giant rectangle as an argument, one much larger than actually needed. An example
would be setting the physical screen to all spaces (that is, clearing it). Rather
than supply a rectangle exactly the size of the screen, which might vary from
one display to another, it's easier to just use a rectangle much larger than
any screen. In **display.h**, a **RECT** variable is defined for such uses:

```
extern RECT GIANT_RECT;
```

For a similar reason, occasionally a giant row number or column number is
needed, so a symbolic constant is defined for that, too:

```
#define GIANT 9999
```

GIANT_RECT is initialized in **dsputil.c**:

```
RECT GIANT_RECT = {0, 0, GIANT, GIANT};
```

Another common operation is finding the smallest rectangle that
completely encloses two other rectangles (which might or might not intersect
each other). In Fig. 2–4, rectangle C encloses rectangles A and B. The
function **enclose** in **dsputil.c** computes an enclosing rectangle:

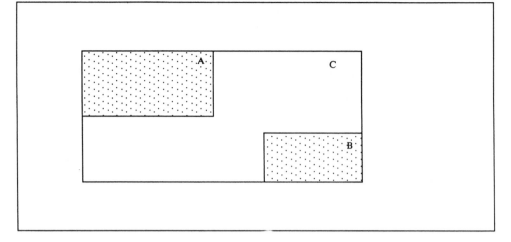

Fig. 2−4. Rectangle C encloses rectangles A and B.

```
/*-----------------------------------------------------------------
     enclosing - rectangle enclosing 2 rectangles
-----------------------------------------------------------------*/
void enclosing(srcp1, srcp2, dstp)
RECT *srcp1;                          /* first source rectangle */
RECT *srcp2;                          /* second source rectangle */
RECT *dstp;                           /* enclosing rectangle */
{
    dstp->r1 = MIN(srcp1->r1, srcp2->r1);
    dstp->c1 = MIN(srcp1->c1, srcp2->c1);
    dstp->r2 = MAX(srcp1->r2, srcp2->r2);
    dstp->c2 = MAX(srcp1->c2, srcp2->c2);
}
```

2.7. Portability

We want the programs in this book to be as portable as possible, in four ways:

1. *Across display types.* This is handled by the multiple implementations of the physical screen interface and is discussed thoroughly in Chapter 3.

2. *Across computer types.* This is achieved by coding the programs carefully enough to avoid unnecessary machine dependencies, such as integer and pointer sizes, or byte-ordering within a word. To chase down accidental machine dependencies, the programs in this book have been tested on four different processor families: Intel 8086, Motorola 68000, DEC VAX−11, and AT&T 3B2/3B20. On the Intel 8086, tests were run with 16-bit integers and 16-bit pointers, and also with 16-bit integers and 32-bit pointers.

3. *Across different operating systems.* Only the UNIX and MS–DOS (PC–DOS) operating systems are supported by the programs in this book, although porting the programs to, say, VAX VMS shouldn't be too hard. Unfortunately there are several versions of UNIX and MS–DOS which aren't entirely compatible, so even this restricted portability is more difficult than it sounds.

4. *Across different versions of C.* Some C compilers handle only the language as defined in *The C Programming Language* [Ker78] which corresponds to the C compiler delivered with UNIX Version 7. Other C compilers handle newer language features that were introduced with UNIX System III. As far as the language itself goes, the problem is handled by programming in Version 7 C, since the newer C is nearly upward-compatible. In fact, the only difference between the two that we care about is the existence of the **void** data type. Other features of System III C, such as the enumerated type (**enum**) and structure assignment, we'll do without, because they're not yet supported by all C compilers.[2] Variations in library functions present more of a challenge. The new ANSI C Standard will eventually help, but at the time of this writing it has had an impact only on compilers for MS–DOS.

To make the operating system and C compiler portability problem tractable, we'll restrict ourselves to five environments: Lattice C on MS–DOS, Microsoft C on MS–DOS, UNIX System III, Xenix, and Berkeley 4BSD. Variations among these five environments are handled via conditional compilation controlled by one of these five symbolic constants:

LATTICE   This means that the computer is an IBM PC or equivalent, that the operating system is MS–DOS or PC–DOS Version 2.0 or higher, and that the compiler is Lattice C [Lat86] configured for the large model (that is, 32-bit pointers and greater than 64K bytes of instructions).

MICROSOFT   This means the same hardware and operating system as **LATTICE**, but the compiler is from Microsoft [Mic86]. The language compiled by the Lattice and Microsoft compilers is essentially the same, but the implementations have different non-ANSI library functions and assembly-language interfaces.[3]

---

[2]The types **void** and **enum** are explained in Sec. 1.10 of [Roc85].

[3]With minor changes the programs can also be compiled by other popular C compilers for MS–DOS, but the display methods used in Chapter 3 will work only on computers that are 100 percent IBM compatible.

SYS3   This means that the operating system and C compiler are based on AT&T UNIX System III. *This includes System V, so there is no separate SYS5 symbol.* Newer versions of Xenix are also based on System III (or System V).

XENIX   This refers to the version of Xenix based on UNIX Version 7. This operating system is obsolete, but still in widespread use. The C compiler is the one that comes with Xenix. This symbol will also work on newer versions of Xenix, since they are upward-compatible from Version 7 (not true of AT&T versions of UNIX). However, for newer versions of Xenix the symbol **SYS3** should be used instead.

BSD4   This means that the operating system is Berkeley 4.2BSD or 4.3BSD.

Note that, in keeping with the spirit of UNIX, we aren't concerned with the hardware on which the System III, Xenix, or Berkeley 4BSD systems run. And, in keeping with the spirit of MS−DOS, we *are* concerned with the hardware on which it runs. This is because, unlike UNIX, the MS−DOS system does not efficiently manage all the hardware (e.g., the screen), and because the prevailing performance standards for MS−DOS software are so high that direct hardware interfacing is mandatory.

In this book, when we use the term "UNIX," we mean the union of **SYS3**, **XENIX**, and **BSD4**. This probably covers over 99 percent of the computers running UNIX today. The **LATTICE** and **MICROSOFT** symbols cover a few million personal computers.

When the programs in this book are compiled, one of the five symbols **LATTICE**, **MICROSOFT**, **SYS3**, **XENIX**, or **BSD4** must be defined. On UNIX, it might be done this way:

```
$ cc -c -DSYS3 port.c
```

For convenience in programming, four more symbolic constants are derived in the header file **port.h**:

UNIX   This means that the operating system is UNIX (as opposed to MS−DOS).

MSDOS   This means that one of the symbols **LATTICE** or **MICROSOFT** was defined.

OLDTTY   This means that the UNIX device driver for terminals is compatible with Version 7, rather than System III. This is true for **XENIX** and **BSD4**, and false for **SYS3**.

NOVOID   This means that the C compiler lacks the **void** data type. This is true for **XENIX**, and false for **SYS3** and **BSD4**.

The derivation of these four symbolic constants is easily handled by the C preprocessor:

```
#ifdef LATTICE
#undef MSDOS
#define MSDOS
#endif

#ifdef MICROSOFT
#undef MSDOS
#define MSDOS
#endif

#ifdef SYS3
#define UNIX
#endif

#ifdef XENIX
#define UNIX
#define OLDTTY
#define NOVOID
#endif

#ifdef BSD4
#define UNIX
#define OLDTTY
#endif
```

We undefine some symbols before defining them, in case they are already defined, to avoid a warning from the C preprocessor.

For the **NOVOID** compilers, we define a **void** data type:

```
#ifdef NOVOID
#define void int
#endif
```

To localize portability issues, we have an ironclad rule that the symbols **OLDTTY** and **NOVOID** are used only in the files **port.h** and **port.c** (to be discussed shortly). We'd also like to confine the operating system symbols (**UNIX, MSDOS, SYS3, XENIX**, and **BSD4**), and therefore operating system dependencies, to as few files as possible, primarily the ones introduced in this and the next two chapters. The idea is to restrict all such dependencies to a low-level layer that implements an abstract, portable operating environment.

Most operating system dependencies are in the file **port.c**, which handles these tasks:

1. *Moving large areas of memory.* Although this can be done portably and need not be operating-system-dependent, we do want to take advantage of some extremely fast functions that come with the Lattice and Microsoft C compilers because the speed of these operations greatly affects the speed with which rectangles (Sec. 2.6) can be moved and filled.

2. *Printing error messages* from UNIX system calls. Some of the information we want to print is not available under MS–DOS.

3. *Reading the keyboard.* This is surprisingly complicated. We must be able to determine if a keystroke is ready, to read it if it is, to read a character without blocking when one isn't ready, and to turn terminal *raw mode* on and off.[4] MS–DOS and the different UNIX versions differ markedly in how these keyboard tasks are implemented.

The first two groups of functions (moving memory and printing error messages) will be discussed in the next two sections of this chapter. Keyboard functions will be deferred to Chapter 4.

2.8. Memory Operations

We want to move contiguous areas of memory so that these requirements are met:

1. Fast hardware block-move instructions are used.

2. Overlapping source and destination areas are properly handled, by starting the move at either the right or left end of the source depending on which will prevent a source byte from being overwritten before it is read.

The System V and ANSI C function **memcpy** does not necessarily obey the second requirement, so it can't be used under UNIX. The Lattice and Microsoft versions of this function do handle overlaps correctly, and this important property is stated clearly in their reference manuals. We'll refer to their restricted **memcpy** as **movmem**, which is a traditional Lattice version of this function, except that the order of the source and destination arguments is reversed. For Microsoft C, a macro in **port.h** gives us **movmem**:

```
#ifdef MICROSOFT
#define movmem(s, d, n) memcpy(d, s, n)
#endif
```

For UNIX, we'll have to code our own **movmem**:

---

[4]When raw mode is on, characters typed on the keyboard are transmitted immediately without waiting for a full line to be entered. No characters—such as Control–S or Control–D—are special. This is what we want for interactive applications because the display must be updated as the characters are typed. Raw mode is explained fully in Sec. 4.5 of [Roc85].

```
#ifndef MSDOS
/*-------------------------------------------------------------------
    movmem - move block of memory

    Move starts at left or right end as appropriate, in case source
    and destination blocks overlap.  UNIX memcpy doesn't do this.
-------------------------------------------------------------------*/
void movmem(s, d, n)
char *s;                                /* pointer to source block */
char *d;                                /* pointer to destination block */
int n;                                  /* number of bytes to move */
{
    if (s > d)
        while (n-- > 0)
            *d++ = *s++;
    else {
        s += n - 1;
        d += n - 1;
        while (n-- > 0)
            *d-- = *s--;
    }
}
#endif
```

If you like, you can code a hardware-specific version of **movmem** in assembly language for your local UNIX system.

Two additional memory operations we'll need are filling an area with a constant byte value and filling an area with a constant group of bytes. Again, Lattice C comes with functions to do this: **setmem** and **repmem**. System V, ANSI C, and Microsoft C all define a function **memset**, which is equivalent to **setmem** with the source and destination arguments reversed. They don't have an equivalent to **repmem**.

Here's how we'll handle this: We'll ignore the fact that System V has **memset** (it isn't used that much in this book anyway), and code a portable version of **setmem** for use in all UNIX systems:

```
#ifndef MSDOS
/*-------------------------------------------------------------------
    setmem - set memory to character value
-------------------------------------------------------------------*/
void setmem(d, n, c)
char *d;                                /* pointer to destination block */
int n;                                  /* number of bytes to set */
char c;                                 /* character value */
{
    while (n-- > 0)
        *d++ = c;
}
#endif
```

For Microsoft C, we'll use a macro, as we did for **movmem**:

```
#ifdef MICROSOFT
#define setmem(p, n, c) memset(p, c, n)
#endif
```

For all environments except Lattice, we'll code our own **repmem**:

```
#ifndef LATTICE
/*-------------------------------------------------------------------
    repmem - replicate values through memory
-------------------------------------------------------------*/
void repmem(d, v, lv, nv)
char *d;                            /* pointer to destination block */
char *v;                            /* pointer to values */
int lv;                            /* number of bytes of values */
int nv;                            /* number of replications
                                      (lv * nv bytes will be moved) */
{
    int i;

    while (nv-- > 0)
        for (i = 0; i < lv; i++)
            *d++ = v[i];
}
#endif
```

What an incredible amount of trouble to go to for just a few simple memory functions that can easily be coded in portable C! It's worth it, however, because experiments have shown that using the memory functions supplied with Lattice and Microsoft C makes a big difference in performance. This justification, along with the desire to make sure things at least work, are the only two reasons for using conditional compilation to achieve portability. Conditional compilation is otherwise undesirable because it makes the program harder to write and read, and because it creates extra paths to be tested. And you have to recompile the program to get to these extra paths, not just make up a separate set of test data. That's why we did not define **BOOLEAN** like this:

```
#ifdef HAVE_ENUMS
typedef enum {FALSE, TRUE} BOOLEAN;
#else
typedef int BOOLEAN;
#define FALSE    0
#define TRUE     1
#endif
```

This bit of extra pain would have bought us absolutely nothing. Since the second definition is universal, we just did it that way.

2.9. Error-Handling

When a UNIX system call returns −1, which indicates that an error has occurred, additional information about the error is available in the external variables **errno**, **sys_nerr**, and **sys_errlist**. The function **syserr** prints this information along with a message supplied by the caller. More details are given in Sec. 1.9 of [Roc85].

```
#ifdef UNIX
/*-------------------------------------------------------------------
      syserr - print system call error message and terminate
               Taken from Advanced UNIX Programming, Sec 1.9.
------------------------------------------------------------------*/
void syserr(msg)
char *msg;                              /* message to be printed */
{
    extern int errno, sys_nerr;
    extern char *sys_errlist[];

    fprintf(stderr, "ERROR: %s (%d", msg, errno);
    if (errno > 0 && errno < sys_nerr)
        fprintf(stderr, "; %s)\n", sys_errlist[errno]);
    else
        fprintf(stderr, ")\n");
    exit(1);
}
#endif
```

For other, non-system-call errors, we frequently want to simply print a message and terminate processing by calling a function named **fatal**. In these cases the error is so rare and so catastrophic that is isn't worth trying to patch things up so execution can continue. Before we exit, however, we must clean up loose ends. This includes closing files, taking the terminal out of raw mode, and other actions that are application-dependent. To keep **fatal** as general as possible, it calls the function **cleanup**. Each application must supply its own version of **cleanup**, perhaps in the same file that contains the **main** function. Since **fatal** is portable, it's defined in **dsputil.c** (rather than **port.c**):

```
/*-------------------------------------------------------------------
      fatal - clean up, print error message, and terminate
------------------------------------------------------------------*/
void fatal(msg)
char *msg;
{
    cleanup();
    fprintf(stderr, "ERROR: %s\n", msg);
    exit(1);
}
```

2.10. Allocating Memory

The standard C function **malloc** is used to allocate dynamic memory. It's available in all environments that concern us.

Often we want to terminate processing when memory is exhausted, so this common operation is encapsulated into the portable function **xmalloc**, defined in **dsputil.c**:[5]

---

[5]We didn't use **calloc**, which automatically clears the allocated block because during the debugging of the programs in this book, **xmalloc** was used with a diagnostic memory allocation module (not described here) that lacks that function.

```
/*-------------------------------------------------------------------
     xmalloc - allocate zeroed memory; terminate on error
     RETURN: Pointer to memory, or NULL on error.
----------------------------------------------------------------*/
char *xmalloc(n)
int n;                                  /* number of bytes to allocate */
{
     char *p;

     if ((p = malloc((unsigned)n)) == NULL)
          fatal("out of memory");
     setmem(p, n, '\0');
     return(p);
}
```

When we want to recover from an allocation error, we'll call **malloc** directly.

2.11. String Functions

A few general purpose string functions are in **dsputil.c**. The function **strrep** builds a string made up of a repeated character. It's used for such things as drawing lines.

```
/*-------------------------------------------------------------------
     strrep - build string from repeated character
----------------------------------------------------------------*/
void strrep(d, c, n)
char *d;                                 /* destination string */
char c;                                  /* character to repeat */
int n;                                   /* number of repetitions */
{
     while (n-- > 0)
          *d++ = c;
     *d = '\0';
}
```

The function **strtok** breaks up a string into tokens that are separated by a span of characters taken from a set of delimiters. This function is actually present in System III, but since it's not in all the other environments, we'll include it for ourselves:

```
/*-------------------------------------------------------------------
     in - test for character in string (used only by strtok)
     RETURN: Is character present?
----------------------------------------------------------------*/
static BOOLEAN in(c, delim)
char c, *delim;
{
     for (; *delim != '\0'; delim++)
          if (c == *delim)
               return(TRUE);
     return(FALSE);
}
```

```
/*--------------------------------------------------------------------
      strtok - get next token (UNIX compatible)
                  Set first arg to NULL after one token is returned.
                  Source string is destroyed (planted with NUL bytes).
      RETURN: Pointer to token or NULL if none left.
--------------------------------------------------------------------*/
char *strtok(src, delim)
char *src, *delim;
{
    static char *s;
    char *rtn;

    if (src != NULL)
        s = src;
    rtn = s;
    while (*s != '\0') {
        if (in(*s, delim)) {
            *s = '\0';
            while (in(*++s, delim))
                ;
            return(rtn);
        }
        s++;
    }
    if (rtn == s)
        return(NULL);
    return(rtn);
}
```

Here's an example program that uses strtok:

```
#include "display.h"

void main()
{
    static char string[] = "   one two    three    four";
    char *s, *tok;

    s = string;
    while ((tok = strtok(s, " ")) != NULL) {
        s = NULL;
        printf("Got token <%s>\n", tok);
    }
    exit(0);
}
```

It printed this:

```
                    Got token <>
                    Got token <one>
                    Got token <two>
                    Got token <three>
                    Got token <four>
```

2.12. Summary

This chapter introduced the fundamental objects and attributes that can be displayed on physical screens, windows, and virtual screens. The objects are 8-bit characters that include the displayable ASCII characters, augmented with line-drawing characters such as **C_H** (horizontal line) and **C_LR** (lower right corner).   Attributes are inverse, blinking, underlined, intense, and normal. We coded additional definitions for character cells (each containing a character and attribute), directions, and rectangles.   We showed some functions to perform common rectangle calculations.

Next, we tackled the problem of portability. All of the modules in this book will be implemented under the MS–DOS and UNIX operating systems. Three major categories of UNIX systems are supported: Systems III and V, Xenix, and BSD 4.2 and 4.3. We established several C preprocessor symbols to define the operating system and version so that we can use alternative coding in the places where the environments differ.

These differences are confined to a few utility functions given in this chapter and a few more that will be given in Chapter 4. The functions handle memory operations, error-reporting, and keyboard input. We also supplied some handy functions for memory allocation and string manipulation that don't depend on the environment.

With the basic building blocks defined, and with a reasonably portable environment established, this chapter has prepared us to begin programming the display software itself, starting, in the next chapter, with the physical screen.

CHAPTER 3

The Physical Screen

3.1. Introduction

In this chapter we'll present the lowest level of display software: the physical screen. We'll define a display-independent interface to the physical screen and give an example program to show how the interface is used. Application programs may be designed to use this interface directly when the fancier services of the window or virtual screen layers aren't needed. In Chapter 5, we'll show such an application: a screen editor.

Next, we'll implement this interface five ways for these display architectures:

1. Zenith Z-19 terminal
2. UNIX Termcap
3. UNIX Curses
4. IBM PC BIOS
5. IBM PC memory-mapped video

Each of these physical screen implementations has an important job: to allow the higher software layers to be display-independent without sacrificing display speed. This job is particularly challenging for the IBM PC because that computer has an extraordinarily fast display. If our physical screen implementation is not optimal, programmers won't want to use it for critical applications, which would defeat our goal of allowing high-performance display applications to be portable across display types. So the code in Sec. 3.7 is fairly tricky. Some of it is even written in Intel 8086 assembly language.

We'll try our best to make the other implementations fast, too, but there's no way to get around the speed limit imposed by the communication lines commonly used with ASCII terminals. Even at 9600 bits per second, it takes about two seconds to rewrite the entire screen, and most terminals don't run nearly that fast. On the IBM PC, using memory-mapped video, it takes only a sixth of a second.

3.2. Physical Screen Interface

3.2.1. Properties of the Physical Screen

The physical screen has these properties:

1. It consists of a rectangular arrangement of characters that is the same size as the actual display. There is only one physical screen per user.

2. The number of rows and columns varies, but there are usually at least twenty-four rows and eighty columns. Of course, it's best if application programs are written to adapt to any screen size, but for some applications this may not be practical.

3. All of the characters defined in Sec. 2.2 may be used. Displayable ASCII characters (codes 32 through 126) are guaranteed to appear properly. Not so for the others—a different character may be substituted, or a space may appear instead.

4. All of the attributes defined in Sec. 2.3 may be used, but all of the non-normal attributes may be displayed as inverse.

5. There is a cursor that indicates a particular position on the display, usually by a blinking underscore or an inverse block. The cursor can be moved about. It can also be made to disappear, but sometimes this operation is ineffective—the cursor is always there. A program using the interface cannot inquire as to the location of the cursor; instead, the program must keep track of the cursor location itself. (In practice, this limitation is of small consequence.)

6. The physical screen can be accessed only via the interface presented in the next section. "Back door" tricks—such as sending an escape sequence to a display that you know is, say, a VT–100—probably won't work. Such kludges also violate the modular structure of the display software in this book.

The physical screen interface doesn't provide a way to divide the screen into separate windows. It also doesn't provide a virtual screen that might be bigger than the actual screen. These important capabilities are provided instead by the window (Chap. 6) and virtual screen (Chap. 7) modules.

3.2.2. Physical Screen Interface Functions

You access the physical screen via function calls. These are declared in the header file **pscreen.h**, which should be included in any source file that uses the interface.[1]

The first physical screen call must be to **PSbegin**, which initializes the display. The last call must be to **PSend**, which puts the display back into the state it was in before **PSbegin** was called, and clears it.

```
/*------------------------------------------------------------------
      PSbegin - initialize display
------------------------------------------------------------------*/
void PSbegin()
/*------------------------------------------------------------------
      PSend - terminate display
------------------------------------------------------------------*/
void PSend()
```

The display is not necessarily updated immediately when characters are written or when rectangles are filled or slid. For some implementations, changes are buffered and output all at once. You must call **PSsynch** to bring the display up to date. For an interactive application, such as a text editor, you will usually want to call **PSsynch** just before you read the keyboard. Note that an implementation is not required to do anything when **PSsynch** is called; the display might in fact be updated continuously.

```
/*------------------------------------------------------------------
      PSsynch - bring screen up to date
------------------------------------------------------------------*/
void PSsynch()
```

---

[1]To save space, we generally won't show function declarations since they add nothing (for human readers) that the function definitions don't show. We're also not showing that there are two declarations for each function, one with argument types, for those C compilers that support ANSI C prototypes, and one without. You set a compiler flag to indicate which declarations you want. Further details are provided with the software package described in Appendix C.

An application program can get the height in rows and the width in columns by calling **PSheight** and **PSwidth**:

```
/*-----------------------------------------------------------------
     PSheight - get height of physical screen
-----------------------------------------------------------------*/
int PSheight()
/*-----------------------------------------------------------------
     PSwidth - get width of physical screen
-----------------------------------------------------------------*/
int PSwidth()
```

Note that the bottom row is **PSheight()−1** and the rightmost column is **PSwidth()−1**. These are functions rather than macros so that the implementation can get the dimensions dynamically, at run time, rather than having them bound into the program at compile time. For example, the Termcap implementation will not know the size of the screen until it is actually executed on a particular terminal.

You write a null-terminated string of characters to the display with **PSwrite**. The string is written at the row and column you specify—it's not necessary to position the cursor first. However, **PSwrite** is allowed to disturb the position of the cursor, so it's a good idea to reposition the cursor after you've written to the display (perhaps just before each call to **PSsynch**).

```
/*-----------------------------------------------------------------
     PSwrite - write string
-----------------------------------------------------------------*/
void PSwrite(row, col, ncols, str, att)
int row;                              /* starting row */
int col;                              /* starting column */
int ncols;                            /* number of columns to write */
char *str;                            /* string */
int att;                              /* attribute */
```

The entire string is written with the specified attribute. To change the attribute of an already-displayed character, you must rewrite the character. The number of characters written is limited by the end of **str** or by **ncols**, whichever is less. If **row** is off the screen or **col** is greater than the last column, nothing at all is written. If **col** is less than zero or if the string would extend past the last column, only the part of the string that intersects the screen is written. If you want to write the entire string without worrying about how long it is, you can use **GIANT** (Sec. 2.6) for **ncols**, as in this example:

```
PSwrite(20, 15, GIANT, "Hello world!", A_INVERSE);
```

If you have a display buffer consisting of **CELL** structures (Sec. 2.4), you can call **PSwrtcells** to output a vector of **CELL**s directly. Without this function, you would first have to collect the characters into a null-terminated string in preparation for calling **PSwrite**, which would waste time with some implementations.   (With others, it would make no difference.) Also, with **PSwrtcells**, each character can have its own attribute.

```
/*-----------------------------------------------------------------
     PSwrtcells - write vector of CELLs
-----------------------------------------------------------------*/
void PSwrtcells(row, col, captr, ncols)
int row;                                /* starting row */
int col;                                /* starting column */
CELL *captr;                            /* CELLs */
int ncols;                              /* number of columns to write */
```

PSwrtcells treats out-of-range **row** and **col** arguments as **PSwrite** does, except that a negative **col** causes an immediate return with no output. **PSwrtcells** will rarely be used directly in application programs; it is intended primarily for the benefit of the window and virtual-screen layers.

You can fill a rectangle on the physical screen with the same character and attribute by calling **PSfill**. The rectangle you supply can be partially or entirely off the screen, in which cases only the part that intersects the screen will be filled.

```
/*-----------------------------------------------------------------
     PSfill - fill a rectangle
-----------------------------------------------------------------*/
void PSfill(srectp, chr, att)
RECT *srectp;                           /* rectangle */
char chr;                               /* fill character */
int att;                                /* fill attribute */
```

PSfill handles a variety of common screen editing functions:[2]

1. Clearing the screen.

```
        PSfill(&GIANT_RECT, ' ', A_NORM);
```

2. Clearing a row (row 20).

```
        RECT rect;

        RASG(&rect, 20, 0, 20, GIANT);
        PSfill(&rect, ' ', A_NORM);
```

3. Drawing a horizontal line.

```
        RASG(&rect, 20, 10, 20, 39);
        PSfill(&rect, C_H, A_NORM);
```

---

[2]**GIANT_RECT, RECT**, and **RASG** were defined in Sec. 2.6.

4. Drawing a vertical line.

```
RASG(&rect, 5, 40, 19, 40);
PSfill(&rect, C_V, A_NORM);
```

In fact, on a terminal like the Zenith Z–19, the single function **PSfill** replaces about a half-dozen different escape sequences. It's far more general than the escape sequences it replaces, too.

With **PSslide**, you can slide a rectangle in any of four directions: **DIR_UP, DIR_DOWN, DIR_LEFT**, or **DIR_RIGHT**.[3]

```
/*------------------------------------------------------------------
    PSslide - slide a rectangle
    RETURN: Was slide performed?
----------------------------------------------------------------*/
BOOLEAN PSslide(srectp, dir, dist)
RECT *srectp;                           /* rectangle */
int dir;                                /* direction */
int dist;                               /* distance */
```

The rectangle is clipped to its intersection with the screen if necessary, just as with **PSfill**. Sliding is destructive in that any characters in the path of the slide may be changed arbitrarily. Furthermore, the vacated area is not cleared. If you want it cleared, you can do so with a separate call to **PSfill**.

An implementation need not perform **PSslide** at all, and if it does, it need not perform it in all four directions. For any particular call, the return value indicates whether the slide took place. When the call fails, you must update the screen using an alternate approach, usually by making several calls to **PSwrite** or **PSwrtcells** instead. **PSslide** is optional because some displays do not allow characters on the screen to be moved about. The implementation for such a display could keep its own display buffer and do sliding by rewriting the affected area, but we prefer not to force the implementation to dedicate memory for this purpose. This is mainly because the virtual-screen layer (Chap. 7) will keep a display buffer anyway. That layer's equivalent function (**VSslide**) will always succeed even if it can't use **PSslide**.

PSslide (when it's implemented fully) handles the following common functions. Note the use of **PSwrite** and **PSfill** to clear the vacated character positions.

1. Deleting a character (at row 10, column 50).

```
RECT rect;

RASG(&rect, 10, 51, 10, GIANT);
PSslide(&rect, DIR_LEFT, 1);
PSwrite(10, PSwidth() - 1, 1, " ", A_NORM);
```

---

[3]These symbolic constants were defined in Sec. 2.5.

2. Inserting a character (at row 10, column 50).

```
RASG(&rect, 10, 50, 10, PSwidth() - 2);
PSslide(&rect, DIR_RIGHT, 1);
PSwrite(10, 50, 1, " ", A_NORM);
```

3. Deleting a row (row 10).

```
RASG(&rect, 11, 0, GIANT, GIANT);
PSslide(&rect, DIR_UP, 1);
RASG(&rect, PSheight() - 1, 0, GIANT, GIANT);
PSfill(&rect, ' ', A_NORM);
```

4. Inserting a row (above row 10).

```
RASG(&rect, 10, 0, PSheight() - 2, GIANT);
PSslide(&rect, DIR_DOWN, 1);
RASG(&rect, 10, 0, 10, GIANT);
PSfill(&rect, ' ', A_NORM);
```

Scrolling of the entire screen or any rectangular region of it (which might be a window), vertically or horizontally, can also be easily accomplished by calling **PSslide**.

You position the cursor to a row and column with **PSsetcur**.

```
/*---------------------------------------------------------------
    PSsetcur - set cursor position
---------------------------------------------------------------*/
void PSsetcur(row, col)
int row;                          /* row */
int col;                          /* column */
```

An implementation is allowed to change the cursor position arbitrarily whenever **PSwrite**, **PSwrtcells**, **PSfill**, or **PSslide** is called.

PSshowcur turns the cursor on or off, but it's not always implemented. When it is, the cursor is initially off.

```
/*---------------------------------------------------------------
    PSshowcur - turn cursor on or off
---------------------------------------------------------------*/
void PSshowcur(on)
BOOLEAN on;                       /* switch */
```

Finally, you can startle the user with **PSbeep**.

```
/*---------------------------------------------------------------
    PSbeep - sound bell
---------------------------------------------------------------*/
void PSbeep()
```

These twelve functions are the only way the programs in this book display anything on the physical screen. The functions are straightforward to implement, especially since **PSslide** is optional. The hard part is implementing them so that they are *fast*!

Sometimes with display packages there is a tendency for designers to implement as many functions as they can think of in order to be competitive in terms of quantity of features. Our goal is the opposite: We want to come up with the *fewest* number of functions that will allow us to implement real-world applications. By limiting ourselves to just a dozen functions, we reduce the work of implementing them, we make them easier to test, we save space, and we simplify the task of mastering their use.

3.2.3. *Example Program*

To illustrate how the physical screen interface may be used, here's a simple program that produces the screen in Fig. 3-1 and then waits for the user to type a character. Then it slides things around to look like the screen in Fig. 3-2.

```
#include "display.h"
#include "pscreen.h"
/*------------------------------------------------------------------
    Example using the physical screen interface.
-------------------------------------------------------------*/
main()
{
    RECT rect1, rect2;

    PSbegin();

    PSfill(&GIANT_RECT, ' ', A_NORM);
    RASG(&rect1, 2, 10, 11, 29);
    PSfill(&rect1, 'X', A_NORM);
    RASG(&rect2, 13, 10, 22, 49);
    PSfill(&rect2, 'O', A_NORM);
    PSwrite(24, 10, GIANT, "Before sliding", A_NORM);
    PSsynch();
    /* display at this point is shown in Fig. 3-1 */

    cget();
    if (!PSslide(&rect1, DIR_RIGHT, 40) || !PSslide(&rect2, DIR_UP, 11))
        fatal("can't slide");
    RASG(&rect1, 12, 0, 23, GIANT);
    PSfill(&rect1, ' ', A_NORM);
    PSwrite(24, 10, GIANT, " After", A_NORM);
    PSsynch();
    /* display at this point is shown in Fig. 3-2 */

    PSend();
}
```

3.3. Terminal-Specific (Z-19) Implementation

Our first implementation of the physical screen interface will be for the Zenith Z-19 terminal. This terminal was chosen because it's widely used, easy to understand, and as suitable for our purposes as any other.[4] The code

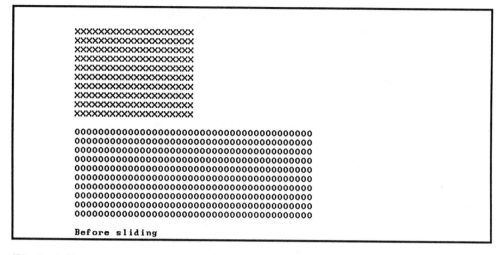

Fig. 3-1. First screen from physical screen interface example.

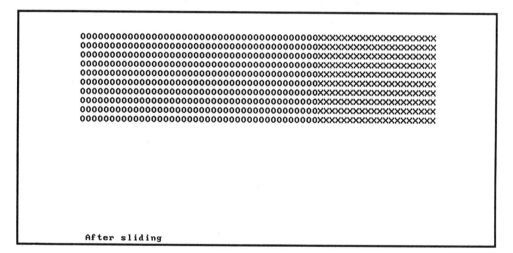

Fig. 3-2. Second screen from physical interface example.

presented here can be adapted for most common terminals without too much difficulty. But you won't want to do so, particularly on UNIX, because the Termcap (Sec. 3.4) implementation is more general.

---

[4]Also, I have one in my office.

3.3.1. Z–19 Control Codes and Escape Sequences

This will be a partial description of how the Z–19 works. We'll leave out some control codes and escape sequences that we have no need to use. For a complete description of the Z–19, you'll need to consult the reference manual that comes with it. If you do, bear in mind that we number rows and columns starting with zero, whereas Zenith numbers them starting with one. So our row 24 is their row (or line) 25.

The Z–19 has a 25-row by 80-column screen, but the last row is awkward to use, so we'll treat it like a 24-row terminal. It can show all of the ASCII displayable characters plus special symbols that match some of the line-drawing characters defined in Sec. 2.2. For simplicity, we won't use the special symbols. The only attributes supported are normal and inverse, a typical state of affairs for terminals.

Displayable ASCII characters are placed onto the screen at the cursor, overwriting what's currently there. Then the cursor moves one position to the right (like a typewriter). You can choose what happens after the eightieth character is displayed by turning wrap-around on or off. When it's on, the cursor goes to column 0 of the next line; when it's off, the cursor stays in column 79. Initially, wrap-around is off. For implementing the physical screen interface, it usually doesn't matter which mode is on because we'll reposition the cursor before each write, and because we are allowed to mess up the cursor position after a write. However, wrap-around from the last row causes the entire screen to scroll up, which is unacceptable. So we'll make sure wrap-around is off.

The following list gives some of the ASCII control characters (codes below 32) that affect the Z–19's screen. Decimal ASCII codes are given in parentheses.

BEL—Bell (7)
> Rings the bell.

BS—Backspace (8)
> Moves the cursor one position to the left. Does nothing if the cursor is already in column 0.

HT—Horizontal Tab (9)
> Moves the cursor to the next tab position. Tab positions are set at eight column intervals, with the first tab position in column 8.

LF–Line Feed (10)
> Moves the cursor to the next line, but leaves the column alone. If the cursor is in row 23, a Line Feed leaves it on that row, but all of the text on the screen is scrolled up one row. The

contents of row zero are scrolled off the top of the screen and
are lost. Row 23 is cleared.

CR—Carriage Return (13)

Moves the cursor to column zero, but leaves the row alone.

ESC—Escape (27)

Indicates that the next few characters are to be interpreted as
a control sequence, and are not to be treated normally (for
example, displayed). This is called an *escape sequence*. The
length of an escape sequence varies and can be determined only
by knowing what the sequence actually is. On the Z−19,
lengths vary from two to four characters.

A few other ASCII control codes also do things to the Z−19, but we won't
use them in this book.

Here is a partial list of Z−19 escape sequences, only a few of which are
needed to implement the physical screen interface. In this list, the symbol
ESC stands for the Escape control character. Spaces are used in escape
sequences for clarity; they are not part of the sequence. In reviewing this
list, you will note that the escape sequences seem to have been chosen at
random. With the possible exception of the first six sequences, the letters
chosen make no sense whatsoever.

Cursor Up **ESC A**

Moves the cursor up one row. Does nothing if the cursor is
already in row 0.

Cursor Down **ESC B**

Moves the cursor down one row. Does nothing if the cursor is
already in row 23. Note that this behaves differently from Line
Feed, which would cause scrolling.

Cursor Right **ESC C**

Moves the cursor right one column. Does nothing if the cursor
is already in column 79.

Cursor Left **ESC D**

Moves the cursor left one column. Does nothing if the cursor is
already in column 0.

Cursor Home **ESC H**

Moves the cursor to row 0, column 0.

Reverse Index **ESC I**

Same as Cursor Up, but the screen scrolls down when a
Reverse Index is issued with the cursor already in row 0. This

means that rows 0 through 22 are moved down, the old row 23 is lost, and row 0 is cleared.

Direct Cursor Addressing **ESC** Y *r c*

Moves the cursor to row *r*, column *c*. These two numbers are encoded by adding 32, which is the ASCII code for space. Thus the escape sequence is always made of displayable characters (not that they're actually displayed, of course). You can position the cursor like this (Escape is 33 in octal):

```
int row, col;
printf("\033Y%c%c", row + 32, col + 32);
```

For example, to move the cursor to row 17, column 53, the sequence sent would be **ESC Y 1 U**.

Normally, the cursor can't be moved lower than row 23. But if row 24 is enabled (see Set Modes, below) the cursor can be moved to that row. Direct cursor addressing is the only way to move the cursor to row 24.

Save Cursor Position **ESC j**

The cursor position is saved, so it can be restored with ...

Restore Cursor Position **ESC k**

Moves the cursor to the position previously saved.

Cursor Position Report **ESC n**

The terminal reports the current cursor position by sending an escape sequence *back* to the host. This four-character escape sequence is identical in format to the Direct Cursor Addressing sequence described previously in this list. Note that a newline character is not appended to the sequence, so the program receiving the sequence must not expect to read a full line of text.

Clear Display and Home Cursor **ESC E**

All but row 24 of the screen are cleared and the cursor is moved to row 0, column 0.

Erase to End of Page **ESC J**

The character at the cursor, the rest of that row, and all rows below it except for row 24 are cleared.

Erase to End of Line **ESC K**

The character at the cursor and the rest of that row are cleared.

Insert Line **ESC L**

The screen from the current row through row 22 is moved down one row. The old contents of row 23 are lost, the current row is cleared, and the cursor is moved to column 0.

Delete Line **ESC M**

> The screen from the next row through row 23 is moved up one row. The old contents of the current row are lost, row 23 is cleared, and the cursor is moved to column 0.

Delete Character **ESC N**

> The contents of the current row from the next character through column 79 are moved left one character. The current character is lost, a space is displayed in column 79, and the cursor stays where it is.

Enter Insert Character Mode **ESC @**

> Puts the Z−19 into a mode where displaying a character causes the character at the cursor and the rest of the row to be moved to the right. The old character in column 79 is lost. This is in contrast to the normal case, in which displaying a character simply overwrites the current character.

Exit Insert Character Mode **ESC O**

> Puts the Z−19 back into normal, overwrite mode. As an example, the common operation of inserting a space can be done like this:

```
printf("\033@ \033O");
```

Erase To Beginning Of Display **ESC b**

> All rows above the current row and the current row up through the current character are cleared.

Erase Entire Line **ESC l**

> The current line is cleared. This is the recommended way to clear row 24. The other clearing sequences tend to behave erratically when issued in that row.

Erase to Beginning Of Line **ESC o**

> The current row up through the current character are cleared.[5]

Enter Inverse Video Mode **ESC p**

> Subsequent characters sent to the terminal are displayed in inverse video.

Exit Inverse Video Mode **ESC q**

> Subsequent characters are displayed normally.

---

[5]If you think the Z−19 has an excessive number of ways to erase, you're in agreement with me.

Set Mode—Enable Row 24 **ESC** **x 1**

Nothing happens to the screen right away, but the cursor is allowed to be moved to row 24 with Direct Cursor Addressing (see above).

Reset Mode—Disable Row 24 **ESC** **y 1**

Row 24 is cleared and disabled. The cursor can't be moved there until it is enabled again.

Set Mode—Cursor Off **ESC** **x 5**

The cursor disappears from view, although the need to position it before displaying characters remains.

Reset Mode—Cursor On **ESC** **y 5**

The cursor is made visible.

Wrap-Around At End Of Line **ESC** **v**

This puts the terminal in wrap-around mode: After a character is displayed in column 79, the cursor moves to column 0 of the next row. If the next row would be row 24, the screen scrolls up and the cursor remains in row 23.

Discard At End Of Line **ESC** **w**

Wrap-around mode is exited, so that when a character is displayed in column 79, the cursor remains in that column and in that row.

Reset **ESC** **z**

The Z-19 is reset to its power-up configuration. The following is a partial list of what happens: the screen is cleared; the cursor moves to row 0, column 0; the cursor appears; wrap-around mode is exited; insert character mode is exited; inverse video is exited; row 24 is disabled and cleared.

3.3.2. *Z-19 Implementation of the Physical Screen Interface*

The Z-19 implementation of the physical screen interface is in the file **ps_z19.c**. It begins like this:

```
#include "display.h"
#include "pscreen.h"

#define MAXROW 23
#define MAXCOL 79
#define BEL '\007'

#define putstr(s) fputs(s, stdout)
#define putchr(c) fputc(c, stdout)
```

The macros **putstr** and **putchr** are defined so that we can easily change how characters are sent to the terminal. For now, we'll use the standard C functions **fputs** and **fputc**. We'll have more to say about output shortly.

Since any 8-bit character code can be used in calls to **PSwrite**, **PSwrtcells**, and **PSfill**, we need to map the non-ASCII codes to a code that the Z−19 can display. A 256-element translation table does this quickly. Any character that can't be reasonably mapped becomes a question mark.

```
static char map[] = {
    /* 0 */     '?', '?', '?', '?', '?', '?', '?', '?', '?', '?',
    /* 10 */    '?', '?', '?', '?', '?', '?', '?', '?', '?', '?',
    /* 20 */    '?', '?', '?', '?', '?', '?', '?', '?', '?', '?',
    /* 30 */    '?', '?', ' ', '!', '"', '#', '$', '%', '&', '\'',
    /* 40 */    '(', ')', '*', '+', ',', '-', '.', '/', '0', '1',
    /* 50 */    '2', '3', '4', '5', '6', '7', '8', '9', ':', ';',
    /* 60 */    '<', '=', '>', '?', '@', 'A', 'B', 'C', 'D', 'E',
    /* 70 */    'F', 'G', 'H', 'I', 'J', 'K', 'L', 'M', 'N', 'O',
    /* 80 */    'P', 'Q', 'R', 'S', 'T', 'U', 'V', 'W', 'X', 'Y',
    /* 90 */    'Z', '[', '\\', ']', '^', '_', '`', 'a', 'b', 'c',
    /* 100 */   'd', 'e', 'f', 'g', 'h', 'I', 'j', 'k', 'l', 'm',
    /* 110 */   'n', 'o', 'p', 'q', 'r', 's', 't', 'u', 'v', 'w',
    /* 120 */   'x', 'y', 'z', '(', '|', ')', ' ', '?', '?', '?',
    /* 130 */   '?', '?', '?', '?', '?', '?', '?', '?', '?', '?',
    /* 140 */   '?', '?', '?', '?', '?', '?', '?', '?', '?', '?',
    /* 150 */   '?', '?', '?', '?', '?', '?', '?', '?', '?', '?',
    /* 160 */   '?', '?', '?', '?', '?', '?', '?', '?', '?', '?',
    /* 170 */   '?', '?', '?', '?', '?', '?', ' ', ' ', ' ', '|',
    /* 180 */   '|', '?', '?', '?', '?', '|', '|', '=', '=', '?',
    /* 190 */   '?', '-', '-', '-', '-', '|', '-', '-', '?', '?',
    /* 200 */   '=', '=', '=', '=', '|', '=', '=', '?', '?', '?',
    /* 210 */   '?', '?', '?', '?', '?', '?', '?', '-', '-', '?',
    /* 220 */   '?', '?', '?', '?', '?', '?', '?', '?', '?', '?',
    /* 230 */   '?', '?', '?', '?', '?', '?', '?', '?', '?', '?',
    /* 240 */   '?', '?', '?', '?', '?', '?', '?', '?', '?', '?',
    /* 250 */   '?', '?', '?', '?', '?', ' ' };
```

To map the character **ch**, we can use the expression:

```
map[ch & 0377]
```

Masking off all but the low-order 8 bits counters the effect of sign extension that might take place with some C compilers if the character code is greater than 127.

Because we often need to map all or part of a string, here's a handy function to do that:

```
/*-------------------------------------------------------------------
    mapstr - map string to 7-bit ASCII
    RETURN: 1st argument.
-------------------------------------------------------------------*/
static char *mapstr(buf, str, n)
char *buf;                              /* buffer to hold mapped string */
char *str;                              /* source string */
int n;                                  /* number of characters to map */
{
    char *b;

    b = buf;
    while (n-- > 0)
        *b++ = map[*str++ & 0377];
```

```
        *b = '\0';
        return(buf);
    }
```

Now we can begin with the interface functions themselves. Here are the first five:

```
/*------------------------------------------------------------------
    PSbegin - initialize display
--------------------------------------------------------------------*/
void PSbegin()
{
    static char buf[BUFSIZ];

    setbuf(stdout, buf);
    putstr("\033E\033y1"); /* clear screen & home cursor; disable row 24 */
    putstr("\033w\0330\033q"); /* exit wrap-around, insert, inverse */
    PSshowcur(FALSE);
}

/*------------------------------------------------------------------
    PSend - terminate display
--------------------------------------------------------------------*/
void PSend()
{
    PSshowcur(TRUE);
    putstr("\033E\033y1"); /* same sequence as for PSbegin() */
    putstr("\033w\0330\033q");
    PSsynch();
}

/*------------------------------------------------------------------
    PSsynch - bring screen up to date
--------------------------------------------------------------------*/
void PSsynch()
{
    fflush(stdout);
}

/*------------------------------------------------------------------
    PSheight - get height of physical screen
    RETURN: Height.
--------------------------------------------------------------------*/
int PSheight()
{
    return(MAXROW + 1);
}

/*------------------------------------------------------------------
    PSwidth - get width of physical screen
    RETURN: Width.
--------------------------------------------------------------------*/
int PSwidth()
{
    return(MAXCOL + 1);
}
```

To speed up processing, we use **setbuf** to force the Standard I/O Library to buffer output into groups of **BUFSIZ** characters. (**BUFSIZ** is defined in **stdio.h**.) **PSsynch** is the perfect place to flush the buffer. Remember that the buffer will also be flushed automatically if it gets full before a call to **PSsynch**, so screen output doesn't necessarily wait until then.

Next comes **PSwrite**. Most of the code is concerned with adjusting **col**, **ncols**, and the starting point in **str** in case they are out of range. (You may want to review the rules in Sec. 3.2.2). Note how **mapstr** neatly clips the string to a width of **ncols** for us.

```
/*-------------------------------------------------------------------
        PSwrite - write string
-----------------------------------------------------------------*/
void PSwrite(row, col, ncols, str, att)
int row;                                /* starting row */
int col;                                /* starting column */
int ncols;                              /* number of columns to write */
char *str;                              /* string */
int att;                                /* attribute */
{
    int slen;
    char buf[MAXCOL + 2];

    if (row < 0 || row > MAXROW || col > MAXCOL)
        return;
    if (col + ncols > MAXCOL + 1)
        ncols = MAXCOL + 1 - col;
    slen = strlen(str);
    if (col < 0) {
        if (-col >= slen)
            return;
        str = &str[-col];
        ncols += col;
        col = 0;
    }
    ncols = MIN(ncols, slen);
    if (att != A_NORM)
        putstr("\033p"); /* enter inverse video */
    PSsetcur(row, col);
    putstr(mapstr(buf, str, ncols));
    if (att != A_NORM)
        putstr("\033q"); /* exit inverse video */
}
```

PSwrtcells is a little more complicated than **PSwrite**, because characters alternate with attributes. We map and output the characters one by one. We take care to output the inverse video escape sequences only when necessary, or else the number of characters output would become excessive.

```
/*-------------------------------------------------------------------
        PSwrtcells - write vector of CELLs
-----------------------------------------------------------------*/
void PSwrtcells(row, col, captr, ncols)
int row;                                /* starting row */
int col;                                /* starting column */
CELL *captr;                            /* CELLs */
int ncols;                              /* number of columns to write */
{
    int i;
    BOOLEAN normal = TRUE;

    if (row < 0 || row > MAXROW || col < 0 || col > MAXCOL)
        return;
    if (col + ncols > MAXCOL + 1)
        ncols = MAXCOL + 1 - col;
    PSsetcur(row, col);
```

```
    for (i = 0; i < ncols; i++) {
        if (captr[i].att == A_NORM) {
            if (!normal) {
                putstr("\033q"); /* exit inverse video */
                normal = TRUE;
            }
        }
        else
            if (normal) {
                putstr("\033p"); /* enter inverse video */
                normal = FALSE;
            }
        putchr(map[captr[i].chr & 0377]);
    }
    if (!normal)
        putstr("\033q"); /* exit inverse video */
}
```

This is a case where **PSwrtcells** isn't substantially more efficient than several calls to **PSwrite**, but later in this chapter we'll get to implementations where it is.

In **PSfill**, we take advantage of the fact that its most common use is to clear all or part of the screen. This is when the character is a space and the attribute is normal; we set the variable **canclear** accordingly. There are two special cases: when the rectangle extends the full width of the screen and down to the last row, and when the rectangle extends to the last column, but is either not full width or else does not go all the way down. In the former case we can use the Erase to End of Page sequence, and in the latter the Erase to End of Line sequence.

```
/*---------------------------------------------------------------------
      PSfill - fill a rectangle
  ---------------------------------------------------------------------*/
void PSfill(srectp, chr, att)
RECT *srectp;                           /* rectangle */
char chr;                               /* fill character */
int att;                                /* fill attribute */
{
    RECT srect;
    int r, ncols;
    char buf[MAXCOL + 2];
    BOOLEAN canclear;

    if (!intersect(srectp, MAXROW, MAXCOL, &srect))
        return;
    canclear = (chr == ' ' && att == A_NORM);
    ncols = RWIDTH(&srect);
    if (canclear && srect.r2 == MAXROW && ncols == MAXCOL + 1) {
        PSsetcur(srect.r1, 0);
        putstr("\033J"); /* erase to end of screen */
    }
    else {
        if (!canclear || srect.c2 != MAXCOL) {
            if (att != A_NORM)
                putstr("\033p"); /* enter inverse video */
            setmem(buf, ncols, map[chr & 0377]);
            buf[ncols] = '\0';
        }
        for (r = srect.r1; r <= srect.r2; r++) {
            PSsetcur(r, srect.c1);
```

```
                if (canclear && srect.c2 == MAXCOL)
                    putstr("\033K"); /* erase to end of line */
                else
                    putstr(buf);
        }
    }
    if (att != A_NORM)
        putstr("\033q"); /* exit inverse video */
}
```

In **PSslide** we want to make as much use as possible of characters that are already on the screen. The Z−19 lacks an actual slide escape sequence, but some sliding can be done with insert line paired with delete line and insert character paired with delete character. These are the cases that can be handled:

1. If the rectangle is full width and the direction is up, delete rows above the rectangle and insert rows below it. The area below the rectangle will seem to bounce as it goes up and then back down where it came from, but this is better than not being able to slide at all.

2. Similarly, if the rectangle is full width and the direction is down, delete rows below the rectangle and insert rows above it.

3. If the direction is left, delete characters to the left of the rectangle. If the rectangle did not extend all the way to the last column, insert characters to the rectangle's right to move the right part of the screen back into position. This operation is done for each row in the rectangle. It's very fast on each row, but there's still a little sideways bounce. On some Z−19s, the whole screen jiggles for a moment, in addition to bouncing.

4. Similarly, if the direction is right, delete characters to the right of the rectangle and insert characters to the left. If the rectangle extends all the way to the last column, the deletion can be skipped.

When we pair a deletion with an insertion, it's crucial that the deletion be done first. Otherwise needed characters might roll off the screen and be lost.

If none of these cases applies, **PSslide** returns **FALSE** and the caller will have to accomplish the screen update by rewriting all or part of it with **PSwrite** or **PSwrtcells**.

```
/*-----------------------------------------------------------------
    PSslide - slide a rectangle
    RETURN: Was slide performed?
-----------------------------------------------------------------*/
BOOLEAN PSslide(srectp, dir, dist)
RECT *srectp;                           /* rectangle */
int dir;                                /* direction */
int dist;                               /* distance */
{
    RECT srect;
    int r, c;
```

```
    if (!intersect(srectp, MAXROW, MAXCOL, &srect))
        return(TRUE);
    switch(dir) {
    case DIR_UP:
        if (srect.cl != 0 || srect.c2 != MAXCOL)
            return(FALSE);
        PSsetcur(srect.rl - dist, 0);
        for (r = 0; r < dist; r++)
            putstr("\033M"); /* delete line */
        if (srect.r2 < MAXROW) {
            PSsetcur(srect.r2 + 1, 0);
            for (r = 0; r < dist; r++)
                putstr("\033L"); /* insert line */
        }
        return(TRUE);
    case DIR_DOWN:
        if (srect.cl != 0 || srect.c2 != MAXCOL)
            return(FALSE);
        PSsetcur(srect.r2 + 1, 0);
        for (r = 0; r < dist; r++)
            putstr("\033M"); /* delete line */
        PSsetcur(srect.rl, 0);
        for (r = 0; r < dist; r++)
            putstr("\033L"); /* insert line */
        return(TRUE);
    case DIR_LEFT:
        for (r = srect.rl; r <= srect.r2; r++) {
            PSsetcur(r, srect.cl - dist);
            for (c = 0; c < dist; c++)
                putstr("\033N"); /* delete character */
            if (srect.c2 < MAXCOL) {
                PSsetcur(r, srect.c2 - dist + 1);
                for (c = 0; c < dist; c++)
                    putstr("\033@ \0330"); /* insert blank character */
            }
        }
        return(TRUE);
    case DIR_RIGHT:
        for (r = srect.rl; r <= srect.r2; r++) {
            if (srect.c2 < MAXCOL - 1) {
                PSsetcur(r, srect.c2 + 1);
                for (c = 0; c < dist; c++)
                    putstr("\033N"); /* delete character */
            }
            PSsetcur(r, srect.cl);
            for (c = 0; c < dist; c++)
                putstr("\033@ \0330"); /* insert blank character */
        }
        return(TRUE);
    }
}
```

Finally, here are the last three functions. Note the trouble we go to in
PSsetcur to avoid calling **printf**, which is too slow.

```
/*-------------------------------------------------------------------
      PSsetcur - set cursor position
--------------------------------------------------------------------*/
void PSsetcur(row, col)
int row;                                    /* row */
int col;                                    /* column */
{
    static char *seq = "\033Yrc";
```

```
        seq[2] = 32 + row;
        seq[3] = 32 + col;
        putstr(seq); /* position cursor */
}

/*-------------------------------------------------------------------
        PSshowcur - turn cursor on or off
-------------------------------------------------------------------*/
void PSshowcur(on)
BOOLEAN on;                                      /* switch */
{
        if (on)
            putstr("\033y5"); /* cursor on */
        else
            putstr("\033x5"); /* cursor off */
}

/*-------------------------------------------------------------------
        PSbeep - sound bell
-------------------------------------------------------------------*/
void PSbeep()
{
        putchr(BEL);
}
```

All of the optimizations in **PSfill** and **PSslide** depended on the rectangle's touching a border of the screen. There's a tendency these days for designers to draw frames around windows on the screen, so that the application never actually displays anything in the first and last rows or columns. This looks great, and it makes hardly any difference on a personal computer where the screen is extremely fast. But it really slows down ordinary terminals. If possible, design the screen so that the main area is full width and extends to the last row. For example, in a text editor, put status messages and prompts at the top of the screen rather than the bottom, and give the user all eighty columns to type in. Then most optimizations can be exploited, and vertical and horizontal bounce will be minimized.

3.3.3. Generalizations to Other Terminals

As popular as the Z−19 may be, it's still true that most terminals aren't Z−19s and their escape sequences are likely to be quite different. How can the Z−19 physical screen implementation be enhanced to support other terminals? Three approaches come to mind:

1. Using the Z−19 version as a guide, code versions for other terminals: **ps_vt100.c, ps_adm3a.c,** and so on. For each application, create a separate executable program for each terminal type by linking with the appropriate implementation. This method has several disadvantages: You need to be a C programmer to be able to support a new terminal, and you need to be able to relink and retest the application. It isn't practical for a software vendor to support users who do this for themselves, because they can foul up the application if they don't code their physical screen implementation correctly. All those executable

programs take up too much space. Finally, under UNIX, if several users have different terminals, the kernel won't share the instruction segments of the application processes, since each is running a distinct program.

2.   Pick three or four of the most popular terminal types and code a single implementation that handles all of them by determining the terminal type and branching appropriately (at run time, not at compile time). An environment variable (**TERM**, say) can be set by a user to indicate the terminal type. This approach might be reasonable in a situation where the terminals are fairly new, since it's common these days for terminals to emulate one of the dominant terminal types (usually a DEC VT–100 or VT–52). But this method still isn't as flexible as we'd like.

3.   Go all the way: Build a database with an entry for practically every terminal ever made. List the characteristics of each terminal and give the escape sequences for each operation. Design a set of retrieval functions to access the data for a particular terminal. Don't gear the physical screen implementation towards any specific terminal, but rather take all of the information from the terminal database at runtime. This method is certainly general enough, but it's very hard to know what characteristics and operations the database should record, not to mention the problem of gathering accurate information to populate the database.

The last method is the best in theory, but it sounds like so much work that we're tempted to rule it out as being impractical. Fortunately, someone's already done it: It's called Termcap, and we'll describe it in the next section.

3.4. UNIX Termcap

Termcap is a database of terminal capabilities along with a set of accessing functions that are called from C programs. It was designed by William Joy at Berkeley, originally as a part of his **vi** text editor. Today Termcap comes not only with Berkeley 4BSD UNIX but with most other versions, too. AT&T has redesigned Termcap for System V (theirs is called Terminfo), but the principles—and the accessing functions—are the same. Only the database format is different. We'll discuss the Berkeley design here, and interested readers can learn about the AT&T changes from the System V documentation. All of our code runs correctly under System V, however.

Termcap allows a program to determine at runtime how a terminal works, instead of embedding specific escape sequences in the code as we did for the Z–19 in the previous section. The program accesses the environment

variable **TERM** to get the name of the terminal and then goes to the Termcap database to find out its capabilities. With the Berkeley shell **csh**, **TERM**
can be set like this:

```
% setenv TERM z19
```

or like this:

```
% set term=z19
```

(The shell variable **term** is automatically copied to the environment variable
TERM.) With the AT&T Bourne shell **sh**, you do it like this:

```
$ TERM=z19
$ export TERM
```

In practice you won't actually execute these commands directly, but
rather place them in your login profile so they will be executed automatically
each time you log in. How do you know whether your terminal is supported
and what its name is? You can just try an obvious name or two, and you may
get lucky. Or you can scan through the Termcap database to see what's
there.

Termcap is often confused with the much more widely known Curses
(Sec. 3.5). Termcap only supplies information about capabilities and escape
sequences; the programmer still has to figure out how and when to use them.
Curses is a higher-level package that implements a virtual terminal. Operations on that virtual terminal are then translated to specific escape sequences
to be sent out, which Curses gets from Termcap. Should you use Termcap or
Curses? This is a difficult question to answer in general, but we'll try in Sec.
3.8. Whichever you pick, it will affect only the internals of your program
—the user deals with the Termcap database and the **TERM** variable in
either case.

We'll begin our treatment of Termcap with the terminal capability
database itself. It's too complicated to explain completely in this book, and
we won't try. We'll give just enough detail to enable us to use it to implement
the physical screen interface. Indeed, you may never have to look at the
database yourself, since any terminal you use probably already has an entry.
If you do want the details, you can find them in the "termcap" pages in your
UNIX manual (usually in section 5).

Next, we'll explain how to access the database from a C program using
the handy functions supplied for that purpose. Then we'll be ready to implement the physical screen interface using Termcap.

3.4.1. Termcap Database

The Termcap database is kept in an ordinary text file whose path is
/etc/termcap. Each terminal's entry takes up several lines, and the entries

follow one another in an arbitrary order. Since a given entry has to be found by sequentially scanning the file, and since it's often over 100,000 bytes long, it pays to put the most frequently accessed entries near the top.

There are over 370 entries on the University of Colorado's 4.3BSD system. Here's one for the Z−19 (are you sitting down?):

```
kb|h19|heath|h19-b|h19b|heathkit|heath-19|z19|zenith|heathkit h19:\
    :cr=^M:nl=^J:bl=^G:\
    :al=1*\EL:am:le=^H:bs:cd=\EJ:ce=\EK:cl=\EE:cm=\EY%+ %+ :co#80:dc=2\EN:\
    :dl=1*\EM:do=\EB:ei=\EO:ho=\EH:im=\E@:li#24:mi:nd=\EC:as=\EF:ae=\EG:\
    :ms:ta=^I:pt:sr=\EI:se=\Eq:so=\Ep:up=\EA:vs=\Ex4:ve=\Ey4:\
    :kb=^h:ku=\EA:kd=\EB:kl=\ED:kr=\EC:kh=\EH:kn#8:\
    :kl=\ES:k2=\ET:k3=\EU:k4=\EV:k5=\EW:\
    :16=blue:17=red:18=white:k6=\EP:k7=\EQ:k8=\ER:\
    :es:hs:ts=\Ej\Ex5\Exl\EY8%+ \Eo:fs=\Ek\Ey5:ds=\Eyl:
```

All but the last line end with a backslash; leading tabs don't matter.

The entry begins with a list of synonyms for the terminal, separated by bars and terminated with a colon. By convention, the first name is two characters long (required by older versions of UNIX), the second name is the most common name, and the last name is the longest and most descriptive. But any of the names may be used to retrieve the entry.

Next come the capabilities themselves, separated by colons. Hence, the first three capabilities for the Z−19 are:

```
cr=^M
nl=^J
bl=^G
```

A capability name is always two characters long. Its value may be one of three types:

1. *Numeric.* A numeric capability consists of the name, a pound sign (#), and an integer. An example (from the third line of the Z−19 entry) is:

    ```
    co#80
    ```

    which states that there are 80 columns.

2. *Boolean.* A Boolean capability consists only of the name, indicating that the terminal has that capability. An example (also from the third line) is:

    ```
    am
    ```

    which indicates that the terminal has automatic margins (that is, the cursor wraps around to the next line from column 80).

3. *String.* A string capability (the most common type) consists of a name, an equals sign (=), and a string of characters (terminated by a colon). An example is:

    ```
    ce=\EK
    ```

which indicates that the sequence to clear to the end of the row is **ESC K.**

Because the Termcap file should contain only displayable ASCII characters, some special codes are provided that stand for ASCII control characters:

\E	**ESC**
\b	backspace
\f	form feed
\n	line feed (newline)
\r	carriage return
\t	horizontal tab
\\	\
\^	^
\nnn	character whose code is nnn in octal
\072	:
\200	null character

The cursor motion (**cm**) capability is special because the actual sequence sent isn't constant—it depends on the row and column numbers desired. Termcap uses a technique reminiscent of **printf** to format the sequence. For the Z–19, the capability is:

```
cm=\EY%+ %+
```

This means that the row and column numbers are to be added to the ASCII code for a space (this is explained in Sec. 3.3.1). Other format codes are defined to handle all of the different ways of encoding row and column numbers that terminals use. We won't describe these in detail here.

At this point you may wish to review the Z–19 entry above. It should be much more readable now. Of course, we still don't know what the two-letter capability names mean, but we'll get to that shortly.

Some terminals take so long to execute certain operations (such as insert line) that they'll lose track of a few characters that immediately follow. To make up for this, some sequences should be followed by padding characters—usually nulls—that have no effect on the terminal. No harm is done if these are lost. A string capability may have an integer right after the equals sign to indicate the number of milliseconds of padding required. An example is:

```
dc=2\EN
```

This means that after sending the sequence **ESC N** to delete a character, two milliseconds of nulls should be sent. Sometimes the padding delay depends on the number of rows affected by the operation. In this case the number is followed by an asterisk (*) and is interpreted as the number of milliseconds per row. An example is:

```
al=1*\EL
```

After inserting a row, the terminal needs a delay of one millisecond per affected row. If the row is inserted above row 10, say, then there are about fourteen affected rows, so fourteen milliseconds of nulls should be sent.

The actual number of padding characters sent depends on the speed of the terminal. For example, at 1200 bits per second, each character takes about 8.33 milliseconds. So two null characters should be sent for a fourteen-millisecond delay. Fortunately, you don't have to do these calculations because the transmission of padding characters is handled automatically by the Termcap access functions. You do have to be aware of which capabilities might require a delay and figure out how many rows are affected.

Today's terminals are much faster than those of the past, and they often have buffers to guard against losing characters, so delays are seldom required. In a few years, perhaps this awkward problem will go away completely.

Termcap doesn't care what the actual capability names are; any collection of names can be used. Which names are meaningful is determined by the programs that use Termcap, the most important of which are the Curses package and **vi**. About 112 capabilities are currently defined in the Termcap manual, but not all of these are actually used. We will describe only twenty-eight capabilities that our implementation of the physical screen interface needs. These include two new capabilities to turn the cursor on and off so we can implement **PSshowcur**. It's not necessary to modify the Termcap database for our programs, however; the entries already there will work just fine. Without the new capabilities, the cursor will simply stay on.

The following chart lists each capability name, its type (**N** for numeric, **B** for Boolean, and **S** for string), whether padding is supported, and a brief description. **P** in the *Pad* column means that padding is independent of the number of affected rows; **P*** means it is dependent.

Name	Type	Pad	Description
al	S	P*	insert line above
am	B		has automatic margins (wrap around)
bc	S		backspace (if BS won't work)
cd	S	P*	clear to end of display
ce	S	P	clear to end of line
cl	S	P*	clear screen
co	N		number of columns
cm	S	P	cursor motion
dl	S	P*	delete line
dc	S	P*	delete character
dm	S		enter delete mode
ed	S		end delete mode
ei	S		end insert mode
hc	B		is hardcopy terminal
ic	S	P	insert character

Name	Type	Pad	Description
im	S		enter insert mode
ip	S	P*	post-insert padding
li	N		number of rows
pc	S		pad character
sc	S		show cursor (on)
se	S		end standout mode
so	S		enter standout mode
te	S		end cursor addressing mode
ti	S		enter cursor addressing mode
up	S		cursor up
ve	S		end visual mode
vs	S		enter visual mode
zc	S		zap cursor (off)

Capabilities **sc** and **zc** aren't defined in the Berkeley Termcap documentation—they were invented for this book.

If the terminal has automatic margins (capability **am**) you can't put anything in the lower right corner of the display. If you do, the terminal will try to wrap to the next row and will scroll the screen up to make room, thus throwing everything out of position. We'll see how this is taken into account in Sec. 3.4.3.

The various insert character capabilities need some additional explanation. Some terminals, like the Z–19, enter an insert mode in which displayed characters push the rest of the line to the right. Capability **im** enters this mode and **ei** exits it. To open up a character position, a space is sent while in this mode. Other terminals use a single sequence to insert a space; this is done by **ic**. Generally, a terminal will define **im** and **ei**, or **ic**, but not both. The following procedure can be used to insert N positions on either type of terminal:

1. Send the **im** sequence, if any.

2. Send the **ic** sequence, if any.

3. Send a space. If **ic** did anything, this does no harm since it overlays the space just opened up.

4. Send the **ip** sequence for any required post-insert padding.

5. Go back to step 2, unless *N* spaces have already been opened.

6. Send the **ei** sequence, if any.

We'll show this in C in Sec. 3.4.3.

3.4.2. Termcap Access Functions

Termcap comes with functions that make it easy to access the database and send the appropriate sequences to the terminal. To link with them, you must use a **−l** (*library*) argument on the **cc** command line:

```
$ cc main.o ps_termc.o -ltermcap
```

If you have the new version of Curses (see Sec. 3.5), the Termcap and Curses libraries are combined, so you link like this:

```
$ cc main.o ps_termc.o -lcurses
```

This assumes, of course, that your system has Termcap installed. If you have **vi**, you probably already have Termcap, or you can get it from your operating system vendor.

To use the access functions, you must first declare four external variables:

```
/*-------------------------------------------------------------------
    External variables needed by tgoto() and tgets()
--------------------------------------------------------------------*/
char *BC;                       /* backspace ("bc" capability) */
char *UP;                       /* cursor up ("up" capability) */
char PC;                        /* pad character ("pc" capability) */
short ospeed;                   /* terminal speed (from ioctl()) */
```

You must make **BC** and **UP** point to the **bc** and **up** capability strings before you call **tgoto**. Similarly, you must set **PC** to the first character of the **pc** string and **ospeed** to the speed of the terminal, before you call **tgets**. We'll explain how these variables are used by those functions shortly. The value in **ospeed** is actually the encoding of the speed as returned by the **ioctl** system call.[6] To see how it's set, look at the **setraw** function in Sec. 4.1.1.

The first Termcap call is to **tgetent**, which tries to retrieve the appropriate entry from the database:

```
/*-------------------------------------------------------------------
    tgetent - get Termcap entry
    RETURN: -1 or 0 on error; 1 on success
--------------------------------------------------------------------*/
int tgetent(bp, name)
char *bp;                       /* buffer to hold entry */
char *name;                     /* name of terminal */
```

The returned value is −1 if the database can't be opened, 0 if an entry for the specified terminal can't be found, and 1 if all went well. Before the call, **bp** must point to a buffer that's large enough to hold the entry. The Termcap documentation states that 1024 bytes is enough. You must not deallocate or otherwise modify this buffer while the Termcap access functions are being used.

The second argument is the name of the terminal, obtained from any source at all. You should do what most other screen software does and get it from the **TERM** variable in the environment, using the standard UNIX function **getenv**:

---

[6]See Sec. 4.4 of [Roc85].

```
char tcbuf[1024], *getenv();

switch (tgetent(tcbuf, getenv("TERM"))) {
case -1:
    fatal("can't open termcap file");
case 0:
    fatal("terminal not defined");
case 1:
    break;
default:
    fatal("bad return from tgetent");
}
```

After you call **tgetent,** you can retrieve the capabilities themselves. Use **tgetnum** to retrieve a numeric capability:

```
/*-------------------------------------------------------------------
    tgetnum - get numeric capability
    RETURN: capability or -1 if absent
--------------------------------------------------------------------*/
int tgetnum(id)
char *id;                               /* capability name */
```

Here's an example:

```
int cols;

if ((cols = tgetnum("co")) == -1)
    printf("co capability is absent\n");
else
    printf("There are %d columns\n", cols);
```

Boolean capabilities are retrieved with **tgetflag:**

```
/*-------------------------------------------------------------------
    tgetflag - get Boolean capability
    RETURN: 1 if present; 0 if absent
--------------------------------------------------------------------*/
int tgetflag(id)
char *id;                               /* capability name */
```

as shown in this example:

```
if (tgetflag("am"))
    printf("Has automatic margins\n");
else
    printf("No automatic margins\n");
```

You get string capabilities with **tgetstr:**

```
/*-------------------------------------------------------------------
    tgetstr - get string capability
    RETURN: pointer to capability or NULL if absent
--------------------------------------------------------------------*/
char *tgetstr(id, area)
char *id;                               /* capability name */
char **area;                            /* address of buffer pointer */
```

You should maintain a pointer to a buffer large enough to hold all the string capabilities that you will use. The address of this pointer is passed to **tgetstr**, and it will automatically advance it to the next available byte after each string capability is retrieved. The Termcap documentation doesn't say how big this buffer should be, but Curses assumes that 512 bytes is sufficient for *all* string capabilities for any single terminal. Thus, by allowing room for 512 bytes you may be assured that, if your program blows up, then programs using Curses will blow up, too. (Small comfort!)

Backslash encodings (such as \E) are replaced by their byte values by **tgetstr**, but the special coding for **cm** and padding numbers are left alone.

You might use **tgetstr** like this:

```
char capbuf[512], *area, *CL, *CM, *tgetstr();

area = capbuf;
CL = tgetstr("cl", &area);
CM = tgetstr("cm", &area);
```

Don't forget that the second argument is a *pointer* to a pointer, not a plain pointer.

To format a cursor motion (**cm**) string for a specific row and column, you can use **tgoto** to make the appropriate calculations and substitutions:

```
/*-------------------------------------------------------------------
    tgoto - format cursor motion capability
    RETURN: cursor motion sequence
 -----------------------------------------------------------------*/
char *tgoto(cm, destcol, destrow)
char *cm;                           /* cursor motion capability */
int destcol;                        /* column */
int destrow;                        /* row */
```

The string returned by **tgoto** is cleverly constructed so as not to contain certain ASCII control characters, such as line feed, EOT (Control-D), or null. These characters might be interpreted incorrectly by UNIX device drivers, by modems, or by communication processors. Additionally, a null character can't appear in a C string because it acts as the string terminator. So, when any of these dangerous characters would appear in the sequence, **tgoto** instead sends the cursor just past or below the target point and then backspaces or goes up from there. That's why it needs the **bc** and **up** sequences in the global variables **BC** and **UP**.

In case of error, **tgoto** returns a very strange error indication: the string **OOPS**. If you ever run a screen program that displays that on your terminal, you'll know where it came from!

Once you have a string capability from **tgetstr** or, in the case of **cm**, from **tgoto**, you output it with **tputs**. You could output it with a standard output function, such as **fputs**, but it might begin with a padding code which would have to be stripped off and replaced with the appropriate padding characters. The function **tputs** does the whole job for you.

```
/*-----------------------------------------------------------------
      tputs - send sequence and padding to terminal
------------------------------------------------------------------*/
void tputs(cp, affcnt, outc)
char *cp;                          /* sequence to send */
int affcnt;                        /* number of affected rows */
int (*outc)();                     /* pointer to output function */
```

If the capability to be sent can take padding that depends on the number of affected rows, you must supply the correct number as the second argument. If the padding is independent, or if none applies, the second argument can be 1. To figure out how many pad characters to send, **tputs** needs to know the terminal's speed, which it gets from **ospeed**. It pads with null characters or whatever **PC** is set to.

The third argument is the address of a function that will output one character in whatever way you think appropriate. It will be called by **tputs** for each character in the sequence and for each pad character. You can't use **putchar** for the third argument because it's a macro, not a function. You can't use **fputc** because it takes two arguments (the second is the stream pointer), and **tputs** only calls it with one. So you need to define your own output function:

```
            static void outc(ch)
            char ch;
            {
                putchar(ch);
            }
```

Then you can call **tputs** like this to clear the screen and move the cursor to row 17, column 53:

```
            char *tgoto();

            tputs(CL, 1, outc);
            tputs(tgoto(CM, 53, 17), 1, outc);
```

More examples of how these functions are used are in the next section.

3.4.3. *Termcap Implementation of the Physical Screen Interface*

Now we're ready to implement the physical screen interface using Termcap. Some terminals are unbelievably weird, and a few obscure capabilities are defined only to handle one or two odd terminals.[7] We'll make no attempt to handle every terminal ever made, like **vi** does. Our implementation will work only on terminals that can be defined in terms of the twenty-eight capabilities listed in Sec. 3.4.1. This includes most terminals already in use

---

[7]For example: Some Hazeltines can't display a tilde (~). Some terminals (such as Televideos) can't change to inverse video without using up a screen position.

and nearly all the new ones. If you're unfortunate enough to use one of the oddballs, you can make the enhancements yourself.

If you've skipped Sec. 3.3, you might want to review it now because the Termcap implementation is based on the Z–19 implementation.

The file **ps_termc.c** begins this way:

```
#include "display.h"
#include "pscreen.h"

char *getenv(), *tgetstr(), *tgoto();

#define MAXCOLS 132
#define BEL '\007'
```

MAXCOLS is just used to allocate some buffers—it doesn't indicate the size of the screen, although it is an upper bound.

Next come four output macros:

```
#define putctln(s, n) (s != NULL ? tputs(s, n, outc) : 0)
#define putctl(s) putctln(s, 1)
#define putstr(s) fputs(s, stdout)
#define putchr(c) putchar(c)
```

The first two are used to output string capabilities that might require padding. If the padding is row independent, **putctl** can be used; otherwise, **putctln** is used with the number of affected rows as the second argument. The function **outc** was shown in the previous section. The macro **putstr** is used to output regular strings (that is, characters to be displayed), and **putchr** is used to output single characters. As we did with the Z–19, we'll let the Standard I/O Library buffer output and we'll flush the buffer in **PSsynch**.

We'll keep the capabilities we need in global variables:

```
char *AL;                    /* insert line */
BOOLEAN AM;                  /* automatic margins (wrap around) */
char *BC;                    /* backspace (if not BS) */
char *CD;                    /* clear to end of display */
char *CE;                    /* clear to end of line */
char *CL;                    /* clear screen */
int CO;                      /* number of columns */
char *CM;                    /* cursor motion */
char *DC;                    /* delete character */
char *DL;                    /* delete line */
char *DM;                    /* enter delete mode */
char *ED;                    /* end delete mode */
char *EI;                    /* end insert mode */
BOOLEAN HC;                  /* hardcopy terminal */
char *IC;                    /* insert character */
char *IM;                    /* enter insert mode */
char *IP;                    /* post-insert padding */
int LI;                      /* number of rows */
char PC, *PCstr;             /* pad character and string */
char *SC;                    /* show cursor (on) */
char *SE;                    /* end standout mode */
char *SO;                    /* enter standout mode */
char *TE;                    /* end cursor addressing mode */
```

```
char *TI;                              /* enter cursor addressing mode */
char *UP;                              /* cursor up */
char *VE;                              /* end visual mode */
char *VS;                              /* enter visual mode */
char *ZC;                              /* zap cursor (off) */
```

These will be initialized in **PSbegin** by calling **getcaps**:

```
/*--------------------------------------------------------------------
        getcaps - get all needed capabilities
--------------------------------------------------------------------*/
static void getcaps()
{
    static char capbuf[512];
    char tcbuf[1024], *area;

    switch (tgetent(tcbuf, getenv("TERM"))) {
    case -1:
        fatal("can't open termcap file");
    case 0:
        termfatal("is not defined");
    case 1:
        break;
    default:
        fatal("bad return from tgetent");
    }
    area = capbuf;
    AL = tgetstr("al", &area);
    AM = tgetflag("am");
    BC = tgetstr("bc", &area);
    CD = tgetstr("cd", &area);
    CE = tgetstr("ce", &area);
    CL = tgetstr("cl", &area);
    CO = tgetnum("co");
    CM = tgetstr("cm", &area);
    DC = tgetstr("dc", &area);
    DL = tgetstr("dl", &area);
    DM = tgetstr("dm", &area);
    ED = tgetstr("ed", &area);
    EI = tgetstr("ei", &area);
    HC = tgetflag("hc");
    IC = tgetstr("ic", &area);
    IM = tgetstr("im", &area);
    IP = tgetstr("ip", &area);
    LI = tgetnum("li");
    PCstr = tgetstr("pc", &area);
    SC = tgetstr("sc", &area);
    SE = tgetstr("se", &area);
    SO = tgetstr("so", &area);
    TE = tgetstr("te", &area);
    TI = tgetstr("ti", &area);
    UP = tgetstr("up", &area);
    VE = tgetstr("ve", &area);
    VS = tgetstr("vs", &area);
    ZC = tgetstr("zc", &area);
    if (PCstr != NULL)
        PC = PCstr[0];
    else
        PC = '\0';
    if (LI == -1 || HC)
        termfatal("is not a CRT");
    CO = MIN(CO, MAXCOLS);
}
```

We set **PC** to the first character of the **pc** capability string, for use by **tputs**. If the terminal doesn't have an **li** (number of lines) capability, or if it's actually specified as a hardcopy terminal, we exit with a message. Unlike **vi**, our software won't work on non-CRT terminals. Lastly, we limit the number of columns in case the screen is unusually wide.

The function **termfatal** constructs and outputs an error message that includes the name of the terminal:

```
/*-------------------------------------------------------------------
        termfatal - add terminal name to fatal message
----------------------------------------------------------------*/
static void termfatal(msg)
char *msg;
{
    char buf[100];

    sprintf(buf, "Terminal %s %s\n", getenv("TERM"), msg);
    fatal(buf);
}
```

We need to map all characters to 7-bit codes, just as we did for the Z-19, so we'll use the same **map** table and **mapstr** functions that we defined in Sec. 3.3.2. We won't repeat the code for these here.

Now we're ready for **PSbegin**, **PSend**, **PSsynch**, **PSheight**, and **PSwidth**:

```
/*-------------------------------------------------------------------
        PSbegin - initialize display
----------------------------------------------------------------*/
void PSbegin()
{
    static char buf[BUFSIZ];

    setraw();
    setbuf(stdout, buf);
    getcaps();
    putctl(TI);
    putctl(VS);
    PSshowcur(FALSE);
}


/*-------------------------------------------------------------------
        PSend - terminate display
----------------------------------------------------------------*/
void PSend()
{
    PSshowcur(TRUE);
    putctl(CL);
    putctl(VE);
    putctl(TE);
    unsetraw();
}
```

```
/*-------------------------------------------------------------------
     PSsynch - bring screen up to date
  -----------------------------------------------------------------*/
void PSsynch()
{
     fflush(stdout);
}

/*-------------------------------------------------------------------
     PSheight - get height of physical screen
     RETURN: Height.
  -----------------------------------------------------------------*/
int PSheight()
{
     return(LI);
}

/*-------------------------------------------------------------------
     PSwidth - get width of physical screen
     RETURN: Width.
  -----------------------------------------------------------------*/
int PSwidth()
{
     return(CO);
}
```

PSbegin puts the terminal into raw mode so that output characters won't be transformed by the UNIX terminal device driver. The functions **setraw** and **unsetraw** will be explained in Sec. 4.1.1. Note that **setraw** initializes **ospeed** for us, so we don't even have to declare it here.

Capabilities **ti** and **vs** initialize the terminal. In **PSend**, capabilities **ve** and **te** restore the terminal to the way it was. Note that the **putctl** macro will output nothing if any of these capabilities are undefined.

PSwrite and **PSwrtcells** are a lot like the implementations for the Z–19:

```
/*-------------------------------------------------------------------
     PSwrite - write string
  -----------------------------------------------------------------*/
void PSwrite(row, col, ncols, str, att)
int row;                                /* starting row */
int col;                                /* starting column */
int ncols;                              /* number of columns to write */
char *str;                              /* string */
int att;                                /* attribute */
{
     int slen;
     char buf[MAXCOLS + 1];

     if (row < 0 || row >= LI || col >= CO)
         return;
     if (col + ncols > CO)
         ncols = CO - col;
     slen = strlen(str);
```

```
        if (col < 0) {
            if (-col >= slen)
                return;
            str = &str[-col];
            ncols += col;
            col = 0;
        }
        ncols = MIN(ncols, slen);
        if (row == LI - 1 && col + ncols == CO && AM)
            ncols--; /* skip lower right corner */
        if (att != A_NORM)
            putctl(SO);
        PSsetcur(row, col);
        putstr(mapstr(buf, str, ncols));
        if (att != A_NORM)
            putctl(SE);
    }


/*--------------------------------------------------------------------
    PSwrtcells - write vector of CELLs
--------------------------------------------------------------------*/
void PSwrtcells(row, col, captr, ncols)
int row;                                 /* starting row */
int col;                                 /* starting column */
CELL *captr;                             /* CELLs */
int ncols;                               /* number of columns to write */
{
    int i;
    BOOLEAN normal = TRUE;

    if (row < 0 || row >= LI || col < 0 || col >= CO)
        return;
    if (col + ncols > CO)
        ncols = CO - col;
    if (row == LI - 1 && col + ncols == CO && AM)
        ncols--; /* skip lower right corner */
    PSsetcur(row, col);
    for (i = 0; i < ncols; i++) {
        if (captr[i].att == A_NORM) {
            if (!normal) {
                putctl(SE);
                normal = TRUE;
            }
        }
        else
            if (normal) {
                putctl(SO);
                normal = FALSE;
            }
        putchr(map[captr[i].chr & 0377]);
    }
    if (!normal)
        putctl(SE);
}
```

When the terminal has automatic margins (capability **am**), we avoid displaying the last character in the string or the vector of **CELL**s if it would appear in the last column of the last row.

PSfill uses the same optimizations as the one for the Z–19, except the clearing sequences can only be sent if they exist. Another change is that we turn inverse video on and off separately for each row because some terminals

automatically turn it off when a new row is begun. We also have to watch
out for the lower right corner, as we did with **PSwrite** and **PSwrtcells**.

```
/*-------------------------------------------------------------------
    PSfill - fill a rectangle
---------------------------------------------------------------*/
void PSfill(srectp, chr, att)
RECT *srectp;                           /* rectangle */
char chr;                               /* fill character */
int att;                                /* fill attribute */
{
    RECT srect;
    int r, ncols, nrows;
    char buf[MAXCOLS + 1];
    BOOLEAN canclear;

    if (!intersect(srectp, LI - 1, CO - 1, &srect))
        return;
    canclear = (chr == ' ' && att == A_NORM);
    ncols = RWIDTH(&srect);
    nrows = RHEIGHT(&srect);
    if (CL != NULL && canclear && ncols == CO && nrows == LI)
        putctln(CL, nrows);
    else if (CD != NULL && canclear && srect.r2 == LI - 1 && ncols == CO) {
        PSsetcur(srect.r1, 0);
        putctln(CD, nrows);
    }
    else {
        buf[0] = '\0';
        for (r = srect.r1; r <= srect.r2; r++) {
            PSsetcur(r, srect.c1);
            if (att != A_NORM)
                putctl(SO);
            if (CE != NULL && canclear && srect.c2 == CO - 1)
                putctl(CE);
            else {
                if (buf[0] == '\0') {
                    setmem(buf, ncols, map[chr & 0377]);
                    buf[ncols] = '\0';
                }
                if (r == LI - 1 && srect.c2 == CO - 1 && AM)
                    buf[ncols - 1] = '\0'; /* skip lower right corner */
                putstr(buf);
            }
            if (att != A_NORM)
                putctl(SE);
        }
    }
}
```

PSslide is also like the one for the Z-19, except we have to make sure
that we can insert and delete rows and characters before using those actions
to slide the rectangle.

```
/*-------------------------------------------------------------------
    PSslide - slide a rectangle
    RETURN: Was slide performed?
---------------------------------------------------------------*/
BOOLEAN PSslide(srectp, dir, dist)
RECT *srectp;                           /* rectangle */
int dir;                                /* direction */
int dist;                               /* distance */
{
```

```
RECT srect;
int r, c;

if (!intersect(srectp, LI - 1, CO - 1, &srect))
    return(TRUE);
switch(dir) {
case DIR_UP:
    if (AL == NULL || DL == NULL || srect.cl != 0 || srect.c2 != CO - 1)
        return(FALSE);
    PSsetcur(srect.rl - dist, 0);
    for (r = 0; r < dist; r++)
        putctln(DL, LI - srect.rl + dist);
    if (srect.r2 < LI - 1) {
        PSsetcur(srect.r2 + 1, 0);
        for (r = 0; r < dist; r++)
            putctln(AL, LI - srect.r2);
    }
    return(TRUE);
case DIR_DOWN:
    if (AL == NULL || DL == NULL || srect.cl != 0 || srect.c2 != CO - 1)
        return(FALSE);
    PSsetcur(srect.r2 + 1, 0);
    for (r = 0; r < dist; r++)
        putctln(DL, LI - srect.r2);
    PSsetcur(srect.rl, 0);
    for (r = 0; r < dist; r++)
        putctln(AL, LI - srect.rl);
    return(TRUE);

case DIR_LEFT:
    if ((IC == NULL && IM == NULL) || DC == NULL)
        return(FALSE);
    for (r = srect.rl; r <= srect.r2; r++) {
        PSsetcur(r, srect.cl - dist);
        putctl(DM);
        for (c = 0; c < dist; c++)
            putctl(DC);
        putctl(ED);
        if (srect.c2 < CO - 1) {
            PSsetcur(r, srect.c2 - dist + 1);
            putctl(IM);
            for (c = 0; c < dist; c++) {
                putctl(IC);
                putctl(IP);
                putchr(' ');
            }
            putctl(EI);
        }
    }
    return(TRUE);
case DIR_RIGHT:
    if ((IC == NULL && IM == NULL) || DC == NULL)
        return(FALSE);
    for (r = srect.rl; r <= srect.r2; r++) {
        if (srect.c2 < CO - 2) {
            PSsetcur(r, srect.c2 + 1);
            putctl(DM);
            for (c = 0; c < dist; c++)
                putctl(DC);
            putctl(ED);
        }
        PSsetcur(r, srect.cl);
        putctl(IM);
        for (c = 0; c < dist; c++) {
            putctl(IC);
            putctl(IP);
            putchr(' ');
```

```
            }
            putctl(EI);
        }
        return(TRUE);
    }
}
```

The insertion algorithm used here was explained in Sec. 3.4.1.

Finally, here are the last three functions:

```
/*-------------------------------------------------------------------
      PSsetcur - set cursor position
--------------------------------------------------------------------*/
void PSsetcur(row, col)
int row;                                 /* row */
int col;                                 /* column */
{
    char *cmseq;

    cmseq = tgoto(CM, col, row);
    if (strcmp(cmseq, "OOPS") == 0)
        termfatal("lacks cursor addressing");
    putctl(cmseq);
}

/*-------------------------------------------------------------------
      PSshowcur - turn cursor on or off
--------------------------------------------------------------------*/
void PSshowcur(on)
BOOLEAN on;                              /* switch */
{
    if (on)
        putctl(SC);
    else
        putctl(ZC);
}

/*-------------------------------------------------------------------
      PSbeep - sound bell
--------------------------------------------------------------------*/
void PSbeep()
{
    putchr(BEL);
}
```

3.5. UNIX Curses

The Termcap implementation in Sec. 3.4.3 is superior to the Z−19 implementation in Sec. 3.3.2, but it still has two problems:

1. **PSsetcur** is called too many times: with every call to **PSwrite** and **PSwrtcells,** and several times for **PSfill** and **PSslide.** It may send a half-dozen or so characters to the terminal with every call. This is wasteful, because the cursor is often already close to where it needs to go—a simple carriage return, newline, backspace, or non-destructive space (capability **nd**), or a combination of them, would do the trick.

2. Since the screen doesn't have to be updated until **PSsynch** is called, some display operations that are superseded by others could be skipped. For example, many applications clear a part of the screen (**PSfill**) and then rewrite it with text (**PSwrite**). There's no need to actually clear a row if it is about to be filled with text.

Because display speed is so critical to many interactive applications, these problems really hurt when terminals are operated at low speeds (300 or 1200 bits per second), as they usually are. When speeds approach 9600 bits per second, these inefficiencies become much less important.

The Curses package, designed by Ken Arnold at Berkeley, corrects these problems. It's extremely clever about moving the cursor (hence its name), outputting the full cursor motion sequence only if the "shortcut" would actually be longer. Furthermore, it keeps images of the current screen and the updated screen and sends only the sequences necessary to bring the two together. Many redundant updates are automatically eliminated.

Of course, all of these smarts take up time and space. The Curses routines can add about 10,000 bytes of instructions and data to a program, and it takes lots of CPU time to perform the optimizations. Sometimes, Curses even makes things worse. For example, if you call the function **deleteln** to delete a row, most versions of Curses won't realize that the **dl** capability can be used—they will rewrite most of the screen instead. So the decision to use Curses instead of plain Termcap is not at all clear-cut. We'll come back to this quandary in Sec. 3.8.

There are actually two versions of Curses: The old one, direct from Berkeley, is the one most commonly found. The new one, heavily modified by AT&T, is available only on some versions of System V. The actual function-calls and macros are upwardly compatible from old to new, but the new one does a much smarter job of deciding how to update the display. With a single exception, we won't use any functions added in new Curses, so our implementation of the physical screen interface will work with both. The exception is the function **idlok**, which tells new Curses to use the insert and delete line capabilities. As we'll see in Sec. 3.8, this makes an important difference in performance.

Which Curses do you have on your system? If it's not System V, you undoubtedly have the old one. If you do have System V, you may or may not have the old one. A test that seems to work is to see if the symbolic constant **A_UNDERLINE** is defined in the Curses header file:

```
$ grep A_UNDERLINE /usr/include/curses.h
#define A_UNDERLINE    0000400
$
```

If it is, you have new Curses. Also, new Curses seems to be associated with the Terminfo database of terminal information (Terminfo is in the directory **/usr/lib/terminfo**). Of course, all of these facts are subject to change as

System V is revised and as new Curses propagates to AT&T licensees.

When we refer to Curses without specifying old or new, we mean old Curses. Hence, if we say that "Curses doesn't do such-and-such," it may be that new Curses does do it. If we say that "Curses *does* do such-and-such," this applies to both.

Just as we did for Termcap, we'll first describe Curses itself and then present an implementation for the physical screen interface. Everything we said in Sec. 3.4 about the Termcap database applies here too, since Curses uses Termcap.

3.5.1. Curses Windows

Curses uses two predefined windows, and more if you define your own. The first predefined window is named **curscr** and represents the current contents of the physical screen, that is, what is actually visible. The second is named **stdscr** and represents the work space that you change with the various Curses screen functions. Changes that you make to **stdscr** don't appear on **curscr** until you call **refresh**.

The predefined windows are always the same size as the physical screen. Or, more precisely, their size is determined by the **co** (columns) and **li** (lines) capabilities. You can create additional windows the same size as or smaller than the physical screen with the function **newwin**. You can then apply a screen function to one of these instead of to **stdscr**. Calling **wrefresh** updates the portion of **curscr** covered by the window.

The Curses definition of window is different from the definition we're using in this book. Although Curses windows can overlap, you can't update an overlapped window without bringing it to the front; when you call **wrefresh**, the entire window is updated, not just the visible part. So it's not possible for several processes to be writing to windows simultaneously if they overlap. Also, there's no window manager to resize, move, and activate windows.

We won't use Curses windows to implement windows in this book, and we won't describe the window features of Curses in any detail. We don't really need them—our windowing layer operates on top of the physical screen interface. It doesn't use Curses inefficiently because, when you call **refresh**, it is already smart enough to only look at the rectangle that actually changed. The processing load is the same as if you had actually written to a Curses window explicitly.

You don't ever actually write to the predefined window **curscr**—Curses does that for you, in its own way. So the only Curses window we will deal with is **stdscr**. Most of the Curses functions that we'll introduce operate on it by default. The two that don't (**scrollok** and **clearok**) will require a first argument of **stdscr**.

3.5.2. Curses Access Functions

Curses functions are kept in their own library, so to link you need to do something like this:

```
$ cc main.o ps_curse.o -lcurses -ltermcap
```

You need both libraries because Curses uses Termcap. For new Curses, the libraries have been combined, so you link like this:

```
$ cc main.o ps_curse.o -lcurses
```

Each source file that calls Curses functions must include the header **curses.h**, which defines constants, structures, variables, and macros. In fact, many "functions" that we'll describe are really macros that are defined there. Unfortunately, **curses.h** redefines **TRUE** and **FALSE**, which we have already defined in **display.h** (Sec. 2.5). New Curses also redefines **A_BLINK**. Fortunately, the definitions for **TRUE** and **FALSE** are the same, and we won't be using **A_BLINK**, so our symbols can be undefined when both headers are included:

```
#include "display.h"
#undef TRUE
#undef FALSE
#undef A_BLINK
#include <curses.h>
```

Your first Curses call must be to **initscr**, which initializes data structures and allocates memory for the **stdscr** buffer:

```
/*-----------------------------------------------------------------
    initscr - initialize Curses
    RETURN: (WINDOW *)ERR if out of memory; otherwise OK
-----------------------------------------------------------------*/
WINDOW *initscr()
```

This function also initializes two global integer variables: **LINES** contains the number of screen rows (from the **li** capability), and **COLS** contains the number of screen columns (from the **co** capability). **WINDOW, ERR, OK, LINES**, and **COLS** are defined in **curses.h**.

You can follow **initscr** with optional calls that set certain modes, such as whether returns can be sent without mapping them to line feeds, whether the terminal is to be in raw mode, and whether the screen will scroll:

```
/*-----------------------------------------------------------------
    nonl - turn off mapping of CR to LF
-----------------------------------------------------------------*/
void nonl()

/*-----------------------------------------------------------------
    raw - put terminal into raw mode
-----------------------------------------------------------------*/
void raw()
```

```
/*-----------------------------------------------------------------------
     scrollok - allow or disallow scrolling
-------------------------------------------------------------------*/
void scrollok(win, flag)
WINDOW *win;                            /* window (should be stdscr) */
BOOLEAN flag;                           /* should scrolling be allowed? */
```

There seems to be some flexibility here, but my experience has been that it's best to always call **nonl** and **raw**, and never **scrollok**—I know that Curses works well that way, and I'm less sure about the other combinations. (Run your own experiments, if you like.) There's another reason for calling **raw**: The keyboard functions in Chapter 4 will have to run in raw mode, so they will establish it even if Curses doesn't. If you don't call **raw**, Curses doesn't realize that the terminal is in raw mode and screen output gets fouled up. It's OK to set the terminal to raw mode twice, but make sure that you restore it in the opposite order. That is, do it like this:

> *initialize Curses*
> *initialize keyboard module*
>
> ...
>
> *terminate keyboard module*
> *terminate Curses*

rather than like this:

> *initialize Curses*
> *initialize keyboard module*
>
> ...
>
> *terminate Curses*
> *terminate keyboard module*

If you do it the second way, the keyboard module will leave the terminal in raw mode, because that's the mode it was in when that module was initialized.

If you don't allow scrolling (and you should not), you can't use the lower right position of the screen (the same problem we had with Termcap).[8] Curses will refuse to put anything there and will return **ERR** from those functions that attempt to do so. In the return value descriptions that follow, this is referred to as *scrolling illegally*.

We'll see **initscr**, **nonl**, and **raw** used in Sec. 3.5.3, and we'll see how

---

[8]Theoretically, you should be able to use that position as long as capability **am** (automatic margins) isn't defined, but Curses doesn't take that flag into account. Even if it did, you'd still be in trouble if you moved to a terminal that did define **am**.

the physical screen module and the keyboard module are initialized and terminated in Chapter 5.

For new Curses only, you should call **idlok** to allow it to exploit the insert and delete line capabilities:

```
/*-------------------------------------------------------------------
    idlok - allow or disallow insert/delete line
            New Curses only.
------------------------------------------------------------------*/
void idlok(win, flag)
WINDOW *win;                            /* window (should be stdscr) */
BOOLEAN flag;                           /* should insert/delete be allowed? */
```

For compatibility, you should make this call only when **A_UNDERLINE** is defined (see Sec. 3.5.3).

When you're done with Curses (normally, just before your program exits), you call **endwin**:

```
/*-------------------------------------------------------------------
    endwin - terminate Curses
------------------------------------------------------------------*/
void endwin()
```

The physical screen (window **curscr**) doesn't get written until you call **refresh**, which is a lot like **PSsynch**:

```
/*-------------------------------------------------------------------
    refresh - update physical screen
    RETURN: ERR if window would scroll illegally; otherwise OK
------------------------------------------------------------------*/
int refresh()
```

You should call **refresh** whenever the screen should be brought up to date, usually just before you read the keyboard.

As **stdscr** is updated, Curses keeps track of which rows have been changed, and, for each changed row, the leftmost and rightmost changed columns. When **refresh** is called, it operates only on the changed rows.[9] It scans backward from the end of the row to see if trailing blanks can be output by clearing to the end of the line (only possible if capability **ce** is defined). Then it outputs any remaining characters between the leftmost and rightmost changed columns.

During the execution of **refresh**, or any other time the cursor has to be moved (by **move**, for example), Curses tries to discover the shortest sequence that will do the job. Tricks it uses include homing the cursor and moving right and down from there, moving right or left from the current position and then up or down, homing down to the bottom of the screen and then moving

---

[9]Here's where its myopia prevents Curses from discovering that rows may have been inserted or deleted. Old Curses never uses the insert line (**al**), delete line (**dl**), insert character (**im**, **ic**), or delete character (**dc**) capabilities.

right and up, and returning to column 0 of the current row and then moving right and up or down. When moving right, tabs are used if possible. Of course, these tricks are only viable if the corresponding capabilities are defined (for example, homing down requires the **ll** capability).

In addition to all of this, Curses knows that outputting a character moves the cursor to the right for free, and, on terminals with automatic margins (capability **am**), going past the last column gives a carriage return and line feed for free. Thus, the cursor is often either already where it belongs or can be moved there with only one or two control characters. Naturally, the tricky sequence is only used if it's shorter than conventional cursor motion (capability **cm**).

Occasionally, it's desirable to force Curses to rewrite the screen without making use of anything that might already be there. This is done by calling **clearok** any time before the next **refresh**:

```
/*---------------------------------------------------------------
      clearok - force screen rewrite
-------------------------------------------------------------*/
void clearok(win, flag)
WINDOW *win;                          /* window (should be stdscr) */
BOOLEAN flag;                         /* should scrolling be allowed? */
```

It's a good idea for every application using Curses to give the user a way to force the screen to be rewritten. This is needed if the communication hardware loses some characters, if another process (or the system administrator) writes to the screen, or if Curses just updates the screen incorrectly and the user is lucky enough to notice it. With **vi**, this is done by the Control–L command. That's something of an informal standard, so you might consider using Control–L, too.

The functions that follow are used to update the screen (**stdscr**). Don't forget that nothing happens until **refresh** is called. These functions are so simple that their usage should be clear from the comments.

```
/*---------------------------------------------------------------
      move - position cursor
      RETURN: ERR if window would scroll illegally; otherwise OK
-------------------------------------------------------------*/
int move(row, col)
int row;                              /* row number */
int col;                              /* column number */

/*---------------------------------------------------------------
      addch - output character at current cursor position
      RETURN: ERR if window would scroll illegally; otherwise OK
-------------------------------------------------------------*/
int addch(ch)
int ch;                               /* character */
```

```
/*-----------------------------------------------------------------
     mvaddch - combination of move() and addch()
     RETURN: ERR if window would scroll illegally; otherwise OK
-----------------------------------------------------------------*/
int mvaddch(row, col, ch)
int row;                                 /* row number */
int col;                                 /* column number */
int ch;                                  /* character */


/*-----------------------------------------------------------------
     addstr - output string at current cursor position
     RETURN: ERR if window would scroll illegally; otherwise OK
-----------------------------------------------------------------*/
int addstr(str)
char *str;                               /* null-terminated string */


/*-----------------------------------------------------------------
     mvaddstr - combination of move() and addstr()
     RETURN: ERR if window would scroll illegally; otherwise OK
-----------------------------------------------------------------*/
int mvaddstr(row, col, str)
int row;                                 /* row number */
int col;                                 /* column number */
char *str;                               /* null-terminated string */


/*-----------------------------------------------------------------
     insch - insert character at current cursor position, sliding rest
             of line to the right
     RETURN: ERR if window would scroll illegally; otherwise OK
-----------------------------------------------------------------*/
int insch(ch)
int ch;                                  /* character */


/*-----------------------------------------------------------------
     insertln - insert row above current row, moving lower rows down,
                losing last row, clearing new row, and leaving cursor
                where it is
     RETURN: ERR if window would scroll illegally; otherwise OK
-----------------------------------------------------------------*/
int insertln()


/*-----------------------------------------------------------------
     delch - delete character at current cursor position, sliding rest
             of line to the left and making last character a space
-----------------------------------------------------------------*/
void delch()


/*-----------------------------------------------------------------
     deleteln - delete current row, moving lower rows up, making last
                row blank, and leaving cursor where it is
-----------------------------------------------------------------*/
void deleteln()


/*-----------------------------------------------------------------
     erase - clear entire screen and home cursor
-----------------------------------------------------------------*/
void erase()


/*-----------------------------------------------------------------
     clrtobot - clear screen from cursor to last row
-----------------------------------------------------------------*/
void clrtobot()


/*-----------------------------------------------------------------
     clrtoeol - clear row from cursor to end
-----------------------------------------------------------------*/
void clrtoeol()
```

```
/*-------------------------------------------------------------------
     standout - enter standout mode (usually, inverse video)
-------------------------------------------------------------------*/
void standout()

/*-------------------------------------------------------------------
     standend - exit standout mode
-------------------------------------------------------------------*/
void standend()
```

The use of these functions will be made more clear in the next section when we implement the physical screen interface.

We've shown only a fraction of the functions available with Curses. Other functions manipulate windows, read characters from the keyboard and the screen, sense the position of the cursor, and format input and output in the manner of **printf**. The Curses manual pages only list the functions —they don't provide enough details so you can actually use them. For that you'll have to find a copy of [Arn]. However, if you use the physical screen interface you won't need to deal with Curses directly.

3.5.3. Curses Implementation of the Physical Screen Interface

If you've studied the physical screen interface implementations for the Z–19 and Termcap, you're practically an expert by now, so you should have no trouble understanding the implementation for Curses. It's the simplest one of all because Curses handles so much of the tough parts automatically. If you didn't bother reading Sec. 3.3.2, you should do so now; we won't repeat the explanations we gave there.

The file **ps_curse.c** begins like this:

```
#include "display.h"
#undef TRUE
#undef FALSE
#undef A_BLINK
#include <curses.h>
#include "pscreen.h"

#define MAXCOLS 132
#define BEL "\007"

static BOOLEAN changed = FALSE;        /* has screen been changed? */
```

We'll use the variable **changed** to indicate whether any functions have changed the screen. In **PSsynch**, we want to call **refresh** only if there's work to do. Curses takes time to discover that nothing has happened.

We need to do the same character mapping that we did in the Z–19 and Termcap implementations. We won't show the array **map**; you can find it in Sec. 3.3.2. We don't need the function **mapstr** because we'll send characters to Curses one at a time.

The first few functions are what you'd expect:

```
/*-------------------------------------------------------------------
    PSbegin - initialize display
-------------------------------------------------------------------*/
void PSbegin()
{
    if (initscr() == (WINDOW *)ERR)
        fatal("initscr - insufficient memory");
    nonl();
    raw();
#ifdef A_UNDERLINE
    idlok(stdscr, TRUE);
#endif
    PSshowcur(FALSE);
}

/*-------------------------------------------------------------------
    PSend - terminate display
-------------------------------------------------------------------*/
void PSend()
{
    erase();
    clearok(stdscr, TRUE);
    refresh();
    endwin();
}

/*-------------------------------------------------------------------
    PSsynch - bring screen up to date
-------------------------------------------------------------------*/
void PSsynch()
{
    if (changed) {
        refresh();
        changed = FALSE;
    }
}

/*-------------------------------------------------------------------
    PSheight - get height of physical screen
    RETURN: Height.
-------------------------------------------------------------------*/
int PSheight()
{
    return(LINES);
}

/*-------------------------------------------------------------------
    PSwidth - get width of physical screen
    RETURN: Width.
-------------------------------------------------------------------*/
int PSwidth()
{
    return(COLS);
}
```

Next come **PSwrite** and **PSwrtcells**:

```
/*-------------------------------------------------------------------
    PSwrite - write string
-------------------------------------------------------------------*/
void PSwrite(row, col, ncols, str, att)
int row;                            /* starting row */
int col;                            /* starting column */
int ncols;                          /* number of columns to write */
char *str;                          /* string */
int att;                            /* attribute */
{
```

88

```
    int i, slen;

    if (row < 0 || row >= LINES || col >= COLS)
        return;
    changed = TRUE;
    if (col + ncols > COLS)
        ncols = COLS - col;
    slen = strlen(str);
    if (col < 0) {
        if (-col >= slen)
            return;
        str = &str[-col];
        ncols += col;
        col = 0;
    }
    ncols = MIN(ncols, slen);
    if (att != A_NORM)
        standout();
    for (i = 0; i < ncols; i++)
        mvaddch(row, col + i, map[str[i] & 0377]);
    if (att != A_NORM)
        standend();
}


/*-------------------------------------------------------------------
    PSwrtcells - write vector of CELLs
-------------------------------------------------------------------*/
void PSwrtcells(row, col, captr, ncols)
int row;                                /* starting row */
int col;                                /* starting column */
CELL *captr;                            /* CELLs */
int ncols;                              /* number of columns to write */
{
    int i;
    BOOLEAN normal = TRUE;

    if (row < 0 || row >= LINES || col < 0 || col >= COLS)
        return;
    changed = TRUE;
    if (col + ncols > COLS)
        ncols = COLS - col;
    for (i = 0; i < ncols; i++) {
        if (captr[i].att == A_NORM) {
            if (!normal) {
                standend();
                normal = TRUE;
            }
        }
        else
            if (normal) {
                standout();
                normal = FALSE;
            }
        mvaddch(row, col + i, map[captr[i].chr & 0377]);
    }
    if (!normal)
        standend();
}
```

Note that **PSwrtcells** is simpler than it was for the other two implementations because it doesn't much matter how often we call **standout** and **standend**. They don't output anything; they only set attributes in **stdscr**.

PSfill is also quite simple because we don't need to discover whether any of the special screen-clearing capabilities should be used. Curses will figure this out for itself when **refresh** is called.

```
/*------------------------------------------------------------------
     PSfill - fill a rectangle
--------------------------------------------------------------*/
void PSfill(srectp, chr, att)
RECT *srectp;                              /* rectangle */
char chr;                                  /* fill character */
int att;                                   /* fill attribute */
{
    RECT srect;
    int r, c;

    if (!intersect(srectp, LINES - 1, COLS - 1, &srect))
        return;
    changed = TRUE;
    if (att != A_NORM)
        standout();
    chr = map[chr & 0377];
    for (r = srect.r1; r <= srect.r2; r++)
        for (c = srect.c1; c <= srect.c2; c++)
            mvaddch(r, c, chr);
    if (att != A_NORM)
        standend();
}
```

PSslide is almost identical in structure to the implementations for the Z–19 and Termcap in that it tries to use insert row, delete row, insert character, and delete character. However, this doesn't buy us much here, because **refresh** won't use the corresponding capabilities when it actually updates the screen. A minor benefit is that fewer calls will be made to Curses functions than if **PSslide** simply returned **FALSE** all the time, letting its caller redisplay the affected area. You may want to save space in your version of **ps_curse.c** by throwing away all the code in **PSslide** except for the last **return** statement.[10]

```
/*------------------------------------------------------------------
     PSslide - slide a rectangle
     RETURN: Was slide performed?
--------------------------------------------------------------*/
BOOLEAN PSslide(srectp, dir, dist)
RECT *srectp;                              /* rectangle */
int dir;                                   /* direction */
int dist;                                  /* distance */
{
    RECT srect;
    int r, c;

    if (!intersect(srectp, LINES - 1, COLS - 1, &srect) || dist <= 0)
        return(TRUE);
    changed = TRUE;
    switch(dir) {
```

---

[10]Another reason for doing this is that some very early versions of Curses lack **insch** and **delch**.

```
            case DIR_UP:
                if (srect.cl != 0 || srect.c2 != COLS - 1)
                    return(FALSE);
                move(srect.rl - dist, 0);
                for (r = 0; r < dist; r++)
                    deleteln();
                if (srect.r2 < LINES - 1) {
                    move(srect.r2 - dist + 1, 0);
                    for (r = 0; r < dist; r++)
                        insertln();
                }
                return(TRUE);
            case DIR_DOWN:
                if (srect.cl != 0 || srect.c2 != COLS - 1)
                    return(FALSE);
                move(srect.r2 + 1, 0);
                for (r = 0; r < dist; r++)
                    deleteln();
                move(srect.rl, 0);
                for (r = 0; r < dist; r++)
                    insertln();
                return(TRUE);
            case DIR_LEFT:
                for (r = srect.rl; r <= srect.r2; r++) {
                    move(r, srect.cl - dist);
                    for (c = 0; c < dist; c++)
                        delch();
                    if (srect.c2 < COLS - 1) {
                        move(r, srect.c2 - dist + 1);
                        for (c = 0; c < dist; c++)
                            insch(' ');
                    }
                }
                return(TRUE);
            case DIR_RIGHT:
                for (r = srect.rl; r <= srect.r2; r++) {
                    move(r, srect.c2 + 1);
                    for (c = 0; c < dist; c++)
                        delch();
                    move(r, srect.cl);
                    for (c = 0; c < dist; c++)
                        insch(' ');
                }
                return(TRUE);
        }
        return(FALSE);
}
```

Here's the rest of the implementation:

```
/*-----------------------------------------------------------------------
    PSsetcur - set cursor position
-----------------------------------------------------------------------*/
void PSsetcur(row, col)
int row;                                /* row */
int col;                                /* column */
{
    move(row, col);
}
```

```
/*-----------------------------------------------------------------
    PSshowcur - turn cursor on or off
-----------------------------------------------------------------*/
void PSshowcur(on)
BOOLEAN on;                                    /* switch */
{
    /* not available with Curses */
}

/*-----------------------------------------------------------------
    PSbeep - sound bell
-----------------------------------------------------------------*/
void PSbeep()
{
    if (write(2, BEL, 1) == -1)
        syserr("write");
}
```

To make sure the bell gets rung without unnecessary buffering, we use the system call **write**. Writing to file descriptor 2 (standard diagnostic output) ensures that the output won't be redirected.[11]

3.5.4. Efficiency Improvements

Since Curses keeps the screen buffer **stdscr** in internal memory, it seems wasteful to use so many calls to **mvaddch, standout, insertln,** and so on, to update it. It would be more efficient to directly change the internal data structures used by Curses (which are pointed to by **stdscr**), as we'll do in the memory-mapped video implementation in Sec. 3.7. As is so often the case, this efficiency comes at the expense of violating an important software design principle: We ought to use an interface to a module as it's defined, not access information that's supposed to be hidden. Someone who modifies Curses in the future is not obligated to maintain the same internal storage structures, although he or she will certainly try to maintain the same function calls. In fact, AT&T did make changes to the internals for their version of Curses (a character is stored in 16 bits instead of 8).

Still, the speed of this physical screen implementation is so critical that it seems a shame to make sacrifices for such an abstract notion as maintainability. Normally, I feel as strongly about good design practices as anyone, but I don't like interactive programs that write the screen slower than they might. Not everyone has a million-instruction-per-second workstation—most folks have slow personal computers or use time-sharing systems that are overloaded.

There are two solutions to this dilemma. The first is for the keepers of Curses (if there is such a group) to add four functions to do the work of **PSwrite, PSwrtcells, PSfill,** and **PSslide.** Then the tricks we wanted to perform would be inside the Curses module, and everything is still on the up-and-up. The second solution is the reverse: to merge Curses with our physi-

---

[11] See Secs. 2.2 and 2.7 of [Roc85].

cal screen implementation. We could then bypass the Curses interface itself (the physical screen interface is simpler, faster, and more portable) while keeping the cursor motion and screen update optimizations. This new implementation would run on top of Termcap. In essence, this would be augmenting the Termcap implementation of the physical screen with Curses-like optimizations.

3.6. IBM PC Basic I/O System (BIOS)

The IBM PC's Basic I/O System, or BIOS, is a collection of low-level subroutines that manage various devices such as printers, serial communication lines, disks, the clock, the keyboard, and, of most interest to us, the display. The BIOS is permanently resident in the PC's read-only memory, so it's often referred to as the ROM BIOS. The MS–DOS operating system runs on top of the BIOS. A few BIOS services are also available via MS–DOS system calls, but we will concern ourselves here only with the BIOS proper.

As a practical matter, you can consider the BIOS to be part of MS–DOS because you can count on its being available only when MS–DOS is in control. Other operating systems for the PC generally bypass the ROM BIOS, most commonly because it is not re-entrant and is therefore unsuitable for multitasking. The upshot of this is that you can't use the BIOS with versions of UNIX for the IBM PC and, even if you could, it would handle only the primary display, not any terminals. For UNIX, you should use the Termcap or Curses methods.

In the next section, we'll introduce only the BIOS entry points that we need to implement the physical screen. See [IBM84], [Nor85], or [Dun86] for more information about the rest of the BIOS.

3.6.1. BIOS Access Functions

You access the BIOS from Intel 8086 assembly language by executing an interrupt instruction. For example, this code moves the cursor to row 12, column 5:

```
        mov     ah,2            ; set cursor-position function number
        mov     dh,12           ; row number
        mov     dl,5            ; column number
        mov     bh,0            ; display page
        int     10h             ; video interrupt - go to BIOS
```

Don't worry if you don't understand this assembly language—it's the spirit we're trying to convey, not the details.

With Lattice or Microsoft C, you don't actually have to write in assembler, because the function **int86** is supplied to allow you to load registers, issue an interrupt, and fetch results from registers—all without leaving C. You still have to understand how each BIOS interrupt uses the registers, however. We can move the cursor with **int86** like this:

```
union REGS inr, outr; /* REGS defined in "dos.h" */

inr.h.ah = 2;
inr.h.dh = 12;
inr.h.dl = 5;
inr.h.bh = 0;
int86(0x10, &inr, &outr);
```

This is better than assembly language, but still fairly grungy. We don't want things like registers and functions named **int86** in our programs. So we'll use a still higher-level interface that allows each BIOS service to be invoked via a simple C subroutine, this way:

```
                    BVsetcpos(12, 5);
```

The code for these BIOS access functions is in the file **bios.c**, which appears in Appendix A. We'll present only the function headers here, just as we did for Termcap and Curses. Video functions start with the letters BV, and keyboard functions (which will be explained in Sec. 4.1.3) start with BK.

The first two functions set and get the video mode, which is a number from 0 to 7 (or higher if some newer modes are in effect). The mode indicates whether the IBM Monochrome Display Adapter or the Color Graphics Adapter is installed—or being emulated—and whether, in the case of the CGA, we're showing graphics or characters.[12] It also indicates the current resolution in characters or pixels. We're interested in the video mode for two reasons. First, if the CGA is in use, we want to make sure the screen is 80-by-25. This will require us to get the mode and, if it's a CGA number, force it to the right value. Second, in the memory-mapped implementation (Sec. 3.7) we need to find out whether the MDA or CGA is in use because the frame buffer addresses are different.

Here's how to set the video mode:

```
/*------------------------------------------------------------------
    BVsetmode - set video mode
       CGA modes:
          0    40 x 25 BW
          1    40 x 25 color
          2    80 x 25 BW
          3    80 x 25 color
          4    320 x 200 color
          5    320 x 200 BW
          6    640 x 200 BW
       MDA mode:
          7    80 x 25
    --------------------------------------------------------------*/
void BVsetmode(mode)
int mode;                                /* mode */
```

[12]For characters, it doesn't matter whether the CGA or the Enhanced Graphics Adapter (EGA) is installed. The latter emulates the former, with the same modes, but the characters are clearer. If we were concerned with graphics, we would have to consider the special EGA modes.

We get the mode with **BVgetstate**. It is also capable of giving us the number of columns and the video page number (there can be several frame buffers), but we're not concerned with those in this book.

```
/*-------------------------------------------------------------------
    BVgetstate - get current video state
                 Arguments aren't used if NULL.
-----------------------------------------------------------------*/
void BVgetstate(modep, numcolsp, pagep)
int *modep;                             /* returned mode */
int *numcolsp;                          /* returned number of columns */
int *pagep;                             /* returned page */
```

The next function sets the size of the cursor in terms of the starting and ending scan lines. The IBM PC generally has 200 scan lines for the CGA and 350 for the MDA. Since there are twenty-five rows of characters, there are eight or fourteen scan lines per row. The cursor can occupy all scan lines in a row (block cursor), or just two at the bottom (underscore cursor), or anything in between.

```
/*-------------------------------------------------------------------
    BVsetctype - set cursor type
-----------------------------------------------------------------*/
void BVsetctype(startline, endline)
int startline;                          /* starting scan line */
int endline;                            /* ending scan line */
```

Here are some typical cursor sizes:

	Monochrome		Color	
Cursor Shape	Start	End	Start	End
Underscore	11	12	6	7
Block	0	13	0	7
Invisible	32	0	32	0

Fig. 3-3 shows an underscore cursor on a color display.

Note that we can set a block cursor or turn the cursor off in a way that's independent of the monitor type, since an ending scan line of 13 is OK for the color monitor, too. But for an underscore cursor, we have to first find out what adapter is installed by calling **BVgetstate**.

We've already seen **BVsetcpos**:

```
/*-------------------------------------------------------------------
    BVsetcpos - set cursor position
-----------------------------------------------------------------*/
void BVsetcpos(row, col)
int row;                                /* row */
int col;                                /* column */
```

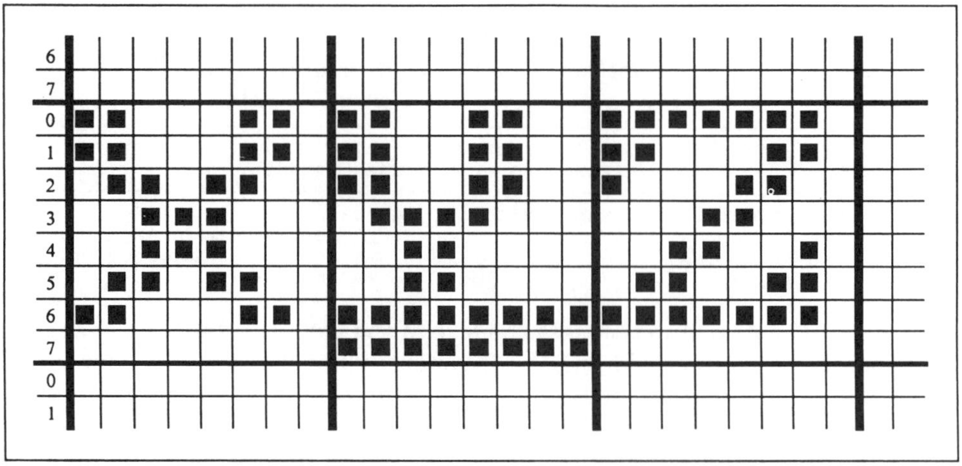

Fig. 3-3. Underscore cursor on letter Y. Eight scan lines per character row.

The next function gets the cursor position and its size in terms of the
starting and ending scan lines:

```
/*-------------------------------------------------------------------
     BVrdcpos - read cursor position
 -----------------------------------------------------------------*/
void BVrdcpos(rowp, colp, startlinep, endlinep)
int *rowp;                              /* row */
int *colp;                              /* column */
int *startlinep;                        /* starting scan line */
int *endlinep;                          /* ending scan line */
```

We have no need for the first two arguments in this book because the
physical screen interface has no function to determine the cursor's position.
But we'll use the cursor size arguments to find out what the cursor looks like
when the physical screen is initialized, so it can later be restored to the way
it was.[13]
    There may be several 25-row display pages on the controller card. You
can tell the BIOS to make one of them active with **BVselpage**:

```
/*-------------------------------------------------------------------
     BVselpage - select active display page
 -----------------------------------------------------------------*/
void BVselpage(page)
int page;                               /* page number */
```

We'll always use page 0. In fact, our BIOS interface assumes that only that
page is used. It's a good idea to select page 0 when your program starts in
case a previous program activated another page.

---

[13]There's a bug in some versions of the BIOS that gives erroneous results for this service,
but the interface in Appendix A circumvents it.

The BIOS has functions to scroll an arbitrary screen rectangle vertically but not horizontally.

```
/*------------------------------------------------------------------
    BVsclup - scroll up
-----------------------------------------------------------------*/
void BVsclup(amt, row1, col1, row2, col2)
int amt;                                /* number of rows to scroll */
int row1;                               /* top row */
int col1;                               /* left column */
int row2;                               /* bottom row */
int col2;                               /* right column */

/*------------------------------------------------------------------
    BVscldn - scroll down
-----------------------------------------------------------------*/
void BVscldn(amt, row1, col1, row2, col2)
int amt;                                /* number of rows to scroll */
int row1;                               /* top row */
int col1;                               /* left column */
int row2;                               /* bottom row */
int col2;                               /* right column */
```

Scrolling is different from sliding: When a rectangle is scrolled up, its position on the screen doesn't change at all. Instead, each scroll causes the top row of the rectangle to be lost, the second through last rows to be moved up, and the last row to be cleared. A similar definition holds for scrolling down. For example, to *slide* rows 10 through 15 up a distance of 3, you can use the BIOS to *scroll* rows 7 through 15 up by 3 rows. We'll show the code for this translation in the next section.

You can display replications of a single character and attribute, at the current cursor position, with **BVwtac**:

```
/*------------------------------------------------------------------
    BVwtac - write attribute and character
-----------------------------------------------------------------*/
void BVwtac(amt, chr, att)
int amt;                                /* number of characters to write */
char chr;                               /* character to write */
int att;                                /* attribute */
```

The attributes defined in **display.h** (Sec. 2.3) can be used since their values were chosen specially for the IBM PC. As an example, this sequence will display a blinking horizontal line in row 10, from columns 20 through 40:

```
                    BVsetcpos(10, 20);
                    BVwtac(21, C_H, A_BLINK);
```

You can also display a single character as though writing to a dumb terminal:

```
/*------------------------------------------------------------------
    BVwttty - write teletype
-----------------------------------------------------------------*/
void BVwttty(chr)
char chr;                               /* character to write */
```

A few ASCII control characters are acted upon by **BVwtty**: carriage return, line feed, backspace, and bell. After a character is written, the cursor moves right. If it moves past column 79, it automatically wraps to column 0 of the next row. If there is no next row, the screen scrolls up.

We can't use **BVwtty** to implement the physical screen interface because **PSwrite** and **PSwrtcells** don't interpret ASCII control characters and they don't do wrap-around. We could use **BVwtac**, but it's too inefficient to call it and **int86** for every character. What's worse, with **BVwtac** we have to reposition the cursor separately for every character, thus doubling the function-call overhead. So we've speeded things up considerably by providing two special interfaces to the BIOS that take a string and a vector of **CELL**s. They issue the appropriate BIOS interrupts directly from assembly language. Their only purpose is to save C function-call overhead—they still make BIOS system calls.

The code for **wrtstr** and **wrtcell** is in Appendix B. This is how they're called from C:

```
/*------------------------------------------------------------------
      wrtstr - write string
   -----------------------------------------------------------------*/
void wrtstr(row, col, str, ncols, att)
int row;                               /* starting row */
int col;                               /* starting column */
char *str;                             /* string to write */
int ncols;                             /* number of columns to write */
int att;                               /* attribute */

/*------------------------------------------------------------------
      wrtcell - write vector of CELLs
   -----------------------------------------------------------------*/
void wrtcell(row, col, cellptr, ncols)
int row;                               /* starting row */
int col;                               /* starting column */
CELL *cellptr;                         /* vector to write */
int ncols;                             /* number of columns to write */
```

For both functions, exactly **ncols** characters are written. The argument **str** to **wrtstr** need not be null-terminated, and, if it is, its length had better be at least **ncols**.

If we had to grade the BIOS for its suitability for implementing the physical screen interface, its report card would look like this:

Cursor control	A
Displaying text	C
Scrolling vertically	A
Scrolling horizontally	F

A GPA of only 2.5 isn't nearly good enough for topnotch PC software, so it's no surprise that the BIOS isn't used by programmers who know better, except in unusual cases (described in Sec. 3.8.3). The best PC software uses memory-mapped video, which we'll describe in Sec. 3.7. Its GPA is 4.0.

3.6.2. BIOS Implementation of the Physical Screen Interface

For the first time we can fully implement the physical screen interface, in that all 256 character codes and all attributes can be displayed directly and faithfully. There are twenty-five screen rows. The only glitches are that **PSwrite** and **PSwrtcells** are a little slow, and **PSslide** can't go sideways. We still consider this a full implementation, because **PSslide** isn't *required* to go sideways.

The file **ps_bios.c** begins in the usual way:

```
#include <dos.h>
#include "display.h"
#include "pscreen.h"

#define MAXROW 24
#define MAXCOL 79
#define BEL '\007'
```

Because we're going to have to set the cursor position often, we don't want the cursor flying around the screen as we update the display. We want to turn the cursor off before each display operation and then restore it to the way it was. We can do this with **curoff** and **curprev**, used in pairs:

```
static int prevstart, prevend;        /* to save cursor size */

/*---------------------------------------------------------------------
    curoff - turn cursor off, saving previous size
----------------------------------------------------------------*/
static void curoff()
{
    int dummyrow, dummycol;

    BVrdcpos(&dummyrow, &dummycol, &prevstart, &prevend);
    PSshowcur(FALSE);
}

/*----------------------------------------------------------------
    curprev - restore cursor to previous size
----------------------------------------------------------------*/
static void curprev()
{
    BVsetctype(prevstart, prevend);
}
```

We'll see these functions in use shortly.

The function **cursize** is for setting the cursor's size explicitly (it's called from **PSshowcur**). It remembers the cursor's size when the physical screen is initialized so **PSend** can restore the cursor exactly. The cursor on entry could be an underscore, a block, or something else, and we don't want to mess it up because the user may have gone to some trouble to adjust it.

```
/*----------------------------------------------------------------
    cursize - set cursor size, saving initial size
-----------------------------------------------------------------*/
static void cursize(startline, endline)
int startline, endline;
{
    static int savestart = -1, saveend;
    int dummyrow, dummycol;

    if (savestart == -1)
        BVrdcpos(&dummyrow, &dummycol, &savestart, &saveend);
    if (startline == -1) {
        startline = savestart;
        endline = saveend;
    }
    BVsetctype(startline, endline);
}
```

We can restore the cursor with **cursize(–1, 0)**.

Now we can code **PSbegin**, **PSend**, **PSsynch** (simple and easy to maintain), **PSheight**, and **PSwidth**:

```
/*----------------------------------------------------------------
    PSbegin - initialize display
-----------------------------------------------------------------*/
void PSbegin()
{
    int mode;

    BVgetstate(&mode, NULL, NULL);
    if (mode != 7)
        BVsetmode(3); /* 80 by 25 color text */
    BVselpage(0);
    PSshowcur(FALSE);
}

/*----------------------------------------------------------------
    PSend - terminate display
-----------------------------------------------------------------*/
void PSend()
{
    PSfill(&GIANT_RECT, ' ', A_NORM);
    BVsetbdr(0);
    PSsetcur(MAXROW, 0);
    cursize(-1, 0); /* restore size */
}

/*----------------------------------------------------------------
    PSsynch - bring screen up to date
-----------------------------------------------------------------*/
void PSsynch()
{
}

/*----------------------------------------------------------------
    PSheight - get height of physical screen
    RETURN: Height.
-----------------------------------------------------------------*/
int PSheight()
{
    return(MAXROW + 1);
}
```

```
/*-------------------------------------------------------------------
    PSwidth - get width of physical screen
    RETURN: Width.
-------------------------------------------------------------------*/
int PSwidth()
{
    return(MAXCOL + 1);
}
```

Recall from Sec. 3.2.2 that we're not obligated to buffer screen updates. A good thing, too, because the BIOS doesn't work that way.

PSwrite and **PSwrtcells** are easy, thanks to **wrtstr** and **wrtcell**:

```
/*-------------------------------------------------------------------
    PSwrite - write string
-------------------------------------------------------------------*/
void PSwrite(row, col, ncols, str, att)
int row;                                /* starting row */
int col;                                /* starting column */
int ncols;                              /* number of columns to write */
char *str;                              /* string */
int att;                                /* attribute */
{
    int slen;

    if (row < 0 || row > MAXROW || col > MAXCOL)
        return;
    if (col + ncols > MAXCOL + 1)
        ncols = MAXCOL + 1 - col;
    slen = strlen(str);
    if (col < 0) {
        if (-col >= slen)
            return;
        str = &str[-col];
        ncols += col;
        col = 0;
    }
    ncols = MIN(ncols, slen);
    curoff();
    wrtstr(row, col, str, ncols, att);
    curprev();
}

/*-------------------------------------------------------------------
    PSwrtcells - write vector of CELLs
-------------------------------------------------------------------*/
void PSwrtcells(row, col, captr, ncols)
int row;                                /* starting row */
int col;                                /* starting column */
CELL *captr;                            /* CELLs */
int ncols;                              /* number of columns to write */
{
    if (row < 0 || row > MAXROW || col < 0 || col > MAXCOL)
        return;
    curoff();
    if (col + ncols > MAXCOL + 1)
        ncols = MAXCOL + 1 - col;
    wrtcell(row, col, captr, ncols);
    curprev();
}
```

Note that we carefully set **ncols** in **PSwrite** because **wrtstr** doesn't stop on the null byte at the end of **str**.

PSfill is simple, too, because **BVwtac** serves its needs beautifully:

```
/*------------------------------------------------------------------
      PSfill - fill a rectangle
------------------------------------------------------------------*/
void PSfill(srectp, chr, att)
RECT *srectp;                           /* rectangle */
char chr;                               /* fill character */
int att;                                /* fill attribute */
{
    RECT srect;
    int r;

    if (!intersect(srectp, MAXROW, MAXCOL, &srect))
        return;
    curoff();
    for (r = srect.r1; r <= srect.r2; r++) {
        BVsetcpos(r, srect.cl);
        BVwtac(RWIDTH(&srect), chr, att);
    }
    curprev();
}
```

PSslide can slide any rectangle up or down, even if it isn't full width (contrast this with the Z−19, Termcap, and Curses implementations). But it can't slide sideways at all.

```
/*------------------------------------------------------------------
      PSslide - slide a rectangle
      RETURN: Was slide performed?
------------------------------------------------------------------*/
BOOLEAN PSslide(srectp, dir, dist)
RECT *srectp;                           /* rectangle */
int dir;                                /* direction */
int dist;                               /* distance */
{
    RECT srect;

    if (!intersect(srectp, MAXROW, MAXCOL, &srect) || dist <= 0)
        return(TRUE);
    switch(dir) {
    case DIR_UP:
        BVsclup(dist, srect.r1 - dist, srect.cl, srect.r2, srect.c2);
        return(TRUE);
    case DIR_DOWN:
        BVscldn(dist, srect.r1, srect.cl, srect.r2 + dist, srect.c2);
        return(TRUE);
    default:
        return(FALSE);
    }
}
```

Here's the rest of the implementation:

```
/*------------------------------------------------------------------
      PSsetcur - set cursor position
------------------------------------------------------------------*/
void PSsetcur(row, col)
int row;                                /* row */
int col;                                /* column */
{
```

```
        BVsetcpos(row, col);
}

/*-----------------------------------------------------------------
        PSshowcur - turn cursor on or off
-------------------------------------------------------------------*/
void PSshowcur(on)
BOOLEAN on;                                      /* switch */
{
    if (on)
        cursize(0, 13);
    else
        cursize(32, 0);
}

/*-----------------------------------------------------------------
        PSbeep - sound bell
-------------------------------------------------------------------*/
void PSbeep()
{
    BVwttty(BEL);
}
```

We always run with a block cursor. Fourteen scan lines may be too many, but the BIOS will clip it to the right number for whatever monitor is installed.

3.7. IBM PC Memory-Mapped Video

The IBM PC's CPU can directly access the same memory that the display controller uses to refresh the screen. Any changes made to that memory are shown instantly. Because no I/O or system calls are required, and because the CPU has extremely fast memory manipulation instructions, the physical screen implementation for the IBM PC is complete and unbelievably fast. Writing application programs that use this implementation is a pleasure.
    There aren't any access functions to describe here. We'll start by explaining the structure and location of display memory, and for color monitors, some complications that make display memory troublesome to access. Then we'll present the code for the physical screen implementation.

3.7.1. Accessing Display Memory

The PC's display memory, in character mode, consists of twenty-five rows of eighty 16-bit words, each of which contains a character and an attribute. The **CELL** structure introduced in Sec. 2.4 describes each word exactly. Thus, display memory looks like this:

                            CELL dspmem[25][80];

This array is located at address 0xB0000 for the monochrome controller, and 0xB8000 for the color controller. It probably wasn't IBM's intention for these addresses to become so well known and so relied upon, but, in deference to the fact that thousands of PC programs have them hard-coded in, IBM has officially promised to preserve them in future hardware (and they have, so far). So you can safely build them into programs without fear of obsolescence. Use a symbolic constant, of course, just in case.

In C, you can update display memory by setting a pointer to the appropriate address. The following program writes a blinking *Hello* starting at row 15, column 30:[14]

```
#include "display.h"

#define MONO_ADDR    0xB0000000
#define COLR_ADDR    0xB8000000

void main()
{
    struct Dspmem {
        CELL dspmem[25][80];
    } *a;
    int mode;

    BVgetstate(&mode, NULL, NULL);
    if (mode == 7)
        a = (struct Dspmem *)MONO_ADDR;
    else
        a = (struct Dspmem *)COLR_ADDR;
    a->dspmem[15][30].chr = 'H';
    a->dspmem[15][30].att = A_BLINK;
    a->dspmem[15][31].chr = 'e';
    a->dspmem[15][31].att = A_BLINK;
    a->dspmem[15][32].chr = 'l';
    a->dspmem[15][32].att = A_BLINK;
    a->dspmem[15][33].chr = 'l';
    a->dspmem[15][33].att = A_BLINK;
    a->dspmem[15][34].chr = 'o';
    a->dspmem[15][34].att = A_BLINK;
    exit(0);
}
```

If you run this program on the color monitor, it will work, but you'll see snow on the screen for the brief interval when the CPU is writing display memory. That's because the controller is unable to get at memory while the CPU is using it. To avoid this objectionable snow, it's necessary for the CPU to access display memory only when the controller doesn't need it.

One such period is during the horizontal retrace, when the CRT beam has finished a scan line and is on its way back to the left edge. This period is only long enough to transfer one byte. A longer interval occurs during the vertical retrace, when the beam is moving from the end of the last scan line

---

[14]The long constants **MONO_ADDR** and **COLR_ADDR** reflect the fact that the Lattice and Microsoft large models use 32-bit pointers. For Lattice C, it's necessary to compile the program with the "s" option so that the pointers can be assigned literally to the variable **a**. The command to compile should be **lc -mls dspmem.c**.

all the way back to the top. Then you can move 480 bytes (240 characters and attributes). So the procedure to transfer data to display memory would be:[15]

1. Wait for the vertical retrace to start, by interrogating the controller's status port.
2. Transfer 480 bytes.
3. Wait for a horizontal retrace.
4. Transfer one byte.
5. Loop back to step 3 until 188 bytes are transferred.
6. Loop back to step 1.

This procedure is continued until the entire block is transferred. In case you're wondering where these magic numbers (480 and 188) came from, they came from experimentation.

These numbers work for the slowest type of PC with an Intel 8088 running at 4.77 MHz. They will work for faster CPUs, too, but so will somewhat larger numbers. (In fact, a warm controller allows larger numbers than a cold one!) With newer color controllers, such as IBM's Enhanced Graphics Adapter (EGA), you don't even have to wait for the retrace. In short, a colossal mess—just the kind of thing the operating system or BIOS ought to handle for you (but doesn't). The simplest approach is to just use our conservative numbers, since experience has shown that they always work.

It's too much trouble to apply this procedure when display-memory rectangles are slid. Not only does the coding get messy, but, when you're both reading and writing display memory, you need to wait for the retrace *twice*, which slows the display even more. It's better to keep a display buffer in your program's address space and do all memory manipulations there, and transfer data to display memory only when **PSsynch** is called.

Keeping a display buffer is a good idea even for the monochrome display, which doesn't require waiting for the retrace intervals. Changes snap onto the screen all at once instead of being painted on in pieces. If you clear an area and then write to it, you won't see it flash as it goes blank and then fills up. It might seem as though the extra copying would be too slow, but the PC can transfer contiguous blocks of memory so fast that it really doesn't matter. It takes only a sixth of a second to transfer an entire 4000-byte screen buffer!

For the monochrome display, we could copy the display buffer to display memory with **movmem** (Sec. 2.8), but that won't do for the color monitor.

---

[15]The procedure presented here was developed by Augie Hansen [Han86]. The routine **wrtscrn** is based on code supplied by him.

The single function **wrtscrn** handles both cases transparently; the assembler code for this function is shown in Appendix B.

```
/*-----------------------------------------------------------------
    wrtscrn - update IBM PC display memory
-------------------------------------------------------------*/
void wrtscrn(srcptr, start, nwords)
char *srcptr;                           /* pointer to 4000-byte screen buffer */
int start;                              /* offset in buffer, display memory */
int nwords;                             /* number of words to write */
```

You can transfer as much or as little as you want by setting **start** and **nwords** appropriately. In the physical screen implementation, we'll keep track of the lowest and highest addresses in our screen buffer that actually got changed, and transfer only that segment to display memory.

Our earlier example can now be changed so it's snow-free and monitor-type independent:

```
#include "display.h"

void main()
{
    CELL dspbuf[25][80];
    dspbuf[15][30].chr = 'H';
    dspbuf[15][30].att = A_BLINK;
    dspbuf[15][31].chr = 'e';
    dspbuf[15][31].att = A_BLINK;
    dspbuf[15][32].chr = 'l';
    dspbuf[15][32].att = A_BLINK;
    dspbuf[15][33].chr = 'l';
    dspbuf[15][33].att = A_BLINK;
    dspbuf[15][34].chr = 'o';
    dspbuf[15][34].att = A_BLINK;
    wrtscrn((char *)dspbuf, &dspbuf[15][30].chr - (char *)dspbuf, 5);
    exit(0);
}
```

3.7.2. Memory-Mapped Implementation of the Physical Screen Interface

Now we're ready to implement the physical screen interface. We'll do all modifications to a display buffer and call **wrtscrn** from **PSsynch** to update the display. The file **ps_mm.c** begins like this:

```
#include "display.h"
#include "pscreen.h"

#define MAXROW 24
#define MAXCOL 79
#define BEL '\007'

static union {                          /* must match display memory layout */
    CELL cell;
    short word;
} dspbuf[MAXROW + 1][MAXCOL + 1];
```

```
static BOOLEAN changed = FALSE;      /* has screen been changed? */
static char *minptr;                 /* start of changed region in dspbuf */
static char *maxptr;                 /* end of changed region in dspbuf */
```

We want to be able to reference a **CELL** two ways: as a **CELL** (that is, with members **chr** and **att**) and as a 16-bit word.[16] We want the word so we can transfer a character and an attribute together, using a word assignment instead of two byte assignments. (We can't use a **CELL**, because some versions of Lattice C don't have structure assignment.) This is only slightly faster, but it occurs often enough to matter.

The flag **changed** keeps track of whether the display buffer is changed; **PSsynch** will update the display only when necessary. The pointers **minptr** and **maxptr** bound the region of **dspbuf** that was changed, so we can call **wrtscrn** appropriately. Each of the updating functions will reduce **minptr** and increase **maxptr** in accordance with the amount of data they write. Initially, we want them set to their extremes, which is done by **minmaxinit**:

```
/*-------------------------------------------------------------------
    minmaxinit - initialize minptr and maxptr
-------------------------------------------------------------------*/
static void minmaxinit()
{
    minptr = (char *)&dspbuf[MAXROW][MAXCOL];
    maxptr = (char *)&dspbuf[0][0];
}
```

PSsynch calls **wrtstr** to copy the changed part of display buffer (**dspbuf**) to screen memory:

```
/*-------------------------------------------------------------------
    PSsynch - bring screen up to date
-------------------------------------------------------------------*/
void PSsynch()
{
    if (changed) {
        wrtscrn((char *)dspbuf, minptr - (char *)dspbuf,
          (maxptr - minptr + 2) / 2);
        changed = FALSE;
    }
    minmaxinit();
}
```

We would expect that **minptr** and **maxptr** would be even (that is, point to **CELL**s), but we round their difference up to the next higher word just in case. In this decidedly non-portable file, we've safely used the constant 2 as the number of bytes per word.

The BIOS is called for cursor control and setting the screen mode, so **PSbegin**, **PSend**, **PSheight**, **PSwidth**, **PSsetcur**, **PSshowcur**, and

---

[16]No need to be portable here—this file is only for Intel 8086-type processors. However, machine dependencies will be allowed only here, in **ps_bios.c**, and in **port.c**.

PSbeep are identical to the BIOS versions in **ps_bios.c** (**cursize** is used here, too). They were shown in Sec. 3.6.2.

Next comes **PSwrite**:

```
/*------------------------------------------------------------------
    PSwrite - write string
------------------------------------------------------------------*/
void PSwrite(row, col, ncols, str, att)
int row;                              /* starting row */
int col;                              /* starting column */
int ncols;                            /* number of columns to write */
char *str;                            /* string */
int att;                              /* attribute */
{
    int i;
    short *p1 = NULL, *p2;

    if (row < 0 || row > MAXROW || col > MAXCOL)
        return;
    if (col + ncols > MAXCOL + 1)
        ncols = MAXCOL + 1 - col;
    for (i = 0; i < ncols && str[i] != '\0'; i++)
        if (col + i >= 0) {
            p2 = &dspbuf[row][col + i].word;
            if (p1 == NULL)
                p1 = p2;
            *p2 = (att << 8) | (str[i] & 0377);
        }
    if (p1 != NULL) {
        changed = TRUE;
        minptr = MIN(minptr, (char *)p1);
        maxptr = MAX(maxptr, (char *)p2);
    }
}
```

To make this function as fast as possible, we OR the attribute and the character into a word and assign it to the **word** member of the **CELL** union, instead of individually to the **chr** and **att** fields. We AND each character with octal 377 so that sign extension won't occur if the code is above 127. As we go along, **p1** and **p2** keep track of the starting and ending addresses, so we can set **minptr** and **maxptr**.

PSwrtcells is even simpler because the vector of **CELL**s is already in the same form as the corresponding part of **dspbuf**. We only have to move the data into position:

```
/*------------------------------------------------------------------
    PSwrtcells - write vector of CELLs
------------------------------------------------------------------*/
void PSwrtcells(row, col, captr, ncols)
int row;                              /* starting row */
int col;                              /* starting column */
CELL *captr;                          /* CELLs */
int ncols;                            /* number of columns to write */
{
    char *p1, *p2;
    int nbytes;

    if (row < 0 || row > MAXROW || col < 0 || col > MAXCOL)
        return;
    changed = TRUE;
```

```
        if (col + ncols > MAXCOL + 1)
            ncols = MAXCOL + 1 - col;
        p1 = (char *)&dspbuf[row][col];
        nbytes = sizeof(CELL) * ncols;
        movmem((char *)captr, p1, nbytes);
        p2 = p1 + nbytes - 1;
        minptr = MIN(minptr, p1);
        maxptr = MAX(maxptr, p2);
    }
```

PSfill and **PSslide** are less straightforward because there are some nifty optimizations that are worth exploiting.

PSfill has three cases:

1. The rectangle is the full width of the physical screen.

2. The rectangle is only one character wide (for example, a vertical line).

3. The rectangle's width is between these extremes.

In the first case, we can fill the rectangle as though the rows were strung together end to end into a linear array. A single call to **repmem** propagates a word containing the character and attribute throughout the entire rectangle. In the second case, a simple assignment statement handles each row. The third case is similar to the second, but **repmem** is called for each row.

```
/*--------------------------------------------------------------------
      PSfill - fill a rectangle
--------------------------------------------------------------------*/
void PSfill(srectp, chr, att)
RECT *srectp;                           /* rectangle */
char chr;                               /* fill character */
int att;                                /* fill attribute */
{
    RECT srect;
    short word;
    int r;
    char *p1, *p2;

    if (!intersect(srectp, MAXROW, MAXCOL, &srect))
        return;
    changed = TRUE;
    word = (att << 8) | (chr & 0377);
    if (RWIDTH(&srect) == MAXCOL + 1)
        repmem((char *)&dspbuf[srect.r1][0], (char *)&word, sizeof(CELL),
            RHEIGHT(&srect) * (MAXCOL + 1));
    else if (RWIDTH(&srect) == 1)
        for (r = srect.r1; r <= srect.r2; r++)
            dspbuf[r][srect.c1].word = word;
    else
        for (r = srect.r1; r <= srect.r2; r++)
            repmem((char *)&dspbuf[r][srect.c1], (char *)&word,
                sizeof(CELL), RWIDTH(&srect));
    p1 = (char *)&dspbuf[srect.r1][srect.c1];
    p2 = (char *)&dspbuf[srect.r2][srect.c2];
    minptr = MIN(minptr, p1);
    maxptr = MAX(maxptr, p2);
}
```

The third case is general enough to handle the other two cases as well, but we want **PSfill** to be as fast as possible.

For **PSslide**, we have even more tricks up our sleeve. If the rectangle is the full width of the screen, sliding up, down, left, or right can be done with a *single* call to **movmem**. This is because the rows are contiguous in memory, and we can consider the entire rectangle to be a linear array just as we did in **PSfill**.

Up and down sliding can be achieved by moving this array a multiple of eighty **CELL**s, as shown in Fig. 3–4. We have to be careful to start from the lowest memory address when moving up, and from the highest address when moving down, or else we'll overwrite memory before we have a chance to move it out of the way. Fortunately, **movmem** starts from the appropriate end automatically (see Sec. 2.8).

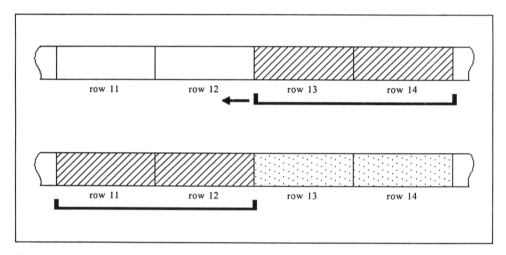

Fig. 3–4. Sliding rows 13 and 14 up two rows. Vacated (dotted) memory is undefined.

Left and right sliding of a full-width rectangle is a little more subtle. If we slide memory an amount less than a full row, it will have the effect of sliding each row that amount, as shown in Fig. 3–5. Data that slides off the screen actually appears on the previous or the next row, depending on the direction of movement. This is OK, because **PSslide** is allowed to leave garbage there.

If the rectangle is less than full width, we have to treat each row separately. Vertical sliding is done by copying each row to the row above or below, and horizontal sliding is done by moving the data within each row.

Here then is the code for **PSslide**:

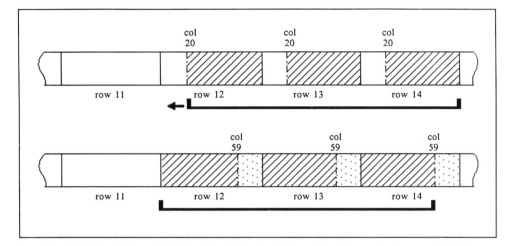

Fig. 3-5. Sliding rows 12-24, columns 20-79 left. Vacated memory (columns 60-79) is undefined.

```
/*--------------------------------------------------------------------
    PSslide - slide a rectangle
    RETURN: Was slide performed?
--------------------------------------------------------------------*/
BOOLEAN PSslide(srectp, dir, dist)
RECT *srectp;                           /* rectangle */
int dir;                                /* direction */
int dist;                               /* distance */
{
    RECT srect;
    int r;
    char *p1, *p2;

    if (!intersect(srectp, MAXROW, MAXCOL, &srect) || dist <= 0)
        return(TRUE);
    changed = TRUE;
    switch(dir) {
    case DIR_UP:
        if (RWIDTH(&srect) == MAXCOL + 1)
            movmem((char *)&dspbuf[srect.r1][0],
                (char *)&dspbuf[srect.r1 - dist][0],
                sizeof(CELL) * RHEIGHT(&srect) * RWIDTH(&srect));
        else
            for (r = srect.r1; r <= srect.r2; r++)
                movmem((char *)&dspbuf[r][srect.c1],
                    (char *)&dspbuf[r - dist][srect.c1],
                    sizeof(CELL) * RWIDTH(&srect));
        p1 = (char *)&dspbuf[srect.r1 - dist][srect.c1];
        p2 = (char *)&dspbuf[srect.r2 - dist][srect.c2];
        break;
    case DIR_DOWN:
        if (RWIDTH(&srect) == MAXCOL + 1)
            movmem((char *)&dspbuf[srect.r1][0],
                (char *)&dspbuf[srect.r1 + dist][0],
                sizeof(CELL) * RHEIGHT(&srect) * RWIDTH(&srect));
```

```
        else
            for (r = srect.r2; r >= srect.r1; r--)
                movmem((char *)&dspbuf[r][srect.cl],
                    (char *)&dspbuf[r + dist][srect.cl],
                    sizeof(CELL) * RWIDTH(&srect));
        pl = (char *)&dspbuf[srect.r1 + dist][srect.cl];
        p2 = (char *)&dspbuf[srect.r2 + dist][srect.c2];
        break;
    case DIR_LEFT:
        if (srect.c2 == MAXCOL && srect.cl == dist)
            movmem((char *)&dspbuf[srect.r1][srect.cl],
                (char *)&dspbuf[srect.r1][srect.cl - dist],
                sizeof(CELL) * (RHEIGHT(&srect) * (MAXCOL + 1) - dist));
        else
            for (r = srect.r1; r <= srect.r2; r++)
                movmem((char *)&dspbuf[r][srect.cl],
                    (char *)&dspbuf[r][srect.cl - dist],
                    sizeof(CELL) * RWIDTH(&srect));
        pl = (char *)&dspbuf[srect.r1][srect.cl - dist];
        p2 = (char *)&dspbuf[srect.r2][srect.c2 - dist];
        break;
    case DIR_RIGHT:
        if (srect.c2 + dist == MAXCOL && srect.cl == 0)
            movmem((char *)&dspbuf[srect.r1][srect.cl],
                (char *)&dspbuf[srect.r1][srect.cl + dist],
                sizeof(CELL) * (RHEIGHT(&srect) * (MAXCOL + 1) - dist));
        else
            for (r = srect.r1; r <= srect.r2; r++)
                movmem((char *)&dspbuf[r][srect.cl],
                    (char *)&dspbuf[r][srect.cl + dist],
                    sizeof(CELL) * RWIDTH(&srect));
        pl = (char *)&dspbuf[srect.r1][srect.cl + dist];
        p2 = (char *)&dspbuf[srect.r2][srect.c2 + dist];
    }
    minptr = MIN(minptr, pl);
    maxptr = MAX(maxptr, p2);
    return(TRUE);
}
```

Note that the full-width and less-than-full-width algorithms both move the same amount of data when the rectangle is full width. So why treat the full-width case specially? The answer is that there's considerable overhead in calling **movmem**, both for the subroutine call itself and for setting up the CPU's registers in preparation for the block move instruction. So a single **movmem** is much faster than several equivalent **movmems**.

3.8. Choosing an Implementation

Of the five physical screen implementations presented in this chapter, which one is best? We'll try to answer that question by running some tests and measuring the performance of each implementation in terms of executable program size, CPU time used, and time to update the display. However, you need not base your choice on the results given here. Since the interface to the physical screen is identical for all implementations, you can choose your implementation late in the development of your application. You can run your own tests, using your own user interface (the real one, not a mock-up), your own computer system, and your own terminal and communication hardware. You may even want to supply your users with two versions of your application (say, one using Termcap and one using Curses) and let *them* decide.

Nonetheless, the results given here will still be of interest because they do indicate roughly what you can expect. You may be able to determine before you even start that your design will never work satisfactorily, and that's surely the best time to get such unpleasant news. These results also point out the sharp contrast in display performance between, say, a thousand-dollar PC and a terminal connected to a ten-million-dollar mainframe. On one of our tests, the PC would be about 300 times faster!

3.8.1. *Tests and Results*

What constitutes a valid test of display performance? Probably no test or series of tests can be entirely valid, and, since you can run your own tests on your own application, it isn't important to agree on a general test. Instead, we'll run a few tests that point out the differences in performance between the implementations—we're just trying to gain some insight, not give out trophies!

These four tests were run:

1. *A program that exercises each physical screen function.* I originally wrote this program to debug the physical screen implementations.

2. *A demonstration program that shows off the windowing and virtual screen features that will be discussed later in this book.* This program does lots of sliding of rectangles that are less than a full screen wide.

3. *A program that displays twenty-nine screens of text, one after the other.* This simulates repeated use of the page-down key in a screen editor.

4. *A program that scrolls through a text file containing 713 lines.* For each scroll, the last twenty-three rows on the screen are slid up one row, and a new last row is displayed. This simulates repeated use of the down-arrow key in a screen editor.

The Z-19 implementation wasn't tested because it is unlikely to be used and because its performance would be nearly identical to the Termcap implementation. The four test programs were linked with each of the four other implementations: UNIX Termcap, UNIX Curses, IBM PC BIOS, and IBM PC memory-mapped video. Both old and new Curses were tested.

The UNIX programs were run with a specially-designed terminal that counted how many characters were sent to the display. This is a more realistic measure of elapsed time than actual wall-clock time because it eliminates the effect of communication speed. Theory would predict that at, say, 1200 bps it would take eighty-three seconds to send 10,000 characters, and this is exactly what it did take.

The terminal used for the UNIX tests was the Z–19, which has insert-line and delete-line. This allowed Termcap to do its best, whereas old Curses, unable to use these features, was at its worst. The "IBM PC" was actually an AT. The UNIX machine for the Termcap and old Curses trials was a VAX-11/780 running Berkeley 4.3BSD. The new Curses trials were run on an AT&T 3B2/400 with System V. A CPU test established that the 3B2 was about five percent slower than the VAX, so the actual 3B2 times were reduced by this amount to allow the speed of the old and new Curses implementations to be compared.[17]

The following chart summarizes the results from the sixteen trials. For UNIX, the chart shows user and system time in seconds,[18] the number of characters transmitted, and the predicted elapsed time at 9600 bps. For the IBM PC, the actual elapsed time in seconds is shown.

We'll discuss the UNIX and IBM PC environments separately in the next two sections.

PHYSICAL SCREEN IMPLEMENTATION

Test	UNIX Termcap	UNIX Old Curses	UNIX New Curses	IBM PC BIOS	IBM PC Memory Mapped
1. Physical Screen Test	.4 user .2 sys 9.9 elapsed 9,541 ch	3.4 user .5 sys 10.2 elapsed 9,805 ch	7.7 user .4 sys 9.2 elapsed 8,870 ch	1.04 elapsed	.64 elapsed
2. Window Demo	18.7 user 3.2 sys 164.4 elapsed 157,822 ch	35.6 user 2.7 sys 65.9 elapsed 63,267 ch	77.0 user 2.8 sys 63.8 elapsed 61,284 ch	50.31 elapsed	16.58 elapsed
3. Show 29 Pages	1.7 user .4 sys 28.5 elapsed 27,368 ch	11.5 user 1.0 sys 20.5 elapsed 19,690 ch	19.4 user 1.3 sys 18.6 elapsed 17,864 ch	11.92 elapsed	4.83 elapsed

[17]That CPU test used the windowing demonstration program linked with an implementation of the physical screen that did nothing at all—the functions (**PSwrite**, **PSfill**, and so on) just returned. This test is much more applicable to our present needs than any other benchmark.

[18]User time is the time spent executing instructions in the program itself, and system time is the time spent executing in the kernel on behalf of the program. For more information, see Chap. 9 of [Roc85].

Test	UNIX Termcap	UNIX Old Curses	UNIX New Curses	IBM PC BIOS	IBM PC memory mapped
4. Scroll 713 Lines	2.4 user 1.2 sys 35.0 elapsed 33,569 ch	84.5 user 17.8 sys 469.9 elapsed 451,058 ch	80.8 user 3.5 sys 22.6 elapsed 21,712 ch	18.79 elapsed	11.87 elapsed

3.8.2. Comparing UNIX Implementations

Old Curses sometimes displays fewer characters than Termcap, and is always slower. New Curses always displays fewer characters than Termcap, and is always much slower.

There are two reasons why Curses displays fewer characters than Termcap:

1. When one operation supplants another, such as clearing the screen and then filling it with text, Curses updates the screen only once, when **refresh** is called. Termcap updates the screen continuously.

2. If a revised screen is similar to the existing one, Curses may output only a small set of differences. Termcap would output the revisions even if some of the screen were unchanged.

How much these two optimizations help in practice depends on the nature of the screen updates and on how clever the program using Termcap is. If the program never unnecessarily displays anything, then Curses can't optimize the output because it's already minimal. On the other hand, the program might use insert-line and delete-line effectively via Termcap, whereas old Curses would never use them.

The differences between Termcap and Curses are most apparent in tests 3 and 4. When displaying pages of text, Curses could often use characters that were already on the screen. But when scrolling, old Curses had to rewrite the screen for every new line, whereas Termcap and new Curses could physically scroll twenty-three lines up by deleting the top line. In many applications, such as text editors or spreadsheets, scrolling is common, and old Curses would probably be too irritating to use.

The behavior of new Curses on test 3 was amazing. It frequently used multiple insert-line and delete-line sequences to move text from place to place on the screen in totally unpredictable ways. It was fascinating to watch it cleverly make use of an existing row, even if it was far away. These tricks allowed it to transmit ten percent fewer characters than old Curses.

In test 2, both old and new Curses displayed less than half as many characters as Termcap. This was mainly because the program cleared the windows and moved them around quite a bit, and the Curses optimization helped out. Test 1 was more tightly controlled by the program, with very little redundant output. Termcap and Curses both did about the same amount of work.

In all cases, even when outputting fewer characters, old Curses used significantly more CPU time than Termcap. All that optimization is expensive. Additionally, the old Curses library routines added about 8500 bytes to the size. So you wouldn't want to use old Curses if it only did about as well as Termcap, and you certainly wouldn't want to use it if did much worse.

New Curses is even more expensive than old, in terms of time and space. But at least the investment pays off.

Here are some recommendations on whether to use Termcap or Curses:

1. Clearing part of the screen and then filling it with text is expensive when you're using Termcap, and bothersome to the user because the screen may seem to flash. Try to design your programs so that unnecessary clearing does not occur. If you can do this, Termcap is likely to work well.

2. If scrolling must be fast (as in a text editor) old Curses will probably be unsatisfactory.

3. If your terminal is very fast, say 19,200 bps or more, Termcap is probably the best choice. Small improvements achieved by Curses are unimportant at high speeds, but disasters like test 4 still hurt. Note that old Curses couldn't have finished test 4 in less than 100 seconds no matter how fast the terminal was, because that's how much CPU time was used.

4. Conversely, if your CPU is fast and underutilized, and your terminal is slow, old Curses may be the best choice and new Curses certainly would be.

5. If size is important, as it might be on a 16-bit computer, you can save some space by using Termcap.

6. If your terminal doesn't have insert-line and delete-line, the gap between Termcap and Curses will be much narrower. For example, Termcap and old and new Curses would all flunk test 4.

7. Most versions of Curses still have a few bugs that cause the screen to be updated incorrectly now and then. For example, new Curses did very well in test 2, but the 61,284 characters it transmitted weren't the *right* characters. The screen was almost, but not quite, updated correctly. (The test was run three times to rule out transmission errors.)

These recommendations are intended only to provide some things to think about. The most valid test is to compare Termcap and Curses using your actual application.

My own experience is that when I'm sloppy about updating the screen redundantly, Curses makes my program look pretty good, whereas Termcap shows all of my wasteful output. When I take the time to optimize my own program, I'm happier with Termcap because I can more readily control exactly what happens.

3.8.3. Comparing IBM PC Implementations

The memory-mapped implementation is much faster than the BIOS implementation, always. What's more, it can slide rectangles sideways, whereas the BIOS can't.

The memory-mapped implementation is bigger, however, by about 5000 bytes. Of this, 4000 bytes are for the display buffer (the array **dspbuf** in **ps_mm.c**). The rest are simply because all of the work is done in user code, while the BIOS implementation calls functions that are in ROM. There was a time when 5000 bytes meant a lot (on a 64K machine), but those days are gone forever. Most PCs today have 256K or more, and 5000 bytes devoted to significantly improved display speed seems like a bargain.

There seem to be only two reasons for preferring the BIOS implementation:

1. Under some windowing systems, such as IBM's TopView or Microsoft's Windows, the BIOS implementation can run in a window, whereas the memory-mapped implementation would take over the full screen. Furthermore, because the operating system can't fully control a program that writes directly to display memory, multitasking is suspended while such a program is active.

2. A few MS–DOS computers that aren't completely compatible with the IBM PC will support the BIOS functions, although they do not have memory-mapped video (or it's incompatible with the IBM PC). An example is the Tandy 2000. Machines like this are no longer being designed, and the ones that exist don't sell very well, so the increased universality of the BIOS implementation is of little practical value.

Neither of these reasons is important to most people, and therefore the memory-mapped implementation is the one to use.

Actually, either of the IBM PC implementations is so much faster than the UNIX implementations that one could argue that software developed first for the PC may not be portable to UNIX because the display can't be updated fast enough! A user interface with windows, menus, and pop-up dialog boxes may be great on a PC, but on a 1200 bps terminal it would be gruesome. At that speed, most users would be better off with a command-driven interface, very brief error messages, and a paper manual nearby. Sounds like a typical time-sharing system, doesn't it?

3.9. Summary

In this very long chapter we introduced the physical screen interface, which allows us to write strings, fill rectangles, slide rectangles, and adjust the cursor. This interface is interesting for two reasons: It has an amazing absence of features, and it can be implemented for widely divergent environments.

We implemented the physical screen interface five times: for the Z–19 terminal, for Curses and Termcap under UNIX, and for the IBM PC BIOS and video memory map under MS–DOS. While doing so, a lot of details were given about Curses, Termcap, and the innards of the IBM PC.

Our challenge in these implementations was to maintain the interface and at the same time execute the physical screen functions as fast as possible. We had to use a lot of coding tricks to meet this challenge, so the programs in this chapter are quite complex. But they work.

We closed with a comparison of the implementations. We saw that Curses is often inferior to Termcap, especially the older, Berkeley version of Curses. The little-known Termcap library package deserves wider visibility. It's harder to program for than Curses, but the physical screen module makes this disadvantage moot. On the IBM PC, there's hardly any reason to use the BIOS, because the memory-mapped implementation is small, complete, and blazingly fast. These days many computers are accurate clones of the IBM PC, so the memory-mapped version is suitably portable, too.

As soon as we've figured out how to read the keyboard, which we're about to do, we'll be ready to use the physical screen module in a real application, a screen editor.

CHAPTER 4

Keyboards

Is reading the keyboard really so difficult that we need an entire chapter to explain how to do it? After all, you can just use the **read** system call. You don't even have to open a file because file descriptor 0 is already open to the standard input:

```
char ch;

switch (read(0, &ch, 1)) {
case 1:
    /* got character */
    ...
case 0:
    /* end of file */
    ...
case -1:
    /* error */
    ...
}
```

One problem with reading the keyboard this way is that the operating system (UNIX or MS–DOS) does too much processing that we don't want: Characters typed by the user are echoed back to the screen, assembled into complete lines to allow editing, and translated automatically (for example, carriage returns are replaced by line feeds). We don't want any of this help for interactive programs. We just want each character exactly as it was typed, as soon as it was typed, and without echoing anything to the screen.

We also don't get some features that we do want. We'd like to be able to ask whether a character is ready, but on most UNIX systems there's no straightforward way to do so. And we'd like a simple, portable way to read function keys that transmit several characters at a time so that our programs can be keyboard-independent. For instance, we'd like the arrow cursor keys to transmit a standard code regardless of what terminal they're on, just as, say, the tab key does.

So reading the keyboard isn't a matter of just calling **read**. It's going to take some hard work to make things easy. The next section explains how to read the keyboard without any unwanted processing by the operating system, and how to tell if a character is ready. As usual, the functions we'll define will behave identically on UNIX and MS–DOS, although their implementations will differ. Then we'll present a simple keyboard interface for use in application programs. Finally, we'll show how to handle a wide variety of keyboards in a uniform way. We'll show two hard-coded mapping functions: a Wordstar-like generic scheme (Control–E is cursor up, Control–C is next page, and so on), and a scheme just for the IBM PC. We'll then present a table-driven method that supports function keys on any keyboard and even allows the user to change which keys do what.

4.1. Reading the Keyboard

4.1.1. Line Mode vs. Raw Mode

We'll distinguish between line mode and raw mode by listing the processing that does or does not occur in each case. These modes are most apparent on UNIX, but they exist on MS–DOS, too, especially when C library routines are used.

Normally, unless you take special care, a program runs in line mode:

1.   The program gets no input—it blocks—until a complete line has been typed. A line is completed by pressing the carriage return key. The program can then read as many or as few characters as it wants, but at most one line can be read with a single **read** request.

2.   The user can erase (backspace over) keystrokes or kill the entire line, but the program will be unaware that this is occurring (it's handled entirely by the device driver).

3.   Characters typed by the user are echoed back to the display. If a special key is typed, such as an up arrow, the echo might cause the cursor to

move to a strange place. This isn't screen editing, however, because the device driver doesn't know that such a thing has occurred.

4. Certain characters are translated to other characters. For example, the terminating carriage return is translated to a line feed. Other characters, such as a Delete or a Control–C, may cause a signal to be sent.

For line-by-line interaction, performing these services in the device driver makes sense because the process can stay blocked for a relatively long time while the user is typing. But for screen-oriented interaction, we don't want any of this processing at all. It's all designed for lines, and we don't have lines. Instead we want to operate in *raw* mode:

1. Every keystroke is available to the program right away. It's OK if the operating system clumps rapidly-typed characters together, but only if the resulting delay is imperceptible.

2. No editing occurs on the input, since a typed character has already been made available to the program and can't be withdrawn.

3. Nothing is automatically echoed to the screen. The program has total control over what is shown. Of course, it can echo characters if it wants to.

4. No character translations occur, and no keystrokes cause signals to be sent.

You might think that telling the operating system to leave you alone would be easy, but it isn't. In older versions of UNIX (based on Version 7) you could set a *raw* bit in a structure maintained by the terminal driver, but, in versions based on System III, that bit is gone. You need to suppress each processing feature independently. On MS–DOS, you don't actually set a mode. Instead, what processing you get is determined by which system call you use to read the keyboard. This means that a character can't be processed until it is read, which is why on MS–DOS you don't see characters echoed when you type ahead of the program.

We'll tackle UNIX first, because it's harder. The mode of a UNIX terminal, affecting both the keyboard and the display, is controlled by the **ioctl** system call. You call **ioctl** once to retrieve the current settings into a structure, save a copy so the mode can be restored later, change the appropriate bits, and then make a second call to **ioctl**. The details concerning **#include** files, structures, bits and **ioctl** commands are different for Version-7-based systems and System-III-based systems. For our purposes, Berkeley 4BSD falls into the Version 7 category, System V falls into the System III category, and newer versions of Xenix fall into both categories since their terminal drivers are compatible with both. Berkeley 4BSD also has an old and a new driver (the new one supports job control), but they're compatible as far as the mode bits go.

Hence, there are only two possibilities to worry about, and the **OLDTTY** symbol (introduced in Sec. 2.7) tells us which one to use. The file **port.c** tests that flag to define the appropriate structure:

```
#include <errno.h>

#ifdef OLDTTY

#include <sgtty.h>
static struct sgttyb tbufsave;

#else

#include <sys/types.h>
#include <sys/ioctl.h>                       /* not really needed for System V */
#include <termio.h>
static struct termio tbufsave;

#endif

short ospeed;                                /* terminal speed from ioctl(); needed
                                                by Termcap (see "ps_termc.c") */
```

Recall from Sec. 3.4.2 that the Termcap implementation of the physical screen interface needs the speed of the terminal in the variable **ospeed**. Here's a good place to initialize **ospeed** since we're calling **ioctl** anyhow.

The function **setraw** puts the keyboard and the display into raw mode. We called it from the Termcap implementation of **PSbegin** (Sec. 3.4.3) for its effect on the display, and we'll call it again from **Kbegin** (Sec. 4.2) for its effect on the keyboard. A static variable inside **setraw** permits only the first call to be effective. This is crucial because, if **setraw** were executed twice, the saved terminal modes would be overwritten by the second call. Here is the code for **setraw**, with dual implementations for the **OLDTTY** and non-**OLDTTY** cases:[1]

```
    static BOOLEAN now_raw = FALSE;

    /*-------------------------------------------------------------------
        setraw - put terminal into raw mode
                 Taken from Advanced UNIX Programming, Sec 4.5.
                 Extended for Version 7 terminal driver (OLDTTY).
                 Error ignored in case standard input is a pipe.
        -----------------------------------------------------------------*/
    void setraw()
    {
#ifdef OLDTTY
        struct sgttyb tbuf;
```

---

[1]This is an enhanced version of the **setraw** in Sec. 4.5 of [Roc85]. The details of the various flags for System III (non-**OLDTTY**) are explained there; you also may wish to see the "tty" manual page in Sec. 4 of a System III manual, or the "termio" manual page in Sec. 7 of a System V manual. For the **OLDTTY** flags and structure members, see the "tty" manual page in Sec. 4 of a Version 7 or Berkeley 4BSD manual.

```
#else
    struct termio tbuf;
#endif
    static BOOLEAN first = TRUE;

    if (!first)
        return;
    first = FALSE;
#ifdef OLDTTY
    if (ioctl(0, TIOCGETP, &tbuf) == -1) /* may be pipe */
        return;
    if (ioctl(0, TIOCGETP, &tbufsave) == -1)
        syserr("setraw - ioctl");
    ospeed = tbuf.sg_ospeed;
    tbuf.sg_flags |= RAW | CBREAK;
    tbuf.sg_flags &= (CRMOD | ECHO);
    if (ioctl(0, TIOCSETP, &tbuf) == -1)
        syserr("setraw - ioctl2");
#else
    if (ioctl(0, TCGETA, &tbuf) == -1) /* may be pipe */
        return;
    tbufsave = tbuf;
    ospeed = tbuf.c_cflag & CBAUD;
    tbuf.c_iflag &= (INLCR | ICRNL | IUCLC | ISTRIP | IXON | BRKINT);
    tbuf.c_oflag &= OPOST;
    tbuf.c_lflag &= (ICANON | ISIG | ECHO);
    tbuf.c_cc[4] = 5; /* MIN */
    tbuf.c_cc[5] = 2; /* TIME */
    if (ioctl(0, TCSETAF, &tbuf) == -1)
        syserr("setraw - ioctl");
#endif
    now_raw = TRUE;
}
```

The external flag **now_raw** records whether raw mode was actually set; we'll see how it's used shortly.

At the conclusion of processing, you should call **unsetraw** to put the terminal back the way you found it. It uses the **tbufsave** structure saved by **setraw**.[2]

```
/*-------------------------------------------------------------------
    unsetraw - restore terminal flags
                Taken from Advanced UNIX Programming, Sec 4.4.8 (restore).
                Extended for Version 7 terminal driver (OLDTTY).
                Error ignored in case standard input is a pipe.
---------------------------------------------------------------*/
void unsetraw()  /* restore terminal flags */
{
    static BOOLEAN first = TRUE;

    if (!first || !now_raw)
        return;
    first = FALSE;
#ifdef OLDTTY
    (void)ioctl(0, TIOCSETP, &tbufsave); /* may be pipe */
```

2The function **unsetraw** is based on the function **restore** in Sec. 4.4.8 of [Roc85]. The name **unsetraw** is more suggestive of what it does.

```
#else
    (void)ioctl(0, TCSETAF, &tbufsave); /* may be pipe */
#endif
#ifndef XENIX
    setblock(0, TRUE);
#endif
    now_raw = FALSE;
}
```

You should call **unsetraw** from your **cleanup** function, as explained in Sec. 2.9. If **setraw** never saved the modes, the **now_raw** flag ensures that **unsetraw** doesn't attempt to restore them, since they were never captured. This is important if you have to abort your program during its initialization, in which case **cleanup** (and hence **unsetraw**) may be called before **setraw**.

On MS–DOS, you don't have to set a mode in order to read the keyboard in raw mode—you just have to use an appropriately low-level system call to do the reading, as we'll see in the next section. So **setraw** and **unsetraw** are empty:

```
/*--------------------------------------------------------------------
      setraw, unsetraw - not necessary on MS-DOS
                         See UNIX code for what they don't do.
    ---------------------------------------------------------------*/
void setraw()
{
}

void unsetraw()
{
}
```

4.1.2. Checking for and Reading Keystrokes on UNIX

We sometimes want to see if a keystroke is ready without actually reading it. This may be because we don't want to block on a read while we're waiting for input, or it may be because we have some discretionary work to do, such as updating the screen, that we might as well do while the user is thinking about what key to press. Only Xenix has a system call that does exactly what we want:

```
/*--------------------------------------------------------------------
      rdchk - check to see if data is ready (Xenix only)
        RETURN: 1 if yes or EOF; 0 if no; -1 on error
    ---------------------------------------------------------------*/
int rdchk(fd)
int fd;                              /* file descriptor */
```

When **rdchk** returns 1, it's safe to issue a **read** system call. Either a character is available, or a 0 count will be returned, indicating an end of file.

On other versions of UNIX, you can't directly ask whether data is ready, but you can put the file descriptor into non-blocking mode. A **read** will then return with a 0 or −1 if no data is ready. It will actually read a character if one is ready, of course, which we didn't want—we just wanted to *ask*. The unwanted character can simply be saved until we actually want to read.

We'll build up the routines we need in stages. First, we'll implement the function **setblock**, which turns blocking on or off. Next, we'll implement **readcond**, which reads either with or without blocking. It uses **rdchk** on Xenix systems and **setblock** otherwise, so it can be used on all versions of UNIX. Finally, we'll implement **cready**, which tells us whether a character is ready, and **cget**, which gets a character for us.

The first call to **setblock** obtains the file descriptor's flags with **fcntl** and forms a set of flags for blocking and a set for nonblocking. Each call then uses **fcntl** to flip the switch the desired way.

```
#ifndef XENIX
#include <fcntl.h>

/*------------------------------------------------------------------
    setblock - turn blocking on or off
               Taken from Advanced UNIX Programming, Sec 4.3.
               Enhanced for 4.2 and 4.3 BSD.
               Impossible to implement on Version 7 Xenix.
---------------------------------------------------------------*/
static void setblock(fd, on)
int fd;                                 /* file descriptor */
BOOLEAN on;                             /* blocking on or off? */
{
    static int blockf, nonblockf;
    static BOOLEAN first = TRUE;
    int flags;
#ifdef SYS3
    static int ndelay = O_NDELAY;
#endif
#ifdef BSD4
    static int ndelay = FNDELAY;
#endif

    if (first) {
        first = FALSE;
        if ((flags = fcntl(fd, F_GETFL, 0)) == -1)
            syserr("fcntl");
        blockf = flags &  ndelay; /* make sure O_NDELAY is off */
        nonblockf = flags | ndelay; /* make sure O_NDELAY is on */
    }
    if (fcntl(fd, F_SETFL, on ? blockf : nonblockf) == -1)
        syserr("fcntl2");
}
#endif
```

Note that because **setblock** gets the flags on only the first call, it really can't be used on several file descriptors unless their flags are the same. This makes no difference to us, because we're concerned only with file descriptor 0. For other purposes, however, you may want to fix this bug.

---

[3]The techniques used here are explained more fully in Sec. 4.3 of [Roc85], from which **setblock, cready,** and **cget** were adapted.

Now we can implement a variant of **read** that has a fourth argument telling it whether to block or not. The point of **readcond** is to hide the differences between Xenix and the other versions of UNIX.

```
/*-------------------------------------------------------------------
    readcond - conditional read with or without blocking
    RETURN: Number of bytes read; 0 on no data or EOF; -1 on error.
            On 4.2 and 4.3 BSD, no data is an error (EWOULDBLOCK).
-------------------------------------------------------------------*/
static int readcond(fd, buf, nbytes, block)
int fd;                                  /* file descriptor */
char *buf;                               /* buffer address */
unsigned nbytes;                         /* number of bytes to read */
BOOLEAN block;                           /* should it block? */
{
#ifdef XENIX
    if (!block && rdchk(fd) == 0)
        return(0);
#else
    setblock(fd, block);
#endif
    return(read(fd, buf, nbytes));
}
```

Note that on System III and System V, **read** returns 0 when no data is ready, which is indistinguishable from an end-of-file. On Berkeley UNIX, it returns −1 and sets **errno** to **EWOULDBLOCK** (defined in **errno.h**). The ambiguity on System III doesn't matter to us, because we will always read file descriptor 0 in raw mode, and it's impossible to generate an end-of-file from the keyboard (Control−D is read literally).

We have enough mechanism now to code **cready** and **cget**. Note that **cget** always blocks if no character is ready.

```
/*-------------------------------------------------------------------
    cready - see if keyboard character is ready, without returning it
             Taken from Advanced UNIX Programming, Sec. 4.3.
             Changed to use readcond() instead of setblock().
    RETURN: Is character ready?
-------------------------------------------------------------------*/
#define EMPTY '\0'
static char cbuf = EMPTY;

BOOLEAN cready()
{
    extern int errno;

    if (cbuf != EMPTY)
        return(TRUE);
    switch (readcond(0, &cbuf, 1, FALSE)) {
    case -1:
#ifdef BSD4
        if (errno == EWOULDBLOCK)
            return(FALSE);
#endif
        syserr("read");
    case 0:
        return(FALSE); /* could be EOF too */
    default:
        return(TRUE);
    }
}
```

```
/*----------------------------------------------------------------
      cget - get a character from keyboard
             Taken from Advanced UNIX Programming, Sec. 4.3.
             Changed to use readcond() instead of setblock().
      RETURN: Character, or -1 on EOF (impossible in raw mode).
      --------------------------------------------------------------*/
int cget()
{
    char c;

    if (cbuf != EMPTY) {
        c = cbuf;
        cbuf = EMPTY;
        return(c & 0377); /* prevent sign extension */
    }
    switch (readcond(0, &c, 1, TRUE)) {
    case -1:
        syserr("read");
    case 0:
        return(-1); /* must be EOF */
    default:
        return(c & 0377);
    }
}
```

4.1.3. Checking for and Reading Keystrokes on MS-DOS

As we've come to expect by now, it's much easier to figure out how to code **cready** and **cget** on MS-DOS than on UNIX. Actually, the problem is that there are too *many* ways to access the keyboard, but then that's better than too *few*. You can use MS-DOS system calls or BIOS interrupts. We'll use the BIOS, mainly because we accessed it for the physical screen implementations (Sec. 3.6.1), and we've already explained how to do so.

We want to add two new functions to the file **bios.c** that we introduced in Sec. 3.6.1 (this file is shown in Appendix A).[4] First, **BKavail** tells us whether a keystroke is ready:

```
/*----------------------------------------------------------------
      BKavail - determine if keyboard character is available
      RETURN: Is it?
      --------------------------------------------------------------*/
BOOLEAN BKavail()
```

Next, **BKread** gets the next character and the keyboard scan code:

```
/*----------------------------------------------------------------
      BKread - read keyboard character and scan code
      RETURN: Character read.
      --------------------------------------------------------------*/
int BKread(scanp)
int *scanp;                                    /* scan code */
```

---

[4]For Microsoft C, **BKavail** is coded in assembly language, because its **int86** function doesn't return the flag that tells whether the character is ready.

For ASCII characters, the value of **BKread** indicates which key was pressed. For special keys on the IBM PC keyboard (such as F1, PgDn, Del), **BKread** returns 0 and the scan code indicates which key was pressed. Generally, scan codes are the same as those described in [IBM84], but **BKread** treats the gray asterisk, minus, and plus keys on the numeric keypad differently, in order to distinguish them from the same characters on the white keys. These three keys cause **BKread** to return 0, instead of the corresponding ASCII codes. Thus, they act more like function keys than ASCII keys (their scan codes are, respectively, 54, 74, and 78). We'll give more details about the actual values returned by **BKread** at the end of Sec. 4.4.

Function keys create a slight complication for **cget**. We'll do what MS-DOS does: A function key actually returns *two* characters, a zero and a scan code. Thus, when **cget** returns a zero, it must be called again. Actually, this isn't so different from how most terminals treat function keys, which typically return an Escape character followed by one or more additional characters. When **BKread** returns a zero, we'll just save the scan code for the next call in the variable **nextch**:

```
static int nextch = 0;                     /* character saved by cget() */

/*-------------------------------------------------------------------
    cget - get a character from keyboard
            If zero, next call gets scan code.
    RETURN: Character.
------------------------------------------------------------------*/
int cget()
{
    int ch;

    if (nextch != 0) {
        ch = nextch;
        nextch = 0;
    }
    else {
        ch = BKread(&nextch);
        if (ch != 0)
            nextch = 0;
    }
    return(ch);
}
```

It's straightforward to code **cready** for MS-DOS. Either we know a character is ready because **nextch** is non-zero, or we can call **BKavail**:

```
/*-------------------------------------------------------------------
    cready - see if keyboard character is ready, without returning it
    RETURN: Is character ready?
------------------------------------------------------------*/
BOOLEAN cready()
{
    BOOLEAN BKavail();

    return((BOOLEAN)(nextch != 0 || BKavail()));
}
```

4.2. Keyboard Interface and Implementation

We now have the four building blocks we need to handle the keyboard: **setraw, unsetraw, cready,** and **cget.** What's more, they work on all versions of UNIX and on MS−DOS. We'd still like to hide details such as the necessity of putting the terminal into raw mode, however, so we'll interface to these four functions through a keyboard module, in the file **keyboard.c**. You initialize and terminate the keyboard with **Kbegin** and **Kend**:

```
/*-----------------------------------------------------------------
     Kbegin - initialize keyboard
-------------------------------------------------------------------*/
void Kbegin()
{
    setraw();
}
/*-----------------------------------------------------------------
     Kend - terminate keyboard
-------------------------------------------------------------------*/
void Kend()
{
    unsetraw();
}
```

You call **Kget** to get a character. The function **keycode** isn't necessary yet, but we'll need it in Sec. 4.4, so we're putting it in now as a place holder.[5]

```
/*-----------------------------------------------------------------
     Kget - get keyboard code
     RETURN: Keyboard code.
-------------------------------------------------------------------*/
int Kget()
{
    return(keycode());
}
/*-----------------------------------------------------------------
     keycode - get key code
     RETURN: Key code.
-------------------------------------------------------------------*/
int keycode()
{
    return(cget());
}
```

You can call **Kready** to find out whether a character is available:

---

[5]For reasons that will become clear later, this version of **keycode** is in the file **kc_real.c** rather than in **keyboard.c**.

```
/*-------------------------------------------------------------------
      Kready - check if keyboard code is ready
      RETURN: Is it?
-----------------------------------------------------------------*/
BOOLEAN Kready()
{
      return(cready());
}
```

Finally, you can call **Ksynch** instead of **PSsynch** if you want to update the display only when no character has been typed:

```
/*-------------------------------------------------------------
      Ksynch - update display if keyboard isn't ready
---------------------------------------------------------------*/
void Ksynch()
{
      if (!Kready())
          PSsynch();
}
```

All programs in the rest of this book access the keyboard through this interface. The functions **setraw, unsetraw, cready,** and **cget** are never called directly.

4.3. The Virtual Keyboard

We have a clean, portable, easy-to-use interface to the keyboard that solves most of the problems outlined at the start of this chapter. We can read every keystroke with no interference from the operating system. Now we can tackle an even worse problem: Reading every keystroke is exactly what we do *not* want to do! While the ordinary ASCII keys are simple enough to read, the function keys may transmit several characters which vary from terminal to terminal.

To illustrate this problem, and to provide a simple tool to explore various keyboards, here's a program (**keysee.c**) that displays the codes transmitted by each key:

```
#include "display.h"
#include "keyboard.h"

/*-------------------------------------------------------------
      Show keyboard code sequences.
---------------------------------------------------------------*/
void main()
{
      int k;

      Kbegin();
      while (TRUE) {
          if ((k = Kget()) == 'q')
              break;
          printf("%d ", k);
```

```
    if (!Kready())
        printf("\r\n");
}
Kend();
exit(0);
}
```

Since we start a new line only when no keystrokes are pending, we can see the entire sequence generated by each key on a single line of output (provided we type slowly, that is). As a test, we pressed these ten keys:

h   e   l   l   o   *up-arrow   down-arrow   F1   F2*   **q**

On a terminal connected to a UNIX system, this is the output we got:

```
104
101
108
108
111
27 91 65
27 91 66
27 91 77
27 91 78
```

Apparently, function keys start with the two characters <u>ESC</u> [. On the IBM PC, the same ten keystrokes generated this output:

```
104
101
108
108
111
0 72
0 80
0 59
0 60
```

We could have found a dozen more terminals that generated a dozen more variations.

The headache caused by function keys actually has two separate sources:

1. Some keys generate more than one character. This complicates the treatment of keystroke input because a simple **switch** statement can't be used to process the values returned by **Kget**. You need a more elaborate arrangement of nested **switch** statements or table lookups. Worse, some terminals don't even transmit sequences of a fixed length. The program must somehow know when one sequence ends and another begins.

2. The sequences generated vary from terminal to terminal (just as display sequences do). Sometimes even the same terminal can generate different sequences, depending on how it's configured.

We'll attack the first problem by defining a virtual keyboard in which every keystroke is assigned a unique integer—always exactly one code per key. We'll attack the second problem in two ways. In Sec. 4.4 we'll propose a scheme (inspired by Wordstar) that can generate the virtual keyboard codes entirely from the ASCII keyboard. No function keys will be used even if they are available. In Sec. 4.5 we'll implement a table-driven scheme that can handle any function keys of almost any terminal. Because the defining table is an ordinary text file, the end user has the additional freedom to redefine the keyboard to suit his or her own tastes.[6]

The first 128 codes on the virtual keyboard are identical to the ASCII codes. Codes 128 through 299 aren't used (this isn't a problem, because numbers are in plentiful supply). Function keys start at 301 and go up as high as necessary, although currently the highest code actually used is 396. The assignments of function keys to codes are defined in the header file **keycode.h**. It begins with symbols for the ASCII control characters, but, since these are standardized, the symbols needn't be used (in C, for example, **\r** can be used for carriage return).

```
#define K_CTL_A      1          /* control A */
#define K_CTL_B      2
#define K_CTL_C      3
#define K_CTL_D      4
#define K_CTL_E      5
#define K_CTL_F      6
#define K_CTL_G      7
#define K_BEL        7          /* bell */
#define K_CTL_H      8
#define K_BS         8          /* backspace */
#define K_CTL_I      9
#define K_TAB        9          /* horizontal tab */
#define K_CTL_J      10
#define K_LF         10         /* line feed (newline) */
#define K_CTL_K      11
#define K_CTL_L      12
#define K_CTL_M      13
#define K_RET        13         /* return */
#define K_CTL_N      14
#define K_CTL_O      15
#define K_CTL_P      16
#define K_CTL_Q      17
#define K_CTL_R      18
#define K_CTL_S      19
#define K_CTL_T      20
#define K_CTL_U      21
#define K_CTL_V      22
#define K_CTL_W      23
#define K_CTL_X      24
#define K_CTL_Y      25
#define K_CTL_Z      26
```

---

[6]From a human-factors point of view, this is probably a lousy idea for most interactive applications because it invalidates help screens, user manuals, and training materials, and because it becomes more difficult for new users to get help from their colleagues or from the software vendor. On the other hand, the ability to reconfigure the keyboard gives a user who is forced to use several incompatible products a way to make them appear reasonably consistent.

```
#define K_CTL_LB    27          /* control [ */
#define K_ESC       27          /* escape    */
#define K_CTL_BSLSH 28          /* control \ */
#define K_CTL_RB    29          /* control ] */
#define K_CTL_CFLEX 30          /* control ^ */
#define K_CTL_UNDER 31          /* control _ */
#define K_DEL       127         /* delete */
```

Next come codes useful for applications like text editors and form-entry systems. The virtual keyboard doesn't impose a meaning on any of these codes—that's up to the application. But the symbolic name suggests the most common usage of the key. We'll see how most of these symbols are used in the screen editor in the next chapter.

```
#define K_UP        301         /* up arrow */
#define K_DOWN      302         /* down arrow */
#define K_RIGHT     303         /* right arrow */
#define K_LEFT      304         /* left arrow */
#define K_PREV      305         /* previous screen */
#define K_NEXT      306         /* next screen */
#define K_LHOME     307         /* line home */
#define K_LEND      308         /* line end */
#define K_HOME      309         /* home */
#define K_END       310         /* end */
#define K_INS       312         /* insert */
#define K_WLEFT     313         /* word left */
#define K_WRIGHT    314         /* word right */
#define K_BTAB      315         /* back tab */
#define K_SCL_UP    321         /* scroll window up */
#define K_SCL_DOWN  322         /* scroll window down */
#define K_SCL_RIGHT 323         /* scroll window right */
#define K_SCL_LEFT  324         /* scroll window left */
#define K_ZOOM_OUT  325         /* zoom out */
#define K_ZOOM_IN   326         /* zoom in */
```

Line home and *line end* mean to go to the leftmost and rightmost positions on the line.

Next come ten function keys to be used any way an application sees fit.

```
#define K_F1        331         /* function key 1 */
#define K_F2        332
#define K_F3        333
#define K_F4        334
#define K_F5        335
#define K_F6        336
#define K_F7        337
#define K_F8        338
#define K_F9        339
#define K_F10       340
```

The IBM PC actually has thirty more function keys triggered by using the Control, Shift, and Alternate keys together with the ten normal function keys (F1 through F10). We'll include definitions for them, but we won't use them in applications in this book, nor will we worry about supporting them on UNIX terminals.

```
#define K_S_F1      341            /* shift F1 */
#define K_S_F2      342
#define K_S_F3      343
#define K_S_F4      344
#define K_S_F5      345
#define K_S_F6      346
#define K_S_F7      347
#define K_S_F8      348
#define K_S_F9      349
#define K_S_F10     350
#define K_C_F1      351            /* control F1 */
#define K_C_F2      352
#define K_C_F3      353
#define K_C_F4      354
#define K_C_F5      355
#define K_C_F6      356
#define K_C_F7      357
#define K_C_F8      358
#define K_C_F9      359
#define K_C_F10     360
#define K_A_F1      361            /* alternate F1 */
#define K_A_F2      362
#define K_A_F3      363
#define K_A_F4      364
#define K_A_F5      365
#define K_A_F6      366
#define K_A_F7      367
#define K_A_F8      368
#define K_A_F9      369
#define K_A_F10     370
```

Finally, there are twenty-six alternate alphabetic codes that can be used for mnemonic keystrokes, such as **K_ALT_S** for search. These are modeled after the popular use of the Alternate key on the IBM PC keyboard, which acts like a second shift key.[7]

```
#define K_ALT_A     371            /* alternate A */
#define K_ALT_B     372
#define K_ALT_C     373
#define K_ALT_D     374
#define K_ALT_E     375
#define K_ALT_F     376
#define K_ALT_G     377
#define K_ALT_H     378
#define K_ALT_I     379
#define K_ALT_J     380
#define K_ALT_K     381
#define K_ALT_L     382
#define K_ALT_M     383
#define K_ALT_N     384
#define K_ALT_O     385
#define K_ALT_P     386
#define K_ALT_Q     387
#define K_ALT_R     388
#define K_ALT_S     389
#define K_ALT_T     390
#define K_ALT_U     391
#define K_ALT_V     392
#define K_ALT_W     393
#define K_ALT_X     394
#define K_ALT_Y     395
#define K_ALT_Z     396
```

---

[7]We're deliberately postponing the problem of generating all of these codes from terminals that may lack certain function keys. This is a *virtual* keyboard!

For codes above 127, application programs should refer only to the **K_** symbols, never to the actual code numbers, and never to the actual sequences transmitted by specific keyboards. This will make handling keystrokes easy and portable. Mapping of actual keystrokes to virtual key codes will be explained in the next two sections.

4.4. Hard-Coded Virtual Keyboard Mapping

A scheme that assigns virtual keyboard codes to control characters is nearly universal because every popular ASCII terminal has a control key. Most keyboards have function keys, too—particularly arrow keys—and most users would prefer to use what they've paid for rather than awkward control key combinations. We'll cater to this desire in the next section; for now, we'll satisfy ourselves with a generic approach that nearly always works and is nearly always sub-optimal.

There are thirty-two ASCII codes that can be generated with the control key. In addition to the twenty-six codes represented by Control-A through Control-Z, there are Control-@, Control-[(better known as Escape), Control-\, Control-], Control-^, and Control-_. We'll ignore these six codes because they're too hard for users to remember. Of the alphabetic control codes, three are assigned to ASCII functions that we need in most applications (text editing, certainly): Control-H (backspace), Control-I (tab), and Control-M (carriage return). We're left with twenty-three control codes that we can use to generate the fifty-six function codes on the virtual keyboard.

We don't have enough keys to assign a separate one to each function code, so we'll use Control-Q as the lead-in code for two character sequences. We'll assign **K_ALT_A** to Control-Q Control-A, **K_ALT_B** to Control-Q Control-B, and so on, through Control-Q Control-Z. We'll assign **K_F1** through **K_F10** to Control-Q 1 through Control-Q 0. (Digits are typed without the control key.)

With Control-Q gone, we're left with twenty-two control codes to handle twenty virtual keyboard codes. The following scheme works about as well as any:

Control Code	*Function*
Control-A	**K_WLEFT**
Control-B	**K_BTAB**
Control-C	**K_NEXT**
Control-D	**K_RIGHT**
Control-E	**K_UP**
Control-F	**K_WRIGHT**
Control-G	unused
Control-H	Backspace

(Table continues)

Control Code	Function
Control—I	Tab
Control—J	**K_SCL_DOWN**
Control—K	**K_SCL_LEFT**
Control—L	**K_SCL_RIGHT**
Control—M	Return
Control—N	unused
Control—O	**K_ZOOM_OUT**
Control—P	**K_ZOOM_IN**
Control—Q	lead-in for **K_ALT_A**, etc.
Control—R	**K_PREV**
Control—S	**K_LEFT**
Control—T	**K_LHOME**
Control—U	unused
Control—V	**K_INS**
Control—W	**K_HOME**
Control—X	**K_DOWN**
Control—Y	**K_LEND**
Control—Z	**K_END**

In this alphabetized list, the virtual keyboard codes appear to have been randomly assigned, but they actually make some sense, particularly on the left part of the keyboard. The diamond pattern for the cursor directions was taken from the popular microcomputer word processing program Wordstar. The arrangement here, however, is not intended to be completely compatible with Wordstar.

It's pretty easy to write a C function called **keycode** that translates from actual keyboard codes, as returned by **cget**, to virtual keyboard codes. There's one **switch** statement to handle the single-character codes (such as Control–A) and one nested **switch** statement to handle the second character of the codes starting with Control-Q. Here's the file **kc_gnrc.c**:

```c
#include "display.h"
#include "keycode.h"
#include "pscreen.h"

/*--------------------------------------------------------------------
    keycode - get key code
              Hard-wired virtual keyboard in the style of Wordstar.
    RETURN: Key code as defined in keycode.h.
--------------------------------------------------------------------*/
int keycode()
{
    int ch;

    while (TRUE)
        switch (ch = cget()) {
        case 0:
            (void)cget(); /* toss out IBM PC function keys */
            PSbeep();
            continue;
        case K_CTL_A:
            return(K_WLEFT);
        case K_CTL_B:
            return(K_BTAB);
```

```
case K_CTL_C:
    return(K_NEXT);
case K_CTL_D:
    return(K_RIGHT);
case K_CTL_E:
    return(K_UP);
case K_CTL_F:
    return(K_WRIGHT);
case K_CTL_J:
    return(K_SCL_DOWN);
case K_CTL_K:
    return(K_SCL_LEFT);
case K_CTL_L:
    return(K_SCL_RIGHT);
case K_CTL_O:
    return(K_ZOOM_OUT);
case K_CTL_P:
    return(K_ZOOM_IN);
case K_CTL_Q:
    switch (cget()) {
    case '1':
        return(K_F1);
    case '2':
        return(K_F2);
    case '3':
        return(K_F3);
    case '4':
        return(K_F4);
    case '5':
        return(K_F5);
    case '6':
        return(K_F6);
    case '7':
        return(K_F7);
    case '8':
        return(K_F8);
    case '9':
        return(K_F9);
    case '0':
        return(K_F10);
    case K_CTL_A:
        return(K_ALT_A);
    case K_CTL_B:
        return(K_ALT_B);
    case K_CTL_C:
        return(K_ALT_C);
    case K_CTL_D:
        return(K_ALT_D);
    case K_CTL_E:
        return(K_ALT_E);
    case K_CTL_F:
        return(K_ALT_F);
    case K_CTL_G:
        return(K_ALT_G);
    case K_CTL_H:
        return(K_ALT_H);
    case K_CTL_I:
        return(K_ALT_I);
    case K_CTL_J:
        return(K_ALT_J);
    case K_CTL_K:
        return(K_ALT_K);
    case K_CTL_L:
        return(K_ALT_L);
    case K_CTL_M:
        return(K_ALT_M);
```

```
                    case K_CTL_N:
                        return(K_ALT_N);
                    case K_CTL_O:
                        return(K_ALT_O);
                    case K_CTL_P:
                        return(K_ALT_P);
                    case K_CTL_Q:
                        return(K_ALT_Q);
                    case K_CTL_R:
                        return(K_ALT_R);
                    case K_CTL_S:
                        return(K_ALT_S);
                    case K_CTL_T:
                        return(K_ALT_T);
                    case K_CTL_U:
                        return(K_ALT_U);
                    case K_CTL_V:
                        return(K_ALT_V);
                    case K_CTL_W:
                        return(K_ALT_W);
                    case K_CTL_X:
                        return(K_ALT_X);
                    case K_CTL_Y:
                        return(K_ALT_Y);
                    case K_CTL_Z:
                        return(K_ALT_Z);
                    default:
                        PSbeep();
                        continue;
                    }
            case K_CTL_R:
                return(K_PREV);
            case K_CTL_S:
                return(K_LEFT);
            case K_CTL_T:
                return(K_LHOME);
            case K_CTL_U:
                return(K_SCL_UP);
            case K_CTL_V:
                return(K_INS);
            case K_CTL_W:
                return(K_HOME);
            case K_CTL_X:
                return(K_DOWN);
            case K_CTL_Y:
                return(K_LEND);
            case K_CTL_Z:
                return(K_END);
            case K_CTL_BSLSH: /* emergency exit */
                cleanup();
                exit(0);
            case K_CTL_CFLEX:
                return(cget()); /* literal character */
            default:
                return(ch);
            }
        }
```

Note that we trap keyboard sequences starting with zero in case this function is used on an IBM PC. We don't want a scan code (see Sec. 4.1.3) to be interpreted as an ordinary character. So we read and ignore one character whenever a zero comes in.

We've also provided a way to input actual control characters, since we've

preempted most of them. The character Control-^ causes the next character
to be taken literally.   Thus, to input, say, Control-A, you would type
Control-^ Control-A.

Recall from Sec. 4.2 that the keyboard interface function **Kget** actually
calls **keycode**, not **cget**. When we link with this version of **keycode**, we will
get the virtual keyboard codes (**K_UP** and so forth) when we call **Kget**.

It's handy to use a testing program to check out our keyboard mapping.
We generated a long but boring test program by taking the file **keycode.h**
and massaging it with a text editor. We won't show the whole thing, but it
begins like this:

```
#include "display.h"
#include "keyboard.h"
#include "keycode.h"

void main()
{
    int k;

    Kbegin();
    while (TRUE)
        switch (k = Kget()) {
        case K_CTL_A:       printf("K_CTL_A\r\n");           break;
        case K_CTL_B:       printf("K_CTL_B\r\n");           break;
        case K_CTL_C:       printf("K_CTL_C\r\n");           break;
        case K_CTL_D:       printf("K_CTL_D\r\n");           break;
        case K_CTL_E:       printf("K_CTL_E\r\n");           break;
        case K_CTL_F:       printf("K_CTL_F\r\n");           break;
        case K_CTL_G:       printf("K_CTL_G (K_BEL)\r\n");   break;
        case K_CTL_H:       printf("K_CTL_H (K_BS)\r\n");    break;
        case K_CTL_I:       printf("K_CTL_I (K_TAB)\r\n");   break;
        case K_CTL_J:       printf("K_CTL_J (K_LF)\r\n");    break;
        case K_CTL_K:       printf("K_CTL_K\r\n");           break;
        case K_CTL_L:       printf("K_CTL_L\r\n");           break;
```

and ends like this:

```
        case K_ALT_X:       printf("K_ALT_X\r\n");           break;
        case K_ALT_Y:       printf("K_ALT_Y\r\n");           break;
        case K_ALT_Z:       printf("K_ALT_Z\r\n");           break;
        default:
            printf("code %d\r\n", k);
            if (k == 'q') {
                Kend();
                exit(0);
            }
        }
}
```

You can use your imagination for the middle part.

We linked this program with the keyboard module (**keyboard.c**) and
the generic version of **keycode** (**kc_gnrc.c**). We then pressed these thirteen
keys to mirror the ten keys we pressed in Sec. 4.3:

h e l l o *Control-E Control-X Control-Q* **1** *Control-Q* **2 q**

Here's the output we got:

```
                                        code 104
                                        code 101
                                        code 108
                                        code 108
                                        code 111
                                        K_UP
                                        K_DOWN
                                        K_F1
                                        K_F2
                                        code 113
```

Rather than map the key codes with **switch** statements, it's sometimes desirable to encode the mappings into a table and translate them by a simple look-up procedure.   We'll show a hard-coded implementation of **keycode** using that approach, this time for the IBM PC keyboard. Note that the codes in the table are the scan codes returned as the second character of sequences starting with zero. This is the file **kc_ibmpc.c**:

```c
#include "display.h"
#include "keycode.h"
#include "pscreen.h"

#define MINCODE 15  /* K_BTAB */
#define MAXCODE 119 /* K_LHOME */
#define UNUSED  0

static int kmap[] = {
    /* 15 */    K_BTAB,             /* 16 */    K_ALT_Q,
    /* 17 */    K_ALT_W,            /* 18 */    K_ALT_E,
    /* 19 */    K_ALT_R,            /* 20 */    K_ALT_T,
    /* 21 */    K_ALT_Y,            /* 22 */    K_ALT_U,
    /* 23 */    K_ALT_I,            /* 24 */    K_ALT_O,
    /* 25 */    K_ALT_P,            /* 26 */    UNUSED,
    /* 27 */    UNUSED,             /* 28 */    UNUSED,
    /* 29 */    UNUSED,             /* 30 */    K_ALT_A,
    /* 31 */    K_ALT_S,            /* 32 */    K_ALT_D,
    /* 33 */    K_ALT_F,            /* 34 */    K_ALT_G,
    /* 35 */    K_ALT_H,            /* 36 */    K_ALT_J,
    /* 37 */    K_ALT_K,            /* 38 */    K_ALT_L,
    /* 39 */    UNUSED,             /* 40 */    UNUSED,
    /* 41 */    UNUSED,             /* 42 */    UNUSED,
    /* 43 */    UNUSED,             /* 44 */    K_ALT_Z,
    /* 45 */    K_ALT_X,            /* 46 */    K_ALT_C,
    /* 47 */    K_ALT_V,            /* 48 */    K_ALT_B,
    /* 49 */    K_ALT_N,            /* 50 */    K_ALT_M,
    /* 51 */    UNUSED,             /* 52 */    UNUSED,
    /* 53 */    UNUSED,             /* 54 */    UNUSED,
    /* 55 */    UNUSED,             /* 56 */    UNUSED,
    /* 57 */    UNUSED,             /* 58 */    UNUSED,
    /* 59 */    K_F1,               /* 60 */    K_F2,
    /* 61 */    K_F3,               /* 62 */    K_F4,
    /* 63 */    K_F5,               /* 64 */    K_F6,
    /* 65 */    K_F7,               /* 66 */    K_F8,
    /* 67 */    K_F9,               /* 68 */    K_F10,
    /* 69 */    UNUSED,             /* 70 */    UNUSED,
    /* 71 */    K_HOME,             /* 72 */    K_UP,
    /* 73 */    K_PREV,             /* 74 */    K_ZOOM_OUT,
    /* 75 */    K_LEFT,             /* 76 */    UNUSED,
    /* 77 */    K_RIGHT,            /* 78 */    K_ZOOM_IN,
```

```
        /* 79 */      K_END,              /* 80 */      K_DOWN,
        /* 81 */      K_NEXT,             /* 82 */      K_INS,
        /* 83 */      K_DEL,              /* 84 */      K_S_F1,
        /* 85 */      K_S_F2,             /* 86 */      K_S_F3,
        /* 87 */      K_S_F4,             /* 88 */      K_S_F5,
        /* 89 */      K_S_F6,             /* 90 */      K_S_F7,
        /* 91 */      K_S_F8,             /* 92 */      K_S_F9,
        /* 93 */      K_S_F10,            /* 94 */      K_C_F1,
        /* 95 */      K_C_F2,             /* 96 */      K_C_F3,
        /* 97 */      K_C_F4,             /* 98 */      K_C_F5,
        /* 99 */      K_C_F6,             /* 100 */     K_C_F7,
        /* 101 */     K_C_F8,             /* 102 */     K_C_F9,
        /* 103 */     K_C_F10,            /* 104 */     K_A_F1,
        /* 105 */     K_A_F2,             /* 106 */     K_A_F3,
        /* 107 */     K_A_F4,             /* 108 */     K_A_F5,
        /* 109 */     K_A_F6,             /* 110 */     K_A_F7,
        /* 111 */     K_A_F8,             /* 112 */     K_A_F9,
        /* 113 */     K_A_F10,            /* 114 */     UNUSED,
        /* 115 */     K_WLEFT,            /* 116 */     K_WRIGHT,
        /* 117 */     K_LEND,             /* 118 */     UNUSED,
        /* 119 */     K_LHOME
};


/*---------------------------------------------------------------------
    keycode - get key code
                    Hard-wired virtual keyboard for the IBM PC.
    RETURN: Key code as defined in keycode.h.
-----------------------------------------------------------------------*/
int keycode()
{
    int ch, code;

    while (TRUE)
        switch (ch = cget()) {
        case 0:
            ch = cget();
            if (ch >= MINCODE && ch <= MAXCODE) {
                code = kmap[ch - MINCODE];
                if (code != UNUSED)
                    return(code);
            }
            PSbeep();
            continue;
        case K_CTL_J:
            return(K_SCL_DOWN);
        case K_CTL_K:
            return(K_SCL_LEFT);
        case K_CTL_L:
            return(K_SCL_RIGHT);
        case K_CTL_U:
            return(K_SCL_UP);
        case K_CTL_CFLEX:
            return(cget()); /* literal character */
        default:
            return(ch);
        }
}
```

We've left the four scrolling codes as control codes rather than use
special IBM PC keys. All other control codes are read literally, but we've still
retained the Control–^ mechanism that we used in **kc_gnrc.c,** just in case.

4.5. Table-Driven Virtual Keyboard Mapping

It's straightforward to develop additional hard-coded keyboard mapping functions for any keyboard you like. By linking appropriately, you can produce a separate version of your application for each terminal. We proposed the same idea for the physical screen implementation in Sec. 3.3.3. A different physical screen implementation, based on that for the Z–19 terminal, could be produced for each supported terminal.

But for displays, we pointed out that the table-driven approach used by Termcap (Sec. 3.4) was much more flexible.[8] We'd like an equally flexible table-driven approach for the keyboard, too. As a bonus, the end-user can modify the table to change how the keyboard is used, something users rarely care to do with displays.

It's harder to design a table-driven approach for the keyboard than for the screen because the problem for the keyboard is *recognition*, whereas the problem for the screen is *generation*. For the screen, we had a function we wanted to perform, such as *insert line*, and all we had to do was look in the Termcap database to find out what sequence to send to the terminal. But for the keyboard, we have sequences of indeterminate length coming in, and we have to figure out when a sequence matches an entry in some table. We have a many-to-one mapping, which is harder to program than a one-to-many mapping.

Basically, here's what we'll do: A keyboard definition table (the file **kbdef.tbl**) will contain a list of virtual keyboard codes and their corresponding input sequences. The virtual keyboard codes are the integers contained in **keycode.h** (such as 301 for up arrow). The input sequences can include any characters at all, using a full eight bits. Null characters are allowed, too. At run-time, we'll read the table in and organize the sequences into a finite-state machine that can recognize the defined sequences and report an error on undefined sequences. When a code is requested via a call to the function **keycode**, we'll run the finite-state machine against successive input characters until a virtual keyboard code is recognized or an error results.

There are three issues to deal with: designing the defining table, constructing the finite-state machine (that is, compiling the table), and running the machine when a code is requested.

---

[8]Termcap has a rudimentary way of handling function keys in the capability database, but this is for the benefit of the **vi** editor. The Termcap access functions don't support those capabilities, nor do most versions of Curses (the newest AT&T version does). In any event, it's not nearly as flexible as the scheme presented here.

4.5.1. Keyboard Definition Table

Each line of the table consists of an integer virtual keyboard code followed by white space (spaces and/or tabs) followed by the input sequence consisting of any number of actual keyboard codes. Individual codes in the input sequence are separated by white space. For example, the line for up arrow might be coded like this:

301 27 91 65

This means, "when the sequence of values 27, 91, and 65 comes in, recognize it as virtual keyboard code 301." (The ASCII characters corresponding to 27, 91, and 65 are Escape, [, and A.)

To make it easier to write a keyboard definition table, some additional ways to encode characters are allowed. Here are the rules:

1. Any single character, except space, tab, and #, stands for itself. Thus, the example sequence could have been coded as:

301 27 [A

2. A two-character symbol starting with ^ stands for a control character. For example, **^A** or **^a** stands for Control–A. The example sequence could have been coded as:

301 ^[[A

3. A sequence of two or more digits is interpreted as an integer value, as in the example. If an integer starts with a zero, it is interpreted as an octal number. The example could have been coded as:

301 033 91 65

4. An integer (decimal or octal) can have a leading plus sign. This is essential for coding decimal integers less than ten, because a single digit alone would be taken as an ASCII character under Rule 1. Thus, a tab character could be coded as **+9** (or as **^I**) but not as plain **9**.

5. A # starts a comment. It and the rest of the line are skipped. If a line consists of nothing but a comment, or is empty, it is skipped.

6. The three characters space, tab, and # can't be coded literally. They can be coded as the integers **32**, **+9**, and **35**.

7. Input characters that are their own virtual keyboard codes (such as carriage return, **A, =**) need not be coded in the table at all. When the **keycode** function is reading characters and is about to begin a new sequence, a character that doesn't match any sequence is returned as is. But when the finite-state machine is in the middle of some candidate

sequences, a non-matching character signals a typing error. The impact of this rule is that the table need not be cluttered up with definitions for the 128 ASCII codes. However, these codes may be translated if desired.

Here is a keyboard definition table that blends together the generic (Wordstar-like) and IBM PC keyboard mappings from the previous section. (Except for testing, such a blending isn't usually desirable, so you'll probably want to whittle this table down before using it.) Note that it's perfectly OK for several input sequences to be translated to the same virtual keyboard code.

```
# Symbols in parentheses are the ones used in keycode.h.  Labels in square
# brackets are those found on the IBM PC keyboard.

# First group of virtual keyboard codes are portable between the IBM PC and
# all ASCII terminals.  Sequences starting with +0 are for the IBM PC.
# Other sequences work on the IBM PC or on any ASCII terminal.

127 +0 83   # Delete              (K_DEL)          [Del]
301 +0 72   # Cursor Up           (K_UP)           [up arrow]
301 ^e
302 +0 80   # Cursor Down         (K_DOWN)         [down arrow]
302 ^x
303 +0 77   # Cursor Right        (K_RIGHT)        [right arrow]
303 ^d
304 +0 75   # Cursor Left         (K_LEFT)         [left arrow]
304 ^s
305 +0 73   # Previous Screen     (K_PREV)         [PgUp]
305 ^r
306 +0 81   # Next Screen         (K_NEXT)         [PgDn]
306 ^c
307 +0 119  # Line Home           (K_LHOME)        [Control-Home]
307 ^t
308 +0 117  # Line End            (K_LEND)         [Control-End]
308 ^y
309 +0 71   # Home                (K_HOME)         [Home]
309 ^w
310 +0 79   # End                 (K_END)          [End]
310 ^z
312 +0 82   # Insert              (K_INS)          [Ins]
312 ^v
313 +0 115  # Word Left           (K_WLEFT)        [Control-left arrow]
313 ^a
314 +0 116  # Word Right          (K_WRIGHT)       [Control-right arrow]
314 ^f
315 +0 15   # Back Tab            (K_BTAB)         [Shift-Tab]
315 ^b
321 ^u      # Scroll Window Up    (K_SCL_UP)
322 ^j      # Scroll Window Down  (K_SCL_DOWN)
323 ^l      # Scroll Window Right (K_SCL_RIGHT)
324 ^k      # Scroll Window Left  (K_SCL_LEFT)
325 +0 74   # Zoom out            (K_ZOOM_OUT)     [numeric pad -]
325 ^o
326 +0 78   # Zoom in             (K_ZOOM_IN)      [numeric pad +]
326 ^p
331 +0 59   # Function Key F1     (K_F1)
331 ^q 1
332 +0 60   # Function Key F2     (K_F2)
332 ^q 2
333 +0 61   # Function Key F3     (K_F3)
333 ^q 3
```

```
334 +0 62   # Function Key F4     (K_F4)
334 ^q 4
335 +0 63   # Function Key F5     (K_F5)
335 ^q 5
336 +0 64   # Function Key F6     (K_F6)
336 ^q 6
337 +0 65   # Function Key F7     (K_F7)
337 ^q 7
338 +0 66   # Function Key F8     (K_F8)
338 ^q 8
339 +0 67   # Function Key F9     (K_F9)
339 ^q 9
340 +0 68   # Function Key F10    (K_F10)
340 ^q 0
371 +0 30   # Alternate A         (K_ALT_A)
371 ^q ^a
372 +0 48   # Alternate B         (K_ALT_B)
372 ^q ^b
373 +0 46   # Alternate C         (K_ALT_C)
373 ^q ^c
374 +0 32   # Alternate D         (K_ALT_D)
374 ^q ^d
375 +0 18   # Alternate E         (K_ALT_E)
375 ^q ^e
376 +0 33   # Alternate F         (K_ALT_F)
376 ^q ^f
377 +0 34   # Alternate G         (K_ALT_G)
377 ^q ^g
378 +0 35   # Alternate H         (K_ALT_H)
378 ^q ^h
379 +0 23   # Alternate I         (K_ALT_I)
379 ^q ^i
380 +0 36   # Alternate J         (K_ALT_J)
380 ^q ^j
381 +0 37   # Alternate K         (K_ALT_K)
381 ^q ^k
382 +0 38   # Alternate L         (K_ALT_L)
382 ^q ^l
383 +0 50   # Alternate M         (K_ALT_M)
383 ^q ^m
384 +0 49   # Alternate N         (K_ALT_N)
384 ^q ^n
385 +0 24   # Alternate O         (K_ALT_O)
385 ^q ^o
386 +0 25   # Alternate P         (K_ALT_P)
386 ^q ^p
387 +0 16   # Alternate Q         (K_ALT_Q)
387 ^q ^q
388 +0 19   # Alternate R         (K_ALT_R)
388 ^q ^r
389 +0 31   # Alternate S         (K_ALT_S)
389 ^q ^s
390 +0 20   # Alternate T         (K_ALT_T)
390 ^q ^t
391 +0 22   # Alternate U         (K_ALT_U)
391 ^q ^u
392 +0 47   # Alternate V         (K_ALT_V)
392 ^q ^v
393 +0 17   # Alternate W         (K_ALT_W)
393 ^q ^w
394 +0 45   # Alternate X         (K_ALT_X)
394 ^q ^x
395 +0 21   # Alternate Y         (K_ALT_Y)
395 ^q ^y
396 +0 44   # Alternate Z         (K_ALT_Z)
396 ^q ^z
```

```
# Next group are currently defined only for the IBM PC.  Until corresponding
# generic sequences are defined, they should not be used in programs
# intended to be portable.
```

```
341 +0 84    # Shift F1                    (K_S_F1)
342 +0 85    # Shift F2                    (K_S_F2)
343 +0 86    # Shift F3                    (K_S_F3)
344 +0 87    # Shift F4                    (K_S_F4)
345 +0 88    # Shift F5                    (K_S_F5)
346 +0 89    # Shift F6                    (K_S_F6)
347 +0 90    # Shift F7                    (K_S_F7)
348 +0 91    # Shift F8                    (K_S_F8)
349 +0 92    # Shift F9                    (K_S_F9)
350 +0 93    # Shift F10                   (K_S_F10)
351 +0 94    # Control F1                  (K_C_F1)
352 +0 95    # Control F2                  (K_C_F2)
353 +0 96    # Control F3                  (K_C_F3)
354 +0 97    # Control F4                  (K_C_F4)
355 +0 98    # Control F5                  (K_C_F5)
356 +0 99    # Control F6                  (K_C_F6)
357 +0 100   # Control F7                  (K_C_F7)
358 +0 101   # Control F8                  (K_C_F8)
359 +0 102   # Control F9                  (K_C_F9)
360 +0 103   # Control F10                 (K_C_F10)
361 +0 104   # Alternate F1                (K_A_F1)
362 +0 105   # Alternate F2                (K_A_F2)
363 +0 106   # Alternate F3                (K_A_F3)
364 +0 107   # Alternate F4                (K_A_F4)
365 +0 108   # Alternate F5                (K_A_F5)
366 +0 109   # Alternate F6                (K_A_F6)
367 +0 110   # Alternate F7                (K_A_F7)
368 +0 111   # Alternate F8                (K_A_F8)
369 +0 112   # Alternate F9                (K_A_F9)
370 +0 113   # Alternate F10               (K_A_F10)
```

```
# Next group generates literal control characters.
```

```
^@   ^^  ^@    # Control-@
^a   ^^  ^a    # Control-a
^b   ^^  ^b    # Control-b
^c   ^^  ^c    # Control-c
^d   ^^  ^d    # Control-d
^e   ^^  ^e    # Control-e
^f   ^^  ^f    # Control-f
^g   ^^  ^g    # Control-g
^h   ^^  ^h    # Control-h
^i   ^^  ^i    # Control-i
^j   ^^  ^j    # Control-j
^k   ^^  ^k    # Control-k
^l   ^^  ^l    # Control-l
^m   ^^  ^m    # Control-m
^n   ^^  ^n    # Control-n
^o   ^^  ^o    # Control-o
^p   ^^  ^p    # Control-p
^q   ^^  ^q    # Control-q
^r   ^^  ^r    # Control-r
^s   ^^  ^s    # Control-s
^t   ^^  ^t    # Control-t
^u   ^^  ^u    # Control-u
^v   ^^  ^v    # Control-v
^w   ^^  ^w    # Control-w
^x   ^^  ^x    # Control-x
^y   ^^  ^y    # Control-y
^z   ^^  ^z    # Control-z
^[   ^^  ^[    # Control-[
^\   ^^  ^\    # Control-\
```

```
^]   ^^ ^]   # Control-]
^^   ^^ ^^   # Control-^
^_   ^^ ^_   # Control-_

# End of keyboard definition table.
```

4.5.2. Building and Running the Finite-State Machine

We'll now explain how to generate, from a keyboard definition, a finite-state machine that can recognize incoming sequences. We'll track the generation with this fragment as an example:

```
301 27 [ A
302 27 [ B
303 [ C
304 [ D
305 27 ) A
306 27 ) B 2
307 27 X
308 27 ) C
309 27 Y
310 27 ) B 1
```

Here's the algorithm:

1. Bypass empty lines and comment lines, and strip comments from the end of the remaining lines.

2. Convert all values to binary integers. This involves translating the various encoding schemes described in the previous section (plain characters, control sequences starting with ^, octal numbers, and decimal numbers). We end up with a table of integer virtual keyboard codes and their associated integer input sequences:

```
301: 27 91 65
302: 27 91 66
303: 91 67
304: 91 68
305: 27 41 65
306: 27 41 66 50
307: 27 88
308: 27 41 67
309: 27 89
310: 27 41 66 49
```

3. Sort the table according to the input sequences (not the virtual keyboard codes). Now we have:

                    305: 27 41 65
                    310: 27 41 66 49
                    306: 27 41 66 50
                    308: 27 41 67
                    307: 27 88
                    309: 27 89
                    301: 27 91 65
                    302: 27 91 66
                    303: 91 67
                    304: 91 68

4. Now divide the table into sub-tables according to the first number in
   each input sequence. Make each sub-table a separate state. Construct
   a transition from the start state to each new state, and label it with the
   number that distinguishes that sub-table. For our example, we would
   have something like this:

                    On 27, go to state 1:
                         305: (27) 41 65
                         310: (27) 41 66 49
                         306: (27) 41 66 50
                         308: (27) 41 67
                         307: (27) 88
                         309: (27) 89
                         301: (27) 91 65
                         302: (27) 91 66
                    On 91, go to state 2:
                         303: (91) 67
                         304: (91) 68

   We introduce the term *i-sub-table* to refer to a sub-table of
   consecutive sequences in which at least the first i characters are
   identical. (The identical characters are shown in parentheses.) Thus,
   each sub-table created at this point is a 1-sub-table. The original,
   complete table could be called a 0-sub-table.

5. Within each state, divide again according to the second number in each
   input sequence to create 2-sub-tables. Construct a transition to each
   new state. This gives:

                    On 27, go to state 1:
                    On 41, go to state 1.1:
                         305: (27 41) 65
                         310: (27 41) 66 49
                         306: (27 41) 66 50
                         308: (27 41) 67

```
            On 88, go to state 1.2:
                307: (27 88)
            On 89, go to state 1.3:
                309: (27 89)
            On 91, go to state 1.4:
                301: (27 91) 65
                302: (27 91) 66
        On 91, go to state 2:
            On 67, go to state 2.1:
                303: (91 67)
            On 68, go to state 2.2:
                304: (91 68)
```

Continue to subdivide states until every final state consists of just a
virtual keyboard code.   All input sequences have been absorbed into
state transitions and are entirely within parentheses.   There is exactly
one input sequence per sub-table.   We end up with:

```
        On 27, go to state 1:
            On 41, go to state 1.1:
                On 65, go to state 1.1.1:
                    305: (27 41 65)
                On 66, go to state 1.1.2:
                    On 49, go to state 1.1.2.1:
                        310: (27 41 66 49)
                    On 50, go to state 1.1.2.2:
                        306: (27 41 66 50)
                On 67, go to state 1.1.3:
                    308: (27 41 67)
            On 88, go to state 1.2:
                307: (27 88)
            On 89, go to state 1.3:
                309: (27 89)
            On 91, go to state 1.4:
                On 65, go to state 1.4.1:
                    301: (27 91 65)
                On 66, go to state 1.4.2:
                    302: (27 91 66)
        On 91, go to state 2:
            On 67, go to state 2.1:
                303: (91 67)
            On 68, go to state 2.2:
                304: (91 68)
```

During the construction of the finite-state machine, if two input sequences in a sub-table are discovered to be identical, or if one sequence is a prefix of the other, then an ambiguous definition has been coded, and an appropriate error message is generated.

Given the completed, unambiguous, finite-state machine, it's easy to recognize input sequences as they are read (with **cget**). When a character is read, the appropriate state transition is taken. When a state is reached with only a virtual keyboard code (that is, the entire sequence is parenthesized), that code has been recognized and it is returned. When no transition matches a character, the character is discarded, the bell is rung, and the machine reverts to the start state. An exception is that when the machine is already in the start state, the unmatched character is returned as is. This allows simple ASCII characters to be left out of the defining table, as mentioned in the previous section.

If you study the sorted table shown in step 3, you can visualize the machine that will result without actually performing the subdividing in steps 4 and 5. In fact, we can skip the subdividing entirely and just use the sorted table to process the incoming character sequences. This also neatly avoids the problem of designing storage structures to represent the finite-state machine in memory.

Here's how to run input sequences against the sorted table: There is an integer variable i that keeps track of where we are in the input sequence being recognized. It starts at zero and is incremented by one each time we input a character. The current sub-table of candidate sequences is thus an i-sub-table. The next character to be read will be matched against character number i of those sequences (characters are numbered starting with 0). For example, suppose we have read the two characters Escape and) (codes 27 and 41). The variable i is 2, and this is the current 2-sub-table (characters already read are parenthesized):

> 305: (27 41) 65
> 310: (27 41) 66 49
> 306: (27 41) 66 50
> 308: (27 41) 67

The next character to be read will be matched against the third character (65, 66, or 67). If it's 65 or 67, we have recognized virtual keyboard codes 305 or 308. If it's 66, we create a 3-sub-table and read another character.

More precisely, here are the steps to be followed:

1. Set i to 0. The 0-sub-table of candidate sequences is the entire table, since we haven't read anything yet. The table is already sorted.

2. Read a character.

3. Scan the current i-sub-table for the *first* sequence whose ith character matches the input character.

4. Continue scanning for the *last* sequence whose ith character matches the input. The consecutive sequences scanned become the new (i+1)-sub-table. During this scan, if we find a sequence that is short (no ith character), it means that that sequence is identical to a prefix of some other sequence. The keyboard definition is therefore ambiguous, and an appropriate error is signaled.

5. If the i-sub-table is empty, then no sequence's ith character matched the input. If i is zero (we haven't started a sequence yet), just return the input as a plain ASCII character. Otherwise, signal an error.

6. If the i-sub-table consists of only one sequence, and if its ith character (the one we just matched) is its last character, then we have found a unique sequence that matches the input. Return the virtual keyboard code corresponding to the sequence.

7. Increment i by one.

8. Go back to step 2 and continue processing with the new i-sub-table.

Sequence recognition with this algorithm is slower than if we had actually built a finite-state machine, because of the scanning in steps 3 and 4. Unlike a finite-state machine, our algorithm's running time depends not only on the length of the input but also on the number of states. But the difference doesn't seem to matter much in practice because computers are pretty good at scanning linear lists, and because recognizing keystroke sequences is such a small part of the total processing that interactive applications do.

A simple but significant speed-up can be gained by keeping track of the minimum and maximum characters that occur at the start of the defined input sequences. When starting to recognize a sequence, a character that's outside these bounds can be returned right away. There's no need to scan the table to find out that nothing will match. For the IBM PC, this helps a lot because *all* sequences in the table start with zero (the minimum and the maximum). So the table is used only when a zero character is read. On other keyboards the benefits are less spectacular, but still worthwhile, because most sequences will start with control codes between 0 and 31.

If even more efficiency is desired, the look-up algorithm can be converted to one that actually produces a finite-state machine.

4.5.3. Implementing the Finite-State Machine

Now we'll show an implementation of **keycode** that reads in a keyboard definition table, converts all of the symbols to binary integers, sorts the resulting table, and uses the algorithm from the previous section to recognize input sequences.

The file **kc_table.c** starts like this:

```
#include "display.h"
#include "pscreen.h"
#include "keycode.h"

#define TBLGRANULE   10              /* amount to increase table by */
#define SEQGRANULE   3               /* amount to increase sequence by */
#define MAXINT       32767           /* maximum virtual keyboard code */

typedef struct {                     /* compiled keyboard definition table */
    short code;                      /* virtual keyboard code to return */
    char len;                        /* length of sequence */
    char seq[SEQGRANULE];            /* input sequence of keystrokes */
} KEYSEQ;

static KEYSEQ **table;               /* definition table */
static int tablelen;                 /* number of definitions */
static int maxtablelen;              /* maximum number of definitions */
static int minchar = 255;            /* minimun initial char in any seq. */
static int maxchar = 0;              /* maximun initial char in any seq. */

static char *filename = "kbdef.tbl";/* table file name */
static int linenum = 0;              /* line number in table */
static FILE *fin;                    /* stream for input */
```

Each input sequence and virtual keyboard code is kept in a **KEYSEQ** structure. At first, **table** points to storage large enough for **TBLGRANULE** sequences, each of which can be up to **SEQGRANULE** characters long. (We'll see this allocation a little later.) If more sequences are present in the table, the storage pointed to by **table** is reallocated to hold an additional **TBLGRANULE** sequences. The table continues to expand by this amount as needed, until all sequences in the keyboard definition table have been read in. Similarly, if an individual sequence is longer than **SEQGRANULE** characters, its **KEYSEQ** structure is reallocated to add room for an additional **SEQGRANULE** characters. Additional reallocations are made until the entire sequence fits. Thus, there is no fixed limit on the number of sequences or the size of a sequence, and very little storage is wasted.

As the table grows, **maxtablelen** keeps track of its capacity, and **tablelen** keeps track of its current length. The variables **minchar** and **maxchar** will be used to record the minimum and maximum initial character values in sequences. We'll set these as we compile the table, and we'll check them as we input characters. The last three variables are used in reading in the keyboard definition table. We'll see this shortly.

Here's the **keycode** function itself:

```
/*-------------------------------------------------------------------
      keycode - get key code
                Table-driven virtual keyboard using "kbdef.tbl" file.
      RETURN: Key code as defined in keycode.h.
-------------------------------------------------------------------*/
int keycode()
{
    static BOOLEAN first = TRUE, translate;
    int k;

    if (first) {
        first = FALSE;
        if ((translate = compile()) && tablelen <= 0)
            fatal("Error compiling keyboard table");
    }
```

```
        if (translate) {
            while ((k = lookup(table, tablelen, 0)) == -1)
                PSbeep();
            return(k);
        }
        return(cget());
    }
```

It compiles the table the first time it's called. If there is no table, **compile**
returns **FALSE** and characters are simply passed through literally. If there
is a table, **lookup** is called to match input sequences against the sorted table,
as described in the previous section. We'll look first at **compile**, and come
back to **lookup** later.

```
/*--------------------------------------------------------------------
    compile - compile keyboard definition table
--------------------------------------------------------------------*/
static BOOLEAN compile()
{
    char *getenv(), buf[100], *s;

    if ((fin = fopen(filename, "r")) == NULL)
        if ((filename = getenv("KBDEF")) == NULL)
            return(FALSE);
        else if ((fin = fopen(filename, "r")) == NULL)
            kfatal("can't open");
    tablelen = 0;
    maxtablelen = TBLGRANULE;
    table = (KEYSEQ **)xmalloc(TBLGRANULE * sizeof(KEYSEQ *));
    while (fgets(buf, sizeof(buf), fin) != NULL) {
        linenum++;
        buf[strlen(buf) - 1] = '\0'; /* clip newline */
        s = strtok(buf, "#");
        if (s != NULL && s[0] != '\0') {
            tablelen++;
            doline(s);
        }
    }
    if (ferror(fin))
        kfatal("read error");
    fclose(fin);
    qsort((char *)table, tablelen, sizeof(KEYSEQ *), compare);
    linenum = -1; /* so kfatal doesn't display line numbers */
    return(TRUE);
}
```

The global variable **filename** is set initially to **kbdef.tbl**. If a file with
such a name can be opened, the table in the current directory is used. If not,
the environment variable **KBDEF** is used to find the table's path. If this
variable isn't set, there is no table and **compile** just returns **FALSE** to
arrange for characters to be input literally. If **KBDEF** is set, but the path
can't be opened, a fatal error is issued by calling **kfatal**, which is defined like
this:

```
/*------------------------------------------------------------------
    kfatal - printf-like fatal
------------------------------------------------------------------*/
static void kfatal(fmt, a, b, c, d)
char *fmt;                              /* format */
char *a, *b, *c, *d;                    /* some arguments */
{
    char buf1[100], buf2[100];

    sprintf(buf1, fmt, a, b, c, d);
    if (linenum > 0)
        sprintf(buf2, "\"%s\", line %d - %s", filename, linenum, buf1);
    else
        sprintf(buf2, "\"%s\" - %s", filename, buf1);
    fatal(buf2);
}
```

We'll see a **printf**-like usage of **kfatal** later on. Note that this function isn't strictly portable because it plays fast and loose with argument types, but it works.

Getting back to **compile**, it next allocates a **TBLGRANULE**-long array of pointers to **KEYSEQ** structures, which will grow as needed. The structures themselves aren't allocated here; we'll allocate them as we need them.

Next, we read the file, bypassing comments and empty lines. (The function **strtok** was shown in Sec. 2.11.) The actual processing of each line is done by **doline**, which we'll get to in a moment. Let's first finish with **compile**.

When all lines have been processed, the standard UNIX function **qsort** is called to sort the table. Its synopsis is:

```
/*------------------------------------------------------------------
    qsort - sort array of objects
------------------------------------------------------------------*/
void qsort(array, numelts, eltsize, compare)
char *array;                            /* base address of array */
unsigned numelts;                       /* number of elements */
unsigned eltsize;                       /* size of each element */
int (*compare)();                       /* comparison function */
```

The function **compare** is called with two arguments which are pointers to elements in the array to be sorted:

```
/*------------------------------------------------------------------
    compare - compare two elements of array
    RETURN: <0 if first is less, 0 if equal, >0 if second is less
------------------------------------------------------------------*/
int compare(a, b)
char *a;                                /* pointer to first element */
char *b;                                /* pointer to second element */
```

The actual technique used by **compare** is up to us, which is what makes **qsort** so general. In this case, the array to be sorted is **table**, which is an array of pointers to **KEYSEQ** structures. So the arguments passed to **compare** are pointers to pointers to **KEYSEQ**s. We want to base the comparison on the input sequences, so here is our **compare**:

```
/*---------------------------------------------------------------
    compare - comparison routine for qsort
---------------------------------------------------------------*/
static int compare(a, b)
KEYSEQ **a;                              /* pointer to first element */
KEYSEQ **b;                              /* pointer to second element */
{
    int i;

    for (i = 0; i < (*a)->len; i++) {
        if (i >= (*b)->len)
            return(1);
        if ((*a)->seq[i] != (*b)->seq[i])
            return(((*a)->seq[i] & 0377) - ((*b)->seq[i] & 0377));
    }
    return(i >= (*b)->len ? 0 : -1);
}
```

Note that we ANDed each character with 0377 to prevent sign extension.
Now, we're ready for **doline**, which processes each input line:

```
/*---------------------------------------------------------------
    doline - process one line of table
---------------------------------------------------------------*/
static void doline(s)
char *s;                                 /* line to be processed */
{
    char *tok;
    int tablei, toknum, maxseq, n;

    if (tablelen > maxtablelen) {
        maxtablelen += TBLGRANULE;
        if ((table = (KEYSEQ **)realloc((char *)table,
          maxtablelen * sizeof(KEYSEQ *))) == NULL)
            fatal("out of memory");
    }
    tablei = tablelen - 1; /* subscripts start with zero */
    maxseq = SEQGRANULE;
    table[tablei] = (KEYSEQ *)xmalloc(sizeof(KEYSEQ));
    toknum = 0;
    while ((tok = strtok(s, " \t")) != NULL) {
        s = NULL;
        if (tok[0] == '\0') /* leading white space */
            continue;
        toknum++;
        if (toknum > maxseq + 1) {
            if ((table[tablei] = (KEYSEQ *)realloc((char *)table[tablei],
              sizeof(KEYSEQ) + maxseq)) == NULL)
                fatal("out of memory");
            maxseq += SEQGRANULE;
        }
        if (toknum == 1)
            table[tablei]->code = convert(tok, MAXINT);
        else {
            n = convert(tok, 255);
            table[tablei]->seq[toknum - 2] = n;
            if (toknum == 2) {
                minchar = MIN(minchar, n);
                maxchar = MAX(maxchar, n);
            }
        }
    }
}
```

```
    switch (toknum) {
    case 0:
        kfatal("empty line");
    case 1:
        kfatal("keystroke sequence missing");
    }
    table[tablei]->len = toknum - 1;
}
```

Here's where we grow the array of **KEYDEF** structure pointers when it
fills up. Once we have an available slot, we allocate the actual **KEYDEF**
structures.

We consider each line to be a collection of tokens separated by blanks
and tabs which are the delimiters we pass to **strtok** in the **while** condition.
The variable **toknum** keeps track of where we are. When it's one, the token
is the virtual keyboard code. When it's greater than one, we're working on
the input sequence, and **toknum** is two greater than the index of the character in the **seq** array. If **toknum** is two, we check to see whether **minchar** or
maxchar have to be updated.

We have to continually test **toknum** against the capacity of the **seq**
array (variable **maxseq**) because we're only allocating room for
SEQGRANULE characters at a time. We reallocate the **KEYSEQ** structure
as needed.

Each token is converted to binary form by calling **convert**, which looks
like this:

```
/*-------------------------------------------------------------------
    convert - convert string to integer code
              Handles single chars, control chars, and numbers.
    RETURN: Converted code.
--------------------------------------------------------------------*/
static int convert(s, maxval)
char *s;                            /* string to be converted */
int maxval;                         /* maximum allowable value */
{
    int n;

    switch (strlen(s)) {
    case 0:
        kfatal("null token");
    case 1:
        n = s[0];
        break;
    case 2:
        if (s[0] == '^') {
            n = toupper(s[1]) - '@';
            if (n < 0 || n > 31)
                kfatal("invalid character following ^: %c", s[1]);
            break;
        }
        /* fall through */
    default:
        n = cvtint(s);
    }
    if (n > maxval)
        kfatal("integer is too large: %d", n);
    return(n);
}
```

If the length of the token to be converted is zero, we have an impossible situation because **strtok** can only return the null string at the start of its scan, and we've already handled that case in **doline**. If the length is one, the character is taken literally—**convert** just returns its internal code. If the length is two, it might be a control character starting with ^, in which case we just convert the second character. Otherwise, the token is an integer (decimal or octal), and we call **cvtint** to convert it from ASCII to binary:

```
/*-------------------------------------------------------------------
    cvtint - convert string to octal or decimal integer
    RETURN: Converted integer.
-----------------------------------------------------------------*/
static int cvtint(s)
char *s;                            /* string to be converted */
{
    int n, digit, base;
    char *p;

    p = s;
    n = 0;
    if (*p == '+')
        p++;
    if (*p == '0') {
        p++;
        base = 8;
    }
    else
        base = 10;
    for (; *p != '\0'; p++) {
        digit = *p - '0';
        if (digit < 0 || digit >= base)
            kfatal("invalid number: %s", s);
        n = base * n + digit;
    }
    return(n);
}
```

That's all there is to compiling the table. Now, returning to the **keycode** function proper, let's explore **lookup**. The call to it in **keycode** is:

```
while ((k = lookup(table, tablelen, 0)) == -1)
    PSbeep();
```

The arguments to **lookup** define a sub-table. The first argument is the starting address which, for the first sub-table (the only 0-sub-table), is the base of the entire array of **KEYSEQ** pointers. The second argument is the length of the sub-table. The third argument is the index into each **seq** array of the *next* character to be compared with an input character. The index is initially zero, because we haven't read any input characters yet. Note that the third argument to **lookup** is *i*, as in *i-sub-table*.

The function **lookup** returns −1 if the input sequence doesn't match any definition. We ring the bell and keep trying.

Now, we have only to examine **lookup**, and we're done:

```
/*-------------------------------------------------------------------
    lookup - look up one keystroke in sub-table
    RETURN: Virtual keyboard code or -1 if keystroke is invalid.
-------------------------------------------------------------------*/
static int lookup(t, tlen, index)
KEYSEQ *t[];                            /* starting address of sub-table */
int tlen;                               /* length of sub-table */
int index;                              /* input sequence index */
{
    int i, c, seqc, start, end;

    if (tlen <= 0)
        return(-1);
    if (tlen == 1 && index >= t[0]->len)
        return(t[0]->code);
    if ((c = cget()) == K_CTL_BSLSH) { /* emergency exit */
        cleanup();
        exit(0);
    }
    if (index == 0 && (c < minchar || c > maxchar))
        return(c);
    start = end = -1;
    for (i = 0; i < tlen; i++) {
        if (index >= t[i]->len) {
            if (i == tlen - 1)
                kfatal("invalid sort order");
            kfatal("keystrokes for codes %d and %d are ambiguous",
                t[i]->code, t[i + 1]->code);
        }
        seqc = t[i]->seq[index] & 0377;
        if (seqc == c) {
            if (start == -1)
                start = i;
        }
        else if (seqc > c) {
            end = i - 1;
            break;
        }
    }
    if (end == -1)
        end = tlen - 1;
    if (start == -1)
        if (index == 0)
            return(c);
        else
            return(-1);
    return(lookup(&t[start], end - start + 1, index + 1));
}
```

We start with an error check: If the length is negative, there is no sub-table, so the sequence is presumably illegal and we return −1. Actually, this is impossible because we discover empty sub-tables sooner than this, but experienced programmers know that checks for the impossible are nice to have.

If the length of the sub-table is one and all characters in the one and only sequence have been matched, we've found our answer, and we return the virtual keyboard code.

Otherwise, we read a character. Control−\ is an emergency exit that comes in handy because a defective or incomplete keyboard definition table can make it impossible to exit a program that is looking for, say, the F3 function key. (You can remove this safeguard if you don't want it.) The function **cleanup** was discussed in Sec. 2.9.

If we're at the start of a sequence (**index** equals zero), and the input character is outside of the range bounded by **minchar** and **maxchar**, we just return it. The character will not match any sequence.

With the character we have, we start scanning the current sub-table. The variable **start** will record the subscript in the table of the first sequence with a matching character, and **end** will record the subscript of the last sequence. We initialize both to −1.

Ambiguous sequences are detected during the scan by checking the index against the length of each sequence. If it becomes equal to the length, we've got a sequence that's too short. It and the next sequence are ambiguous, and a message to that effect is output. There may be more participants in the ambiguity, but only two are detected. We know that there must be at least one other sequence in the sub-table, because otherwise we would have already returned a virtual keyboard code before we even entered the **for** loop. Furthermore, that other sequence must be *after* the too-short sequence in the table because that's how the sequences are sorted. An impossible situation is for the too-short sequence to be last in the sub-table; in this case, we issue an error.

If **end** is still −1 when we're done with the scan, we set it to the last subscript in the sub-table because we may have run off the end with matching sequences, which is perfectly all right. On the other hand, if **start** is still equal to −1, that means we didn't find a match at all. This is OK if we're only in the 0-sub-table (the entire table), but not if we're farther along.

Finally, if we have both a **start** and an **end**, we call **lookup** recursively to process the next sub-table. We don't bother detecting whether we actually have a match—the recursive call will do it for us.[9]

4.6. Summary

In this chapter we first programmed some low-level functions to give us access to the keyboard in an operating-system-independent way. We showed **cready** to tell us whether a character has been typed, and **cget** to get it for us. These functions operate in raw mode—we get characters immediately and unadulterated, without waiting for a complete line to be typed.

Because different keyboards transmit different characters when a function key is pressed, we defined a rather complete set of virtual key codes which aren't transmitted by any keyboard but which can be mapped into the

---

[9]Since this is *tail recursion*, it's pretty easy to change to a non-recursive implementation. This is left as an exercise.

codes that are. There were codes for cursor keys (such as **K_UP**), editing keys (such as **K_INS**), general-purpose function keys (such as **K_F1**), and so on. At this level of abstraction, we defined the functions **Kready** and **Kget**. Unlike **cready** and **cget**, they return virtual key codes, not real ones.

We showed several methods of mapping real codes to virtual codes. A generic, hard-coded mapping used the keyboard in a Wordstar-like way— clumsy but universal. It made no attempt to use function keys, but settled for control codes: Control–E mapped to **K_UP**, Control–V mapped to **K_INS**, and so on. Next, we used a table-driven scheme with the table inside the C program, in an initialized data structure. This was just for the IBM PC.

The problem with binding the mapping in at compile time is that there isn't enough flexibility to accommodate the wide variety of terminal keyboards. We solved this by designing an external table that's read in at run time and used to build a finite-state machine that recognizes key code sequences for the actual keyboard in use. We showed the programs for reading the table, constructing the machine, and running the recognition algorithm.

CHAPTER 5

A Simple Screen Editor

5.1. Introduction

Let's now use the physical screen module from Chapter 3 and the keyboard module from Chapter 4 to implement a simple screen editor. This will serve two purposes: to provide insight into how screen editors are implemented, and to give an extended example of how the physical screen and keyboard interfaces are used. In Chapter 6 we'll modify the editor to use windows, and in Chapter 7 we'll modify it again to use virtual screens. Of course, the editor is portable between UNIX and MS–DOS and, on UNIX, it will work with any terminal supported by Termcap. Among screen editors, this makes it a freak.

Figure 5–1 shows the editor in use. There is a screenful of text, and the user is in the midst of typing a file name in the upper right hand corner of the screen in response to the prompt. This figure shows the editor as implemented in this chapter. As a preview of coming attractions, Figure 5–2 shows the editor as modified in the next chapter. The user is responding to the same prompt, but this time in a pop-up prompt window.

Our screen editor won't have nearly as many features as most users would like, but it has enough to be usable. There are commands to read and write files, move the cursor around, split and join lines, and insert and delete lines and characters. Because we're primarily interested in the display

```
                                  File: edtex█

void setpos()
{
    struct Bufinfo *bf = bufinfoptr(bufnum);
    int pos, col, prevcol;
    char *t;

    t = ETtext(bufnum, bf->topline + bf->currow);
    col = prevcol = 0;
    bf->curpos = 0;
    for (pos = 0; ; pos++) {
        if (col > bf->curcol)
            break;
        prevcol = col;
        bf->curpos = pos;
        if (t[pos] == '\0')
            break;
        if (t[pos] == '\t')
            col += TABINTERVAL - col % TABINTERVAL;
        else
            col++;
    }
    bf->curcol = prevcol;
```

Fig. 5-1. Editor as implemented with the physical screen module.

```
┌Buffer-1────────────────────────────────────────────────
 void setpos()
 {
     struct Bufinfo *bf = bufinfoptr(bufnum);
     int pos, col, prevcol;
     char *t;            ┌────────────────────────────────┐
                         │ File: edtex█                   │
     t = ETtext(bu       └────────────────────────────────┘
     col = prevcol = 0;
     bf->curpos = 0;
     for (pos = 0; ; pos++) {

┌Buffer-2────────────────────────────────────────────────

 static struct Buffer {              /* info for each buffer */
     char **text;                    /* array of text lines */
     int numlines;                   /* number of lines */
     BOOLEAN changed;                /* has buffer changed since last write? */
 } buf[MAXBUF];

 #define MAXLINES 1000               /* maximum size of buffer */
 #define ALLOCUNIT 10                /* amount to grow line */
```

Fig. 5-2. Editor as implemented with the window module.

aspects of screen editor design, we'll also include two features that are difficult to handle if they aren't incorporated into the design from the start:

1. Tab characters may be entered into the text, are preserved as true tabs (that is, not as spaces), and may be deleted and edited like ordinary characters. This complicates matters because the contents and location of characters in a file may be different from what is on the screen. For example, if a line of text starts with two tabs, the third character of the line must be displayed in column 8 of the screen, assuming that tabs are set at intervals of four columns.

2. The editor can manage multiple buffers, each associated with a different file. The user can read a file into a buffer, edit the buffer, and then write the buffer to the same file or to a different file. No changes are made to a file except under user control. The user can switch instantly between buffers. In Chapter 6, when we modify the editor to use windows, the user will actually be able to view two buffers simultaneously.

We've omitted a long list of features that don't directly affect the display aspects of the editor design. These include overtype mode (typed characters replace existing characters, instead of pushing them to the right); editing of non-printing characters or non-text files; search and replace; marking blocks for copying, moving, and deleting; merging files; reading and writing partial files; printing; word wrap; paragraph reformatting; automatic indenting; user-settable tabs; fancy cursor motions (by word, by paragraph, and such); fancy deletions (of a word, to the end of the line, and such); renaming, copying, and deleting files; running operating system commands; and macros. However, the design presented here is a solid enough foundation to allow these and other features to be added later. Most programmers are quite opinionated about the editors they are forced to use—here's a chance for you to develop your own!

5.2. Using the Editor

This section presents a brief explanation of how the editor is used. It is written under the assumption that you are already familiar with screen editors (or, at least, word processors) in general.

The editor is always in *insert* mode: A typed character pushes the rest of the line to the right, or it extends the line if typed at the end. A carriage return ends a line and begins a new one, opening up a fresh line and pushing the rest of the buffer down, if necessary.

Only ASCII characters from space through tilde (codes 32 through 126), a tab, and a carriage return may be inserted into the buffer. Tab positions are fixed at columns 4, 8, 12, and so on (numbering from 0, as usual). Inserting a tab into a line causes the text to its right to jump to the next tab stop, and deleting a tab causes the text to jump back to the left.

Inserting a carriage return into a line splits the line in two, and deleting a carriage return joins two lines into one. On the screen, a carriage return is displayed as a space, but since a carriage return can occur only at the end of a line, and since every line ends with a carriage return, there is no ambiguity as to what a space at the end of a line means. When a buffer is read or written to or from a text file, appropriate translations are made between the carriage returns in the buffer and the end-of-line sequence required by the operating system. On UNIX, this sequence is a single newline; on MS–DOS it is a carriage return followed by a newline.

The point at which text may be inserted or deleted is indicated by the cursor. The screen (or window) isn't usually big enough to show the entire buffer, so the editor automatically scrolls the text to keep the cursor in view. Hence, one way for the user to explicitly scroll through the buffer is to attempt to move the cursor off the screen.

In this chapter and in Chapter 6, the editor can scroll vertically, but not horizontally. If a line is wider than can be shown, the part off-screen to the right is hidden. It will still be written out to a file, and it will scroll into view if characters are deleted from the visible portion of the line. In Chapter 7, the editor will actually be able to scroll horizontally. It is possible to program an editor so that it can handle long lines without using the virtual screen module, of course, but we won't bother doing so here.

This editor is *modeless*, in the sense that cursor motion and editing commands can be freely intermixed with text entry. It isn't necessary to switch between insert and command modes, as it is with **vi** or with most line editors (such as UNIX's **ed** or MS–DOS's **edlin**). A modeless editor is *much* easier to learn and use, but it does place certain demands on the keyboard: There must be enough keys to go around. The keyboard mapping methods detailed in Chapter 4 will handle this hassle for us very nicely, so we can and will ignore actual keyboard keys in this chapter. Instead, we'll describe usage of the editor purely in terms of the virtual keyboard introduced in Sec. 4.3. That is, to move the cursor down you press (virtually) the **K_DOWN** key. If you like, you can use your imagination and read this as "press the down-arrow key," or "press the Control–X key," or whatever.

Here is what the editing keys do:

K_UP   Moves the cursor up one line, scrolling the screen as necessary to keep the cursor visible. No effect if the cursor is already on the first line. Tries to keep the cursor in the same column, but if necessary will change the column to one that actually contains text.

K_DOWN   Similar to **K_UP**, but moves the cursor down.

K_RIGHT   Moves the cursor one column to the right. Does not wrap to the next line. May or may not scroll the screen sideways, depending on how the editor is implemented. Won't move past the end of the line (that is, you can't position the cursor to a place that has no text). The cursor jumps to the next tab position if it is currently on a tab (the only way to tell when the cursor is on a tab).

K_LEFT	Similar to **K_RIGHT**, but moves left.
K_PREV	Shows the previous screenful of text (that is, it goes backward). No effect if the first line of the buffer is already visible.
K_NEXT	Similar to **K_PREV**, but goes forward.
K_HOME	Moves the cursor to the first character of the buffer.
K_END	Moves the cursor to the last character of the buffer (always a carriage return).
K_LHOME	Moves the cursor to the first character of the current line.
K_LEND	Moves the cursor to the carriage return at the end of the current line.
K_DEL	Deletes the character at the cursor, moving the rest of the line to the left. If a carriage return is deleted, the current line and the next line are joined into one. The last carriage return in the buffer can't be deleted.
K_BS	Moves the cursor left one character and deletes that character. No effect if the cursor is already in the first column.
K_ALT_A	Opens up a new line below the current line and places the cursor there. The new line contains only a carriage return.
K_ALT_B	Switches to the next buffer and shows its text (or a portion thereof). The cursor position is maintained separately for each buffer. (The number of buffers is a symbolic constant set when the editor is compiled.)
K_ALT_D	Deletes the current line and closes up the gap in the buffer. The cursor moves to the first character of the line after the deleted one.
K_ALT_E	Reads a new file into the buffer. If any changes have been made to the current buffer, the user is first asked if it is OK for these changes to be lost. If the answer is no, this command is aborted. If the answer is yes, or if there were no changes, the user is next prompted to type in a file name. A backspace can be used to correct typing errors, and a

carriage return signals completion of the response. The contents of the file are then read in. The name is remembered for use with **K_ALT_W** (see below). If any errors occur (such as unreadable file), a message is displayed and this command is aborted. Prompts used by this and other commands may appear at the top or bottom of the screen or in a pop-up window, depending on how the editor's screen module is implemented (see Sec. 5.3.5).

K_ALT_F   Changes the remembered file name, but has no effect on the contents of the buffer or on any file. The user is prompted as for **K_ALT_E**.

K_ALT_H   Shows a screenful of helpful information about commands. When the user presses a key, the screen is restored to the way it was.

K_F1   Same as **K_ALT_H**.

K_ALT_I   Similar to **K_ALT_A**, but opens up the line above the current line.

K_ALT_K   Kills the current buffer. If there are unsaved changes, the user is given a chance to abort this command, just as for **K_ALT_E**. Then the buffer is emptied (replaced with a line containing only a carriage return) and the remembered file name is forgotten.

K_ALT_S   Displays the editing status: remembered file name (if any), current cursor column and line, total number of lines in the buffer, and buffer number.

K_ALT_V   Toggles the view between one that shows buffers full size (taking up most of the screen), which is the default view, and one that shows two buffers at once. The implementation shown in this chapter (using the physical screen interface) doesn't support this command, but the implementations in Chapter 6 and Chapter 7 do.

K_ALT_W   Writes the buffer to the remembered file name (set by **K_ALT_E**, **K_ALT_F**, or a previous **K_ALT_W**). Prompts for a file name if none was remembered.

K_ALT_X   Exits back to the operating system. If any buffers have unsaved changes, the user is given a chance to stay in the editor.

When the editor is invoked from the command line (the user's shell), a file name can be given as an argument. It is read into the first buffer as though a **K_ALT_E** command had been issued.

5.3. Editor Implementation

The editor is composed of four modules:

1. The *main module* interprets each keystroke as a character to be inserted into the buffer or as an editing command. It calls on the text, input/output, and screen modules to execute each action and to ensure that the buffers and the screen are synchronized.

2. The *text module* stores the text corresponding to each buffer. It provides entry points for use by the main module and the input/output module to insert and delete characters and lines, to retrieve lines, to determine the number of lines and the length of a line, to clear a buffer, and so on. Most importantly, the text module hides the method used to store the text. This allows various approaches to be tried without changing the other modules. Our implementation will store a buffer as an array of strings, but this can easily be replaced by a more sophisticated architecture, if desired. Some possibilities are: storing text lines as a linked list, keeping an array of pointers internally but storing the text on a temporary file, using a virtual memory algorithm that pages text between internal storage and disk, and directly accessing the original file (useful for read-only scanning).

3. The *input/output module* contains the operating system interface needed to read and write files. It accesses and updates the buffer by calling on the text module.

4. The *screen module* handles the arrangement of the screen into text-display areas (for buffers), a message area, and a prompt area. It hides the decision as to whether to use the physical screen, window, or virtual screen interfaces. It also hides decisions about certain user interface issues, such as how messages are displayed, how prompts are handled, what size the windows are, and so on. This module will be rewritten to

use the window interface (Sec. 6.3) and the virtual screen interface (Sec. 7.4).[1]

We'll show the code for the editor top-down. First comes the header files that serve as the interfaces to each module, followed by the main module (**edit.c**), the input/output module (**edio.c**), the text module (**edtext.c**), and finally the screen module (**edscr.c**).

5.3.1. Header Files

We'll just name the various entry points to the four modules here, as we show the corresponding header files. Details of the arguments and the specific actions performed by each will be given when the modules themselves are discussed.

All four modules include the header **edit.h**:

```
#define HIGHASCII 127   /* highest ASCII code */
#define MAXBUF 2 ·       /* number of buffers */
#define MAXLINE 200     /* longest text line that can be stored */

char *EMtext();          /* get text corresp. to row (called from edscr.c) */
```

It defines symbolic constants for the highest ASCII code, the number of buffers, and the maximum length of a text line. This length applies only to the storage of text; how much can be seen on the screen is entirely up to the screen module to decide. It informs the main module of its decision via the function **ESwidth**. The main module provides just one external function, **EMtext**, that gives a displayable version of a text line, with tabs expanded to an appropriate number of blanks, for use by the screen module.

The input/output module has two entry points, to read and to write a file. Its header is **edio.h**:

```
        BOOLEAN EIOreadf();     /* read file into buffer */
        BOOLEAN EIOwritef();    /* write buffer to file */
```

The text module has entry points to handle all access to the buffer. They are declared in **edtext.h**:

---

[1]In this and the next two chapters, this module is shown as if it were three distinct files. In fact, it is a single file (**edscr.c**) that uses conditional compilation to distinguish the three implementations. This is relevant only to those readers who obtain the actual source code files (see Appendix C).

```
void ETbegin();          /* initialize text buffers */
void ETend();            /* terminate text buffers */
int ETlen();             /* get length of line */
void ETinschar();        /* insert character into line */
BOOLEAN ETdelchar();     /* delete character from line */
BOOLEAN ETinsline();     /* insert fresh line into buffer memory */
void ETdelline();        /* delete line of text from buffer memory */
void ETclear();          /* clear out buffer completely */
BOOLEAN ETchanged();     /* determine if buffer changed since last write */
void ETunchanged();      /* turn off buffer's "changed" flag */
int ETnumlines();        /* get number of lines in buffer */
char *ETtext();          /* get line of text */
BOOLEAN ETappend();      /* append new line of text to end of buffer */
void ETreplace();        /* replace line of text with new text */
```

We need so many functions because the actual data structures used must be entirely hidden. Some functions, such as **EMnumlines** could be external variables instead, but I prefer the uniformity of using function calls only.

Finally, **edscr.h** is the interface to the screen module:

```
void ESbegin();          /* initialize screen module */
void ESend();            /* terminate screen module */
int ESheight();          /* get height of area where editor can show text */
int ESwidth();           /* get width of area where editor can show text */
void ESshowrow();        /* show text for row starting at specified column */
void ESshowall();        /* show all rows that are visible */
void ESclear();          /* clear text area */
void ESscrlup();         /* scroll text area up one row */
void ESscrldown();       /* scroll text area down one row */
void ESinschar();        /* insert character into row of text */
void ESdelchar();        /* delete character from row of text */
void ESinsrow();         /* insert blank row into text area */
void ESdelrow();         /* delete row from text area */
void ESsetcur();         /* set cursor position */
void ESshowcur();        /* turn cursor on or off */
void ESmsg();            /* display short message */
void ESmsg2();           /* display message, concatenating two strings */
void ESprompt();         /* prompt user to type in response */
void ESswitch();         /* switch to buffer */
void EShelpstart();      /* prepare screen for help display */
void EShelpfinish();     /* clear help display and restore screen */
void EShelpwrite();      /* write one line of help text */
void ESview();           /* toggle between big and small windows */
```

This module, like the text module, has much to hide, and that takes lots of functions.

5.3.2. Main Program

The main module has to keep track of the following information for each buffer: the file name, if any; the line number of the topmost line on the screen; the current row; the current column; and the current position in the current text line. This information is kept in an array of structures. The file **edit.c** begins like this:

```
#include "display.h"
#include "pscreen.h"
#include "keyboard.h"
#include "keycode.h"
#include "edit.h"
#include "edtext.h"
#include "edio.h"
#include "edscr.h"

#define MAXFNAME 63
#define TABINTERVAL 4

static struct Bufinfo {                  /* info for each buffer */
        char filename[MAXFNAME + 1];     /* file associated with buffer */
        short topline;                   /* number of topmost line on screen */
        short currow;                    /* current cursor row */
        short curcol;                    /* current cursor column */
        short curpos;                    /* current cursor position in text */
} bufinfo[MAXBUF];
```

It's the presence of tabs that might make the current column number different from the current position. The main module will use the column number when interfacing with the screen module, which doesn't understand tabs, and the position when interfacing with the text module, which doesn't have to. Given a column number, the current position is calculated by the function **setpos**, and, given a position, the current column number is calculated by **setcol**. We'll see these functions in a moment.

These global variables keep track of the current buffer number and its size:

```
static int bufnum;                       /* current buffer number */
static int curheight;                    /* height of current buffer's window */
static int curwidth;                     /* width of current buffer's window */
```

The variables **curheight** and **curwidth** are set from information supplied by the screen module each time through the main keystroke processing loop, which we'll look at soon.

Because we often have to reference the **Bufinfo** structure indexed by a buffer number, here's a function to do the translation:

```
/*-----------------------------------------------------------------
    bufinfoptr - convert buffer number to pointer to info structure
    RETURN: Pointer.
-----------------------------------------------------------------*/
static struct Bufinfo *bufinfoptr(bnum)
int bnum;                                /* buffer number */
{
    if (bnum < 0 || bnum >= MAXBUF)
        fatal("bufinfoptr - bad buffer num") ·
    return(&bufinfo[bnum]);
}
```

It includes a check on the sanity of the buffer number, which came in very handy during debugging of the editor. We'll see many more validity checks throughout the code, in this module and in the others.

When we know that we want the cursor in a particular column, such as when **K_DOWN** is pressed, we call **setpos** to calculate the corresponding position in the current line. The two locations are identical when there are no tabs, but when there are, the position may be less than the column number. After calculating the position, we reset the column because there may be no position that corresponds exactly to the given column. An example will clarify this. Suppose these two text lines appear:

```
static struct Bufinfo {            /* info for each buffer */
    char filename[MAXFNAME + 1];   /* file associated with buffer */
```

A tab (not four spaces) begins the second line. Suppose the cursor is on the "a" in "static" and is moved down. There is no position in the *text* of the second line that corresponds to column 2. The function **setpos** will set the position to 0 and then reset the column to 0 also. The cursor will jump to the left as it is moved down. This is necessary, because we always want the cursor on text that actually exists. We can't see it, but column 0 contains the leading tab.

```
/*-------------------------------------------------------------------
    setpos - set current position corresponding to current column
-----------------------------------------------------------------*/
void setpos()
{
    struct Bufinfo *bf = bufinfoptr(bufnum);
    int pos, col, prevcol;
    char *t;

    t = ETtext(bufnum, bf->topline + bf->currow);
    col = prevcol = 0;
    bf->curpos = 0;
    for (pos = 0; ; pos++) {
        if (col > bf->curcol)
            break;
        prevcol = col;
        bf->curpos = pos;
        if (t[pos] == '\0')
            break;
        if (t[pos] == '\t')
            col += TABINTERVAL - col % TABINTERVAL;
        else
            col++;
    }
    bf->curcol = prevcol;
}
```

Note that this function can also be called with a column number past the end of the line. In this case, both the position and the column number will be located at the carriage return.

Some screen editors simplify the handling of tabs to eliminate complexities like those shown by **setpos**. They either convert tabs to spaces, which makes the file harder to edit and wastes disk space, or show tabs as an arrow character occupying only one column, which makes the text hard to look at. Neither approach is attractive.

When we have a position and we want the corresponding column, we call **setcol**:

```
/*---------------------------------------------------------------------
    setcol - set current column corresponding to current position
---------------------------------------------------------------------*/
void setcol()
{
    struct Bufinfo *bf = bufinfoptr(bufnum);
    int pos;
    char *t;

    t = ETtext(bufnum, bf->topline + bf->currow);
    bf->curcol = 0;
    for (pos = 0; t[pos] != '\0'; pos++)
        if (pos == bf->curpos)
            break;
        else if (t[pos] == '\t')
            bf->curcol += TABINTERVAL - bf->curcol % TABINTERVAL;
        else
            bf->curcol++;
    if (bf->curcol >= curwidth) {
        bf->curcol = curwidth - 1;
        setpos();
    }
}
```

If the calculated column is past the visible area (according to the variable **curwidth**), we set it back and then call **setpos** to reset the position and, possibly, to move the column leftward so the cursor stays on the text. We'll see how these two functions make it straightforward to move the cursor around as needed without worrying about the location's being valid.

A related function takes a string and replaces tabs with the appropriate number of blanks:

```
/*---------------------------------------------------------------------
    detab - replace tabs with blanks
    RETURN: Did expanded string fit?
---------------------------------------------------------------------*/
static BOOLEAN detab(src, dst, dstsize)
char *src;                              /* source string */
char *dst;                              /* destination string */
int dstsize;                            /* size of destination string */
{
    int srcpos, dstpos, j;

    dstpos = 0;
    for (srcpos = 0; src[srcpos] != '\0'; srcpos++)
        if (src[srcpos] == '\t')
            for (j = TABINTERVAL - dstpos % TABINTERVAL; j > 0; j--) {
                if (dstpos >= dstsize - 1) {
                    dst[dstpos] = '\0';
                    return(FALSE);
                }
                dst[dstpos++] = ' ';
            }
        else {
            if (dstpos >= dstsize - 1) {
                dst[dstpos] = '\0';
                return(FALSE);
            }
            dst[dstpos++] = src[srcpos];
        }
```

```
        dst[dstpos] = '\0';
        return(TRUE);
    }
```

This function is called by **EMtext**, which supplies a tab-less string for the
screen module to display:

```
/*-----------------------------------------------------------------
    EMtext - get text corresponding to row (called from edscr.c)
    RETURN: Text (blank line if beyond end of buffer).
--------------------------------------------------------------*/
char *EMtext(bnum, row)
int bnum;                               /* buffer number */
int row;                                /* row */
{
    struct Bufinfo *bf = bufinfoptr(bnum);
    char *t;
    static char text[MAXLINE + 1];

    if ((t = ETtext(bnum, bf->topline + row)) == NULL)
        return("");
    if (!hastab(t))
        return(t);
    if (!detab(t, text, sizeof(text))) {
        ESmsg("Line too long");
        PSbeep();
    }
    return(text);
}
```

ETtext gets a text line from the text module. Its second argument is
the line number, which we can calculate by adding the current row to the line
number of the first line on the screen. If this is past the end of the buffer,
ETtext will return **NULL**, so **EMtext** returns a null string. This makes it a
little easier for the screen module to fill the rest of the screen (below the last
line) with blanks. Because **detab** is somewhat slow, we use **hastab** to make
a quick check for the presence of tabs (**strchr** is a standard C function):

```
/*-----------------------------------------------------------------
    hastab - Determine if string contains a tab
    RETURN: Does it?
--------------------------------------------------------------*/
static BOOLEAN hastab(s)
char *s;                                /* string */
{
    char *strchr();

    return((BOOLEAN)(strchr(s, '\t') != NULL));
}
```

Back in **EMtext**, if **detab** complains that the expanded line is too long, we
display a message and ring the bell so the user will know that some text
cannot be seen (it's still in the buffer, however).

The remainder of the main module consists of a central loop, with a
switch statement that switches on each keystroke and a collection of small

service functions that handle various activities corresponding to each editing command. The central editing loop is in the function **edit**. We'll show it with the code for the actual keystroke processing removed for brevity. After discussing the overall function, we'll look at the keystroke processing case by case.

```
/*------------------------------------------------------------------
    edit - main editing loop
--------------------------------------------------------------------*/
static void edit()
{
    struct Bufinfo *bf;
    int key, numlines;

    while (TRUE) {
        bf = bufinfoptr(bufnum);
        curheight = ESheight();
        curwidth = ESwidth();
        normalize();
        ESsetcur(bf->currow, bf->curcol);
        ESshowcur(TRUE);
        Ksynch();
        key = Kget();
        ESshowcur(FALSE);
        ESmsg(NULL);
        if ((key < HIGHASCII && isprint(key)) || key == '\t') {
            inschar(key);
            continue;
        }
        switch (key) {
        case K_UP:
            ...
            continue;
        case K_DOWN:
            ...
            continue;
        ...
        case K_ALT_A:
            ...
            continue;
        case K_ALT_B:
            ...
            continue;
        ...
        case K_ALT_X:
            ...
            continue;
        default:
            PSbeep();
        }
    }
}
```

We process one virtual keystroke (from **Kget**, Sec. 4.2) each time through the **while** loop. At the top of the loop, we take the opportunity to reset things, whether they need it or not—it's safer that way. The variables **curheight** and **curwidth** are set from the screen module just in case a command changed the size of a window. If the cursor has moved off the right end of a text line, or past the end of the buffer, or off the screen, **normalize** slaps it back into position:

```
/*-------------------------------------------------------------------
       normalize - locate cursor sensibly and make sure it's on screen
   -------------------------------------------------------------------*/
   static void normalize()
   {
       struct Bufinfo *bf = bufinfoptr(bufnum);
       int len, numlines;

       if (bf->currow < 0 || bf->currow > curheight || bf->curcol < 0 ||
         bf->curcol >= curwidth)
           fatal("cursor out of bounds");
       numlines = ETnumlines(bufnum);
       if (bf->topline + bf->currow >= numlines) /* caused by delete line */
           if (--bf->currow < 0) {
               bf->topline = MAX(bf->topline - curheight, 0);
               ESshowall();
               bf->currow = numlines - bf->topline - 1;
           }
       len = ETlen(bufnum, bf->topline + bf->currow);
       if (bf->curpos > len) {
           bf->curpos = len;
           setcol();
       }
   }
```

Returning to the function **edit**, we reposition the cursor on the screen (**ESsetcur**), make it visible (**ESshowcur**), and update the display (recall from Sec. 4.2 that **Ksynch** calls **PSsynch** when no keyboard character is ready).

After getting a keystroke, we turn off the cursor so it doesn't show while the editor is "thinking," and clear any message that has been displayed. If the keystroke was a character that can be inserted into the buffer, we call **inschar** (which we'll look at later). Otherwise, the keystroke is an editing command, so we switch on it to the proper case. A bad command causes the bell to ring.

That's the main editing loop. Now let's look at the command cases in detail. Here are the cases to move the cursor up and down:

```
case K_UP:
    if (bf->currow > 0)
        bf->currow--;
    else if (bf->topline > 0) {
        bf->topline--;
        ESscrldown();
    }
    setpos();
    continue;
case K_DOWN:
    numlines = ETnumlines(bufnum);
    if (bf->currow < curheight - 1)
        bf->currow = MIN(bf->currow + 1, numlines - bf->topline - 1);
    else if (bf->topline + curheight < numlines) {
        bf->topline++;
        ESscrlup();
    }
    setpos();
    continue;
```

If the target row is already on the screen, we just change the row number in the **Bufinfo** structure; the cursor will be positioned by the call to **ESsetcur** at the top of the loop. If the target line is off the screen, we call **ESscrldown** or **ESscrlup** to bring it into view (the actual row number can stay the same). If the cursor is already as far up or down as it can go, we do nothing. Once we have the column number, **setpos** recalculates the position, as discussed.

The cases to go right and left are a little simpler, since the editor doesn't have to worry about sideways scrolling—the physical screen and window implementations of the screen module can't do it at all, and the virtual screen implementation does it automatically.

```
case K_RIGHT:
    if (bf->curcol < curwidth - 1) {
        bf->curpos++;
        setcol();
    }
    continue;
case K_LEFT:
    if (bf->curcol > 0) {
        bf->curpos--;
        setcol();
    }
    continue;
```

These cases handle the previous screen and next screen commands:

```
case K_PREV:
    bf->topline = MAX(bf->topline - curheight, 0);
    ESshowall();
    setpos();
    continue;
case K_NEXT:
    numlines = ETnumlines(bufnum);
    bf->topline = MIN(bf->topline + curheight, numlines - curheight);
    bf->topline = MAX(bf->topline, 0);
    ESshowall();
    setpos();
    continue;
```

The function **ESshowall** redisplays everything in a buffer that's visible. When going to the previous screen, we prevent the top line number from going negative. But things are a little trickier when going to the next screen: If incrementing the top line number by the height would take us past the end of the buffer, we instead set the top line to the last line minus the height. However, that might set it negative if the buffer has only a few lines, so we then set it to zero.

Here are the last four cursor motion commands:

```
case K_HOME:
    bf->topline = bf->currow = bf->curcol = bf->curpos = 0;
    ESshowall();
    continue;
case K_END:
    numlines = ETnumlines(bufnum);
    bf->topline = MAX(numlines - curheight, 0);
    bf->currow = numlines - bf->topline - 1;
    bf->curpos = GIANT; /* let normalize() deal with it */
    ESshowall();
    continue;
case K_LHOME:
    bf->curcol = bf->curpos = 0;
    continue;
case K_LEND:
    bf->curpos = GIANT;
    continue;
```

Note how we move the cursor to the end of a line by setting its position to an impossibly large number and letting **normalize** reduce both the position and the column number to the correct values.

A carriage return might just end the current line, or it might split the line in two. Actually, both situations are the same, since a carriage return typed at the end of a line does split it into two pieces, one of which is empty:

```
case K_RET:
    splitline();
    continue;
```

Here is **splitline**:

```
/*------------------------------------------------------------------
    splitline - split line
-----------------------------------------------------------------*/
static void splitline()
{
    struct Bufinfo *bf = bufinfoptr(bufnum);
    int line, len, col, pos;
    char text[MAXLINE + 1];

    line = bf->topline + bf->currow;
    col = bf->curcol;
    pos = bf->curpos;
    len = ETlen(bufnum, line);
    if (len > MAXLINE)
        fatal("splitline - line length");
    strcpy(text, ETtext(bufnum, line));
    bf->currow++;
    if (!insline())
        return;
    if (pos < len) {
        ETreplace(bufnum, line + 1, &text[pos]);
        text[pos] = '\0';
        ETreplace(bufnum, line, text);
        ESshowrow(bf->currow - 1, col);
        ESshowrow(bf->currow, 0);
    }
}
```

We save the current line in the variable **text** before rearranging the buffer, because we want to be able to split it without disturbing the text buffer itself. To preserve the modularity of the text module, we must refrain from manipulating the buffer in any way other than by calling the ET functions. The function **insline** opens up a new line in the buffer and the screen, *above* the current row, so we increment the row number before calling it. (We'll see **insline** when we examine the **K_ALT_A** command.) If the cursor was actually at the end of the line when the carriage return was typed, then opening up a new line has done the whole job. Otherwise (**pos < len**) we call **ETreplace** to change the two affected text lines in the buffer, and **ESshowrow** to update the two corresponding rows on the screen. The first argument to **ESshowrow** is the row to be shown, and the second is the column to start with. It and columns to its right are redisplayed; preceding columns are OK.

Returning to the main **switch** statement in the function **edit**, we're ready to handle deletion of a character. This may involve joining lines if a carriage return is deleted, or just deleting an interior character:

```
case K_DEL:
    if (bf->curpos == ETlen(bufnum, bf->topline + bf->currow))
        joinlines();
    else
        delchar();
    continue;
```

Let's first look at **joinlines**:

```
/*------------------------------------------------------------------
    joinlines - join lines
------------------------------------------------------------------*/
static void joinlines()
{
    struct Bufinfo *bf = bufinfoptr(bufnum);
    int line, saverow, savecol, savepos;
    char text[MAXLINE + 1];

    line = bf->topline + bf->currow;
    if (line >= ETnumlines(bufnum) - 1) {
        PSbeep();
        return;
    }
    if (ETlen(bufnum, line) + ETlen(bufnum, line + 1) > MAXLINE) {
        ESmsg("Line too long");
        PSbeep();
        return;
    }
    saverow = bf->currow;
    savecol = bf->curcol;
    savepos = bf->curpos;
    strcpy(text, ETtext(bufnum, line));
    strcat(text, ETtext(bufnum, line + 1));
    bf->currow++;
    delline();
    bf->currow = saverow;
    bf->curcol = savecol;
    bf->curpos = savepos;
```

```
        ETreplace(bufnum, line, text);
        ESshowrow(bf->currow, bf->curcol);
}
```

If the first line to be joined is the last line, the user has tried to delete the last character in the file, which is illegal, so we just ring the bell and return. Next, we make sure the joined line will fit. If it will, we can do the join by constructing the new, longer line, deleting the second line, and replacing the first line. But first we save the current row, column, and position, because deleting the second line will disrupt them. (We'll look at **delline** when we examine **K_ALT_D**.) We put them back the way they were before finishing the join by calling **ETreplace** and **ESshowrow**.

Now, here is **delchar**, called when a character other than a carriage return is deleted:

```
/*-------------------------------------------------------------------
    delchar - delete character at cursor
--------------------------------------------------------------------*/
static void delchar()
{
    struct Bufinfo *bf = bufinfoptr(bufnum);
    int line;
    char *t;
    BOOLEAN showit;

    line = bf->topline + bf->currow;
    t = &ETtext(bufnum, line)[bf->curpos];
    showit = hastab(t) || strlen(t) > curwidth - bf->curcol;
    if (!ETdelchar(bufnum, line, bf->curpos))
        return;
    if (showit)
        ESshowrow(bf->currow, bf->curcol);
    else
        ESdelchar(bf->currow, bf->curcol);
}
```

The text module has a function, **ETdelchar**, that does exactly what we want, so updating the buffer is no problem. Updating the screen is more complicated because we want to avoid updating more of it than necessary; the editor might be used on a slow terminal, and we want to make sure the terminal's delete-character function can be used if one exists. We call **ESdelchar** if deleting a character on the screen is sufficient. There are two cases where it isn't: when there is a tab to the right of the deleted character (the screen module doesn't know about tabs, which show up as spaces on the screen), and when some of the line is off-screen and one character can be brought into view. In these cases we call **ESshowrow** to update the row to the right of the deleted character.

The same approach of optimizing screen activity when possible is taken by **inschar**, which is called at the top of the main editing loop when an insertable character is typed. If anything, screen speed is even more important here, because this function has to keep up with a fast typist.

```
/*---------------------------------------------------------------------
    inschar - insert character at cursor
-----------------------------------------------------------------------*/
static void inschar(ch)
int ch;                                  /* character */
{
    struct Bufinfo *bf = bufinfoptr(bufnum);
    int line;

    line = bf->topline + bf->currow;
    if (bf->curcol >= curwidth - 1 || ETlen(bufnum, line) + 1 >= MAXLINE) {
        PSbeep();
        return;
    }
    ETinschar(bufnum, line, bf->curpos, ch);
    if (hastab(&ETtext(bufnum, line)[bf->curpos]))
        ESshowrow(bf->currow, bf->curcol);
    else
        ESinschar(bf->currow, bf->curcol, ch);
    bf->curpos++;
    setcol();
}
```

Note that **inschar** prevents the user from typing if the cursor reaches its
rightmost limit or if the line has reached its size limit.

The backspace case is similar to the delete character case, except we
back up the cursor first. Since the cursor can't back up across lines, no
joining is possible:

```
case K_BS:
    if (bf->curpos > 0) {
        bf->curpos--;
        setcol();
        delchar();
    }
    continue;
```

The **K_ALT_A** and **K_ALT_I** commands differ only in where the new
line goes:

```
case K_ALT_A:
    bf->currow++;
    (void)insline();
    continue;
case K_ALT_I:
    (void)insline();
    continue;
```

Their real work is done by **insline**:

```
/*-------------------------------------------------------------------
    insline - insert line
    RETURN: Was there room?
-------------------------------------------------------------------*/
static BOOLEAN insline()
{
    struct Bufinfo *bf = bufinfoptr(bufnum);
    int line;

    line = bf->topline + bf->currow;
    if (!ETinsline(bufnum, line))
        return(FALSE);
    if (bf->currow >= curheight) {
        bf->topline++;
        bf->currow--;
        ESscrlup();
    }
    else
        ESinsrow(bf->currow);
    bf->curcol = bf->curpos = 0;
    return(TRUE);
}
```

If the insertion is below the last visible line, the screen must be scrolled up. Otherwise, the line can be inserted into the midst of the visible lines.

Deleting a line is simpler than inserting one because the line to be deleted must already be visible. Here's the case coding:

```
case K_ALT_D:
    delline();
    continue;
```

and here's the **delline** function:

```
/*-------------------------------------------------------------------
    delline - delete line
-------------------------------------------------------------------*/
static void delline()
{
    struct Bufinfo *bf = bufinfoptr(bufnum);
    int line;

    line = bf->topline + bf->currow;
    ETdelline(bufnum, line);
    ESdelrow(bf->currow);
    bf->curcol = bf->curpos = 0;
}
```

Several commands (**K_ALT_K**, **K_ALT_E**, and **K_ALT_X**) clear a buffer. Two functions are common to these commands: **chgchk** asks the user if unsaved changes can be thrown away, and **clearbuf** does the actual clearing. We'll first see how these are used by **K_ALT_K**:

```
case K_ALT_K:
    killbuf();
    continue;
```

which calls **killbuf**:

```
/*-------------------------------------------------------------------
    killbuf - clear buffer and give it one blank line
---------------------------------------------------------------*/
static void killbuf()
{
    if (clearbuf()) {
        ETappend(bufnum, "");
        ETunchanged(bufnum);
    }
}
```

The user must never be allowed to start editing a completely empty buffer because the various insertion and deletion functions assume that something is always there. So after clearing the buffer, we append a blank line to it via **ETappend**. Since the text module then thinks the buffer has changed, we explicitly set it to an unchanged state with **ETunchanged**. We'll use these two text module entries again when we read-in a file.

Here is the coding for **clearbuf**:

```
/*-------------------------------------------------------------------
    clearbuf - clear buffer completely
    RETURN: OK to clear?
---------------------------------------------------------------*/
static BOOLEAN clearbuf()
{
    struct Bufinfo *bf = bufinfoptr(bufnum);

    if (!chgchk(bufnum))
        return(FALSE);
    ETclear(bufnum);
    bf->topline = bf->currow = bf->curcol = bf->curpos = 0;
    bf->filename[0] = '\0';
    ESclear();
    return(TRUE);
}
```

After checking for unsaved changes, it tells the text and screen modules to clear their parts of the buffer and resets the **Bufinfo** fields to their initial values.

This is **chgchk**:

```
/*-------------------------------------------------------------------
    chgchk - ask user to approve destruction of changed buffer
    RETURN: Is it OK to destroy?
-------------------------------------------------------------------*/
static BOOLEAN chgchk(bnum)
int bnum;                                /* buffer number */
{
    char s[50];

    if (ETchanged(bnum)) {
        if (bnum != bufnum) {
            bufnum = bnum;
            ESswitch(bnum);
        }
        sprintf(s, "Changes to buffer %d not saved!", bnum + 1);
        ESprompt(s, "OK? (y/n)", s);
        ESmsg(NULL);
        return((BOOLEAN)(s[0] == 'y' || s[0] == 'Y'));
    }
    return(TRUE);
}
```

The text module keeps a flag for each buffer that tells whether it
changed. The flag is turned on whenever a call to the text module makes a
change (**ETappend**, **ETreplace**, and the like); it is turned off by calling
ETunchanged which we called from **clearbuf**. If the buffer has changed,
chgchk calls **ESswitch** to make sure the user can see it (the buffer being
checked might not be the current one). Then it calls **ESprompt** to ask the
user a question. The first argument is a message, the second is the actual
question, and the third is the returned response. How this interaction actually takes place is up to the screen module, as we'll see in Sec. 5.3.5.

When we exit the editor, we call **chgchkall** to check all buffers for
unsaved changes:

```
case K_ALT_X:
    if (!chgchkall())
        continue;
    return;
```

The function **chgchkall** simply calls **chgchk** for each buffer, abandoning the
cycle if the user wants to bail out:

```
/*-------------------------------------------------------------------
    chgchkall - check all buffers for changes
    RETURN: Is it OK to destroy all of them?
-------------------------------------------------------------------*/
static BOOLEAN chgchkall()
{
    int bnum;
```

```
        for (bnum = 0; bnum < MAXBUF; bnum++)
            if (!chgchk(bnum))
                return(FALSE);
        return(TRUE);
    }
```

If the user has changed several buffers, **chgchkall** will show them one by
one as it asks for approval to discard them. That way the user can see what
he or she is being asked about.

   The **K_ALT_B** command:

```
    case K_ALT_B:
        nextbuf();
        continue;
```

just calls **nextbuf**:

```
    /*-----------------------------------------------------------------
        nextbuf - make next buffer current
    -------------------------------------------------------------------*/
    static void nextbuf()
    {
        if (++bufnum >= MAXBUF)
            bufnum = 0;
        ESswitch(bufnum);
        status();
    }
```

The function **status** gathers the necessary information into a string and uses
ESmsg to display it:

```
    /*-----------------------------------------------------------------
        status - show editing status
    -------------------------------------------------------------------*/
    static void status()
    {
        struct Bufinfo *bf = bufinfoptr(bufnum);
        char s[100];

        sprintf(s, "%s  Column %d  Line %d of %d  Buffer %d", bf->filename,
            bf->curcol + 1, bf->topline + bf->currow + 1, ETnumlines(bufnum),
            bufnum + 1);
        ESmsg(s);
    }
```

The **K_ALT_S** command shows the status, too:

```
    case K_ALT_S:
        status();
        continue;
```

   The user can toggle between full-size buffers and half-size buffers with
K_ALT_V:

```
    case K_ALT_V:
        ESview();
        bf->currow = MIN(bf->currow, ESheight() - 1);
        bf->curcol = MIN(bf->curcol, ESwidth() - 1);
        setpos();
        continue;
```

The actual work is done by **ESview**. It isn't functional in the physical-screen version of the screen module (as we'll see in Sec. 5.3.5); the user just gets a message indicating that an alternative view isn't possible. Assuming that **ESview** does in fact change the window sizes, however, we have to ensure that the current row and column are within the new window. Then we call **setpos** to find the corresponding position.

The remaining commands all involve input or output. The case coding for **K_ALT_F** is:

```
case K_ALT_F:
    strcpy(bf->filename, getfilename());
    continue;
```

To get a file name, we just use **ESprompt**, which we saw earlier in **chgchk**:

```
/*-------------------------------------------------------------------
    getfilename - ask the user for a file name
    RETURN: File name.
-------------------------------------------------------------------*/
static char *getfilename()
{
    static char filename[MAXFNAME + 1];

    ESprompt("", "File:", filename);
    return(filename);
}
```

There isn't any message, so the first argument is empty.

The **K_ALT_E** command reads in a new file:

```
case K_ALT_E:
    readfile(NULL);
    continue;
```

Here is **readfile**:

```
/*-------------------------------------------------------------------
    readfile - read file, prompting for file name if necessary
-------------------------------------------------------------------*/
static void readfile(filename)
char *filename;                         /* file name (NULL if none) */
{
    struct Bufinfo *bf = bufinfoptr(bufnum);

    if (!clearbuf())
        return;
    if (filename == NULL)
        filename = getfilename();
    if (strlen(filename) > MAXFNAME) {
        ESmsg("File name too long");
        filename[0] = '\0';
    }
    strcpy(bf->filename, filename);
    if (filename[0] == '\0') {
        killbuf();
        return;
    }
```

```
        if (!EIOreadf(bufnum, filename))
            bf->filename[0] = '\0'; /* just to be safe */
        ETunchanged(bufnum);
        ESswitch(bufnum);
        ESshowall();
    }
```

    We saw **clearbuf** earlier; recall that it asks for approval before
discarding a changed buffer.   Normally, **readfile** gets a file name from
getfilename; the exception is when it's called from the **main** function to
simulate a **K_ALT_E** command with the file name given as a command-line
argument.   When prompted for a name, the user might change his or her
mind and enter a null name, in which case we just call **killbuf**. The buffer is
already cleared, but this is a handy way to append a blank line to it. If there
really is a file name, we call **EIOreadf** (in the input/output module) to do the
actual reading. If this call fails with an I/O error, we forget the remembered
file name to ensure that it isn't accidentally overwritten with a **K_ALT_W**
command—what we have in the buffer may be incorrect or incomplete.   Then
we turn off the buffer's changed flag and make sure the screen module is
displaying its text.
    The case coding for **K_ALT_W**:

```
case K_ALT_W:
    writefile();
    continue;
```

calls **writefile**:

```
/*-----------------------------------------------------------------
    writefile - write file, prompting for file name if necessary
------------------------------------------------------------------*/
static void writefile()
{
    struct Bufinfo *bf = bufinfoptr(bufnum);

    if (bf->filename[0] == '\0') {
        strcpy(bf->filename, getfilename());
        if (bf->filename[0] == '\0')
            return;
    }
    if (EIOwritef(bufnum, bf->filename))
        ETunchanged(bufnum);
}
```

It prompts the user for a name if none was remembered (from a previous
K_ALT_E, **K_ALT_F**, or **K_ALT_W**). The user can abort the write by typing
a null name. If we have a name, we call **EIOwrite** to do the writing.   We
turn off the buffer-changed flag only if the writing succeeded.
    The last command is for getting help, by typing either **K_ALT_H** or
K_F1:

```
case K_ALT_H:
case K_F1:
    help();
    continue;
```

The help screen displayed is shown in Fig. 5-3. Here's the **help** function:

```
/*----------------------------------------------------------------
   help - display help screen
----------------------------------------------------------------*/
static void help()
{
    FILE *f;
    char buf[100];
    int r;

    if ((f = fopen("edit.hlp", "r")) == NULL) {
        ESmsg("No help file (edit.hlp)");
        return;
    }
    EShelpstart();
    r = 0;
    while (fgets(buf, sizeof(buf), f) != NULL) {
        buf[strlen(buf) - 1] = '\0'; /* remove trailing newline */
        EShelpwrite(r, buf, r == 0 ? A_INTENSE : A_NORM);
        r++;
    }
    fclose(f);
    EShelpwrite(r + 1, "Press any key to resume editing ...", A_INVERSE);
    PSsynch();
    (void)Kget();
    EShelpfinish();
}
```

```
KEY(S)                      ACTION
arrows                      Go in desired direction.
Home, End                   Go to top or bottom of buffer.
Ctrl-Home, Ctrl-End         Go to left or right of line.
PgUp, PgDn                  Go backward or forward by screenful.
Return                      Get line below current line, or split current line.
Del                         Delete character at cursor, or join lines.
Backspace                   Delete previous character.
Alt-I                       Get new line below current line.
Alt-B                       Switch to next buffer.
Alt-D                       Delete current line.
Alt-E                       Edit another file.
Alt-F                       Set file name.
Alt-H, F1                   Get help.
Alt-I                       Get new line above current line.
Alt-K                       Kill buffer.
Alt-S                       Show editing status.
Alt-V                       Toggle view (1 or 2 windows).
Alt-W                       Write file.
Alt-X                       Exit.

Press any key to resume editing ...
```

Fig. 5-3. Editor help-screen.

It uses three functions supplied by the screen module: **EShelpstart** clears the screen, or pops up a help window, or whatever the screen module wants to do to prepare for help; **EShelpwrite** writes one row to the screen; finally, **EShelpfinish** restores the screen to the way it was before help was invoked. The first line of the help file is supposed to contain a title, so it's displayed with the attribute **A_INTENSE**. The *Press any key* message is displayed in inverse video. Then **PSsynch** is called to update the screen and **Kget** is called to wait for, read in, and throw away the user's next keystroke.

This file, **edit.c**, is the main program for the editor. This is the **main** function itself:

```
/*-------------------------------------------------------------
    main - main program
----------------------------------------------------------*/
void main(argc, argv)
int argc;                              /* argument count */
char *argv[];                          /* argument vector */
{
    ESbegin();
    ETbegin();
    ESswitch(bufnum = 0);
    if (argc > 1)
        readfile(argv[1]);
    else
        ESmsg("Press F1 for help");
    edit();
    cleanup();
    exit(0);
}
```

It initializes the screen and text modules, switches to the first buffer (numbered zero), and reads in a file if one was specified on the command line. If not, the user is notified that help is available. (We're assuming that users unfamiliar with the editor will just type its name without an argument.) Then **edit** is called to bring the editor alive.

The function **cleanup** is our standard way of wrapping things up before exiting:

```
/*-------------------------------------------------------------
    cleanup - prepare for exit
----------------------------------------------------------*/
void cleanup()
{
    static BOOLEAN cleaning = FALSE;

    if (cleaning)
        return;
    cleaning = TRUE;
    ETend();
    ESend();
    cleaning = FALSE;
}
```

We call it explicitly if the user exits from the editor; recall from Sec. 2.9 that it is also called from **fatal** when execution terminates in error. The purpose of the **cleaning** flag is to prevent a recursive call to **cleanup**. Since we have no idea (yet) what **ETend** or **ESend** do, it's entirely possible for an error to occur during cleaning up, in which case **cleanup** would be called again.

5.3.3. Input/Output Module

The input/output module, **edio.c**, has only to supply two entry points:
EIOreadf for use by **readfile** (in **edit.c**), and **EIOwritef** for use by
writefile. It begins this way:

```
#include "display.h"
#include "edit.h"
#include "edtext.h"
#include "edscr.h"
#include "edio.h"

#define EOFMARK '\032'
```

EOFMARK is the character (Control−Z) used by MS−DOS to mark the end
of a text file. UNIX doesn't put a mark at the end of text files.

This is the code for **EIOreadf**:

```
/*-------------------------------------------------------------------
    EIOreadf - read file into buffer
    RETURN: Successful read?
-----------------------------------------------------------------*/
BOOLEAN EIOreadf(bnum, filename)
int bnum;                               /* buffer number */
char *filename;                         /* file name */
{
    FILE *f;
    char s[MAXLINE + 2]; /* room for newline */
    int slen;
    BOOLEAN err = FALSE;

    if ((f = fopen(filename, "r")) == NULL) {
        ESmsg2("Can't open ", filename);
        (void)ETappend(bnum, "");
        return(FALSE);
    }
    ESmsg2("Reading ", filename);
    while (fgets(s, sizeof(s), f) != NULL) {
        slen = strlen(s) - 1;
        if (s[slen] != '\n') {
            ESmsg("Line too long");
            err = TRUE;
            break;
        }
        s[slen] = '\0';
        if (!ETappend(bnum, s)) {
            err = TRUE;
            break;
        }
    }
    if (ferror(f) && !err) {
        ESmsg("Read error");
        err = TRUE;
    }
    if (fclose(f) != 0 && !err) {
        ESmsg("Read error");
        err = TRUE;
    }
```

```
    if (!err)
        ESmsg2("Successfully read ", filename);
    else
        PSbeep();
    if (ETnumlines(bnum) < 1)
        (void)ETappend(bnum, "");
    return((BOOLEAN)(!err));
}
```

The only complications in this function are due to the need to carefully
determine whether an error occurred and to report error conditions accurately to the caller and to the user. Note that if nothing is read, we make
sure that the buffer contains at least one blank line since, as we saw in the
previous section, that's an assumption that many other editing functions
depend on.

EIOwritef is even simpler, because we're not trying to make any
changes to the buffer:

```
/*-------------------------------------------------------------------
    EIOwritef - write buffer to file
    RETURN: Successful write?
-----------------------------------------------------------------*/
BOOLEAN EIOwritef(bnum, filename)
int bnum;                          /* buffer number */
char *filename;                    /* file name */
{
    FILE *f;
    int line;
    char *t;
    BOOLEAN err = FALSE;

    if ((f = fopen(filename, "w")) == NULL) {
        ESmsg2("Can't open ", filename);
        return(FALSE);
    }
    ESmsg2("Writing ", filename);
    for (line = 0; (t = ETtext(bnum, line)) != NULL; line++)
        if (fputs(t, f) == EOF || putc('\n', f) == EOF) {
            err = TRUE;
            break;
        }
#ifdef MSDOS
    if (putc(EOFMARK, f) == EOF)
        err = TRUE;
#endif
    if (fclose(f) == EOF)
        err = TRUE;
    if (err) {
        ESmsg("Write error");
        PSbeep();
        return(FALSE);
    }
    ESmsg2("Successfully wrote ", filename);
    return(TRUE);
}
```

We write the buffer to the same file that it may have been read from.
This is dangerous because, if a write error occurs, we likely will have no valid
copy of the text other than what's in the buffer, which will be lost if the
computer goes down, if the user exits accidentally, or if we are unable to

write at all because of an operating system error. It would be safer to write to a temporary file and then switch the file names in the directory once we established that the write went OK. We could even leave the old file around (under a different name) if we wanted to, thus providing additional protection and giving the user a way to go back to it if necessary.

5.3.4. Text Module

The design of the text module has little to do with either displays or keyboards—the subjects of this book—so we won't concern ourselves with making it too efficient. We'll use a simple approach that works.

Just as the main module had to keep information about each buffer, so does the text module. We need the text itself stored as an array of strings, the number of lines in the buffer, and the buffer-changed flag. So we'll begin the file **edtext.c** like this:

```
#include "display.h"
#include "edit.h"
#include "edscr.h"
#include "edtext.h"

static struct Buffer {          /* info for each buffer */
    char **text;                /* array of text lines */
    int numlines;               /* number of lines */
    BOOLEAN changed;            /* buffer changed since last write? */
} buf[MAXBUF];

#define MAXLINES 1000           /* maximum size of buffer */
#define ALLOCUNIT 10            /* amount to grow line */

static char *blankline = "";    /* blank lines point here */
```

When the text module is initialized, we'll allocate an array of **MAXLINES** character pointers for each buffer. This is wasteful, because not all buffers will get nearly that big, and it's limiting, because some will need to get bigger.

When we actually have text for a line (such as when **ETappend** is called), we'll then allocate space for a string and point to it with the appropriate element of the **text** array. If that line has to grow (when **ETinschar** is called), we'll use **realloc** to make sure the space is large enough. To avoid allocating memory every time a character is inserted, we'll round up the length allocated to a multiple of **ALLOCUNIT**. If the user is typing along, we'll then allocate memory every ten characters or so.

Empty lines are quite common, so we'll just point to **blankline** instead of allocating memory to hold a null character. This has one additional advantage: If we run out of memory, we have a way of making a text pointer point to valid data that doesn't involve allocating memory. It's important in situations like this never to leave the data structures in an invalid state. Since this is a text editor, we can't just exit with a message when memory is exhausted, as we could in other applications (a report generator, say). We have to let the user continue editing.

Here's a function to convert a buffer number into a pointer to a **Buffer** structure (a similar function was in **edit.c**):

```
/*-------------------------------------------------------------------
    bufptr - convert buffer number to pointer to buffer structure
    RETURN: Pointer.
-----------------------------------------------------------------*/
static struct Buffer *bufptr(bnum)
int bnum;                               /* buffer number */
{
    if (bnum < 0 || bnum >= MAXBUF)
        fatal("bufptr - bad buffer num");
    return(&buf[bnum]);
}
```

Next come the functions that implement the memory-management techniques just discussed. When we need to grow a line to a certain length, we call **growline**:

```
/*-------------------------------------------------------------------
    growline - allocate or reallocate memory for line of text
    RETURN: Was there enough memory?
-----------------------------------------------------------------*/
static BOOLEAN growline(b, line, len)
struct Buffer *b;                       /* pointer to buffer structure */
int line;                               /* line number */
int len;                                /* required length (will round up) */
{
    len = ((len + ALLOCUNIT) / ALLOCUNIT) * ALLOCUNIT;
    if (b->text[line] == NULL || b->text[line] == blankline) {
        if ((b->text[line] = malloc(len)) != NULL)
            b->text[line][0] = '\0';
    }
    else
        b->text[line] = realloc(b->text[line], (unsigned)len);
    if (b->text[line] == NULL) {
        b->text[line] = blankline; /* must point to something! */
        ESmsg("Out of memory");
        return(FALSE);
    }
    return(TRUE);
}
```

If the line is brand new, we call **malloc**; if it has already been allocated, we call **realloc**.

Before we free up a line, we have to be careful to make sure it was allocated:

```
/*-------------------------------------------------------------------
    freeline - free memory for line if it points to allocated memory
-----------------------------------------------------------------*/
static void freeline(b, line)
struct Buffer *b;                       /* pointer to buffer structure */
int line;                               /* line number */
{
```

```
    if (b->text[line] != NULL && b->text[line] != blankline) {
        free(b->text[line]);
        b->text[line] = NULL;
    }
}
```

We call **store** to put text into a fresh line:

```
/*--------------------------------------------------------------------
    store - store line of text into buffer memory
    RETURN: Was there enough memory?
--------------------------------------------------------------------*/
static BOOLEAN store(b, line, text)
struct Buffer *b;                       /* pointer to buffer structure */
int line;                               /* line number */
char *text;                             /* text */
{
    b->changed = TRUE;
    if (text[0] == '\0')
        b->text[line] = blankline;
    else if ((b->text[line] = malloc(strlen(text) + 1)) == NULL) {
        b->text[line] = blankline;
        ESmsg("Out of memory");
        return(FALSE);
    }
    else
        strcpy(b->text[line], text);
    return(TRUE);
}
```

We don't round up the length because most lines that are read into a buffer are never changed, so there's no point in getting extra room. If a character is ever inserted, we'll call **growline** to add some growing room then.

All of the rest of the functions in the text module are external entry points called from the main module. A few are called from the text module as well.

ETbegin initializes the text buffers:

```
/*--------------------------------------------------------------------
    ETbegin - initialize text buffers
--------------------------------------------------------------------*/
void ETbegin()
{
    int bnum;

    for (bnum = 0; bnum < MAXBUF; bnum++) {
        buf[bnum].text = (char **)xmalloc(MAXLINES * sizeof(char *));
        buf[bnum].numlines = 0;
        ETclear(bnum);
        (void)ETappend(bnum, "");
        ETunchanged(bnum);
    }
}
```

Note that **xmalloc** (Sec. 2.10) terminates execution if memory is unavailable, so there's no need to check its return. This is OK in **ETbegin** because the

user hasn't done anything yet, nor will the user *ever* be able to do anything.
The three functions **ETclear**, **ETappend**, and **ETunchanged** are used to
set up each buffer with a blank line; we saw them used earlier in the main
module (Sec. 5.3.2) for the same purpose.

At the conclusion of editing, we could clear out all the buffers, but it
takes some time to release all that memory (perhaps thousands of lines), and
it's unnecessary to do so if we are about to exit back to the operating system.
So the code in **ETend** is optional, to be used only if the editor is later embed-
ded in a larger process that calls it as a subroutine. The code is really here
just as a reminder that memory hasn't been freed:

```
/*-------------------------------------------------------------------
    ETend - terminate text buffers
            (Freeing memory takes time, so it's optional.)
    ----------------------------------------------------------------*/
void ETend()
{
#ifdef ENDCLEAR
    int bnum;

    for (bnum = 0; bnum < MAXBUF; bnum++)
        ETclear(bnum);
#endif
}
```

The next group of small functions is so straightforward that it needs no
explanation beyond what the individual comments say:

```
/*-------------------------------------------------------------------
    ETclear - clear out buffer completely
    ----------------------------------------------------------------*/
void ETclear(bnum)
int bnum;                               /* buffer number */
{
    struct Buffer *b = bufptr(bnum);
    int i;

    for (i = 0; i < b->numlines; i++)
        freeline(b, i);
    b->numlines = 0;
    b->changed = FALSE;
}

/*-------------------------------------------------------------------
    ETunchanged - turn off buffer's "changed" flag
    ----------------------------------------------------------------*/
void ETunchanged(bnum)
int bnum;                               /* buffer number */
{
    struct Buffer *b = bufptr(bnum);

    b->changed = FALSE;
}
```

```
/*-------------------------------------------------------------------
    ETchanged - determine if buffer has changed since last write
    RETURN: Has it?
-------------------------------------------------------------------*/
BOOLEAN ETchanged(bnum)
int bnum;                                   /* buffer number */
{
    struct Buffer *b = bufptr(bnum);

    return(b->changed);
}


/*-------------------------------------------------------------------
    ETtext - get line of text
    RETURN: Pointer to text, or NULL if line number is past end.
-------------------------------------------------------------------*/
char *ETtext(bnum, line)
int bnum;                                   /* buffer number */
int line;                                   /* line number */
{
    struct Buffer *b = bufptr(bnum);

    if (line < 0)
        fatal("ETtext - bad line");
    if (line >= b->numlines)
        return(NULL);
    if (b->text[line] == NULL)
        fatal("ETtext - NULL line");
    return(b->text[line]);
}


/*-------------------------------------------------------------------
    ETlen - get length of line
    RETURN: Length, excluding NUL byte.
-------------------------------------------------------------------*/
int ETlen(bnum, line)
int bnum;                                   /* buffer number */
int line;                                   /* line number */
{
    struct Buffer *b = bufptr(bnum);

    if (line < 0 || line >= b->numlines)
        fatal("ETlen - bad line");
    if (b->text[line] == NULL)
        fatal("ETlen - NULL line");
    return(strlen(b->text[line]));
}


/*-------------------------------------------------------------------
    ETnumlines - get number of lines in buffer
    RETURN: Number of lines.
-------------------------------------------------------------------*/
int ETnumlines(bnum)
int bnum;                                   /* buffer number */
{
    struct Buffer *b = bufptr(bnum);

    return(b->numlines);
}
```

What's left are the six functions that actually modify a buffer: **ETinschar**, **ETdelchar**, **ETinsline**, **ETdelline**, **ETappend**, and **ETreplace**.

ETinschar uses **growline** to make sure that the line is big enough to hold one more character, and then uses **movmem** (Sec. 2.8) to spread it apart:

```
/*------------------------------------------------------------------
    ETinschar - insert character into line
-------------------------------------------------------------------*/
void ETinschar(bnum, line, col, ch)
int bnum;                               /* buffer number */
int line;                               /* line number */
int col;                                /* column to insert at */
int ch;                                 /* character to insert */
{
    struct Buffer *b = bufptr(bnum);
    int len;

    if (col < 0 || col > MAXLINE)
        fatal("ETinschar - bad col");
    len = ETlen(bnum, line);
    if (!growline(b, line, len + 1))
        return;
    movmem(&b->text[line][col], &b->text[line][col + 1], len - col + 1);
    b->text[line][col] = (char)ch;
    b->changed = TRUE;
}
```

Similarly, **ETdelchar** uses **movmem** to close up a line:

```
/*------------------------------------------------------------------
    ETdelchar - delete character from line
    RETURN: Was there anything to delete?
-------------------------------------------------------------------*/
BOOLEAN ETdelchar(bnum, line, col)
int bnum;                               /* buffer number */
int line;                               /* line number */
int col;                                /* column to delete */
{
    struct Buffer *b = bufptr(bnum);
    int len;

    if ((len = ETlen(bnum, line)) <= 0)
        return(FALSE);
    movmem(&b->text[line][col + 1], &b->text[line][col], len - col + 1);
    b->changed = TRUE;
    return(TRUE);
}
```

ETinsline has to spread apart the array of text pointers, so it, too, uses **movmem**:

```
/*------------------------------------------------------------------
    ETinsline - insert fresh line into buffer memory
    RETURN: Was there room?
-------------------------------------------------------------------*/
BOOLEAN ETinsline(bnum, line)
int bnum;                               /* buffer number */
int line;                               /* line number */
{
```

```
        struct Buffer *b = bufptr(bnum);

        if (line < 0 || line > b->numlines)
            fatal("ETinsline - bad line");
        if (b->numlines >= MAXLINES) {
            ESmsg("Too many lines");
            return(FALSE);
        }
        if (line < b->numlines)
            movmem((char *)&b->text[line], (char *)&b->text[line + 1],
                (b->numlines - line) * sizeof(b->text[0]));
        if (!store(b, line, ""))
            return(FALSE);
        b->numlines++;
        return(TRUE);
    }
```

And **ETdelline** uses **movmem** to close up the array of text pointers:

```
/*-------------------------------------------------------------------
    ETdelline - delete line of text from buffer memory
-----------------------------------------------------------------*/
void ETdelline(bnum, line)
int bnum;                               /* buffer number */
int line;                               /* line number */
{
    struct Buffer *b = bufptr(bnum);

    if (line < 0 || line >= b->numlines)
        fatal("ETdelline - bad line");
    freeline(b, line);
    movmem((char *)&b->text[line + 1], (char *)&b->text[line],
        (b->numlines - line - 1) * sizeof(b->text[0]));
    b->numlines--;
    if (b->numlines == 0)
        (void)ETappend(bnum, "");
    b->changed = TRUE;
}
```

Once again, we see that **ETdelline** makes sure that the buffer contains at least a blank line.

   ETappend adds a new line, complete with text, to the end of the buffer (no need for **movmem** here):

```
/*-------------------------------------------------------------------
    ETappend - append new line of text to end of buffer
    RETURN: Was there room?
-----------------------------------------------------------------*/
BOOLEAN ETappend(bnum, text)
int bnum;                               /* buffer number */
char *text;                             /* text */
{
    struct Buffer *b = bufptr(bnum);

    if (b->numlines >= MAXLINES) {
        ESmsg("Too many lines");
        return(FALSE);
    }
    if (!store(b, b->numlines, text))
        return(FALSE);
    b->numlines++;
    return(TRUE);
}
```

Note that we leave the number of lines un-incremented if **store** fails.

Lastly, **ETreplace** tosses out the contents of a line and replaces it with new text:

```
/*--------------------------------------------------------------------
    ETreplace - replace line of text with new text
---------------------------------------------------------------*/
void ETreplace(bnum, line, text)
int bnum;                               /* buffer number */
int line;                               /* line number */
char *text;                             /* text */
{
    struct Buffer *b = bufptr(bnum);

    if (line < 0 || line >= b->numlines)
        fatal("ETreplace - bad line");
    freeline(b, line);
    (void)store(b, line, text);
}
```

We could have tried to reuse the memory already allocated, instead of deallocating it and getting a new allocation (via **store**), but the cavalier approach is much easier. As we saw in the main module, **ETreplace** is called only when lines are split or joined, both infrequent events.

You may enjoy redesigning the text module to use some of the more advanced memory management techniques listed in Sec. 5.3.

5.3.5. Screen Module

Now we're ready for the screen module. We are bound to use nothing more than the physical-screen interface, which presents something of a challenge because we still have to handle multiple buffers, help screens, prompts, and messages—all on one screen. No fair implementing a windowing system to better organize things, either, because that's covered in the rest of this book! What we'll do is divide the screen into two fixed-size areas: a text area from row 2 through the end of the screen, and a message/prompt area, on row 0. We'll draw a horizontal line on row 1 to separate the two areas. We'll use the text area for one buffer at a time, and for help screens, too, and just keep overwriting it in its entirety as the main module calls **ESswitch**, **EShelpstart**, or **EShelpfinish**. We'll make no attempt to show two buffers at once, so **ESview** will be ineffective.

The file **edscr.c** begins with symbolic constants for important territorial limits, and some rectangles for the screen areas:

```
#include "display.h"
#include "pscreen.h"
#include "keyboard.h"
#include "keycode.h"
#include "edit.h"
#include "edscr.h"
```

```
#define MAXROW 23                                         /* max row number */
#define MAXCOL 79                                         /* max column number */
#define TEXTROWS 22                                       /* text area height */
#define TEXTROW1 (MAXROW - TEXTROWS + 1)                  /* starting text row */

RECT msgrect = {0, 0, 0, MAXCOL};                         /* message area */
RECT promptrect = {0, MAXCOL / 2 + 2, 0, MAXCOL};         /* user prompt area */
RECT rulerect = {1, 0, 1, MAXCOL};                        /* horizontal rule */
RECT textrect = {TEXTROW1, 0, MAXROW, MAXCOL};            /* text area */

static int curbnum;                                       /* current buffer num */
```

Note that the prompt rectangle occupies the right half of row 0.

We have no need to keep information about buffers, so we have no array of buffer structures as we did in the main and text modules. We just need the current buffer number, and even that we won't use very much. Its only purpose is to tell us what argument to use with **EMtext** (described in Sec. 5.3.2). In later chapters, we'll have much more use for the current buffer number.

We initialize the screen module by initializing the physical-screen and keyboard modules, turning on the cursor, clearing the screen, and drawing the rule that separates the message/prompt row from the text area:

```
/*-------------------------------------------------------------------
     ESbegin - initialize screen module
-------------------------------------------------------------------*/
void ESbegin()
{
    PSbegin();
    PSshowcur(TRUE);
    PSfill(&GIANT_RECT, ' ', A_NORM);
    PSfill(&rulerect, C_H, A_NORM);
    Kbegin();
}
```

ESend terminates the screen module:

```
/*-------------------------------------------------------------------
     ESend - terminate screen module
-------------------------------------------------------------------*/
void ESend()
{
    Kend();
    PSend();
}
```

Since the text area never changes size, **ESheight**, **ESwidth**, and **ESview** are trivial:

```
/*-------------------------------------------------------------------
     ESheight - get height of area where editor can show text
     RETURN: Height.
-------------------------------------------------------------------*/
int ESheight()
{
    return(TEXTROWS);
}
```

```
/*-------------------------------------------------------------------
     ESwidth - get width of area where editor can show text
     RETURN: Width.
-------------------------------------------------------------------*/
int ESwidth()
{
    return(MAXCOL + 1);
}


/*-------------------------------------------------------------------
     ESview - toggle between big and small windows
-------------------------------------------------------------------*/
void ESview()
{
    ESmsg("Full-size windows only");
}
```

ESsetcur requires only that we translate the row number within the
text area to the physical screen coordinate system before calling **PSsetcur**.
ESshowcur just calls **PSshowcur**.

```
/*-------------------------------------------------------------------
     ESsetcur - set cursor position
-------------------------------------------------------------------*/
void ESsetcur(row, col)
int row;                                /* row */
int col;                                /* column */
{
    PSsetcur(TEXTROW1 + row, col);
}


/*-------------------------------------------------------------------
     ESshowcur - turn cursor on or off
-------------------------------------------------------------------*/
void ESshowcur(on)
BOOLEAN on;                             /* switch */
{
    PSshowcur(on);
}
```

Since we have already set up a text rectangle, it's easy to clear the text
area:

```
/*-------------------------------------------------------------------
     ESclear - clear text area
-------------------------------------------------------------------*/
void ESclear()
{
    PSfill(&textrect, ' ', A_NORM);
}
```

To get a row of text to show, we use the function **EMtext**, which is in
the text module. Since it knows the number of the line at the top of the text
area, it can use the row number we give it to calculate the line number.
Recall that it eliminates tabs, so we need not concern ourselves with them
here—we can freely use the column number as a subscript of the character
array **t**.

```
/*-------------------------------------------------------------------
      ESshowrow - show text for row, starting at specified column
-----------------------------------------------------------------*/
void ESshowrow(row, col)
int row;                                  /* row */
int col;                                  /* column */
{
    char *t;
    RECT rect;

    t = EMtext(curbnum, row);
    if (col < strlen(t))
        PSwrite(TEXTROW1 + row, col, GIANT, &t[col], A_NORM);
    RASG(&rect, TEXTROW1 + row, strlen(t), TEXTROW1 + row, MAXCOL);
    PSfill(&rect, ' ', A_NORM);
}
```

Note the use of **PSfill** to clear the right part of the row not covered by text.

Within the screen module, but not outside of it, we'll use a handy function to show a range of lines:

```
/*-------------------------------------------------------------------
      showrange - show range of text rows
-----------------------------------------------------------------*/
static void showrange(row1, row2)
int row1;                                 /* starting row */
int row2;                                 /* ending row */
{
    int row;

    for (row = row1; row <= row2; row++)
        ESshowrow(row, 0);
}
```

When we have to show the entire text area, we'll use a special function, **ESshowall**, rather than merely call **showrange**:

```
/*-------------------------------------------------------------------
      ESshowall - show all rows that are visible
-----------------------------------------------------------------*/
void ESshowall()
{
    int row;

    ESclear();
    for (row = 0; row < TEXTROWS; row++)
        PSwrite(TEXTROW1 + row, 0, GIANT, EMtext(curbnum, row), A_NORM);
}
```

This is because we can clear the text area with a single call to **ESclear**, thereby avoiding calling **PSfill** on each line as we did in **ESshowrow**. This special-case coding is worthwhile because it speeds up display time noticeably.

The code for **ESswitch** shows one place where we use **ESshowall**:

```
/*--------------------------------------------------------------
     ESswitch - switch to buffer
--------------------------------------------------------------*/
void ESswitch(bnum)
int bnum;                              /* buffer number */
{
     curbnum = bnum;
     ESshowall();
}
```

Now we're ready for the scrolling functions, **ESscrlup** and
ESscrldown. These try to use **PSslide** along with a single call to
ESshowrow, but a physical screen implementation is not required to
implement sliding. So we just display the whole text area in that case, with
ESshowall.

```
/*--------------------------------------------------------------
     ESscrlup - scroll text area up one row
--------------------------------------------------------------*/
void ESscrlup()
{
     RECT rect;

     RASG(&rect, TEXTROW1 + 1, 0, MAXROW, MAXCOL);
     if (PSslide(&rect, DIR_UP, 1))
          ESshowrow(TEXTROWS - 1, 0);
     else
          ESshowall();
}

/*--------------------------------------------------------------
     ESscrldown - scroll text area down one row
--------------------------------------------------------------*/
void ESscrldown()
{
     RECT rect;

     RASG(&rect, TEXTROW1, 0, MAXROW - 1, MAXCOL);
     if (PSslide(&rect, DIR_DOWN, 1))
          ESshowrow(0, 0);
     else
          ESshowall();
}
```

We use the same approach with **ESinschar** and **ESdelchar**, only we're
trying to slide sideways this time. This is an important optimization,
because on a slow terminal **PSslide** might use insert- and delete-character
escape sequences. **ESdelchar** and, especially, **ESinschar** are called more
than any other screen module functions. The user will expect them to keep
up with his or her typing.

```
/*--------------------------------------------------------------
     ESinschar - insert character into row of text
--------------------------------------------------------------*/
void ESinschar(row, col, ch)
int row;                               /* row */
int col;                               /* column */
char ch;                               /* character */
{
```

```
    RECT rect;

    RASG(&rect, TEXTROW1 + row, col, TEXTROW1 + row, MAXCOL - 1);
    if (PSslide(&rect, DIR_RIGHT, 1))
        PSwrite(TEXTROW1 + row, col, 1, &ch, A_NORM);
    else
        ESshowrow(row, col);
}

/*-------------------------------------------------------------------
    ESdelchar - delete character from row of text
-------------------------------------------------------------------*/
void ESdelchar(row, col)
int row;                                  /* row */
int col;                                  /* column */
{
    RECT rect;
    RASG(&rect, TEXTROW1 + row, col + 1, TEXTROW1 + row, MAXCOL);
    if (PSslide(&rect, DIR_LEFT, 1))
        PSwrite(TEXTROW1 + row, MAXCOL, 1, " ", A_NORM);
    else
        ESshowrow(row, col);
}
```

We must put a blank at the end of the row when we slide to the left—
PSslide is not required to do this automatically.

   ESinsrow and **ESdelrow** are two more situations in which we try to
slide first. If sliding fails, we show just the range of rows at and below the
current row:

```
/*-------------------------------------------------------------------
    ESinsrow - insert blank row into text area
-------------------------------------------------------------------*/
void ESinsrow(row)
int row;                                  /* row */
{
    RECT rect;

    if (row >= TEXTROWS)
        fatal("ESinsrow - bad row");
    RASG(&rect, TEXTROW1 + row, 0, MAXROW - 1, MAXCOL);
    if (PSslide(&rect, DIR_DOWN, 1)) {
        rect.r2 = rect.r1;
        PSfill(&rect, ' ', A_NORM);
    }
    else
        showrange(row, TEXTROWS - 1);
}

/*-------------------------------------------------------------------
    ESdelrow - delete row from text area
-------------------------------------------------------------------*/
void ESdelrow(row)
int row;                                  /* row */
{
    RECT rect;

    RASG(&rect, TEXTROW1 + row + 1, 0, MAXROW, MAXCOL);
    if (PSslide(&rect, DIR_UP, 1))
        ESshowrow(TEXTROWS - 1, 0);
    else
        showrange(row, TEXTROWS - 1);
}
```

To write a message, we just write it into the message rectangle:

```
/*------------------------------------------------------------------
    ESmsg - display short message
--------------------------------------------------------------------*/
void ESmsg(s)
char *s;                                     /* message */
{
    static BOOLEAN havemsg = FALSE;

    if (havemsg)
        PSfill(&msgrect, ' ', A_NORM);
    havemsg = s != NULL;
    if (havemsg) {
        PSwrite(msgrect.rl, msgrect.cl, GIANT, s, A_INVERSE);
        PSsynch();
    }
}
```

We use the variable **havemsg** to keep track of whether we actually have a
message on the screen. **ESmsg** will be called with a **NULL** argument by the
main module on every keystroke to make a message go away once the user
has had a chance to read it. On a slow terminal, we don't want to blank out
the message area every time. This would be extremely bothersome to the
user. Also, we call **PSsynch** whenever there is a message. This is because
sometimes **ESmsg** is called to show the interim status of some fairly long
operation (see **EIOreadf** in Sec. 5.3.3) and we have to be sure to show each
message. Otherwise, **PSsynch** is called only when we're about to read the
keyboard.

ESmsg2 concatenates two strings and calls **ESmsg**:

```
/*------------------------------------------------------------------
    ESmsg2 - display message, concatenating two strings
--------------------------------------------------------------------*/
void ESmsg2(s1, s2)
char *s1;                                    /* first string */
char *s2;                                    /* second string */
{
    char s[70];

    sprintf(s, "%s%s", s1, s2);
    ESmsg(s);
}
```

The three help functions come next. **EShelpstart** clears the screen, and
EShelpfinish redisplays the text that used to be there:

```
/*------------------------------------------------------------------
    EShelpstart - prepare screen for help display
--------------------------------------------------------------------*/
void EShelpstart()
{
    ESclear();
}
```

```
/*-------------------------------------------------------------------
    EShelpfinish - clear help display and restore screen
--------------------------------------------------------------------*/
void EShelpfinish()
{
    ESshowall();
}
```

EShelpwrite translates the row to physical-screen coordinates (just as
ESshowrow did) and writes out the text:

```
/*-------------------------------------------------------------------
    EShelpwrite - write one line of help text
--------------------------------------------------------------------*/
void EShelpwrite(row, s, att)
int row;                                /* row to be written */
char *s;                                /* text */
int att;                                /* attribute */
{
    PSwrite(TEXTROW1 + row, 0, GIANT, s, att);
}
```

The most complicated function of all is **ESprompt**, because it has to
read the keyboard and provide a little editing (*very* little, because only
backspace and carriage return can be used):

```
/*-------------------------------------------------------------------
    ESprompt - prompt user to type in response
--------------------------------------------------------------------*/
void ESprompt(message, label, response)
char *message;                          /* message for user */
char *label;                            /* label for typing area */
char *response;                         /* user's response */
{
    int startcol, pos, key;
    ESmsg(message);
    response[0] = '\0';
    PSwrite(promptrect.rl, promptrect.cl, GIANT, label, A_INTENSE);
    startcol = promptrect.cl + strlen(label) + 1;
    pos = 0;
    while (TRUE) {
        PSwrite(promptrect.rl, startcol, GIANT, response, A_NORM);
        PSwrite(promptrect.rl, startcol + pos, 1, " ", A_NORM);
        PSsetcur(promptrect.rl, startcol + pos);
        Ksynch();
        ESshowcur(TRUE);
        switch (key = Kget()) {
        case K_BS:
            if (pos > 0)
                response[--pos] = '\0';
            continue;
        case K_RET:
            PSfill(&promptrect, ' ', A_NORM);
            ESmsg(NULL);
            ESshowcur(FALSE);
            return;
```

```
        default:
            if (key <= HIGHASCII && isprint(key) &&
              startcol + pos < promptrect.c2) {
                response[pos++] = (char)key;
                response[pos] = '\0';
            }
            else
                PSbeep();
        }
    }
}
```

To make processing especially simple, we don't bother revising the current display of the user's response on every keystroke. We just display the entire response every time through the loop.

For consistency, it might be better if the same keystrokes used in the rest of the editor could also be used in responding to prompts, where they make sense. You may want to enhance **ESprompt** to allow the use of **K_RIGHT, K_LEFT, K_DEL,** and so on. Such consistency would help to keep our editor as modeless as possible.

5.4. Summary

In this chapter we presented all of the code for a screen editor. It displays text with the physical-screen module of Chapter 3, and it reads the user's input with the virtual-keyboard module of Chapter 4. Perhaps the most interesting feature of this editor is that it has three text buffers, each of which can hold a different file. Without windows, only one buffer can be seen at a time, but the switching is fast.

We divided the editor into four modules: a main module, a text module, an I/O module, and a screen module, which is the only place where the physical screen interface is used. This structure localizes the changes needed to use windows and virtual screens; we'll show these changes in the next two chapters. This structure also provides for replacement of the somewhat toy-like text module with a more capacious one. We've left those modifications for you to do on your own.

CHAPTER 6

Windows

A window is very much like a little screen. You access a window with functions that parallel those in the physical screen interface. For example, instead of **PSwrite**, you use **Wwrite**. But because windows aren't physical, you can do things with them that are much harder to do with physical screens: You can create new windows, dispose of old ones, change their size and location, and, if the windows overlap, decide which one goes on top. You can write to a window even if a chunk of it is covered, without worrying about your text's overflowing into places it doesn't belong.

We'll implement the window module on top of the physical screen interface, so this chapter continues from Chapter 3. We'll begin by discussing windows in general, as they're used here, as well as in other contemporary systems. Next, we'll explain the interface to the window module. To illustrate how it's used, we'll rewrite the screen module of the text editor introduced in Chapter 5. Finally, we'll present the code of the window module itself.

6.1. Properties of Windows

Windows have these properties:

1. A window can be the same size as, or smaller than, the physical screen. If it is smaller, it may or may not have a frame around it (drawn with lines and corner characters).

2. Data written to a window won't go outside the window's boundaries, just as data written to the physical screen won't go off the screen.

3. Part or all of a window can be obscured by other windows. The application writing to the window need not be concerned with this—data that's not supposed to be seen will be suppressed automatically by the window manager.

4. The location of a window on the physical screen can be changed without the application's knowing or caring about it, but the application can find out the location if it wants to. Similarly, the application can decide to be ignorant of the window's size or not, as it wishes.

5. When part of a window has to be redrawn because it just became visible, the application has to help the window manager by supplying the data that is to be shown there. The window manager is unable to remember anything that isn't actually visible.

6. A window has a cursor, at a particular location, which can be moved about and turned on or off.

7. Exactly one window is on top, and it is the only one whose cursor can been seen by the user. However, any window can be written to at any time, even if it's completely covered by other windows. The application need not be aware of the order of windows from back to front, unless it wants to be.

A few of these properties are somewhat inconvenient, particularly numbers one and five. In the next chapter we'll introduce virtual screens that remove these two limitations. A virtual screen can be bigger than the window in which it appears, and it is redrawn automatically as necessary, without the participation of the application.

The term *window* means different things in other contexts. Some systems' windows are less functional than ours, and some are more (equivalent to what we call *virtual screens*). Aside from the fact that our windows contain only characters, not graphics, our definition corresponds closely to what Rob Pike calls *layers* [Pik83]. Also, to many people the word windows suggests features that go way beyond our definition, such as multi-tasking, cut-and-paste, mouse input, drop-down menus. Examples of such windowing systems for the IBM PC are Microsoft's Windows, IBM's TopView, Quarterdeck's DesqView, and Digital Research's GEM. Examples of UNIX windowing systems are Sun's SunView and NeWS, Carnegie-Mellon's Andrew, MIT's X (in the public domain), and AT&T's BLIT (Pike's system). Computers such as Apple's Macintosh, Commodore's Amiga, AT&T's UNIX PC, and IBM's RT also have built-in windowing systems.

All of these windowing systems allow the user, as well the application, to manipulate the windows. For example a text editor might show two

windows each ten rows high by default, and the user might decide to make
one of them larger. This might be done by issuing an editor command, or it
might be done by issuing a meta-command that's intercepted by a *window
manager*. The editor might not even be aware that the window changed size.
The most lavish of these systems implement a *desktop metaphor*, in which
the user shuffles windows around as though they were pieces of paper. We
won't present a window manager in this book, but I have programmed an
experimental one that sits on top of the window module discussed in this
chapter. Our design, then, is not inconsistent with a window manager.

6.2. Window Interface

This section explains how to use the window module in an application. The
design of a few of the function calls is more awkward than it might be; for
example, it takes two calls to create a window (**Wnew** and **Wsetphys**). This
isn't much of a drawback in practice because most applications will interface
with the virtual-screen layer (Chapter 7) rather than with the window layer.

As we've come to expect, you initialize the window module with **Wbegin**
and you terminate it with **Wend**:

```
/*---------------------------------------------------------------------
        Wbegin - initialize window module
   ---------------------------------------------------------------------*/
void Wbegin()

/*---------------------------------------------------------------------
        Wend - terminate window module
   ---------------------------------------------------------------------*/
void Wend()
```

You need not and must not call **PSbegin** or **PSend**—the window module will
do that automatically.

To create a new window, you call **Wnew**, which returns a window
number that must be used in subsequent calls that act on that window:

```
/*---------------------------------------------------------------------
        Wnew - create new window
        RETURN: Window number.
   ---------------------------------------------------------------------*/
int Wnew(drawfcn)
int (*drawfcn)();                       /* redraw function */
```

The window created can't be used yet because it has no size (zero rows and
zero columns). You must call **Wsetphys** (coming up next) before you can
write to the window. A small, fixed amount of memory is allocated to hold
information about the window, but no memory is allocated to hold its

contents. If even this small amount of memory is unavailable, **Wnew** returns a window number of zero. This is actually a real window that is equal in size to the physical screen, and it is always underneath all other windows. So there is no error return from **Wnew**. At most, twenty-five windows can be in existence; a fatal error, with a message, is issued if this limit is exceeded. (If twenty-five isn't enough, the limit can be raised by recompiling the file **window.c**.)

The argument to **Wnew** is the address of a function that will be called by the window module whenever part or all of the window is uncovered and must be redrawn. For example, suppose window 1 is partially obscured by window 2, which covers its right half. As you write to window 1, the window module will clip off anything intended for the covered part. If window 2 is then moved or disposed of, the redraw function associated with window 1 will be called and will be expected to redraw its right half. This is because the window module does not store data that can't immediately be drawn on the physical screen. The function doesn't have to worry about the frame—the window module handles that itself.

More specifically, the redrawing function should be declared like this:

```
/*----------------------------------------------------------------
    redraw - redraw damaged window
--------------------------------------------------------------*/
static void redraw(wnum, wrectp)
int wnum;                               /* window */
RECT *wrectp;                           /* rectangle to be redrawn */
```

The names of the function and its arguments don't matter, of course, as long as the types are correctly declared. The first argument is the number of the window to be repaired in case the same function is used for several windows. The second argument is a pointer to a rectangle, relative to the window, of the part to be written. It's often easier, and perfectly legal, for the function to redraw more than that—perhaps even the whole window. We'll show a simple example using a redrawing function as soon as we've introduced a few more calls.

The argument to **Wnew** can be **NULL**; this means there is no redrawing function, and damage to the interior of the window will not be repaired, although a damaged frame will be. This option can be used when you know that the window will always be fully visible.

A call to **Wnew** must be followed by a call to **Wsetphys** to set the window's size and location on the physical screen:

```
/*----------------------------------------------------------------
    Wsetphys - set window's physical size
--------------------------------------------------------------*/
void Wsetphys(wnum, srectp)
int wnum;                               /* window */
RECT *srectp;                           /* size (including frame) */
```

The rectangle passed to **Wsetphys** is relative to the physical screen, in contrast to the rectangle passed to a redrawing function, which is relative to the window. By default, one row at the top and bottom of the window and one column at the left and right are devoted to the frame. This must be taken into account when sizing the window. For example, suppose you need an area 10 rows by 20 columns, with its upper left corner at row 7, column 25. When you include the frame, the window size will be 12-by-22, with its upper left corner at row 6, column 24. So you might create and size the window with these calls:

```
int wnum;
RECT rect;

wnum = Wnew(NULL);
RASG(&rect, 6, 24, 17, 45);
Wsetphys(wnum, &rect);
```

The character at row 0, column 0 relative to the window is now at row 7, column 25 relative to the physical screen. The upper left corner of the frame itself is at row 6, column 24.

As a special case, the rectangle passed to **Wsetphys** may be just off the screen; that is, starting at row −1, column −1, and extending to row **PSheight()**, column **PSwidth()**. Such a window has an interior that exactly covers the physical screen, but its frame is off-screen. **Wsetphys** handles this in the following way: The window's defining rectangle is reduced by one all around so that the frame is visible, but then the window is *zoomed* so that its interior does indeed match the physical screen, as the caller wished. See the discussion of **Wzoom** for more details.

Wsetphys is separate from **Wnew** because it can be called at any time, as many times as you like, to resize and/or move the window around on the physical screen. A window manager (not itself part of the window module as presented here) would use **Wsetphys** to effect changes in the window's size and location, as directed by the user, perhaps via cursor keys or a mouse.

You can determine the size and location of an existing window with **Wgetphys**:

```
/*-------------------------------------------------------------
    Wgetphys - get window's physical size
-------------------------------------------------------------*/
void Wgetphys(wnum, srectp, inclfrm)
int wnum;                           /* window */
RECT *srectp;                       /* size (returned) */
BOOLEAN inclfrm;                    /* should size include frame? */
```

As with **Wsetphys**, the rectangle returned through **srectp** is relative to the physical screen. You can use the macros **RHEIGHT** and **RWIDTH** (Sec. 2.6) to determine its dimensions, either including or excluding the frame. For example, this program:

```
#include "display.h"
#include "window.h"

/*-------------------------------------------------------------------
    main - window size example program
--------------------------------------------------------------------*/
void main()
{
    int wnum;
    RECT rect;
    FILE *out;

    if ((out = fopen("temp.out", "w")) == NULL)
        fatal("can't create temp.out");
    Wbegin();
    wnum = Wnew(NULL);
    RASG(&rect, 6, 24, 17, 45);
    Wsetphys(wnum, &rect);
    Wgetphys(wnum, &rect, TRUE);
    fprintf(out, "Including frame: height = %d, width = %d\n",
        RHEIGHT(&rect), RWIDTH(&rect));
    Wgetphys(wnum, &rect, FALSE);
    fprintf(out, "Excluding frame: height = %d, width = %d\n",
        RHEIGHT(&rect), RWIDTH(&rect));
    Wend();
    exit(0);
}
```

produced this output on the file **temp.out**:

```
            Including frame: height = 12, width = 22
            Excluding frame: height = 10, width = 20
```

It's convenient to write debugging information like this to a file instead of to the screen because writing to the screen without going through the window module might interfere with the appearance of what you're trying to debug and because the debugging output might be erased before you can see it.

The default frame style is a single line, which looks great on a display with line-drawing characters, such as an IBM PC, and lousy on most terminals, because the ASCII characters | and — are used, as shown in Fig. 6–1. You can select from a few other styles with **Wsetfrm**, which can be called at any time (even several times) after the window is created with **Wnew**.

```
/*-------------------------------------------------------------------
    Wsetfrm - set window's frame appearance
--------------------------------------------------------------------*/
void Wsetfrm(wnum, frmtype, frmatt, title)
int wnum;                               /* window */
FRMTYPE frmtype;                        /* frame type (F_UNFRAMED, F_SINGLE,
                                           F_DOUBLE, F_BLANK, F_AUTO) */
int frmatt;                             /* frame attribute */
char *title;                            /* frame title */
```

Symbolic constants for the **frmtype** argument are defined in the header file **window.h**. These frame styles are supported:

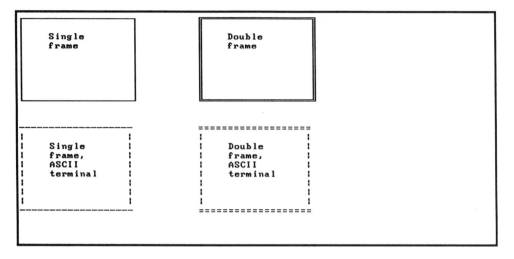

Fig. 6–1. Window frame styles.

F_UNFRAMED   The window has no frame. All of the rectangle given as an argument to **Wsetphys** is available for writing. This style is sometimes used when you want to draw your own frame: You create one window to which you write the frame characters, and a slightly smaller window on top of it to which you write the data to be displayed in the interior. Since windows occupy very little memory, this is quite workable.

F_SINGLE   The window is framed in single lines, as discussed above. This is the default.

F_DOUBLE   The window is framed in double lines. On an ASCII terminal the vertical lines remain the same (|), but the horizontal lines are drawn with = characters.

F_BLANK   The window has a frame, but it's made of blank characters. This is handy when the window frame attribute is **A_INVERSE**. Then the sharp contrast between the window and its surroundings (with the attribute **A_NORM**) makes a line-character frame unnecessary. This looks OK even on a terminal lacking line-drawing characters.

F_AUTO   The window is framed with double lines when it's on top, and single lines otherwise. Switching back and forth between styles is handled automatically by the window manager. The advantage of this type is that the user is reminded which window is on top in a subtle but noticeable way.

The **frmatt** argument gives the attribute for the *frame*, not for the interior of the window. You control the attribute of the interior as you write text there. You can place a title at the top of the frame with the **title** argument, as illustrated in Fig. 6–2. If you don't want a title, the argument can be a null string or a **NULL** pointer.

```
This is row 0 of the window.
This is row 1 of the window.
This is row 2 of the window.
This is row 3 of ┌Window-2─────────────────────────────────────────
This is row 4 of │2222222222222222222222222222222222222222222222222
This is row 5 of │2222222222222222222222222222222222222222222222222
This is row 6 of │2222222222222222222222222222222222222222222222222
This is row 7 of │2222222222222222222222222222222222222222222222222
                 │2222222222222222222222222222222222222222222222222
                 │2222222222222222222222222222222222222222222222222
                 │2222222222222222222222222222222222222222222222222
                 │2222222222222222222222222222222222222222222222222
                 │2222222222222222222222222222222222222222222222222
                 │2222222222222222222222222222222222222222222222222
                 │2222222222222222222222222222222222222222222222222
                 │2222222222222222222222222222222222222222222222222
                 │2222222222222222222222222222222222222222222222222
                 │2222222222222222222222222222222222222222222222222
```

Fig. 6–2. Window 2 partially obscuring window 1.

When you no longer need a window, you can get rid of it with **Wdispose**:

```
/*----------------------------------------------------------------
    Wdispose - eliminate window
------------------------------------------------------------*/
void Wdispose(wnum)
int wnum;                              /* window */
```

Any windows that were covered will be fixed up via calls to their redrawing functions. The memory associated with the disposed-of window is released, and its window number is made available for re-use.

To write into a window, you can use four calls that are similar to calls of the physical screen interface, except that their names start with W instead of PS, and they take a window number as their first argument:

```
/*---------------------------------------------------------------
    Wwrite - write string
------------------------------------------------------------*/
void Wwrite(wnum, wrow, wcol, ncols, str, att)
int wnum;                              /* window */
int wrow;                              /* starting row */
int wcol;                              /* starting column */
```

```
int ncols;                              /* number of columns to write */
char *str;                              /* string */
int att;                               /* attribute */

/*-------------------------------------------------------------------
        Wwrtcells - write vector of CELLs
   -----------------------------------------------------------------*/
void Wwrtcells(wnum, wrow, wcol, captr, ncols)
int wnum;                               /* window */
int wrow;                               /* starting row */
int wcol;                               /* starting column */
CELL *captr;                            /* CELLs */
int ncols;                              /* number of columns to write */

/*-------------------------------------------------------------------
        Wfill - fill rectangle
   -----------------------------------------------------------------*/
void Wfill(wnum, wrectp, chr, att)
int wnum;                               /* window */
RECT *wrectp;                           /* rectangle */
char chr;                               /* fill character */
int att;                               /* fill attribute */

/*-------------------------------------------------------------------
        Wslide -. slide rectangle
        RETURN: Was slide performed?
   -----------------------------------------------------------------*/
BOOLEAN Wslide(wnum, wrectp, dir, dist)
int wnum;                               /* window */
RECT *wrectp;                           /* rectangle */
int dir;                               /* direction */
int dist;                              /* distance */
```

These functions won't write outside of the window on which they're used, even if the length, rectangle, or distance arguments are too large. Thus each window behaves as a separate little screen, as it should. **Wwrite**, like **PSwrite**, does *not* pad its string argument to a length of **ncols**. You may have to precede it or follow it with a call to **Wfill** or **Wwrite** to ensure that the entire row of the window is written properly. Also, note that **Wslide** slides a rectangle *within* the window to another position *within* the window. It does *not* slide the window relative to the physical screen. You can use **Wsetphys** for that.

Now let's use some of the functions we've presented so far in a simple example. This program will display two windows, as shown in Fig. 6–2, and then dispose of the second window, as shown in Fig. 6–3. A redrawing function associated with window 1 repairs the damaged area underneath window 2 when window 2 goes away.

```
#include "display.h"
#include "pscreen.h"
#include "window.h"
#include "keyboard.h"

/*-------------------------------------------------------------------
        redraw - redraw damaged window
   -----------------------------------------------------------------*/
static void redraw(wnum, wrectp)
int wnum;                               /* window */
RECT *wrectp;                           /* rectangle to be redrawn */
{
```

```
    int row;
    char buf[100];

    Wfill(wnum, wrectp, ' ', A_NORM);
    for (row = wrectp->r1; row <= wrectp->r2; row++) {
        sprintf(buf, "This is row %d of the window.", row);
        if (wrectp->c1 < strlen(buf))
            Wwrite(wnum, row, wrectp->c1, RWIDTH(wrectp), &buf[wrectp->c1],
            A_NORM);
    }
}

/*-------------------------------------------------------------------
    main - window redrawing example program
-----------------------------------------------------------------------*/
void main()
{
    int wnum1, wnum2;
    RECT rect;

    Wbegin();
    Kbegin();
    wnum1 = Wnew(redraw);
    RASG(&rect, 0, 0, 9, 35);
    Wsetphys(wnum1, &rect);
    wnum2 = Wnew(NULL);
    RASG(&rect, 4, 18, 19, 69);
    Wsetphys(wnum2, &rect);
    Wsetfrm(wnum2, F_DOUBLE, A_NORM, "Window 2");
    Wfill(wnum2, &GIANT_RECT, '2', A_NORM);
    PSsynch();
    (void)Kget();
    Wdispose(wnum2);
    PSsynch();
    (void)Kget();
    Kend();
    Wend();
    exit(0);
}
```

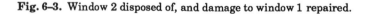

```
This is row 0 of the window.
This is row 1 of the window.
This is row 2 of the window.
This is row 3 of the window.
This is row 4 of the window.
This is row 5 of the window.
This is row 6 of the window.
This is row 7 of the window.
```

Fig. 6–3. Window 2 disposed of, and damage to window 1 repaired.

Returning to the window interface, we note that two more functions are like their physical screen counterparts:

```
/*----------------------------------------------------------------...
    Wsetcur - set cursor position
----------------------------------------------------------------*/
void Wsetcur(wnum, wrow, wcol)
int wnum;                               /* window */
int wrow;                               /* row */
int wcol;                               /* column */


/*-------------------------------------------------------------
    Wshowcur - turn cursor on or off
--------------------------------------------------------------*/
void Wshowcur(wnum, on)
int wnum;                               /* window */
BOOLEAN on;                             /* switch */
```

The cursor position and whether the cursor is visible are remembered automatically by the window module. However, the physical screen has only one cursor, so it can't be shown in more than one window at a time. Only the top window shows the cursor. If that window has the cursor off, no cursor is shown at all. When a window is created, its cursor is located at row 0, column 0, and is off.

The order of windows, from bottom to top, is the same as the order of their creation. You can force a window to the top by disposing of the windows on top of it, or explicitly by calling **Wtop**, which rearranges the order:

```
/*--------------------------------------------------------------
    Wtop - force window to top
-----------------------------------------------------------*/
void Wtop(wnum)
int wnum;                               /* window */
```

This is a fairly expensive operation because the window module has to recalculate which parts of which windows are visible and then call the redrawing function of every affected window.

To determine which window is on top, you can use **Wgettop**:

```
/*----------------------------------------------------------------
    Wgettop - get top window
    RETURN: Window number.
-------------------------------------------------------------*/
int Wgettop()
```

You can make a window disappear, without actually disposing of it, by calling **Whide**:

```
/*--------------------------------------------------------------
    Whide - hide window
------------------------------------------------------*/
void Whide(wnum)
int wnum;                               /* window */
```

No part of a hidden window will be seen and its redrawing function will not be called. You can make it visible again by bringing it to the top via **Wtop** or by changing its size or location via **Wsetphys**. You can write into a window even if it's hidden, although there's no reason to.

It is rare that windows have to be hidden explicitly; usually the natural overlaying of one window by another is sufficient. If you want to temporarily clear the screen of windows, you could hide all existing windows, and then un-hide them when you want them again. But it's easier to leave the windows alone and just create another window that covers the physical screen:

```
wnum = Wnew(NULL);
RASG(&rect, 0, 0, PSheight() - 1, PSwidth() - 1);
Wsetphys(wnum, &rect);
Wsetfrm(wnum, F_UNFRAMED, A_NORM, NULL);
Wfill(wnum, &GIANT_RECT, ' ', A_NORM);
```

Then you can put the screen back the way it was with:

```
Wdispose(wnum);
```

An easy way to enlarge a window to full screen is to zoom it:

```
/*-------------------------------------------------------------------
    Wzoom - make window full screen
-------------------------------------------------------------*/
void Wzoom(wnum)
int wnum;                                     /* window */
```

The size, location, and frame style are saved before zooming the window. While zoomed, it is unframed and its interior is the same size as the physical screen.

You can restore a zoomed window to its former state with **Wunzoom**:

```
/*-------------------------------------------------------------------
    Wunzoom - restore window to former size
-------------------------------------------------------------*/
void Wunzoom(wnum)
int wnum;                                     /* window */
```

And you can even ask whether a window is zoomed:

```
/*-------------------------------------------------------------------
    Wiszoomed - determine if window is zoomed
    RETURN: Is it?
-------------------------------------------------------------*/
BOOLEAN Wiszoomed(wnum)
int wnum;                                     /* window */
```

Wshuffle brings a window to the top without your having to know its number:

```
/*-------------------------------------------------------------------
      Wshuffle - force next window to top
-----------------------------------------------------------------*/
void Wshuffle()
```

You can call **Wshuffle** in a loop to bring the windows to the top one by one. This might be used as a way for the user to specify a window to receive some action. The user would press a function key when the desired window is on top.

Although it isn't actually part of the window interface, one important function must be used with the window calls: **PSsynch**. Until you call it, you must not assume that anything will be seen. See Sec. 3.2.2 for more details about this.

6.3. Screen Editor Implementation Using Windows

There's no better way to show how the window interface is really used than to rewrite the screen module of the editor from Sec. 5.3. We're going to present this implementation as though we were continuing directly from that section. If it isn't fresh in your mind (or if you skipped Chapter 5 entirely), you should review it now.

With windows we'll be able to improve the looks of the editor and make it easier to use, too. Initially the screen will appear as shown in Fig. 6-4. If you switch to buffer 2 with **K_ALT_B** the screen will appear as in Fig. 6-5.

```
┌─Buffer─1──────────────────────────────────────────────────────┐
│void setpos()                                                   │
│{                                                               │
│    struct Bufinfo *bf = bufinfoptr(bufnum);                    │
│    int pos, col, prevcol;                                      │
│    char *t;                                                    │
│                                                                │
│    t = ETtext(bufnum, bf->topline + bf->currow);               │
│    col = prevcol = 0;                                          │
│    bf->curpos = 0;                                             │
│    for (pos = 0; ; pos++) {                                    │
│        if (col > bf->curcol)                                   │
│            break;                                              │
│        prevcol = col;                                          │
│        bf->curpos = pos;                                       │
│        if (t[pos] == '\0')                                     │
│            break;                                              │
│        if (t[pos] == '\t')                                     │
│            col += TABINTERVAL - col % TABINTERVAL;             │
│        else                                                    │
│            col++;                                              │
│    }                                                           │
└────────────────────────────────────────────────────────────────┘
```

Fig. 6–4. Initial editor screen. Buffer 2 is behind buffer 1.

```
┌Buffer─1────────────────────────────────────────────────────────────────────────┐
│┌Buffer─2───────────────────────────────────────────────────────────────────────┐
││    ETinsline - insert fresh line into buffer memory                            │
││    RETURN: Was there room?                                                     │
││ ──────────────────────────────────────────────────────────────────────────*/ │
││ BOOLEAN ETinsline(bnum, line)                                                  │
││ int bnum;                              /* buffer number */                     │
││ int line;                             /* line number */                        │
││ {                                                                              │
││     struct Buffer *b = bufptr(bnum);                                           │
││                                                                                │
││     ▓f (line < 0 !! line > b->numlines)                                        │
││         fatal("ETinsline - bad line");                                         │
││     if (b->numlines >= MAXLINES) {                                             │
││         ESmsg("Too many lines");                                               │
││         return(FALSE);                                                         │
││     }                                                                          │
││     if (line < b->numlines)                                                    │
││         movmem((char *)&b->text[line], (char *)&b->text[line + 1],             │
││             (b->numlines - line) * sizeof(b->text[0]));                        │
││     if (!store(b, line, ""))                                                   │
││         return(FALSE);                                                         │
││     b->numlines++;                                                             │
│└────────────────────────────────────────────────────────────────────────────── ┘
 edtext.c  Column 5  Line 174 of 363  Buffer 2
```

Fig. 6-5. Editor screen after switching to buffer 2.

And if you switch to the two-buffer view with **K_ALT_V** you can see two windows at once, as shown in Fig. 6-6. When more than one window is completely visible, as in this case, one of them is still "on top." It's the one where the cursor appears, if the cursor is being shown, or the one with the double frame, if the frame types are **F_AUTO**. If neither of these techniques is used to distinguish the active window, the application should do something else to make sure the user knows where to look (if it matters).

Recall that the main module (**edit.c**) keeps track of the buffer number and passes it as an argument to most screen module entry points. The screen module will associate a window with each buffer, so it uses an array of integers (**winnum**) to record the window number associated with each buffer number—we can't assume the two numbers are the same. Given a buffer number **bnum**, the window number would be **winnum[bnum]**. There are also global variables to separately store the current buffer and window numbers, and the number of the help window (created by **EShelpstart** and disposed of by **EShelpfinish**). A symbolic constant specifies the width of the prompt window. Here's the start of this version of **edscr.c**:

```
#include "display.h"
#include "pscreen.h"
#include "window.h"
#include "keyboard.h"
#include "keycode.h"
#include "edit.h"
#include "edscr.h"
```

```
static int winnum[MAXBUF];          /* window number for each buffer */
static int curwnum;                 /* current window number */
static int curbnum;                 /* current buffer number */
static int helpwnum;                /* help window num (see EShelpstart) */

#define PROMPTWIDTH 40              /* width of prompt window */
```

```
┌─Buffer─1──────────────────────────────────────────────────────────────┐
│ void setpos()                                                          │
│ {                                                                      │
│     struct Bufinfo *bf = bufinfoptr(bufnum);                           │
│     int pos, col, prevcol;                                             │
│     char *t;                                                           │
│                                                                        │
│     t = ETtext(bufnum, bf->topline + bf->currow);                      │
│     col = prevcol = 0;                                                 │
│     bf->curpos = 0;                                                    │
│     for (pos = 0; ; pos++) {                                           │
│ ┌─Buffer─2──────────────────────────────────────────────────────────┐ │
│ │     ETinsline — insert fresh line into buffer memory              │ │
│ │     RETURN: Was there room?                                        │ │
│ │ ─────────────────────────────────────────────────────────────*/   │ │
│ │ BOOLEAN ETinsline(bnum, line)                                      │ │
│ │ int bnum;                          /* buffer number */             │ │
│ │ int line;                          /* line number */               │ │
│ │ {                                                                  │ │
│ │     struct Buffer *b = bufptr(bnum);                               │ │
│ │                                                                    │ │
│ │     if (line < 0 || line > b->numlines)                            │ │
│ └────────────────────────────────────────────────────────────────────┘ │
└────────────────────────────────────────────────────────────────────────┘
```

Fig. 6–6. Editor screen showing two buffers at once.

The call **ESbegin** creates a window for each buffer:

```
/*---------------------------------------------------------------------
     ESbegin - initialize screen module
 ---------------------------------------------------------------------*/
void ESbegin()
{
    int i;
    char title[20];

    Wbegin();
    Kbegin();
    ESmsg(NULL); /* make message window */
    for (i = 0; i < MAXBUF; i++) {
        winnum[i] = Wnew(redraw);
        sprintf(title, "Buffer %d", i + 1);
        Wsetfrm(winnum[i], F_SINGLE, A_NORM, title);
    }
    bigwindows();
    ESswitch(0);
}
```

(We'll look at **redraw** later.) The size and location of the windows, as shown
in Fig. 6–4, are set by **bigwindows**:

```
/*--------------------------------------------------------------------
    bigwindows - make all windows full size
----------------------------------------------------------------*/
static void bigwindows()
{
    RECT rect;
    int i;

    RASG(&rect, 0, 0, PSheight() - 1 - MAXBUF, PSwidth() - MAXBUF);
    for (i = 0; i < MAXBUF; i++) {
        Wsetphys(winnum[i], &rect);
        rect.r1++;
        rect.r2++;
        rect.c1++;
        rect.c2++;
    }
}
```

Each coordinate of the defining rectangle is incremented to stagger the
windows. This wastes space, especially if there are more than two windows,
but it sure looks terrific!

The function **smallwindows** changes the size of each window with
Wsetphys to be about half-screen in height. The first window is at the top,
and all the other windows share the bottom. That way the first window can
be seen along with one of the other windows.

```
/*--------------------------------------------------------------------
    smallwindows - make windows half size (so two can be seen at once)
----------------------------------------------------------------*/
static void smallwindows()
{
    RECT rect;
    int i;

    RASG(&rect, 0, 0, PSheight() / 2 - 1, PSwidth() - 1);
    Wsetphys(winnum[0], &rect);
    rect.r1 = rect.r2 + 1;
    rect.r2 = PSheight() - 2;
    for (i = 1; i < MAXBUF; i++)
        Wsetphys(winnum[i], &rect);
}
```

This function is called from **ESview**:

```
/*--------------------------------------------------------------------
    ESview - toggle between big and small windows
----------------------------------------------------------------*/
void ESview()
{
    static BOOLEAN big = TRUE;

    switch (big = !big) {
    case TRUE:
        bigwindows();
        break;
    case FALSE:
        smallwindows();
    }
}
```

As long as we get an up-to-date measure each time we use the height and width, the rest of the editor won't be affected by changes in the sizes of the windows. In fact, it would be possible to design a window manager of some sort to let the *user* change the sizes and locations of the windows, and even that wouldn't disrupt anything. This flexibility is attained because we call **ESheight** and **ESwidth** whenever we need the sizes of the current window, rather than store them in variables whose values may persist too long:

```
/*--------------------------------------------------------------------
    ESheight - get height of area where editor can show text
    RETURN: Height.
---------------------------------------------------------------------*/
int ESheight()
{
    RECT rect;

    Wgetphys(curwnum, &rect, FALSE);
    return(RHEIGHT(&rect));
}

/*--------------------------------------------------------------------
    ESwidth - get width of area where editor can show text
    RETURN: Width.
---------------------------------------------------------------------*/
int ESwidth()
{
    RECT rect;

    Wgetphys(curwnum, &rect, FALSE);
    return(RWIDTH(&rect));
}
```

At the end of processing, **ESend** disposes of the windows:

```
/*--------------------------------------------------------------------
    ESend - terminate screen module
---------------------------------------------------------------------*/
void ESend()
{
    int i;

    for (i = 0; i < MAXBUF; i++)
        Wdispose(winnum[i]);
    Kend();
    Wend();
}
```

To switch to a new buffer, and also to a new window, we set the global variables **curbnum** and **curwnum** and, if the window isn't already on top, we force it to the top:

```
/*--------------------------------------------------------------------
    ESswitch - switch to buffer
---------------------------------------------------------------------*/
void ESswitch(bnum)
int bnum;                               /* buffer number */
{
```

```
        curbnum = bnum;
        curwnum = winnum[bnum];
        if (Wgettop() != curwnum)
            Wtop(curwnum);
}
```

ESshowrow and **ESshowall** are similar to the physical screen versions
(see Sec. 5.3.5) except that they use the W functions:

```
/*------------------------------------------------------------------
    ESshowrow - show text for row, starting at specified column
---------------------------------------------------------------------*/
void ESshowrow(row, col)
int row;                                /* row */
int col;                                /* column */
{
    char *t;
    RECT rect;

    t = EMtext(curbnum, row);
    if (col < strlen(t))
        Wwrite(curwnum, row, col, GIANT, &t[col], A_NORM);
    RASG(&rect, row, strlen(t), row, GIANT);
    Wfill(curwnum, &rect, ' ', A_NORM);
}

/*------------------------------------------------------------------
    ESshowall - show all rows that are visible
---------------------------------------------------------------------*/
void ESshowall()
{
    int row, height;

    ESclear();
    height = ESheight();
    for (row = 0; row < height; row++)
        Wwrite(curwnum, row, 0, GIANT, EMtext(curbnum, row), A_NORM);
}
```

The function **showrange** is identical to the one we showed for the
physical screen, since it just calls **ESshowrow** in a loop.

Now we can show the redrawing function that we specified in the call to
Wnew in **ESbegin**. It's a common function that serves to redraw any of the
text windows:

```
/*------------------------------------------------------------------
    redraw - repair damaged window (called from window.c)
---------------------------------------------------------------------*/
static void redraw(wnum, wrectp)
int wnum;                               /* window number */
RECT *wrectp;                           /* rectangle to be redrawn */
{
    int bnum, savewnum, savebnum;

    for (bnum = 0; bnum < MAXBUF; bnum++)
        if (winnum[bnum] == wnum)
            break;
    if (bnum >= MAXBUF)
        Wfill(wnum, wrectp, ' ', A_NORM);
```

```
    else {
        savewnum = curwnum;
        savebnum = curbnum;
        curwnum = wnum;
        curbnum = bnum;
        if (RHEIGHT(wrectp) == ESheight())
            ESshowall();
        else
            showrange(wrectp->r1, wrectp->r2);
        curwnum = savewnum;
        curbnum = savebnum;
    }
}
```

All we know on entry is a window number (**wnum**), so we have to look in the **winnum** array to find the buffer number. If there is none (a supposedly impossible situation) we just fill the rectangle with blanks. Normally we will find the buffer number, so we can call **ESshowall** or **ESshowrow** to redraw all or part of the window. Unfortunately those two functions work on only the current window, which might not be the one **redraw** was called for. So we save the current window and buffer numbers, temporarily change them, and then change them back. Not elegant, but good enough. We're not too picky about repairing more columns than needed, but we do limit ourselves to only the required rows.

Setting the cursor location and turning it on and off come next:

```
/*-------------------------------------------------------------------
    ESsetcur - set cursor position
-------------------------------------------------------------------*/
void ESsetcur(row, col)
int row;                                /* row */
int col;                                /* column */
{
    Wsetcur(curwnum, row, col);
}


/*-------------------------------------------------------------------
    ESshowcur - turn cursor on or off
-------------------------------------------------------------------*/
void ESshowcur(on)
BOOLEAN on;                             /* switch */
{
    Wshowcur(curwnum, on);
}
```

To clear a window we call **Wfill** with the rectangle **GIANT_RECT** and let the window module cut it to size:

```
/*-------------------------------------------------------------------
    ESclear - clear text area
-------------------------------------------------------------------*/
void ESclear()
{
    Wfill(curwnum, &GIANT_RECT, ' ', A_NORM);
}
```

That trick works with **Wslide** too, as shown in **ESscrlup** and **ESscrldown**, which are otherwise similar to the physical screen version:

```
/*-------------------------------------------------------------------
    ESscrlup - scroll text area up one row
--------------------------------------------------------------*/
void ESscrlup()
{
    if (Wslide(curwnum, &GIANT_RECT, DIR_UP, 1))
        ESshowrow(ESheight() - 1, 0);
    else
        ESshowall();
}


    /*-------------------------------------------------------------------
        ESscrldown - scroll text area down one row
    --------------------------------------------------------------*/
    void ESscrldown()
    {
        if (Wslide(curwnum, &GIANT_RECT, DIR_DOWN, 1))
            ESshowrow(0, 0);
        else
            ESshowall();
    }
```

The physical screen version also serves as a model for **ESinschar**, **ESdelchar**, **ESinsrow**, and **ESdelrow**:

```
    /*-------------------------------------------------------------------
        ESinschar - insert character into row of text
    --------------------------------------------------------------*/
    void ESinschar(row, col, ch)
    int row;                                /* row */
    int col;                                /* column */
    char ch;                                /* character */
    {
        RECT rect;

        RASG(&rect, row, col, row, GIANT);
        if (Wslide(curwnum, &rect, DIR_RIGHT, 1))
            Wwrite(curwnum, row, col, 1, &ch, A_NORM);
        else
            ESshowrow(row, col);
    }

    /*-------------------------------------------------------------------
        ESdelchar - delete character from row of text
    --------------------------------------------------------------*/
    void ESdelchar(row, col)
    int row;                                /* row */
    int col;                                /* column */
    {
        RECT rect;

        RASG(&rect, row, col + 1, row, GIANT);
        if (Wslide(curwnum, &rect, DIR_LEFT, 1))
            Wwrite(curwnum, row, ESwidth() - 1, 1, " ", A_NORM);
        else
            ESshowrow(row, col);
    }
```

```
/*-------------------------------------------------------------------
    ESinsrow - insert blank row into text area
---------------------------------------------------------------*/
void ESinsrow(row)
int row;                                /* row */
{
    int height;
    RECT rect;

    height = ESheight();
    if (row >= height)
        fatal("ESinsrow - bad row");
    RASG(&rect, row, 0, GIANT, GIANT);
    if (Wslide(curwnum, &rect, DIR_DOWN, 1)) {
        rect.r2 = rect.r1;
        Wfill(curwnum, &rect, ' ', A_NORM);
    }
    else
        showrange(row, height - 1);
}


/*-------------------------------------------------------------------
    ESdelrow - delete row from text area
---------------------------------------------------------------*/
void ESdelrow(row)
int row;                                /* row */
{
    RECT rect;

    RASG(&rect, row + 1, 0, GIANT, GIANT);
    if (Wslide(curwnum, &rect, DIR_UP, 1))
        ESshowrow(ESheight() - 1, 0);
    else
        showrange(row, ESheight() - 1);
}
```

We'll write messages at the bottom of the screen, instead of at the top as we did in the physical screen version. **ESmsg** creates a frame-less window one row high the first time it's called. Each subsequent call simply writes to that window:

```
/*-------------------------------------------------------------------
    ESmsg - display short message
---------------------------------------------------------------*/
void ESmsg(s)
char *s;                                /* message */
{
    static int wnum = -1;
    static BOOLEAN havemsg = FALSE;
    RECT rect;
    int top;

    if (wnum == -1) {
        top = Wgettop();
        wnum = Wnew(redraw);
        Wsetfrm(wnum, F_UNFRAMED, A_NORM, NULL);
        RASG(&rect, PSheight() - 1, 0, PSheight() - 1, PSwidth() - 1);
        Wsetphys(wnum, &rect);
        if (top > 0)
            Wtop(top);
    }
```

```
    if (havemsg)
        Wfill(wnum, &GIANT_RECT, ' ', A_NORM);
    havemsg = s != NULL;
    if (havemsg) {
        Wwrite(wnum, 0, 0, GIANT, s, A_INVERSE);
        PSsynch();
    }
}
```

The message window will always be visible (except when we're viewing help-text) because the text windows don't reach the bottom row. So there's no need for it to be on top. In fact we don't want it on top, for then the cursor won't appear in the active text window. We solve this problem by getting the number of the top window with **Wgettop** and forcing it back to the top after we create the message window.

ESmsg2 is identical to the version shown in Sec. 5.3.5, since it is independent of the display module used.

For help, we'll create a separate full-screen window when **EShelpstart** is called, write in it when **EShelpwrite** is called, and dispose of it when **EShelpfinish** is called. We don't have to explicitly restore the screen, as we did in the physical screen version, because the window module will call the redrawing function for each text window automatically.

```
/*-----------------------------------------------------------------
    EShelpstart - prepare screen for help display
-----------------------------------------------------------------*/
void EShelpstart()
{
    RECT rect;

    helpwnum = Wnew(NULL);
    RASG(&rect, 0, 0, PSheight() - 1, PSwidth() - 1);
    Wsetphys(helpwnum, &rect);
    Wfill(helpwnum, &GIANT_RECT, ' ', A_NORM);
}

/*-----------------------------------------------------------------
    EShelpfinish - clear help display and restore screen
-----------------------------------------------------------------*/
void EShelpfinish()
{
    Wdispose(helpwnum);
}

/*-----------------------------------------------------------------
    EShelpwrite - write one line of help text
-----------------------------------------------------------------*/
void EShelpwrite(row, s, att)
int row;                              /* row to be written */
char *s;                              /* text */
int att;                              /* attribute */
{
    Wwrite(helpwnum, row, 0, GIANT, s, att);
}
```

We've saved the best for last. **ESprompt** pops up a prompt window on top of whatever is currently showing. When the prompt is completed, the window disappears. It is effects like this that make windowing software so visually exciting. This can be seen by comparing Figs. 5–1 and 5–2. Aside from the fact that it writes into a window, this version of **ESprompt** is very similar to the one using the physical screen interface:

```
/*------------------------------------------------------------------
    ESprompt - prompt user to type in response
--------------------------------------------------------------*/
void ESprompt(message, label, response)
char *message;                          /* message for user */
char *label;                            /* label for typing area */
char *response;                         /* user's response */
{
    int wnum, promptrow, startcol, lastcol, pos, key;
    RECT rect;

    wnum = Wnew(NULL);
    rect.r1 = 5;
    rect.r2 = rect.r1 + (message[0] == '\0' ? 2 : 4);
    rect.c1 = (PSwidth() - PROMPTWIDTH) / 2 - 1;
    rect.c2 = rect.c1 + PROMPTWIDTH - 1;
    promptrow = RHEIGHT(&rect) - 3;
    Wsetphys(wnum, &rect);
    Wshowcur(wnum, TRUE);
    Wfill(wnum, &GIANT_RECT, ' ', A_NORM);
    if (message[0] != '\0')
        Wwrite(wnum, 0, 1, GIANT, message, A_INTENSE);
    lastcol = RWIDTH(&rect) - 3;
    response[0] = '\0';
    Wwrite(wnum, promptrow, 1, GIANT, label, A_INTENSE);
    startcol = strlen(label) + 2;
    pos = 0;
    while (TRUE) {
        Wwrite(wnum, promptrow, startcol, GIANT, response, A_NORM);
        Wwrite(wnum, promptrow, startcol + pos, 1, " ", A_NORM);
        Wsetcur(wnum, promptrow, startcol + pos);
        Ksynch();
        switch (key = Kget()) {
        case K_BS:
            if (pos > 0)
                response[--pos] = '\0';
            continue;
        case K_RET:
            WdIspose(wnum);
            return;
        default:
            if (key <= HIGHASCII && isprint(key) &&
              startcol + pos < lastcol) {
                response[pos++] = (char)key;
                response[pos] = '\0';
            }
            else
                PSbeep();
        }
    }
}
```

6.4.   Window Implementation

Now that we know how to use the window module, we're ready to see how it's implemented. The code is in the file **window.c**, with an associated header file **window.h**. We'll describe these files piece by piece in the following subsections, taking on each of the major design decisions in turn.

6.4.1. Window Description and Geometry

The header **window.h** is accessible to the application using the window module. Besides declarations for the external functions (**Wbegin, Wwrite,** and so on), it includes the frame types and a constant for the maximum number of windows:

```
#define MAXWIND 25

typedef short FRMTYPE;
#define F_UNFRAMED   0          /* no frame */
#define F_AUTO       1          /* single frame, double when on top */
#define F_SINGLE     2          /* single frame */
#define F_DOUBLE     3          /* double frame */
#define F_BLANK      4          /* blank frame */
```

The implementation itself, in **window.c**, begins like this:

```
#include "display.h"
#include "window.h"
#include "pscreen.h"

#define SCR_WIND     0          /* physical screen "window" */

static int maxrow;             /* maximum physical screen row */
static int maxcol;             /* maximum physical screen column */
```

The global variables **maxrow** and **maxcol** are initialized in **Wbegin** from **PSheight** and **PSwidth**, as we'll see. **SCR_WIND** is the background window that's behind all other windows, corresponding to the physical screen. Recall that **Wnew** returns **SCR_WIND** when it is unable to create a new window. We have a background window mainly because some algorithms that we'll use in this module are simpler if we can assume that every screen cell is covered by at least one window.

Windows are fairly complex objects, so we need to maintain quite a bit of information about them. There is an array (**wind**) of **MAXWIND** structures, each of type **WINDOW**. The window number returned by **Wnew** is a subscript into this array.

```
typedef struct {               /* info about window */
    RECT srect;                /* physical screen rectangle */
    RECT svsrect;              /* saved rectangle (for zooming) */
    FRMTYPE frmtype;           /* frame type */
    short frmatt;              /* frame attribute */
    char *title;               /* window title */
    FRMTYPE svfrmtype;         /* saved frame type (for zooming) */
    BOOLEAN zoomed;            /* is window zoomed? */
    short currow;              /* current row in window */
    short curcol;              /* current column in window */
    BOOLEAN showcur;           /* is cursor visible? */
    int (*drawfcn)();          /* redrawing function (void won't work) */
} WINDOW;

static WINDOW *wind[MAXWIND];  /* window info table */
```

The current location relative to the *physical* screen and the size of the window are kept in the **srect** member. This rectangle *includes* the frame. When the window is zoomed to full-screen size, with **Wzoom**, its old, smaller size is kept in **svsrect** so it can be restored when **Wunzoom** is called. The current frame type (**F_SINGLE**, **F_DOUBLE**, and so on) is kept in the **frmtype** member, the frame attribute is kept in **frmatt**, and the frame title is kept in **title**. A zoomed window has its frame type changed to **F_UNFRAMED** because its frame is off the screen; the **svfrmtype** member saves the old frame type. When the frame is **F_UNFRAMED**, the frame attribute and title don't matter, so there's no need to change them and no need to have a member to save their old values. Member **zoomed** indicates whether the window is currently zoomed. The location of the window's cursor and whether it's visible are recorded in **currow**, **curcol**, and **showcur**. Finally, a pointer to the redrawing function supplied as an argument to **Wnew** is kept in the **drawfcn** member. This function should have been declared of type **void**, but some (defective) C compilers won't permit a pointer to such a function to be declared.

Note that the window module doesn't save the actual data written into the window—that's what the redrawing function is for. Hence, the overhead per window is quite small (less than forty bytes on most machines).

We'll often want the row and column numbers of the lower right corner of a window (the upper left is row 0, column 0, of course). Rather than record these as members of the structure, we'll instead use macros:

```
/*-----------------------------------------------------------------
    WROW2, WCOL2 - lower right corner of window, relative to window
    VALUE: Row or column number. (integer)
----------------------------------------------------------------*/
#define WROW2(w)  (RHEIGHT(&(w)->srect) - 1)
#define WCOL2(w)  (RWIDTH(&(w)->srect) - 1)
```

When we want the size of the interior of the window, we have to remember to deduct the space occupied by the frame from the dimensions of the physical rectangle. Also, when the user supplies a row or column number relative to the window (in **Wwrite**, for example), we have to add one for a framed window to translate it to a coordinate relative to the actual rectangle as kept in the **WINDOW** structure. We can eliminate some repetitive code and reduce the incidences of "off-by-one" errors by relegating these details to a function:

```
/*-----------------------------------------------------------
    dimensions - get dimensions of window
----------------------------------------------------------*/
static void dimensions(w, heightp, widthp, offsetp)
WINDOW *w;                        /* window */
int *heightp;                     /* returned height */
int *widthp;                      /* returned width */
int *offsetp;                     /* returned row/col offset */
{
```

```
    *widthp = RWIDTH(&w->srect);
    *heightp = RHEIGHT(&w->srect);
    if (w->frmtype == F_UNFRAMED)
        *offsetp = 0;
    else {
        *widthp -= 2;
        *heightp -= 2;
        *offsetp = 1;
    }
}
```

6.4.2. Ordering of Windows

There is an order to active windows, from bottom (always the **SCR_WIND**
window) to top. A window may be entirely visible (always true of the top
window, and sometimes true of other windows), partially visible, or
completely obscured. Two global variables maintain the number and current
ordering of active windows:

```
static short order[MAXWIND];    /* order of windows, bottom to top */
static short numwinds;          /* number of windows in order array */
```

A subscript of **order** is the position number; the value (**order[i]**) is the
window number (itself a subscript of the **wind** array). The topmost window
always has subscript **numwinds** –1, and there's a handy macro to get its
number:

```
/*------------------------------------------------------------------
    get_top - get number of top window
    VALUE: Window number. (integer)
------------------------------------------------------------------*/
#define get_top() (order[numwinds - 1])
```

We can use this macro only inside the implementation, but the application
can call a function for the same purpose:

```
/*------------------------------------------------------------------
    Wgettop - get top window
    RETURN: Window number.
------------------------------------------------------------------*/
int Wgettop()
{
    return(get_top());
}
```

Another macro determines if a given window is on top:

```
/*------------------------------------------------------------------
    is_top - determine if window is on top
    VALUE: Is it? (BOOLEAN)
------------------------------------------------------------------*/
#define is_top(wnum) (numwinds > 0 && order[numwinds - 1] == wnum)
```

There are two functions which will add a window to, or remove a window from, the **order** array:

```
/*-----------------------------------------------------------------
      addwind - add window to top of order array, if necessary
-----------------------------------------------------------------*/
static void addwind(wnum)
int wnum;                                /* window */
{
    int i;

    for (i = 0; i < numwinds; i++)
        if (order[i] == wnum)
            return;
    order[numwinds++] = wnum;
    if (numwinds > 1)
        drawfrm(order[numwinds - 2], &GIANT_RECT); /* chg to single */
}

/*-----------------------------------------------------------------
      remwind - remove window from order array
-----------------------------------------------------------------*/
static void remwind(wnum)
int wnum;                                /* window */
{
    int i;

    for (i = 0; i < numwinds; i++)
        if (order[i] == wnum) {
            for (i++; i < numwinds; i++)
                order[i - 1] = order[i];
            numwinds--;
            return;
        }
}
```

Note that **addwind** always adds a new window to the top. It also redraws the frame of the window that used to be on top because, when the frame type is **F_AUTO**, its style must be changed from double lines to single lines.

It's possible for an existing window to be removed from the order array and hence be hidden. You can still write to such a window but nothing will be shown on the screen. This function determines whether a window is hidden:

```
/*-----------------------------------------------------------------
      hidden - determine if window is hidden
      RETURN: Is it?
-----------------------------------------------------------------*/
static BOOLEAN hidden(wnum)
int wnum;                                /* window */
{
    int i;

    for (i = 0; i < numwinds; i++)
        if (order[i] == wnum)
            return(FALSE);
    return(TRUE);
}
```

Now we're ready to look at what's involved in bringing a window to the top. Beyond positioning it in the **order** array, we also need to fix up the screen (some of the window may have become visible, thus covering parts of lower windows). Also, the top window is eligible for a visible cursor. These tasks are done by **Wtop**:

```
/*-----------------------------------------------------------------
    Wtop - force window to top
------------------------------------------------------------------*/
void Wtop(wnum)
int wnum;                                    /* window */
{
    WINDOW *w = wind[wnum];

    if (is_top(wnum))
        return;
    remwind(wnum);
    addwind(wnum);
    reset(&w->srect);
    Wsetcur(wnum, w->currow, w->curcol);
    Wshowcur(wnum, w->showcur);
}
```

We'll get to **reset**, the function that updates part of the screen, in Sec. 6.4.3. The part to be updated is given by the rectangle associated with the window that we just brought to the top. No other area is affected, except for having its cursor suppressed.

The steps necessary to hide a window are similar to those that bring a window to the top:

```
/*-----------------------------------------------------------------
    Whide - hide window
------------------------------------------------------------------*/
void Whide(wnum)
int wnum;                                    /* window */
{
    WINDOW *w = wind[wnum];

    remwind(wnum);
    reset(&w->srect);
    w = wind[wnum = Wgettop()];
    Wsetcur(wnum, w->currow, w->curcol);
    Wshowcur(wnum, w->showcur);
}
```

We didn't call **Wtop** to bring a new window to the top because the rectangle to be updated is the one corresponding to the window we hid, not the one corresponding to the new top window.

Here is the strange function **Wshuffle**:

```
/*-----------------------------------------------------------------
    Wshuffle - force next window to top
------------------------------------------------------------------*/
void Wshuffle()
{
    if (numwinds > 1)
        Wtop(order[1]);
}
```

6.4.3. Window Overlap

Some windowing systems require that all windows be entirely visible at all times; this is called *tiling*. Other systems allow windows to partially or entirely obscure other windows; this is called *overlapping*. Of course, a system capable of overlapping need not do so if the windows don't happen to bump into one another, so an overlapping system is more flexible than a tiling one. In both systems there is usually one window that is active. We've been referring to this as the *top* window, although it may not be the only window that's completely uncovered.

Both approaches require that data written to a window be clipped to the rectangular window boundary. In our design, this boundary is given by the **srect** member of the **WINDOW** structure (Sec. 6.4.1). As this region is exactly rectangular, clipping is easy and fast. For a tiling system, that's all the clipping that's ever necessary. But, for an overlapping system, the data must be further clipped so that what's obscured by higher windows won't be shown. Here things aren't so easy, because the clipping boundary may be an arbitrary polygon.

Several approaches can be used to solve the clipping problem. Most graphics-based windowing systems actually store the clipping polygon along with the other information associated with the window, as a variable-length array of coordinates, for example. The clipping polygon must be recalculated for each affected window whenever an event occurs—such as creation, resizing, or moving of a window—that may change what can be seen. When the window is drawn, every row must be checked against the clipping polygon. We'll call this the *polygon method*.

A second method is *overwriting*. We actually write each window to the screen, from the bottom to the top, as though every window were completely visible. (We still have to clip each window to its rectangular boundary.) Each window will physically overwrite the data from the windows it is supposed to hide. With some physical screen implementations, the user will actually see this happening and will be either entertained, confused, or irritated. To prevent that, the windows can be written first to a buffer (as in the memory-mapped physical display implementation of Sec. 3.7), and then the buffer can be written out after the windows have finished overwriting one another off-stage.

Since we're concerned only with character windows in this book, we can use a method that's easier than the polygon method and faster than the overwriting method, which we'll call the *mask method*. We can get away with this because there are only about 2000 cells on a character display, as opposed to 250,000 to 1,000,000 (or more) pixels on a graphics display. We'll simply maintain a rectangular ownership mask that indicates which window owns each character cell. Given a row and column on the physical screen, the corresponding mask element is the number of the window whose data is visible. *Some* window is responsible for every position, even if it's only the **SCR_WIND** window (Sec. 6.4.1). The mask is declared, allocated, and freed like this:

```
static char **mask = NULL;        /* cell ownership mask */

/*-------------------------------------------------------------------------
    allocmask - allocate mask
-------------------------------------------------------------------------*/
static void allocmask()
{
    int row;

    mask = (char **)xmalloc((maxrow + 1) * sizeof(char *));
    for (row = 0; row <= maxrow; row++)
        mask[row] = xmalloc(maxcol + 1);
}

/*-------------------------------------------------------------------------
    freemask - free mask
-------------------------------------------------------------------------*/
static void freemask()
{
    int row;

    if (mask != NULL) {
        for (row = 0; row <= maxrow; row++)
            free(mask[row]);
        free((char *)mask);
        mask = NULL;
    }
}
```

Wbegin calls **allocmask** and **Wend** calls **freemask**. We can't simply declare **mask** as a two-dimensional array because we have to get **maxrow** and **maxcol** dynamically, according to the size of the physical screen. (It's not always 25-by-80.)

It's straightforward to use the mask: Before writing to the display with the physical screen interface functions, you just check each character against the mask and write only the cells that belong to the window being written. As we'll see, a few optimizations speed this up a lot, so it's not as though every character has to be dealt with individually.

But where do the mask values come from? We construct the mask using an algorithm similar to the overwriting method: We go through the windows from bottom to top, only we write each window's *number* to the mask, not its *data*. A covered cell will have its number overwritten by the window (or windows) that cover it. When we're done, the finished mask will tell us who owns which cells. Unlike the overwriting method itself, the time to write a window is proportional only to the number of cells it covers, and to a lesser extent, to how adjacent they are. It does not depend on the *number* of windows. The time to generate the mask does depend on the number of windows as well as on how big they are.

Here's a small example that illustrates how the mask is generated. We begin with the bottom window, numbered 0, which always fills the mask:

```
00000000000000000000000000000000000000
00000000000000000000000000000000000000
00000000000000000000000000000000000000
00000000000000000000000000000000000000
00000000000000000000000000000000000000
00000000000000000000000000000000000000
00000000000000000000000000000000000000
00000000000000000000000000000000000000
00000000000000000000000000000000000000
00000000000000000000000000000000000000
```

Next, we fill the rectangle covered by window 1:

```
00000000011111111111111111111111111100
00000000011111111111111111111111111100
00000000011111111111111111111111111100
00000000011111111111111111111111111100
00000000011111111111111111111111111100
00000000011111111111111111111111111100
00000000000000000000000000000000000000
00000000000000000000000000000000000000
00000000000000000000000000000000000000
00000000000000000000000000000000000000
```

Then comes window 2:

```
00000000011111111111111111111111111100
00000000011111111111111111111111111100
22222222222222222222111111111111111100
22222222222222222222111111111111111100
22222222222222222222111111111111111100
22222222222222222222111111111111111100
22222222222222222222000000000000000000
22222222222222222222000000000000000000
00000000000000000000000000000000000000
00000000000000000000000000000000000000
```

And we finish with the top window, number 3:

```
00000000011111111111111111111111111100
00000000011111111111111111111111111100
22222222222222222222111111111111111100
22222222222222222222111111111111111100
22222222222222222222111111111111111100
22223333333333333333333333333311111100
22223333333333333333333333333300000000
22223333333333333333333333333300000000
00003333333333333333333333333300000000
00000000000000000000000000000000000000
```

If we need to write, say, window 2, this mask tells us exactly which of its cells should be written. The mask stays the same until a window is created (**Wnew**), a window is eliminated (**Wdispose**), a window is resized or moved (**Wsetphys, Wzoom, Wunzoom**), or the order of windows is changed (**Wtop, Whide, Wshuffle**). Whenever the mask is recalculated, every window in the **order** array (Sec. 6.4.2) has to be redrawn. This is done by redrawing its frame and calling its redrawing function. The most-used functions, and the ones that have to be the fastest, are **Wwrite, Wwrtcells, Wfill**, and **Wslide**, and these don't affect the mask at all (they use it, though).

Normally, only a portion of the physical screen is affected by an event that changes the mask. Processing is speeded up a great deal by localizing mask generation and window redrawing to a rectangle on the physical screen. For example, if a window is eliminated, only the rectangle it covered has to be updated. We'll see that the functions in **window.c** to generate the mask and to redraw the frame, as well as the application's redrawing function, all take a rectangle argument that bounds the area to be treated.

The function **reset** is called whenever the mask has been affected:

```
/*--------------------------------------------------------------------
    reset - recalculate mask rectangle and redraw screen
----------------------------------------------------------------*/
static void reset(srectp)
RECT *srectp;                           /* affected rectangle */
{
    RECT srect, srect2;
    WINDOW *w;
    int i;

    if (srectp->r1 > srectp->r2 || srectp->c1 > srectp->c2)
        return;
    if (!intersect(srectp, maxrow, maxcol, &srect))
        return;
    for (i = 0; i < numwinds; i++) {
        w = wind[order[i]];
        RASG(&srect2, MAX(srect.r1, w->srect.r1),
          MAX(srect.c1, w->srect.c1), MIN(srect.r2, w->srect.r2),
          MIN(srect.c2, w->srect.c2));
        setmask(order[i], &srect2);
    }
    draw(&srect);
}
```

First, we check to see if the mask rectangle is null. This can occur as a result of the arithmetic that some routines use to measure the rectangle affected by their activity. Such a routine might not realize that it is calling **reset** with a nonsensical rectangle, so we catch it in **reset**. Next, we clip the mask rectangle to the size of the mask, with **intersect** (see Sec. 2.6). We generate the mask by taking each window in turn, starting with the bottom. For each we set up a physical screen rectangle that is the intersection of its rectangle with the mask rectangle. This isn't exactly the same as what **intersect** does, so we do it with the **MIN** and **MAX** macros (Sec. 2.5) instead. Then we call **setmask** to place the window's number in the appropriate part of the mask. Once the mask is generated, we call **draw** to redraw the affected part of the screen. Here is **setmask** (we'll look at **draw** in Sec. 6.4.4):

```
/*--------------------------------------------------------------
    setmask - fill mask rectangle with window number
----------------------------------------------------------*/
static void setmask(wnum, srectp)
int wnum;                               /* window */
RECT *srectp;                           /* rectangle to fill */
{
```

```
        RECT srect;
        int r;

        if (!intersect(srectp, maxrow, maxcol, &srect))
            return;
        for (r = srect.r1; r <= srect.r2; r++)
            if (srect.c2 >= srect.c1)
                setmem(&mask[r][srect.c1], RWIDTH(&srect), wnum);
    }
```

We intersect the rectangle with the physical screen yet again, although it
isn't necessary to do so, just to be extra safe. Then we write a row of the
mask with **setmem** (Sec. 2.8).

A good way to see the mask in actual use is to look at **Wwrite**:

```
/*-----------------------------------------------------------------
    Wwrite - write string
-------------------------------------------------------------------*/
void Wwrite(wnum, wrow, wcol, ncols, str, att)
int wnum;                                /* window */
int wrow;                                /* starting row */
int wcol;                                /* starting column */
int ncols;                               /* number of columns to write */
char *str;                               /* string */
int att;                                 /* attribute */
{
    WINDOW *w = wind[wnum];
    int c, sr, sc1, sc2, height, width, offset, state, colstop;
    char *s;

    if (wrow < 0 || wcol < 0)
        return;
    dimensions(w, &height, &width, &offset);
    if (wrow >= height || wcol >= width)
        return;
    sr = w->srect.r1 + wrow + offset;
    if (is_top(wnum)) {
        ncols = MIN(ncols, width - wcol);
        PSwrite(sr, w->srect.c1 + wcol + offset, ncols, str, att);
    }
    else {
        state = 1;
        colstop = MIN(width, wcol + ncols);
        for (c = wcol; c < colstop && *str != '\0'; c++, str++) {
            sc2 = w->srect.c1 + c + offset;
            switch (state) {
            case 1:
                if (mask[sr][sc2] == (char)wnum) {
                    sc1 = sc2;
                    s = str;
                    state = 2;
                }
                continue;
            case 2:
                if (mask[sr][sc2] != (char)wnum) {
                    PSwrite(sr, sc1, sc2 - sc1, s, att);
                    state = 1;
                }
            }
        }
        if (state == 2) {
            sc2 = w->srect.c1 + c + offset;
            PSwrite(sr, sc1, sc2 - sc1, s, att);
        }
    }
}
```

We call **dimensions** (Sec. 6.4.1) to get the height, width, and offset of the window. We add the offset to the row and column every time we reference them. (The offset is either 1 or 0, depending on whether the window is framed.) Because most writing is probably to the top window, that's worth a special case. We ignore overlap and just clip **ncols** to the window boundary, without using the mask at all. The actual writing is done by **PSwrite**.

Writing to a window that isn't on top is much more complicated, especially if we want to be fast. The problem is that we can't assume that the entire row can be written; separate pieces of it might be covered by other windows. Still, we want to call **PSwrite** as few times as possible—certainly not for every character, if we can help it. The fancy **for** loop fixes **sc1** and then extends **sc2** as far as it can to include cells in the mask owned by this window. When a foreign cell is encountered, or when the right edge of the window is reached, the substring is written out. If there's more remaining, **sc1** is repositioned and the process repeats. Because more than a few windows is uncommon, usually there will be either no calls to **PSwrite** because the row is completely hidden, or one call because a corner of the window is covered by only one other window. Less often, **PSwrite** will be called several times. Because of this substring optimization, we would write to the top window with a single call to **PSwrite** even if we didn't treat it as a special case. But there is still time to be saved by not consulting the mask for each character in the **for** loop.

Wwrtcells uses a similar strategy:

```
/*-----------------------------------------------------------------
    Wwrtcells - write vector of CELLs
------------------------------------------------------------------*/
void Wwrtcells(wnum, wrow, wcol, captr, ncols)
int wnum;                               /* window */
int wrow;                               /* starting row */
int wcol;                               /* starting column */
CELL *captr;                            /* CELLs */
int ncols;                              /* number of columns to write */
{
    WINDOW *w = wind[wnum];
    int i, sr, sc1, sc2, height, width, offset, state;
    CELL *p;

    if (wrow < 0 || wcol < 0 || ncols <= 0)
        return;
    dimensions(w, &height, &width, &offset);
    if (wrow >= height || wcol >= width)
        return;
    ncols = MIN(ncols, width - wcol);
    sr = w->srect.rl + wrow + offset;
    if (is_top(wnum))
        PSwrtcells(sr, w->srect.cl + wcol + offset, captr, ncols);
```

```
    else {
        state = 1;
        for (i = 0; i < ncols; i++, captr++) {
            sc2 = w->srect.cl + wcol + i + offset;
            switch (state) {
            case 1:
                if (mask[sr][sc2] == (char)wnum) {
                    scl = sc2;
                    p = captr;
                    state = 2;
                }
                continue;
            case 2:
                if (mask[sr][sc2] != (char)wnum) {
                    PSwrtcells(sr, scl, p, sc2 - scl);
                    state = 1;
                }
            }
        }
        if (state == 2) {
            sc2 = w->srect.cl + wcol + i + offset;
            PSwrtcells(sr, scl, p, sc2 - scl);
        }
    }
}
```

The other major window functions (**Wfill**, **Wslide**, and so on) will be presented in Sec. 6.4.9. There are still some thorny issues to be discussed first.

6.4.4. Redrawing Windows

So far, we've dealt with the problem of clipping data to the window boundary and to the polygon defined by overlapping windows. Now let's talk about redrawing a window when part of it that used to be covered gets uncovered. We know how to write to the window—**Wwrite** does that. The issue is knowing *what* to write.

Several approaches might be used:

1. Allocate a two-dimensional array of **CELL**s for each window to hold its entire contents, including the part that's currently obscured. Change **Wwrite** so that it copies data to this array in addition to the screen. When part of the window has to be rewritten, take the data from the array. This is simple, fast, and painless for the application programmer. It uses some extra memory, but on many computer systems that may not be of concern. The chief reason for not using this method here is that it's what the virtual screen module does (among other things). We'll show how this method is programmed, and how it interfaces with the window module, in Chapter 7.

2. Use an array, as in the previous method, but make it just large enough to hold the data that's *not* currently on the screen. The data that is on the screen will be in the physical screen buffer. Obviously this saves

memory, particularly when there are just a few large, mostly non-over-lapped, windows—the most common situation by far. Windows that are completely visible are especially fast to write to because they don't require anything to be written to the array. The programming is extremely complicated, however. Rob Pike invented, and has patented[1], this method; see [Pik83] for further details.

3. Don't worry about repairing damaged areas—let the application figure out what's wrong and deal with it. This approach is OK if the windows are completely static, with nothing popping up or changing size. But it's unworkable in a more dynamic (and more typical) situation.

4. When a portion of a window has to be redrawn, calculate a rectangle, relative to the window, that encloses it, and tell the application to redraw that rectangle. Many windowing systems (such as Apple's Macintosh) use an event queue to tell applications about events that affect them, such as mouse movements, key presses, or messages from other processes. A *window repaint* message is put on the event queue by the window module; the process will receive the message at some point and fix the damage. Our approach doesn't require an event queue. The application designates a redrawing function when a window is created, and we make a repair request by calling that function. If the window module as designed in this book is used in a system with an event queue, and you want to use it for this purpose, you can just program a simple redrawing function that enqueues a message and returns.

The redrawing-function method was explained from the application's point of view in Sec. 6.2. We'll show the implementation here.

Recall that **reset** (from the previous section) calls **draw** once the mask has been brought up to date. This function is given a physical screen rectangle. It figures out which windows own turf in that area, computes a rectangle relative to each one of them, and then calls **drawwind** to do the necessary repairs:

```
/*----------------------------------------------------------- ---------- ---
    draw - draw all windows in physical screen rectangle
----------------------------------------------------------------------------*/
static int draw(srectp)
RECT *srectp;                        /* affected physical screen rect */
{
    WINDOW *w;
    int r, c, i;
    BOOLEAN visible[MAXWIND];
    RECT wrect;
```

---

[1]"Dynamic Generation and Overlaying of Graphic Windows for Multiple Active Program Storage Areas," November 26, 1985, Patent 4,555,775.

```
    for (i = 0; i < MAXWIND; i++)
        visible[i] = FALSE;
    for (r = srectp->r1; r <= srectp->r2; r++)
        for (c = srectp->c1; c <= srectp->c2; c++)
            visible[mask[r][c]] = TRUE;
    for (i = 0; i < numwinds; i++) {
        if (!visible[order[i]])
            continue;
        w = wind[order[i]];
        RASG(&wrect, srectp->r1 - w->srect.r1, srectp->c1 - w->srect.c1,
            srectp->r2 - w->srect.r1, srectp->c2 - w->srect.c1);
        if (!intersect(&wrect, WROW2(w), WCOL2(w), &wrect))
            continue;
        drawwind(order[i], &wrect);
    }
    return(0);
}
```

The **visible** array records which windows own any cells in the rectangle to be drawn. Once we've determined that, we then loop through all the windows in the **order** array. For each, we must calculate a rectangle relative to that window. This is done by translating from physical screen to window coordinates, in the **RASG** statement, and then intersecting the resulting rectangle with the window.

The function **drawwind** fixes up a single window:

```
/*-------------------------------------------------------------------
    drawwind - draw one window's frame and interior
--------------------------------------------------------------------*/
static void drawwind(wnum, wrectp)
int wnum;                               /* window */
RECT *wrectp;                           /* affected window-relative rect */
{
    WINDOW *w = wind[wnum];
    RECT wrect;

    drawfrm(wnum, wrectp);
    RCPY(&wrect, wrectp);
    if (w->frmtype != F_UNFRAMED) {
        wrect.r1--;
        wrect.c1--;
        wrect.r2--;
        wrect.c2--;
        if (!intersect(&wrect, WROW2(w) - 2, WCOL2(w) - 2, &wrect))
            return;
    }
    if (w->drawfcn != NULL)
        (*w->drawfcn)(wnum, &wrect);
}
```

First, it calls **drawfrm** to redraw the part of the frame that lies within the rectangle. We'll look at this function in Sec. 6.4.6. If the window is framed, the rectangle then has to be reduced to cover interior cells only, because those are the only ones that the application can write. There might not be any intersection with the interior—the damage could have affected only the frame. If the interior was damaged, we call the application's redrawing function if there was one.

6.4.5. *Window Sizing*

It's fairly easy for **Wsetphys** to resize a window because the hard work of fixing up the mask and redrawing the screen is already handled by **reset**. The only trick is determining what portion of the physical screen is affected by the change in the window's size. We calculate the fixup rectangle as follows: If the resized window is currently hidden, it currently owns no mask cells, so the fixup rectangle is the same as the new size. (Setting the size with **Wsetphys** un-hides a hidden window.) If the resized window does own mask cells, the fixup rectangle is the one that encloses just the old and new rectangles, as calculated by the function **enclosing** (Sec. 2.6).

One other feature of **Wsetphys** is that it automatically zooms a window if its sizing rectangle is just off the screen, as discussed in Sec. 6.2. Here's the code:

```
/*-------------------------------------------------------------------
    Wsetphys - set window's physical size
-----------------------------------------------------------------*/
void Wsetphys(wnum, srectp)
int wnum;                               /* window */
RECT *srectp;                           /* size (including frame) */
{
    WINDOW *w = wind[wnum];
    RECT srect, srectfixup;
    BOOLEAN needzoom;

    if (srectp->rl < -1 || srectp->rl > maxrow || srectp->cl < -1 ||
      srectp->cl > maxcol || RHEIGHT(srectp) < 1 || RWIDTH(srectp) < 1)
        return;
    needzoom = srectp->rl < 0 && srectp->cl < 0 &&
      RHEIGHT(srectp) > maxrow + 1 && RWIDTH(srectp) > maxcol + 1;
    (void)intersect(srectp, maxrow, maxcol, &srect);
    if (hidden(wnum))
        RCPY(&srectfixup, &srect);
    else
        enclosing(&srect, &w->srect, &srectfixup);
    RCPY(&w->srect, &srect);
    addwind(wnum);
    reset(&srectfixup);
    if (needzoom)
        Wzoom(wnum);
    Wshowcur(wnum, w->showcur);
}
```

A resized window is not moved to the top if it's already in the **order** array; **addwind** puts it on top only if it actually has to be added. If it did get added, we want to turn on the cursor if the window has its cursor on. This is what the call to **Wshowcur** is for.

A window's size can be taken from its **WINDOW** structure, with an appropriate adjustment if the frame isn't to be included:

```
/*-------------------------------------------------------------------
    Wgetphys - get window's physical size
-------------------------------------------------------------------*/
void Wgetphys(wnum, srectp, inclfrm)
int wnum;                                /* window */
RECT *srectp;                            /* size (returned) */
BOOLEAN inclfrm;                         /* should size include frame? */
{
    WINDOW *w = wind[wnum];

    RCPY(srectp, &w->srect);
    if (w->frmtype != F_UNFRAMED && !inclfrm) {
        srectp->r1++;
        srectp->c1++;
        srectp->r2--;
        srectp->c2--;
    }
}
```

Zooming a window means changing it to be unframed and setting its size to that of the physical screen. Its old frame type and size are first saved so it can be unzoomed:

```
/*-------------------------------------------------------------------
    Wzoom - make window full screen
-------------------------------------------------------------------*/
void Wzoom(wnum)
int wnum;                                /* window */
{
    WINDOW *w = wind[wnum];
    RECT srect;

    if (w->zoomed)
        return;
    w->zoomed = TRUE;
    RCPY(&w->svsrect, &w->srect);
    w->svfrmtype = w->frmtype;
    w->frmtype = F_UNFRAMED;
    RASG(&srect, 0, 0, PSheight() - 1, PSwidth() - 1);
    Wsetphys(wnum, &srect);
}
```

Wunzoom just restores the frame type and window size:

```
/*-------------------------------------------------------------------
    Wunzoom - restore window to former size
-------------------------------------------------------------------*/
void Wunzoom(wnum)
int wnum;                                /* window */
{
    WINDOW *w = wind[wnum];

    if (!w->zoomed)
        return;
    w->zoomed = FALSE;
    w->frmtype = w->svfrmtype;
    Wsetphys(wnum, &w->svsrect);
}
```

Wiszoomed is trivial:

```
/*------------------------------------------------------------------
    Wiszoomed - determine if window is zoomed
    RETURN: Is it?
-------------------------------------------------------------------*/
BOOLEAN Wiszoomed(wnum)
int wnum;                                  /* window */
{
    return(wind[wnum]->zoomed);
}
```

6.4.6. Window Frames

Three styles of frames are supported: single lines, double lines, and blanks. Symbols for the line-drawing characters we need are defined in **display.h** (Sec. 2.2). There are six characters used to draw a frame: four corner characters, a horizontal-line character, and a vertical-line character. The following declarations make it easy to pick up the necessary characters by using the frame style and the frame element as subscripts of the array **frame**:

```
#define UL       0                        /* upper left element */
#define UR       1                        /* upper right element */
#define LR       2                        /* lower right element */
#define LL       3                        /* lower left element */
#define H        4                        /* horizontal element */
#define V        5                        /* vertical element */
#define MAXELTS  6                        /* number of elements in frame */

#define FSINGLE  0                        /* single frame style */
#define FDOUBLE  1                        /* double frame style */
#define FBLANK   2                        /* blank frame style */
#define MAXFRAMES 3                       /* number of frame styles */

static char frame[MAXFRAMES][MAXELTS] = {     /* frame elements */
    {C_UL,  C_UR,  C_LR,  C_LL,  C_H,  C_V},  /* single */
    {C_ULD, C_URD, C_LRD, C_LLD, C_HD, C_VD}, /* double */
    {' ',   ' ',   ' ',   ' ',   ' ',  ' '}   /* blank */
};
```

As an example, the lower right corner element of a double frame is given by **frame[FDOUBLE][LR]**. Additional frame styles can be added to the window module by augmenting the **frame** array, without changing the basic drawing algorithm.

Two little routines help to draw horizontal and vertical framing lines:

```
/*------------------------------------------------------------------
    hline - draw horizontal line
-------------------------------------------------------------------*/
static void hline(wnum, wrow, wcol1, wcol2, chr, att)
int wnum;                                  /* window */
int wrow;                                  /* row */
int wcol1;                                 /* starting column */
int wcol2;                                 /* ending column */
char chr;                                  /* character */
int att;                                   /* attribute */
{
```

```
    RECT wrect;

    RASG(&wrect, wrow, wcol1, wrow, wcol2);
    Wfill(wnum, &wrect, chr, att);
}

/*-----------------------------------------------------------------
    vline - draw vertical line
-----------------------------------------------------------------*/
static void vline(wnum, wrow1, wrow2, wcol, chr, att)
int wnum;                               /* window */
int wrow1;                              /* starting row */
int wrow2;                              /* ending row */
int wcol;                               /* column */
char chr;                               /* character */
int att;                                /* attribute */
{
    RECT wrect;

    RASG(&wrect, wrow1, wcol, wrow2, wcol);
    Wfill(wnum, &wrect, chr, att);
}
```

The function **drawfrm** draws the part of the frame that lies within a given rectangle. Initially, when a window is created, that rectangle covers the entire window. Later, when only the damaged part of the frame has to be repaired, **drawfrm** is called from **drawwind** (Sec. 6.4.4) with a smaller rectangle. First, **drawfrm** has to decide which style should be used. For example, if the frame type is **F_AUTO**, the style will be **F_DOUBLE** if the window is on top and **F_SINGLE** otherwise. Then it draws the top line, interspersing the title if there is one. It completes the frame by drawing the sides, with **vline**, the bottom, with **hline**, and the remaining corners. The code for **drawfrm** is complicated by the need to restrict the drawing to the rectangle that requires updating. If the entire frame were drawn every time, things would be much simpler, but tests with this approach showed that too much time was wasted when only a small part of the frame was actually in need of repair. You may not wish to go through every detail of this function— much of it is tedious and not especially enlightening. Note one trick, however. Because we need to write into the frame area, we temporarily change the frame type to **F_UNFRAMED**.

```
/*-----------------------------------------------------------------
    drawfrm - draw complete or partial frame around window
-----------------------------------------------------------------*/
static void drawfrm(wnum, wrectp)
int wnum;                               /* window */
RECT *wrectp;                           /* rectangle to draw within */
{
    WINDOW *w = wind[wnum];
    RECT wrect, wrect2; /* inside */
    FRMTYPE savetype;
    int c, style, wrow2, wcol2;
    char *t;

    wrow2 = WROW2(w);
    wcol2 = WCOL2(w);
```

```
if (wrow2 == 0 || wcol2 == 0)
    return;
if (!intersect(wrectp, wrow2, wcol2, &wrect))
    return;
RASG(&wrect2, MAX(wrect.r1, 1), MAX(wrect.c1, 1),
  MIN(wrect.r2, wrow2 - 1), MIN(wrect.c2, wcol2 - 1));
switch (w->frmtype) {
case F_UNFRAMED:
    return;
case F_AUTO:
    if (is_top(wnum))
        style = FDOUBLE;
    else
        style = FSINGLE;
    break;
case F_SINGLE:
    style = FSINGLE;
    break;
case F_DOUBLE:
    style = FDOUBLE;
    break;
case F_BLANK:
    style = FBLANK;
    break;
}
savetype = w->frmtype;
w->frmtype = F_UNFRAMED; /* allow access to frame itself */
if (wrect.r1 == 0) {
    if (wrect.c1 == 0)
        Wwrite(wnum, 0, 0, 1, &frame[style][UL], w->frmatt);
    if (w->title == NULL)
        t = "";
    else
        t = w->title;
    for (c = 1; c <= wrect2.c2 && *t != '\0'; c++, t++) {
        if (c >= wrect2.c1)
            if (*t == ' ')
                Wwrite(wnum, 0, c, 1, &frame[style][H], w->frmatt);
            else
                Wwrite(wnum, 0, c, 1, t, w->frmatt);
    }
    if (c <= wrect.c2)
        hline(wnum, 0, c, wrect.c2, frame[style][H], w->frmatt);
    if (wrect.c2 == wcol2)
        Wwrite(wnum, 0, wrect.c2, 1, &frame[style][UR], w->frmatt);
}
if (wrect.c1 == 0)
    vline(wnum, wrect2.r1, wrect2.r2, 0, frame[style][V], w->frmatt);
if (wrect.c2 == wcol2)
    vline(wnum, wrect2.r1, wrect2.r2, wrect.c2, frame[style][V],
        w->frmatt);
if (wrect.r2 == wrow2) {
    if (wrect.c1 == 0)
        Wwrite(wnum, wrect.r2, 0, 1, &frame[style][LL], w->frmatt);
    hline(wnum, wrect.r2, wrect2.c1, wrect2.c2, frame[style][H],
        w->frmatt);
    if (wrect.c2 == wcol2)
        Wwrite(wnum, wrect.r2, wrect.c2, 1, &frame[style][LR],
            w->frmatt);
}
w->frmtype = savetype;
}
```

The application sets the frame type with **Wsetfrm** (it's **F_SINGLE** by default):

```
/*-------------------------------------------------------------------
    Wsetfrm - set window's frame appearance
--------------------------------------------------------------------*/
void Wsetfrm(wnum, frmtype, frmatt, title)
int wnum;                                /* window */
FRMTYPE frmtype;                         /* frame type (F_UNFRAMED, F_AUTO,
                                             F_SINGLE, F_DOUBLE, F_BLANK) */
int frmatt;                              /* frame attribute */
char *title;                             /* frame title */
{
    WINDOW *w = wind[wnum];

    w->frmtype = frmtype;
    w->frmatt = frmatt;
    if (title != NULL) {
        if (w->title != NULL)
            free(w->title);
        if ((w->title = malloc(strlen(title) + 1)) != NULL)
            strcpy(w->title, title);
    }
    drawfrm(wnum, &GIANT_RECT);
}
```

6.4.7. Module Initiation and Termination

Wbegin initializes the physical screen module, sets up **maxrow** and **maxcol**, allocates memory for the mask, and creates the background window, **SCR_WIND**:

```
/*-------------------------------------------------------------------
    Wbegin - initialize window module
--------------------------------------------------------------------*/
void Wbegin()
{
    static WINDOW scr_wind;

    PSbegin();
    maxrow = PSheight() - 1;
    maxcol = PSwidth() - 1;
    allocmask();
    RASG(&scr_wind.srect, 0, 0, maxrow, maxcol);
    scr_wind.currow = scr_wind.curcol = 0;
    scr_wind.showcur = FALSE;
    scr_wind.zoomed = FALSE;
    scr_wind.frmtype = F_UNFRAMED;
    scr_wind.frmatt = A_NORM;
    scr_wind.title = NULL;
    scr_wind.drawfcn = draw0;
    wind[SCR_WIND] = &scr_wind;
    Wtop(SCR_WIND);
}
```

The redrawing function for **SCR_WIND** just fills it with spaces:

```
/*-------------------------------------------------------------------
    draw0 - redrawing function for window zero (SCR_WIND)
    RETURN: Nothing (declared int to get through some compilers).
-------------------------------------------------------------------*/
static int draw0(wnum, wrectp)
int wnum;
RECT *wrectp;
{
    Wfill(wnum, wrectp, ' ', A_NORM);
    return(0);
}
```

The call to **Wtop** installs **SCR_WIND** into the **order** array and executes **draw0**. Thus, calling **Wbegin** clears the screen.

    Wend doesn't have much to do at all:

```
/*-------------------------------------------------------------------
    Wend - terminate window module
-------------------------------------------------------------------*/
void Wend()
{
    freemask();
    PSend();
}
```

6.4.8. Window Creation and Elimination

Now we're ready to see how **Wnew** creates a new window:

```
/*-------------------------------------------------------------------
    Wnew - create new window
    RETURN: Window number.
-------------------------------------------------------------------*/
int Wnew(drawfcn)
int (*drawfcn)();                        /* redraw function */
{
    WINDOW *w;
    int wnum;

    if (numwinds == MAXWIND)
        fatal("too many windows");
    for (wnum = 0; wnum < MAXWIND; wnum++)
        if (wind[wnum] == NULL)
            break;
    if (wnum == MAXWIND)
        fatal("Wnew - invalid numwinds");
    if ((wind[wnum] = w = (WINDOW *)malloc(sizeof(WINDOW))) == NULL)
        return(SCR_WIND);
    RASG(&w->srect, 0, 0, 0, 0);
    w->currow = w->curcol = 0;
    w->showcur = w->zoomed = FALSE;
    w->frmtype = F_SINGLE;
    w->frmatt = A_NORM;
    w->title = NULL;
    w->drawfcn = drawfcn;
    return(wnum);
}
```

    The window number is determined by what pointer in the **wind** array is available. (We'll see in a moment that **Wdispose** sets the pointer to **NULL** when it disposes of a window.) Then the **WINDOW** structure itself is allocated and initialized. We won't know the size until **Wsetphys** is called, so we don't insert the window into the **order** array until then; the new window is initially hidden.

To dispose of a window, we have to remove it from the **order** array, reset the screen, and possibly change the frame of the new top window from **F_SINGLE** to **F_DOUBLE** if the disposed-of window used to be on top. Also, a new top window has the right to have its cursor shown. Then we free the space occupied by the **WINDOW** structure and set the pointer to **NULL**, to indicate its availability. Here's the code for **Wdispose**:

```
/*-------------------------------------------------------------------
    Wdispose - eliminate window
-----------------------------------------------------------------*/
void Wdispose(wnum)
int wnum;                                  /* window */
{
    WINDOW *w = wind[wnum], *w2;
    int wnum2;

    if (wnum <= 0)
        return;
    remwind(wnum);
    reset(&w->srect);
    wnum2 = order[numwinds - 1];
    w2 = wind[wnum2];
    drawfrm(wnum2, &GIANT_RECT); /* might be new top window */
    Wsetcur(wnum2, w2->currow, w2->curcol);
    Wshowcur(wnum2, w2->showcur);
    if (w->title != NULL)
        free(w->title);
    free((char *)w);
    wind[wnum] = NULL;
}
```

6.4.9. Remaining Window Operations

Wfill first finds the intersection between the rectangle to be filled and the window's interior. Then, like **Wwrite** and **Wrtcells**, it treats the top window as a special case because the mask doesn't have to be consulted. The rectangle to be filled is translated to physical screen coordinates, and then **PSfill** is called. If the window isn't on top, it is filled by calling **Wwrite** for each row. **Wwrite** will use the mask to ensure that only the proper cells are written to.

```
/*-------------------------------------------------------------------
    Wfill - fill rectangle
-----------------------------------------------------------------*/
void Wfill(wnum, wrectp, chr, att)
int wnum;                                  /* window */
RECT *wrectp;                              /* rectangle */
char chr;                                  /* fill character */
int att;                                   /* fill attribute */
{
```

```
    WINDOW *w = wind[wnum];
    RECT wrect, srect;
    char s[100];
    int i, ncols, height, width, offset;

    dimensions(w, &height, &width, &offset);
    if (!intersect(wrectp, height - 1, width - 1, &wrect))
        return;
    if (is_top(wnum)) {
        RASG(&srect, w->srect.r1 + wrect.r1 + offset,
            w->srect.c1 + wrect.c1 + offset, w->srect.r1 + wrect.r2 + offset,
            w->srect.c1 + wrect.c2 + offset);
        PSfill(&srect, chr, att);
    }
    else {
        ncols = RWIDTH(&wrect);
        if (ncols >= sizeof(s))
            fatal("Wfill 1");
        strrep(s, chr, ncols);
        for (i = wrect.r1; i <= wrect.r2; i++)
            Wwrite(wnum, i, wrect.c1, ncols, s, att);
    }
}
```

Wslide is actually easy to program because we're not obligated to do anything—we have the right to give up and return **FALSE**. This we do if the window isn't on top. It's too much trouble to try to slide it and obey the mask at the same time. Of course, just because the window isn't on top doesn't mean part of it is obscured, but we're not going to worry about that case either. One justification for this is that we're assuming that the user's eyes are focused on the top window, so inefficient sliding of other windows (by rewriting them) might escape notice. If the window is on top, we calculate exactly the proper window-relative rectangle to be slid, translate it to physical screen coordinates, and call **PSslide** (which itself might return **FALSE**).

```
/*-------------------------------------------------------------------
    Wslide - slide rectangle
    RETURN: Was slide performed?
-------------------------------------------------------------------*/
BOOLEAN Wslide(wnum, wrectp, dir, dist)
int wnum;                               /* window */
RECT *wrectp;                           /* rectangle */
int dir;                                /* direction */
int dist;                               /* distance */
{
    WINDOW *w = wind[wnum];
    RECT wrect, srect;
    int height, width, offset;

    if (!is_top(wnum)) /* not worth dealing with */
        return(FALSE);
    dimensions(w, &height, &width, &offset);
    if (!intersect(wrectp, height - 1, width - 1, &wrect))
        return(TRUE);
    switch (dir) {
    case DIR_UP:
        wrect.r1 = MAX(wrect.r1, dist);
        break;
    case DIR_DOWN:
        wrect.r2 = MIN(wrect.r2, height - dist - 1);
        break;
```

```
        case DIR_LEFT:
            wrect.cl = MAX(wrect.cl, dist);
            break;
        case DIR_RIGHT:
            wrect.c2 = MIN(wrect.c2, width - dist - 1);
        }
        if (wrect.rl > wrect.r2 || wrect.cl > wrect.c2)
            return(TRUE);
        RASG(&srect, w->srect.rl + wrect.rl + offset,
            w->srect.cl + wrect.cl + offset, w->srect.rl + wrect.r2 + offset,
            w->srect.cl + wrect.c2 + offset);
        return(PSslide(&srect, dir, dist));
    }
```

Setting a window's cursor position involves updating its **WINDOW** structure and, if it's on top, calling **PSsetcur**:

```
/*-------------------------------------------------------------------
    Wsetcur - set cursor position
-------------------------------------------------------------------*/
void Wsetcur(wnum, wrow, wcol)
int wnum;                                /* window */
int wrow;                                /* row */
int wcol;                                /* column */
{
    WINDOW *w = wind[wnum];
    int height, width, offset;

    dimensions(w, &height, &width, &offset);
    if (wrow < 0 || wrow >= height || wcol < 0 || wcol >= width)
        return;
    w->currow = wrow;
    w->curcol = wcol;
    if (is_top(wnum))
        PSsetcur(w->srect.rl + wrow + offset, w->srect.cl + wcol + offset);
}
```

Similarly, **Wshowcur** updates the **WINDOW** structure and calls **PSshowcur**:

```
/*-------------------------------------------------------------------
    Wshowcur - turn cursor on or off
-------------------------------------------------------------------*/
void Wshowcur(wnum, on)
int wnum;                                /* window */
BOOLEAN on;                              /* switch */
{
    WINDOW *w = wind[wnum];

    w->showcur = on;
    if (is_top(wnum))
        PSshowcur(on);
}
```

6.5. Summary

Our goal in this chapter was to superimpose windows onto the physical screen interface of Chapter 3. Each window behaves much like a small screen, and the window functions for writing strings, filling and sliding rect-angles, and adjusting the cursor parallel those for the physical screen.

Our window module dealt with two primary problems: translating window coordinates to screen coordinates, and clipping displayed text to the region of the window that's visible. Because windows can overlap arbitrarily, the clipping boundary can be an arbitrary polygon. Since we're dealing only with characters, we were able to use a simple mask array to record which window owns each cell on the screen. Bit-oriented windowing systems can't use such a straightforward scheme because there are too many bits.

We didn't have to worry about portability in this chapter, because every-thing we did relied on the abstractions provided by the physical screen and virtual keyboard modules. The pain we went through to achieve portability there finally paid off.

We showed how to program with the window interface by redoing the screen module of the editor described in Chapter 5. The new editor takes the same keyboard commands as the original one (the main module is identical), but now the user can see two buffers at once, each occupying half the screen.

Windows must be smaller than the physical screen, and an application using them has to supply a redrawing function to repair damaged areas that are uncovered by removal or resizing of other windows. In the next chapter we'll introduce virtual screens, which lift these two restrictions.

CHAPTER 7

Virtual Screens

7.1. Properties of Virtual Screens

Virtual screens have two big advantages over windows:

1. They can be of any reasonable size, even larger than the physical screen. At least some of the virtual screen appears in a window, which itself can be of arbitrary size, although not larger than the physical screen. You need not worry about scrolling the virtual screen to make other parts of it visible if you don't want to. The virtual screen module automatically scrolls it as you move the cursor about.

2. Redrawing of a virtual screen's window is done automatically as overlapping windows are taken away. You do not supply a redrawing function. This make programming easier because you can write to the virtual screen just once without making preparations to write the same information again later on.

The impact of these two advantages is that an application can really treat the virtual screen as a giant physical screen, assuming that all of it can be seen and that none of it will be overlapped. Of course, this is only *virtually* true, but scrolling and redrawing do a good job of faking it.

The disadvantage of virtual screens is that the module takes up about

8000 bytes, with additional space to store each virtual screen. There's also a slight speed disadvantage when creating a new virtual screen, but this is counterbalanced by the fact that the window can be redrawn very quickly from the virtual screen storage, usually more quickly than the application could have recalculated the data. Whether a virtual screen or a window is best will vary from application to application, and even from situation to situation within an application. Fortunately, there's no problem mixing virtual screens and windows (virtual screens use windows, after all), so a hybrid approach is often best.

The structure of this chapter parallels that of Chapter 6. We'll describe the virtual screen interface—the VS functions—and use them to rewrite the screen module of the text editor that we coded in Chapter 5. Then we'll look at the code of the module itself. There's also a section on the pragmatics of using virtual screens in applications. This deals with strategic questions like, "How should the size of a virtual screen be determined?" and, "How should the window be moved relative to the virtual screen?"

7.2. Virtual Screen Interface

Much of the virtual screen interface resembles the physical screen and window interfaces, particularly the functions to write strings and fill and slide rectangles. A few functions, such as the one to move a window, are unique.

You should include the header file **vscreen.h** before calling the virtual screen module, although there's nothing in this file other than declarations for the interface functions, all of which are either **void** or **int**. You initialize the virtual screen module with **VSbegin** and terminate it with **VSend**:

```
/*-----------------------------------------------------------------
        VSbegin - initialize virtual screen module
-----------------------------------------------------------------*/
void VSbegin()

/*-----------------------------------------------------------------
        VSend - terminate virtual screen module
-----------------------------------------------------------------*/
void VSend()
```

VSbegin initializes the window and physical screen modules, too, so you must not call **Wbegin** or **PSbegin** yourself. You must not call **Wend** or **PSend**, either. If you're using the keyboard module (Chap. 4), you will have to call **Kbegin** and **Kend**.

You create a new virtual screen (rectangular array of **CELL**s) and a window through which to see it with **VSnew**. It automatically calls **Wnew** to create the window and then **Wsetphys** to set its size according to the physi-

cal screen rectangle that you specify. This does not include the frame even if
the window has one.

```
/*------------------------------------------------------------------
    VSnew - create virtual screen
    RETURN: virtual screen number or -1 on error
--------------------------------------------------------------*/
int VSnew(nrows, ncols, srectp, title, att)
int nrows;                              /* number of rows */
int ncols;                              /* number of columns */
RECT *srectp;                           /* window's physical size & location */
char *title;                            /* window's frame title */
int att;                                /* window's frame attribute */
```

The virtual screen will be **nrows** high and **ncols** wide. It may be
smaller than, bigger than, or the same size as the window. If it's smaller, the
entire virtual screen will be shown pushed up against the upper left corner of
the window, and the excess window area will be blank. If it's bigger, only
part of the virtual screen can be seen at any time—initially, the upper left
corner of it. If the cursor attempts to move outside the window, the window
will move relative to the virtual screen, so the cursor always stays within the
window (even if the cursor is currently turned off). We'll say more about this
side effect of moving the cursor when we discuss **VSsetcur**. The window can
also be explicitly moved relative to the virtual screen (*panned*) by calling
VSpan.

If the argument **title** is **NULL**, the window is unframed (type
F_UNFRAMED). Otherwise, the window has a single frame (**F_SINGLE**),
with the given title (see Sec. 6.2). You can use a null string ("") if you want
an untitled, but framed, window. (It's possible to adjust the frame type with
Wsetfrm using a technique that will be discussed later in this section along
with **VSgetwnum**.) The attribute of the frame is given by the **att** argument,
which affects the frame only; the attributes of the virtual screen's contents
depend on how they're written.

You can have up to twenty-five virtual screens, the same as the
maximum number of windows. **VSnew** returns a virtual screen number
which is used in subsequent virtual screen functions. There is no relationship between a virtual screen number and its associated window number, but
there is a function to get the window number from the virtual screen number
(**VSgetwnum**), along with the inverse function to get the virtual screen
number from the window number (**VSgetvsnum**).

Each virtual screen uses a small amount (about fourteen bytes) of
bookkeeping storage, and a much larger amount of storage for the **CELL**s.
This storage is allocated when **VSnew** is called. **CELL** storage occupies
nrows * ncols * sizeof(CELL) bytes (usually, **sizeof(CELL)** is 2). For
example, a 25-by-80 virtual screen would occupy 4000 bytes, a significant
amount. In some applications, you might want to use the window module
directly, rather than the virtual screen module, to save this memory. Of

course, if you end up allocating just as much in your own program in order to implement the redrawing function (see Sec. 6.2), then you've gained nothing for your trouble. And if this complicates your program excessively, you might have been better off sacrificing the storage.

A virtual screen's **CELL** storage is freed by **VSdispose**:

```
/*-------------------------------------------------------------------
      VSdispose - eliminate virtual screen and window
------------------------------------------------------------------*/
void VSdispose(vsnum)
int vsnum;                                /* virtual screen */
```

Occasionally you may want to operate on a virtual screen's window directly, without affecting the contents of the virtual screen or the location of the window relative to the virtual screen. For example, you may want to change the window's location relative to the *physical screen*, or its size, or its title, and so on. You do these operations by calling appropriate window module functions, as discussed in Sec. 6.2. You'll need the window number, and here's the function to get it:

```
/*-------------------------------------------------------------------
      VSgetwnum - get virtual screen's window number
      RETURN: window number
------------------------------------------------------------------*/
int VSgetwnum(vsnum)
int vsnum;                                /* virtual screen */
```

Changing the size of a virtual screen's *window* is quite different from changing the size of the virtual screen itself. That you can't do. However, as long as the window remains no bigger than the virtual screen, there's no real need to change the virtual screen's size (other than to save storage). Simply avoid using the part you don't need, as we shall do in Sec. 7.4 when we change from a large editing window to two smaller ones.

The window module functions that can sensibly be used with virtual screens are **Wtop, Wshuffle, Wsetphys, Wgetphys, Wzoom, Wunzoom, Wiszoomed, Wsetfrm,** and **Whide.**[1] The ones you should avoid are those that change the contents of the window (**Wwrite, Wslide,** and so on). The problem with these is that the virtual screen module will know nothing about them and will then likely update the window with the wrong data.

You can also get the virtual screen number that corresponds to a window:

---

[1]We could have introduced VS functions for each of the recommended W functions so that the window module could be completely ignored by users of the virtual screen module. We haven't done this because it's assumed that you have been reading this book from the start, and it would have been confusing to have two ways of doing exactly the same thing.

```
/*-------------------------------------------------------------------------
        VSgetvsnum - get window's virtual screen number
        RETURN: virtual screen number
-------------------------------------------------------------------------*/
int VSgetvsnum(wnum)
int wnum;                                    /* window */
```

This function doesn't apply to all windows—only to the ones created by **VSnew**. It's an error to call it with an argument that isn't associated with a virtual screen, so be careful.

Initially, a virtual screen's window is pressed up against the upper left corner of the virtual screen, so row 0, column 0, of the window corresponds to the same row and column of the virtual screen. The window can move from this position later, as we'll see. You can find out its current position with **VSgetwloc**:

```
/*-------------------------------------------------------------------------
        VSgetwloc - get window's location relative to virtual screen
-------------------------------------------------------------------------*/
void VSgetwloc(vsnum, vrowlp, vcollp)
int vsnum;                                   /* virtual screen */
int *vrowlp;                                 /* first row */
int *vcollp;                                 /* first column */
```

This gives the coordinates, relative to the virtual screen, of the upper left character in the interior of window (*not* of the frame). For example, if **vcollp** points to the value 23 after this function returns, it means that 23 columns (numbered 0 through 22) of the virtual screen are unseen, to the left of the window. **VSgetwloc** doesn't give the position of the right or bottom edges of the window. You can calculate these by calling **VSgetwnum** to get the window number, calling **Wgetphys** to get the size of the window, and then doing the necessary arithmetic. Examples of this technique are in the next section and in Sec. 7.5.

You move the window explicitly with **VSpan**:

```
/*-------------------------------------------------------------------------
        VSpan - move window relative to virtual screen
-------------------------------------------------------------------------*/
void VSpan(wnum, dir, dist)
int wnum;                                    /* window */
int dir;                                     /* direction */
int dist;                                    '* distance */
```

Use the symbolic constants defined in **display.h** (Sec. 2.5) for **dir**. The choices are **DIR_UP**, **DIR_DOWN**, **DIR_LEFT**, or **DIR_RIGHT**. If you need to move diagonally, you'll have to call **VSpan** twice. If the specified distance is excessive, the window is moved only as far as it will go. The characters in the window, therefore, are always all part of the virtual screen. Since the cursor must always be in the window, it is dragged along if necessary. The cursor is moved as little as possible, so if it does move it will be located at the edge of the window opposite the movement. For example, if the direction is **DIR_RIGHT** and the cursor had to be moved, it would end up in the first column of the window. You can use **VSgetcur** to find out if the cursor moved and, if so, where.

This function is very different from **VSslide**. **VSpan** never changes the contents of the virtual screen, only your view of it. It is usually a mistake to use **VSslide** to bring an unseen part of the virtual screen into the window. When programming applications, it's best to concentrate on the virtual screen and to imagine that the window is a viewing area that you can pan, as with binoculars. If you concentrate on the window instead, you may be tempted to try moving data into it.

Also, **VSpan** doesn't move the window relative to the *physical* screen. Use **Wsetphys** for that. The part of the virtual screen currently in the window will remain, and will track the movement of the window. To summarize: Use **VSslide** to change the *contents* of the virtual screen; use **VSpan** to move the window relative to the virtual screen; use **Wsetphys** to move the window relative to the physical screen; don't use **Wslide** or **PSslide** at all.

Every virtual screen has a cursor which you can reposition and turn on or off:

```
/*-------------------------------------------------------------------
     VSsetcur - set cursor position relative to virtual screen
-----------------------------------------------------------------*/
void VSsetcur(vsnum, vrow, vcol)
int vsnum;                              /* virtual screen */
int vrow;                               /* row */
int vcol;                               /* column */

/*-------------------------------------------------------------------
     VSshowcur - turn cursor on or off
-----------------------------------------------------------------*/
void VSshowcur(vsnum, on)
int vsnum;                              /* virtual screen */
BOOLEAN on;                             /* switch */
```

The cursor location is always kept in the window (even if the cursor is off). To accomplish this, **VSsetcur** automatically calls **VSpan** as necessary. Hence, some calls to **VSsetcur** are very cheap and some are very expensive. There's some advice in the next section on the usage of **VSpan** and **VSsetcur** to move the window and position the cursor.

With virtual screens you can find out where the cursor is. The window and physical screen modules have no corresponding function.

```
/*-------------------------------------------------------------------
     VSgetcur - get cursor position relative to virtual screen
-----------------------------------------------------------------*/
void VSgetcur(vsnum, vrowp, vcolp)
int vsnum;                              /* virtual screen */
int *vrowp;                             /* row */
int *vcolp;                             /* column */
```

It's rarely necessary to use this function in applications because you nearly always will control the movement of the cursor in your own code (as you process arrow keys, for example). You will know where it is without asking. But sometimes the cursor moves when **VSpan** moves a window, and so **VSgetcur** may be useful to get its new location. However, in my experience with programming editors and data entry systems, moving the window is usually followed by an explicit call to **VSsetcur**, so I seldom care what **VSpan** did to the cursor.

An external event, such as a message that another process sent to your screen, may move the cursor without your being aware of it, but the virtual screen module won't be aware *either*. Remember that there's no way for the virtual screen module to ask the physical screen module where the cursor is. So **VSgetcur** is not useful when this occurs.

Since virtual screens never change size, the number of rows and columns you called **VSnew** with will remain constant. Sometimes, however, a function that needs the size is passed only the virtual screen number. It can then call **VSgetsize**:

```
/*-------------------------------------------------------------------
    VSgetsize - get size of virtual screen
-----------------------------------------------------------------*/
void VSgetsize(vsnum, nrowsp, ncolsp)
int vsnum;                              /* virtual screen */
int *nrowsp;                            /* number of rows */
int *ncolsp;                            /* number of columns */
```

The next three functions, **VSwrite**, **VSfill**, and **VSslide**, are the virtual screen counterparts to similar functions in the physical screen and window interfaces. The virtual screen functions are more convenient, however, because **VSwrite** can pad its string argument to a specified length, and because **VSslide** always succeeds. If they make a change to a visible part of a virtual screen, the changes will be reflected in the window and, if that part of the window is not obscured, on the screen as well. That is, you deal only with the virtual screen, and ignore the other levels.

First, here is **VSwrite**:

```
/*-------------------------------------------------------------------
    VSwrite - write string
-----------------------------------------------------------------*/
void VSwrite(vsnum, vrowl, vcoll, ncols, str, att)
int vsnum;                              /* virtual screen */
int vrowl;                              /* starting row */
int vcoll;                              /* starting column */
int ncols;                              /* number of columns to write */
char *str;                              /* string */
int att;                                /* attribute */
```

The specified string, with the specified attribute, is written to the virtual screen starting at row **vrowl**, column **vcoll**. If **ncols** is less than the length of the string, only that much is written. If it is greater, the written data is padded with blanks. If **ncols** is equal to **GIANT** (defined in **display.h**), the entire string is written until its null byte is encountered. If the starting row or column is off the virtual screen, no writing occurs. However, the written string is clipped to the virtual screen boundary, so the amount written may be less than that specified by the arguments. Writing is *not* clipped to the window boundary, but the part you can see in the window certainly is.

Next comes **VSfill**, which fills virtual screen rectangles just as **Wfill** fills window rectangles and **PSfill** fills physical screen rectangles.

```
/*-------------------------------------------------------------------
     VSfill - fill rectangle
------------------------------------------------------------------*/
void VSfill(vsnum, vrectp, chr, att)
int vsnum;                              /* virtual screen */
RECT *vrectp;                           /* rectangle */
char chr;                               /* fill character */
int att;                                /* fill attribute */
```

It's not necessary to fill a brand new virtual screen with blanks; **VSnew** does this automatically.

Finally, here is **VSslide**. It's not a **BOOLEAN** function, as **Wslide** and **PSslide** are, because it will always be able to slide the rectangle. If its call to **Wslide** fails, because the window wasn't on top or because **PSslide** failed, **VSslide** will update the window from the **CELL** array. This is much slower than sliding, but there's no alternative.

```
/*-------------------------------------------------------------------
     VSslide - slide rectangle (always succeeds)
------------------------------------------------------------------*/
void VSslide(vsnum, vrectp, dir, dist)
int vsnum;                              /* virtual screen */
RECT *vrectp;                           /* rectangle */
int dir;                                /* direction */
int dist;                               /* distance */
```

7.3. Hints On Using Virtual Screens

In many applications, the data to be shown on the screen won't all fit in the window (or even on the physical screen) at the same time. For an effective user interface, you'll have choose the size of the virtual screen wisely, and you'll have to arrange to scroll it so the user finds the interaction natural. The goal is to make things so smooth that the user gets his or her job done without ever once thinking, "Wow, what a wonderful windowing system." In this section, we'll provide some hints on choosing the size of the virtual screen and moving the cursor to control what's visible to the user. This should also help explain the use of virtual screens and reduce confusion about the relationship between windows and virtual screens.

It's best to think of the virtual screen as what the application writes to, and the window as what the user can see. The user can only see something the application wrote if that part of the virtual screen is currently in the window. We'll call the process of making visible a hidden part of the virtual screen *scrolling*, although there's no interface function that does precisely that. As we saw in Chapter 5 and Sec. 6.3, scrolling in general involves sliding some data to another part of the window and writing new data to the vacated part of the window. With virtual screens, scrolling can be handled automatically by the virtual screen module, or you can handle it yourself in your own code. Which is better?

The answer depends on whether the total height and width of everything the user needs to see are fixed at reasonably small sizes, or whether they can extend indefinitely or at least to unreasonably large sizes. Let's take text editing as an example. Suppose the number of lines that can be edited is very large—in the hundreds or thousands. You don't have enough memory to make the virtual screen as tall as the total number of lines, so you will have to scroll in the application, using a combination of **VSslide** and **VSwrite**, as we will do with our screen editor.

Should you make the virtual screen, say, three times as high as the window, so that small amounts of scrolling will be handled automatically, which would require your application to scroll only occasionally? The answer is no. You still have to program for scrolling, so there's no point in wasting virtual screen memory and complicating the program with a two-level scrolling algorithm. If you have to scroll, it's usually best to do all of it.

Handling the width may be another story. Your editor might limit text lines to, say, 200 characters, as ours does. Here it is sensible to make that the width of the virtual screen as well, which allows you to forget about horizontal scrolling entirely. Since it's a little harder to program for horizontal scrolling than for vertical, this is a good deal. But if your editor will allow lines of arbitrary width, then the same considerations apply as for the number of text lines: You'll have to scroll yourself, so you should make the virtual screen and the window the same size.

In the text editor of Chapter 5, we could have up to 1000 lines of up to 200 characters each. The number 1000 should have been much larger, but we wanted to stick with a simple scheme for text storage. Our screen module design ought to be practical for much longer files. So in the next section we'll use a virtual screen about twenty rows high and 200 columns wide. We'll do vertical scrolling ourselves, just as we did in the physical screen and window implementations of the editor, and we'll let the virtual screen module handle all of the horizontal scrolling.

Let's try another example, a form-entry system that displays a fill-in-the-blanks form with labels and typing areas next to them. A real-world form system might limit forms to, say, 200 lines by 150 columns. These limits are quite generous, especially since many successful form-entry systems don't allow forms to be bigger than the screen. Here it's easy, and practical, to just make the virtual screen the size of the form; all scrolling will be handled automatically. You know how big the form is because it has to be defined separately, long before it is actually displayed for the user to fill in the blanks. During *design* of the form, however, you don't know its size, so it may be impractical to create a virtual screen that's large enough. The issues we raised with regard to text editing would probably apply here.

To summarize: If your application has a limited, fairly small height or width, use that to size the virtual screen. Otherwise, scroll it yourself, and make the virtual screen and window the same size to avoid mixing methods.

So much for the issue of *who* does the scrolling. Let's talk about another issue: *when* to scroll. Your application tells the virtual screen module to scroll either by moving the cursor out of the window, with **VSsetcur**, or directly, with **VSpan**. There's often a group of characters you want to make visible, not just one. For example, suppose the user wants to type into this blank on a form:

```
Name: _____
```

Let's say you position the cursor to the first underscore. If this field is currently to the right of the window, the first underscore will be brought into view. But it would be better to bring the entire underscored blank into view at once, not just the first character. Otherwise, the form would scroll on every character typed (very bothersome to watch), and the user would be unsure about how much room was available since the unused part of the blank would be invisible. If the entire field won't fit because the blank is wide and the window is narrow, at least the label (Name:) should be shown so the user knows what to enter.

More generally, assume there is a segment of adjacent columns that you want to make visible, extending from **col1** to **col2**. The first column of the window is column **vcol1** of the virtual screen, and the last column of the window is column **vcol2** of the virtual screen. There are three situations to consider:

1. The entire segment is already visible; that is, this expression is true:

```
col1 >= vcol1 && col2 <= vcol2
```

2. Part or all of the segment is to the left of the window, as diagrammed in Fig. 7-1. This condition is true:

```
col1 < vcol1
```

Assuming that the left end of the segment is more important than the right, use **VSpan** to move the window to the left so that **col1** appears in the first column of the window. The distance to move is:

```
vcol1 - col1
```

This may or may not make **col2** visible, depending on whether the segment fits in the window. We don't care because we've done the best we can.

3. Part or all of the segment is to the right of the window, as diagrammed in Fig. 7-2. This condition is true:

$$\texttt{col1 >= vcol1 \&\& col2 > vcol2}$$

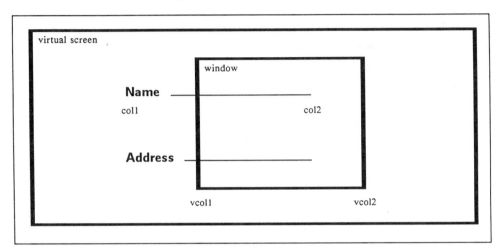

Fig. 7-1. Segment partially to the left of the window.

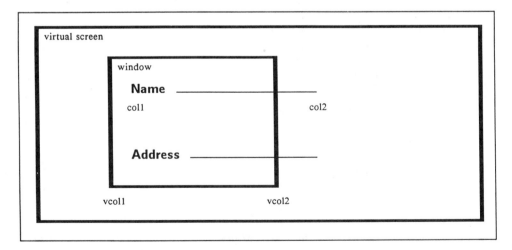

Fig. 7-2. Segment partially to the right of the window.

Move the window to the right until either **col1** reaches the first column of the window or **col2** reaches the last column. That is, move this much:

```
MIN(col2 - vcol2, col1 - vcol1)
```

We're assuming with both leftward and rightward moves that the minimum movement that makes the segment visible is best. This algorithm is embodied in the following handy function that makes a horizontal segment visible:

```
/*------------------------------------------------------------------
    showseg - make horizontal segment visible
------------------------------------------------------------------*/
void showseg(vsnum, col1, col2)
int vsnum;                              /* virtual screen */
int col1;                               /* first col of seg.; always visible */
int col2;                               /* second col; visible if it fits */
{
    RECT rect;
    int wnum, vrow1, vcol1, vcol2;

    VSgetwloc(vsnum, &vrow1, &vcol1);
    wnum = VSgetwnum(vsnum);
    Wgetphys(wnum, &rect, FALSE);
    vcol2 = vcol1 + RWIDTH(&rect) - 1;
    if (col1 >= vcol1 && col2 <= vcol2)
        return;
    if (col1 < vcol1)
        VSpan(wnum, DIR_LEFT, vcol1 - col1);
    else
        VSpan(wnum, DIR_RIGHT, MIN(col2 - vcol2, col1 - vcol1));
}
```

This example also provides us with an opportunity to see how window and virtual screen functions may be used together. The call to **VSgetwloc** gets the location of the first column of the window relative to the virtual screen. We don't care about **vrow1**, since we're only moving sideways. To get **vcol2** we have to determine the width of the window. We get the window number with **VSgetwnum** and then call **Wgetphys** (Sec. 6.2) to get the window's physical screen rectangle. From this we can calculate **vcol2**. The first **if** statement tests to see if the segment is already visible, in which case we're already done. Then we move the window left or right, following the steps listed above.

An analogous algorithm could easily be programmed to make a vertical segment of rows visible by moving the window up or down. We'll leave that as an exercise.

It's also possible to make a segment visible by just calling **VSsetcur**, taking advantage of the fact that this function always makes the cursor visible and always moves the window the minimum distance necessary. We actually call **VSsetcur** *twice*:

1. Position the cursor to the end of the segment, which will move the window if the end isn't already visible. If it is, this call is very fast.

2. Position the cursor to the beginning of the segment. This will move the window only if step 1 failed to make the beginning visible. Also, if the segment is bigger than the window, this will make the left end visible, rather than the right.

This technique is somewhat simpler than using **VSpan** directly, but it requires more processing by the virtual screen module. What's more, there may be two moves instead of one and, with some physical screen implementations—the IBM BIOS, for example—the user will actually see them both, which is not good. Since we've already got **showseg**, the simplicity advantages of the **VSsetcur** method probably don't matter.

7.4. Screen Editor Implementation Using Virtual Screens

In Chapter 5 we presented a simple editor containing a screen module implemented with the physical screen interface of Chapter 3. Then, in Sec. 6.3, we rewrote the screen module to use windows. Now, to show how the virtual screen interface is used, we'll code the screen module for the third time. To a large extent, this version is like the window version, with W functions changed to VS functions. There are some notable differences, however, which we'll emphasize as we go through the code. We'll be comparing the two versions, not explaining everything from scratch, so this section won't make much sense to you if you're unfamiliar with section Sec. 6.3. If you've been skipping the editor stuff up until now, you'd better skip this section, too.

Just as the window version of the screen module had to track the relationship between buffer numbers and window numbers, so does this version have to relate buffer numbers and virtual screen numbers. Except for that difference, it begins in a similar way:

```
#include "display.h"
#include "pscreen.h"
#include "window.h"
#include "vscreen.h"
#include "keyboard.h"
#include "keycode.h"
#include "edit.h"
#include "edscr.h"

static int vscrnum[MAXBUF];        /* vscreen number for each buffer */
static int curvsnum;               /* current vscreen number */
static int curbnum;                /* current buffer number */
static int helpvsnum;              /* help vscreen num (see EShelpstart) */

#define PROMPTWIDTH 40             /* width of prompt window */
```

ESbegin is a little smaller than the window version because **VSnew** puts the title into the frame for us. There's also no redrawing function—the virtual screen module will handle that automatically:

```
/*-------------------------------------------------------------------
    ESbegin - initialize screen module
-------------------------------------------------------------------*/
void ESbegin()
{
    int i;
    char title[20];
    RECT rect;

    VSbegin();
    Kbegin();
    ESmsg(NULL); /* make message window */
    RASG(&rect, 0, 0, 0, 0);
    for (i = 0; i < MAXBUF; i++) {
        sprintf(title, "Buffer %d", i + 1);
        if ((vscrnum[i] = VSnew(PSheight() - 2 - MAXBUF, MAXLINE, &rect,
            title, A_NORM)) == -1)
            fatal("can't create editing vscreen");
    }
    bigwindows();
    ESswitch(0);
}
```

As we said we would do in the previous section, we'll make the virtual screen as high as the tallest window and as wide as the longest possible line (**MAXLINE**). Horizontal scrolling will be automated—all we have to do is position the cursor. Vertical scrolling is our responsibility, just as it was in the window and physical screen versions. Because a virtual screen is created for each buffer at the start of execution, it's safe to call **fatal** (which terminates) if **VSnew** fails. There's no danger of the user's losing text. Rather strangely, we're asking **VSnew** to create a null window. We'll figure out how big it should be in **bigwindows**:

```
/*-------------------------------------------------------------------
    bigwindows - make all windows full size
-------------------------------------------------------------------*/
static void bigwindows()
{
    RECT rect;
    int savebnum;

    savebnum = curbnum;
    RASG(&rect, 0, 0, PSheight() - 1 - MAXBUF, PSwidth() - MAXBUF);
    for (curbnum = 0; curbnum < MAXBUF; curbnum++) {
        curvsnum = vscrnum[curbnum];
        Wsetphys(VSgetwnum(curvsnum), &rect);
        ESshowall(); /* vscreen layer can't repair damage */
        rect.r1++;
        rect.r2++;
        rect.c1++;
        rect.c2++;
    }
    ESswitch(savebnum);
}
```

This version is similar to the window version in that both call **Wsetphys** to arrange a series of staggered rectangles. We had to use **VSgetwnum** to get the window number because all we had in the **vscrnum** array was the virtual screen number.

The call to **ESshowall** requires some explanation. If we use the editor's **K_ALT_V** command to change to a two-buffer view, we'll use only the top half of the virtual screen since that's all that shows in the smaller window. Remember, we're going to scroll vertically ourselves—even when there's more to the virtual screen below what's showing. We'll ignore the lower half of the virtual screen. The problem arises when we toggle **K_ALT_V** again to go back to a big window. The virtual screen module will redraw the window all right, but the lower half of it will be out-of-date because we haven't been tending to it. So we call **ESshowall** ourselves to update the virtual screen with current data. Think of this as redrawing the *virtual screen*, not redrawing the *window*, which we promised we wouldn't have to do.

The function **smallwindows** is even more like the window version. Going to a smaller window doesn't require us to change the virtual screen, so there's no call to **ESshowall**:

```
/*------------------------------------------------------------------
        smallwindows - make windows half size (so two can be seen at once)
------------------------------------------------------------------*/
static void smallwindows()
{
    RECT rect;
    int i;

    RASG(&rect, 0, 0, PSheight() / 2 - 1, PSwidth() - 1);
    Wsetphys(VSgetwnum(vscrnum[0]), &rect);
    rect.rl = rect.r2 + 1;
    rect.r2 = PSheight() - 2;
    for (i = 1; i < MAXBUF; i++)
        Wsetphys(VSgetwnum(vscrnum[i]), &rect);
}
```

ESview is the same as the one in the window version:

```
/*------------------------------------------------------------------
        ESview - toggle between big and small windows
------------------------------------------------------------------*/
void ESview()
{
    static BOOLEAN big = TRUE;

    switch (big = !big) {
    case TRUE:
        bigwindows();
        break;
    case FALSE:
        smallwindows();
    }
}
```

ESheight and **ESwidth** get the dimensions of the area into which the rest of the editor can write text. In this version, the height is that of the window but the width is that of the virtual screen:

```
/*------------------------------------------------------------------
    ESheight - get height of area where editor can show text
    RETURN: Height.
--------------------------------------------------------------------*/
int ESheight()
{
    RECT rect;

    Wgetphys(VSgetwnum(curvsnum), &rect, FALSE);
    return(RHEIGHT(&rect));
}

/*------------------------------------------------------------------
    ESwidth - get width of area where editor can show text
    RETURN: Width.
--------------------------------------------------------------------*/
int ESwidth()
{
    int nrows, ncols;

    VSgetsize(curvsnum, &nrows, &ncols);
    return(ncols);
}
```

It's hard to show it in a book, but the editor really will be able to scroll sideways, and there's no code at the application level to support it!

In **ESend**, we dispose of our virtual screens:

```
/*------------------------------------------------------------------
    ESend - terminate screen module
--------------------------------------------------------------------*/
void ESend()
{
    int i;

    for (i = 0; i < MAXBUF; i++)
        VSdispose(vscrnum[i]);
    Kend();
    VSend();
}
```

When we switch to a different buffer with the editor's **K_ALT_B** command, we make the corresponding virtual screen number the current one. We also have to call **Wtop** to put its window on top, which we can do once we get the window number from **VSgetwnum**:

```
/*------------------------------------------------------------------
    ESswitch - switch to buffer
--------------------------------------------------------------------*/
void ESswitch(bnum)
int bnum;                              /* buffer number */
{
    int wnum;
```

```
    curbnum = bnum;
    curvsnum = vscrnum[bnum];
    if (Wgettop() != (wnum = VSgetwnum(curvsnum)))
        Wtop(wnum);
}
```

Instead of calling **VSgetwnum** so often, we could keep track of both the window and virtual screen numbers corresponding to each buffer, since the relationship between a virtual screen and its window is fixed. But **VSgetwnum** is quite fast, so we chose to do it the simpler way. (The fewer variables—particularly global ones—the better.)

ESshowrow is more streamlined than the window version because **VSwrite** will pad text to a length of **MAXLINE**, the width of the virtual screen:

```
/*------------------------------------------------------------------
    ESshowrow - show text for row, starting at specified column
--------------------------------------------------------------*/
void ESshowrow(row, col)
int row;                                /* row */
int col;                                /* column */
{
    char *t;
    int len;

    t = EMtext(curbnum, row);
    len = strlen(t);
    col = MIN(col, len);
    VSwrite(curvsnum, row, col, MAXLINE, &t[col], A_NORM);
}
```

In the window version, we had to end this function with a call to **Wfill** to finish out the line. Recall that it was to avoid these extra calls that we coded a separate function, **ESshowall**, to show the entire window. It called **Wfill** just once, to clear all rows of the window, thus skipping the individual calls on each row. The virtual screen version doesn't have to take that shortcut, so **ESshowall** is trivial:

```
/*------------------------------------------------------------------
    ESshowall - show all rows that are visible
--------------------------------------------------------------*/
void ESshowall()
{
    showrange(0, ESheight() - 1);
}
```

The function **showrange** is independent of our display method; it is the same one we programmed in Chapter 5:

```
/*------------------------------------------------------------------
    showrange - show range of text rows
----------------------------------------------------------------*/
static void showrange(row1, row2)
int row1;                                /* starting row */
int row2;                                /* ending row */
{
    int row;

    for (row = row1; row <= row2; row++)
        ESshowrow(row, 0);
}
```

ESsetcur, ESshowcur, and **ESclear** do just what you'd expect:

```
/*------------------------------------------------------------------
    ESsetcur - set cursor position
----------------------------------------------------------------*/
void ESsetcur(row, col)
int row;                                 /* row */
int col;                                 /* column */
{
    VSsetcur(curvsnum, row, col);
}


/*------------------------------------------------------------------
    ESshowcur - turn cursor on or off
----------------------------------------------------------------*/
void ESshowcur(on)
BOOLEAN on;                              /* switch */
{
    VSshowcur(curvsnum, on);
}


/*------------------------------------------------------------------
    ESclear - clear text area
----------------------------------------------------------------*/
void ESclear()
{
    VSfill(curvsnum, &GIANT_RECT, ' ', A_NORM);
}
```

We have to scroll the virtual screen vertically when **ESscrlup** or **ESscrldown** are called, by calling **VSslide** and then **ESshowrow** to display the new line at the bottom or top of the window. Unlike the window version, we don't have to handle the case where sliding fails, since **VSslide** will always work.

```
/*------------------------------------------------------------------
    ESscrlup - scroll text area up one row
----------------------------------------------------------------*/
void ESscrlup()
{
    VSslide(curvsnum, &GIANT_RECT, DIR_UP, 1);
    ESshowrow(ESheight() - 1, 0);
}
```

```
/*-------------------------------------------------------------------
      ESscrldown - scroll text area down one row
----------------------------------------------------------------*/
void ESscrldown()
{
    VSslide(curvsnum, &GIANT_RECT, DIR_DOWN, 1);
    ESshowrow(0, 0);
}
```

The four functions to insert and delete characters and rows are also
smaller than their window-version counterparts because they, too, can rely
on horizontal and vertical sliding to work:

```
/*-------------------------------------------------------------------
      ESinschar - insert character into row of text
----------------------------------------------------------------*/
void ESinschar(row, col, ch)
int row;                             /* row */
int col;                             /* column */
char ch;                             /* character */
{
    RECT rect;

    RASG(&rect, row, col, row, GIANT);
    VSslide(curvsnum, &rect, DIR_RIGHT, 1);
    VSwrite(curvsnum, row, col, 1, &ch, A_NORM);
}


/*-------------------------------------------------------------------
      ESdelchar - delete character from row of text
----------------------------------------------------------------*/
void ESdelchar(row, col)
int row;                             /* row */
int col;                             /* column */
{
    RECT rect;

    RASG(&rect, row, col + 1, row, GIANT);
    VSslide(curvsnum, &rect, DIR_LEFT, 1);
    VSwrite(curvsnum, row, ESwidth() - 1, 1, " ", A_NORM);
}


/*-------------------------------------------------------------------
      ESinsrow - insert blank row into text area
----------------------------------------------------------------*/
void ESinsrow(row)
int row;                             /* row */
{
    int height;
    RECT rect;

    height = ESheight();
    if (row >= height)
        fatal("ESinsrow - bad row");
    RASG(&rect, row, 0, GIANT, GIANT);
    VSslide(curvsnum, &rect, DIR_DOWN, 1);
    rect.r2 = rect.r1;
    VSfill(curvsnum, &rect, ' ', A_NORM);
}
```

```
/*------------------------------------------------------------------
      ESdelrow - delete row from text area
   ------------------------------------------------------------------*/
void ESdelrow(row)
int row;                                    /* row */
{
      RECT rect;

      RASG(&rect, row + 1, 0, GIANT, GIANT);
      VSslide(curvsnum, &rect, DIR_UP, 1);
      ESshowrow(ESheight() - 1, 0);
}
```

ESmsg follows the same scheme as the window version except that it
creates a virtual screen instead of window, which is a little easier, as we
mentioned in the discussion of **ESbegin**. Note that we leave the virtual
screen around permanently rather than create it each time, just as we did in
the window version.Virtual screens tie down more storage than windows, but
in this case the message area is too small to worry about. In other situations,
it might make sense to dispose of a virtual screen when it isn't being used.

```
/*------------------------------------------------------------------
      ESmsg - display short message
   ------------------------------------------------------------------*/
void ESmsg(s)
char *s;                                    /* message */
{
      static int vsnum = -1;
      static BOOLEAN havemsg = FALSE;
      RECT rect;
      int top;

      if (vsnum == -1) {
          top = Wgettop();
          RASG(&rect, PSheight() - 1, 0, PSheight() - 1, PSwidth() - 1);
          if ((vsnum = VSnew(1, PSwidth() - 1, &rect, NULL, A_NORM)) == -1)
              fatal("can't create message vscreen");
          if (top > 0)
              Wtop(top);
      }
      if (havemsg)
          VSfill(vsnum, &GIANT_RECT, ' ', A_NORM);
      havemsg = s != NULL;
      if (havemsg) {
          VSwrite(vsnum, 0, 0, GIANT, s, A_INVERSE);
          PSsynch();
      }
}
```

ESmsg2 is independent of the display technique:

```
/*------------------------------------------------------------------
      ESmsg2 - display message, concatenating two strings
   ------------------------------------------------------------------*/
void ESmsg2(s1, s2)
char *s1;                                   /* first string */
char *s2;                                   /* second string */
{
      char s[70];
```

```
    sprintf(s, "%s%s", s1, s2);
    ESmsg(s);
}
```

Just as we did in the window version, we'll pop up a window when
EShelpstart is called, only this time it will have a virtual screen behind it.
All it takes is a call to **VSnew**:

```
/*-------------------------------------------------------------------
    EShelpstart - prepare screen for help display
-----------------------------------------------------------------*/
void EShelpstart()
{
    RECT rect;

    RASG(&rect, 1, 1, PSheight() - 2, PSwidth() - 2);
    if ((helpvsnum = VSnew(RHEIGHT(&rect), RWIDTH(&rect), &rect, "",
      A_NORM)) == -1)
        fatal("can't create help vscreen");
}
```

Both **EShelpfinish** and **EShelpwrite** do the obvious:

```
/*-------------------------------------------------------------------
    EShelpfinish - clear help display and restore screen
-----------------------------------------------------------------*/
void EShelpfinish()
{
    VSdispose(helpvsnum);
}
```

```
/*-------------------------------------------------------------------
    EShelpwrite - write one line of help text
-----------------------------------------------------------------*/
void EShelpwrite(row, s, att)
int row;                          /* row to be written */
char *s;                          /* text */
int att;                          /* attribute */
{
    VSwrite(helpvsnum, row, 0, GIANT, s, att);
}
```

Finally, here's the fancy **ESprompt** that pops up a box for the user to
type into. It closely resembles the window version:

```
/*-------------------------------------------------------------------
    ESprompt - prompt user to type in response
-----------------------------------------------------------------*/
void ESprompt(message, label, response)
char *message;                    /* message for user */
char *label;                      /* label for typing area */
char *response;                   /* user's response */
{
    int vsnum, promptrow, startcol, lastcol, pos, key;
    RECT rect;

    rect.r1 = 6;
    rect.r2 = rect.r1 + (message[0] == '\0' ? 0 : 2);
    rect.c1 = (PSwidth() - PROMPTWIDTH) / 2 - 1;
    rect.c2 = rect.c1 + PROMPTWIDTH - 1;
```

```
if ((vsnum = VSnew(RHEIGHT(&rect), RWIDTH(&rect), &rect, "", A_NORM))
   == -1)
    fatal("can't create prompt vscreen");
VSshowcur(vsnum, TRUE);
VSfill(vsnum, &GIANT_RECT, ' ', A_NORM);
if (message[0] != '\0')
    VSwrite(vsnum, 0, 1, GIANT, message, A_INTENSE);
promptrow = RHEIGHT(&rect) - 1;
lastcol = RWIDTH(&rect) - 1;
response[0] = '\0';
VSwrite(vsnum, promptrow, 1, GIANT, label, A_INTENSE);
startcol = strlen(label) + 2;
pos = 0;
while (TRUE) {
    VSwrite(vsnum, promptrow, startcol, GIANT, response, A_NORM);
    VSwrite(vsnum, promptrow, startcol + pos, 1, " ", A_NORM);
    VSsetcur(vsnum, promptrow, startcol + pos);
    Ksynch();
    switch (key = Kget()) {
    case K_BS:
        if (pos > 0)
            response[--pos] = '\0';
        continue;
    case K_RET:
        VSdispose(vsnum);
        return;
    default:
        if (key <= HIGHASCII && isprint(key) &&
          startcol + pos < lastcol) {
            response[pos++] = (char)key;
            response[pos] = '\0';
        }
        else
            PSbeep();
    }
}
}
```

What we've seen is that the virtual screen version of the editor is a little simpler than the window version, primarily because **VSwrite** can pad text, **VSslide** always slides, and **VSnew** does the whole job of creating a virtual screen. We also were able to skip the window redrawing function. Not only that, but this version of the editor can scroll sideways! In all, a fine bargain.

7.5. Virtual Screen Implementation

In this section we'll look at the code of the virtual screen module. Many of the functions are complicated, more so than those in earlier chapters. You'll most likely want to tread lightly through the programs here, spending time only on the parts that interest you. We'll try to point out which those might be as we go.

The implementation of the virtual screen has to deal with these main issues:

1. Updating the rectangular **CELL** array as the user writes text and fills and slides rectangles. As with windows, everything has to be clipped to the virtual screen boundary. However, the entire virtual screen is always writable—nothing can overlay any part of it. There's no visibility mask as there was in the window module.

2. Calling window functions to update the window if any changes to the virtual screen occur in the area viewable through the window.

3. Keeping track of the location of the window relative to the virtual screen.

4. Supplying the redrawing function as required by the window module, and redrawing portions of the window on demand, by consulting the **CELL** array.

Because it sits on top of the window and physical screen modules, the virtual screen module does *not* have to worry about:

1. Ensuring that the overlapped part of a window is not written to.

2. Knowing when to redraw part of a window, and how much to redraw. The window module will provide the necessary supervision; we just have to follow orders.

3. Physically writing to the display, using whatever method has been selected.

As you read through the code that follows, two themes will recur. First, you'll see that several functions first make a change to the **CELL** array and then make a corresponding change to the window. The techniques used to manipulate the **CELL** array are like those used in the memory-mapped implementation of the physical screen module (Sec. 3.7.2) because the storage layout of the **CELL** array is identical to the layout of that memory map. The second theme is that we'll constantly be dealing with two coordinate systems, one relative to the virtual screen and one relative to the window. Keeping track of these in your own mind will be your greatest challenge as you read through the code. (It certainly was my greatest challenge in writing the code!) To help, we'll adopt the convention that variables storing row or column numbers relative to the virtual screen will begin with **v** and those relative to the window will begin with **w**. Occasionally, we'll have a physical-screen-relative rectangle whose variables will begin with **s**.

Here's the start of the virtual screen module:

```
#include "display.h"
#include "pscreen.h"
#include "window.h"
#include "vscreen.h"

#define MAXVSCREEN MAXWIND      /* maximum number of virtual screens */
#define BADVSCREEN -1           /* error return */
```

MAXVSCREEN will be used to dimension an array of virtual screen information, just as **MAXWIND** was used for a similar purpose in the window module. We'll use the symbolic constant **BADVSCREEN** to return −1 to the user to help make the code clearer. It isn't necessary to include this constant in the header file **vscreen.h**, because −1 is such a common error-return in C programs. (It's the error return from all UNIX system calls.)

Next, we'll define a structure to maintain information about each virtual screen:

```
typedef struct {               /* info about virtual screen; all row & col
                                  numbers are relative to virtual screen */
    short winnum;              /* associated window */
    short vwinrowl;            /* location of window: first row */
    short vwincoll;            /* location of window: first column */
    short vrow2;               /* size of vscreen: last row */
    short vcol2;               /* size of vscreen: last column */
    short vcurrow;             /* cursor row */
    short vcurcol;             /* cursor column */
    CELL **ca;                 /* cell array */
} VSCREEN;

static VSCREEN *vscreen[MAXVSCREEN];      /* vscreen info table */
```

A virtual screen number returned by **VSnew** is a subscript of the **vscreen** array. The array element points to a **VSCREEN** structure.

The first three members of the structure identify the virtual screen's window and its location on the virtual screen. We'll locate a window by the row and column of the upper left corner of its interior. (It will be much easier for you to understand how virtual screens and windows relate if you think of windows moving about on the virtual screen rather than the virtual screen moving underneath the window.) No other information about the window is kept here. If we need to know its size, we will call **Wgetphys**. From that, we can calculate the lower right corner of the window or any other point we want.

Members **vrow2** and **vcol2** are one way to record the size of the virtual screen. We could have simply kept the *number* of rows and columns that were passed to **VSnew**, but it will turn out to be slightly more convenient to do it this way. There will be fewer subtractions of one and, we hope, fewer off-by-one errors. Next come two members to track the cursor location, **vcurrow** and **vcurcol**. We don't record whether the cursor is on or off—we'll let the window module do that for us. You might say that the virtual screen has no cursor of its own—it uses the window's cursor. Last comes a pointer to the **CELL** array to point to storage allocated by **VSnew**. We'll see how this pointer is set up in a moment.

The function **VSgetvsnum** will need the virtual screen number that corresponds to a given window. So whenever we create a new virtual screen, we'll store its number in the array **wtable**, indexed by its window number:

```
static wtable[MAXWIND];                /* window --> vscreen num mapping */
```

The first function is **VSbegin**, which initializes the virtual screen module:

```
/*-----------------------------------------------------------------
    VSbegin - initialize virtual screen module
-------------------------------------------------------------*/
void VSbegin()
{
    int i;
    CELL test[2];

    Wbegin();
    for (i = 0; i < MAXWIND; i++)
        wtable[i] = BADVSCREEN;
    if ((char *)&test[1] - (char *)&test[0] != sizeof(CELL))
        fatal("noncontiguous CELL array");
}
```

We'll be using some algorithms to write to the **CELL** array that assume that its bytes are contiguous (no pad bytes). The **if** statement ensures that this assumption is true. It is true for practically all C compilers, but it's not a requirement of the C language. Since not all C compilers are supported, theoretically the virtual screen module isn't as portable as it could be. Note that a similar limitation applied to the memory-mapped implementation of the physical screen interface (Sec. 3.7.2), but we didn't test for it there because that code was inherently non-portable.

The only thing to do when the virtual screen module terminates is to terminate the window module also:

```
/*-----------------------------------------------------------------
    VSend - terminate virtual screen module
-------------------------------------------------------------*/
void VSend()
{
    Wend();
}
```

Let's now look at **VSnew**, which does a variety of tasks to create a new virtual screen. Look at the function, and then we'll review it step by step.

```
/*-----------------------------------------------------------------
    VSnew - create virtual screen
    RETURN: virtual screen number or BADVSCREEN on error
-------------------------------------------------------------*/
int VSnew(nrows, ncols, srectp, title, att)
int nrows;                          /* number of rows */
int ncols;                          /* number of columns */
RECT *srectp;                       /* window's physical size & location */
char *title;                        /* window's frame title */
int att;                            /* window's frame attribute */
{
    VSCREEN *vs;
    int vsnum, wnum, vr;
    RECT srect;

    if (nrows == 0 || ncols == 0)
        return(BADVSCREEN);
```

```
    for (vsnum = 0; vsnum < MAXVSCREEN; vsnum++)
        if (vscreen[vsnum] == NULL)
            break;
    if (vsnum == MAXVSCREEN)
        fatal("too many virtual screens");
    if ((vscreen[vsnum] = vs = (VSCREEN *)malloc(sizeof(VSCREEN))) == NULL)
        return(BADVSCREEN);
    vs->vrow2 = nrows - 1;
    vs->vcol2 = ncols - 1;
    vs->vcurrow = vs->vcurcol = 0;
    if ((vs->ca = (CELL **)malloc(nrows * sizeof(char *))) == NULL)
        return(BADVSCREEN);
    for (vr = 0; vr < nrows; vr++) {
        if ((vs->ca[vr] = (CELL *)malloc(ncols * sizeof(CELL))) == NULL)
            return(BADVSCREEN);
        repcell(vs->ca[vr], ' ', att, ncols);
    }
    vs->vwinrow1 = vs->vwincol1 = 0;
    vs->vwinnum = wnum = Wnew(redraw);
    wtable[wnum] = vsnum;
    RCPY(&srect, srectp);
    if (title == NULL)
        Wsetfrm(wnum, F_UNFRAMED, att, title);
    else {
        Wsetfrm(wnum, F_SINGLE, att, title);
        srect.r1--;
        srect.c1--;
        srect.r2++;
        srect.c2++;
    }
    Wsetphys(wnum, &srect);
    Wsetcur(wnum, 0, 0);
    Wshowcur(wnum, FALSE);
    return(vsnum);
}
```

First we have to find an available slot in the **vscreen** pointer array. If none are available, we exit with a fatal message. If we find a slot, its subscript, **vsnum**, will be the virtual screen number that we'll return. We then allocate a **VSCREEN** structure and put a pointer to it in the slot. Four members of the structure can now be initialized. The cursor starts at the upper left corner. Allocating the **CELL** array requires that we allocate first a vector of row pointers and then a row for each of them to point to. We can't simply allocate a two-dimensional array of **CELL**s, like this:

```
    if ((vs->ca = (CELL **)malloc(nrows * ncols * sizeof(CELL))) == NULL)
        return(BADVSCREEN);
```

The C language allows an array to be represented by its contents alone only when it's declared explicitly as an array, this way:

```
                            CELL ca[ROWS][COLS];
```

But we can't do that because the dimensions aren't known until **VSnew** is called. So **ca** is declared as a pointer-to-pointer-to-**CELL**, not as an array, and we have to allocate the extra vector of row pointers. As we allocate each row of the **CELL** array, we fill it with spaces by using **repcell**, which will be coming up shortly.

That's all **VSnew** does about the virtual screen proper. The rest has to do with its window. Members **vwinrow1** and **vwincol1** are set to zero, to start the window at the upper left corner of the virtual screen. Then we call **Wnew** to create the window, and use the window number as a subscript of **wtable** to store the virtual screen number. We make a copy of the caller's physical screen rectangle, pointed to by **srectp**, because we may have to change it. If the window is to be framed (for example, if **title** isn't **NULL**), we need to make the rectangle bigger all around because the rectangle passed to **Wsetphys** must include the frame. We finish off by setting the window's cursor to the upper left corner of the window (which corresponds to the upper left corner of the virtual screen), turning the cursor off, and then returning the virtual screen number to the caller.

The redrawing function **redraw** that we passed to **Wnew** will be supplied by the virtual screen module. It will redraw the damaged area by accessing the **CELL** array. This function provides us our first opportunity to see how to translate from virtual-screen-relative coordinates to window-relative ones:

```
/*--------------------------------------------------------------
    redraw - redraw damaged window
--------------------------------------------------------------*/
static int redraw(wnum, wrectp)
int wnum;                          /* window */
RECT *wrectp;                      /* rectangle to be redrawn */
{
    VSCREEN *vs;
    RECT srect, wrect, wrect2;
    int vrow1, vcol1, vrow2, vcol2, vr, vc2;

    Wgetphys(wnum, &srect, FALSE);
    if (!intersect(wrectp, RHEIGHT(&srect) - 1, RWIDTH(&srect) - 1, &wrect))
        return(0);
    vs = vscreen[VSgetvsnum(wnum)];
    vrow1 = vs->vwinrow1 + wrect.r1;
    vcol1 = vs->vwincol1 + wrect.c1;
    vrow2 = vs->vwinrow1 + wrect.r2;
    vcol2 = vs->vwincol1 + wrect.c2;
    for (vr = vrow1; vr <= vrow2; vr++) {
        if (vr > vs->vrow2) {
            wrect.r1 = vr - vs->vwinrow1;
            Wfill(wnum, &wrect, ' ', A_NORM);
            break;
        }
        vc2 = MIN(vcol2, vs->vcol2);
        Wwrtcells(wnum, vr - vs->vwinrow1, wrect.c1, &vs->ca[vr][vcol1],
            vc2 - vcol1 + 1);
        vc2 = MAX(vcol1, vc2 + 1);
        if (vc2 <= vcol2) {
            RASG(&wrect2, vr - vs->vwinrow1, vc2 - vs->vwincol1,
                vr - vs->vwinrow1, wrect.c2);
            Wfill(wnum, &wrect2, ' ', A_NORM);
        }
    }
    return(0);
}
```

There are several RECT variables here. The one starting with **s** is relative to the physical screen (returned by **Wgetphys**); the ones starting with **w** are relative to the window. If the window-relative rectangle we were passed (**wrectp**) has no intersection with the window, we just return. (See Sec. 2.6 for **intersect**.) This isn't supposed to happen, but we're checking for it just the same. The rectangle that does intersect is now in **wrect**; we'll use that from now on. Next we get the virtual screen number corresponding to this window via **VSgetwnum**, and set the pointer **vs** to reference the **VSCREEN** structure, for convenience of notation and for speed.

Now we can calculate the first and last row and column numbers of the window relative to the virtual screen (**wrect** was relative to the *window*). The variables **vrow1**, **vcol1**, **vrow2**, and **vcol2** are the ones that will delimit the part of the virtual screen that we'll need to access. All we have to do is take CELLs from there and write them to the window. We do this by rows, under control of the **for** loop. It's possible for the virtual screen to have fewer rows than the window. If this occurs, we can't access the CELL array (we'd get a subscripting error), and all we need are spaces anyway, so we just update the window with **Wfill**. We fill all the remaining rows together and then exit the loop.

We're ready to copy CELLs to the window, but we have to worry about the virtual screen's being narrower than the window. If it is, we copy what we can with **Wwrtcells** and fill out the rest of the row with **Wfill**. Now you know why we implemented **Wwrtcells** and **PSwrtcells**, which may have perplexed you earlier. They make virtual screens *much* faster than if we had to update the window with calls to **Wwrite**, because different CELLs might have different attributes. In fact, when there's lots of window overlapping activity, using virtual screens is often *faster* than using windows, because the redrawing function supplied by the application is seldom as well optimized as the one we've shown here (although it could be).

We saw in **VSnew** a call to **repcell** to rapidly replicate a CELL throughout a segment of a CELL array. We'll use it several times in this module.

```
/*---------------------------------------------------------------
    repcell - replicate cell
-----------------------------------------------------------------*/
static void repcell(cellp, chr, att, ncols)
CELL *cellp;                     /* vector of CELLs */
char chr;                        /* character to be replicated */
int att;                         /* attribute to be replicated */
int ncols;                       /* columns to replicate */
{
    CELL cell;

    cell.chr = chr;
    cell.att = (char)att;
    repmem((char *)cellp, (char *)&cell, sizeof(CELL), ncols);
}
```

The function **repmem** was shown in Sec. 2.8.

Disposing of a virtual screen involves disposing of its window and freeing its memory, both the **CELL** array and the **VSCREEN** structure. We take care to catch an invalid argument.

```
/*-----------------------------------------------------------------
      VSdispose - eliminate virtual screen and window
  ----------------------------------------------------------------*/
void VSdispose(vsnum)
int vsnum;                              /* virtual screen */
{
    VSCREEN *vs;
    int vr;

    if (vsnum == BADVSCREEN)
        return;
    vs = vscreen[vsnum];
    if (vs != NULL) {
        Wdispose(vs->winnum);
        if (vs->ca != NULL) {
            for (vr = 0; vr <= vs->vrow2; vr++)
                if (vs->ca[vr] != NULL)
                    free((char *)vs->ca[vr]);
            free((char *)vs->ca);
        }
        free((char *)vs);
        vscreen[vsnum] = NULL;
    }
}
```

The next group of functions are each fairly simple. They just retrieve various pieces of information that the virtual screen module keeps right at hand. First, here are **VSgetvsnum** and **VSgetwnum**:

```
/*-----------------------------------------------------------------
      VSgetvsnum - get window's virtual screen number
      RETURN: virtual screen number
  ----------------------------------------------------------------*/
int VSgetvsnum(wnum)
int wnum;                               /* window */
{
    return(wtable[wnum]);
}


/*-----------------------------------------------------------------
      VSgetwnum - get virtual screen's window number
      RETURN: window number
  ----------------------------------------------------------------*/
int VSgetwnum(vsnum)
int vsnum;                              /* virtual screen */
{
    return(vscreen[vsnum]->winnum);
}
```

VSgetwloc can get what it needs directly from the **VSCREEN** structure:

```
/*------------------------------------------------------------------
     VSgetwloc - get window's location relative to virtual screen
---------------------------------------------------------------------*/
void VSgetwloc(vsnum, vrowlp, vcollp)
int vsnum;                            /* virtual screen */
int *vrowlp;                          /* first row */
int *vcollp;                          /* first column */
{
    *vrowlp = vscreen[vsnum]->vwinrowl;
    *vcollp = vscreen[vsnum]->vwincoll;
}
```

The virtual screen's size is easily calculated from the coordinates of its lower right corner:

```
/*------------------------------------------------------------------
     VSgetsize - get size of virtual screen
---------------------------------------------------------------------*/
void VSgetsize(vsnum, nrowsp, ncolsp)
int vsnum;                            /* virtual screen */
int *nrowsp;                          /* number of rows */
int *ncolsp;                          /* number of columns */
{
    if (vsnum == BADVSCREEN)
        return;
    *nrowsp = vscreen[vsnum]->vrow2 + 1;
    *ncolsp = vscreen[vsnum]->vcol2 + 1;
}
```

The function **VSsetcur** is extremely complicated, so we'll look at it later. **VSgetcur** and **VSshowcur**, on the other hand, are trivial:

```
/*------------------------------------------------------------------
     VSgetcur - get cursor position relative to virtual screen
---------------------------------------------------------------------*/
void VSgetcur(vsnum, vrowp, vcolp)
int vsnum;                            /* virtual screen */
int *vrowp;                           /* row */
int *vcolp;                           /* column */
{
    VSCREEN *vs;

    if (vsnum == BADVSCREEN)
        return;
    vs = vscreen[vsnum];
    *vrowp = vs->vcurrow;
    *vcolp = vs->vcurcol;
}
```

```
/*------------------------------------------------------------------
     VSshowcur - turn cursor on or off
---------------------------------------------------------------------*/
void VSshowcur(vsnum, on)
int vsnum;                            /* virtual screen */
BOOLEAN on;                           /* switch */
{
    if (vsnum == BADVSCREEN)
        return;
    Wshowcur(vscreen[vsnum]->winnum, on);
}
```

Now we'll examine **VSwrite**. It has to update both the virtual screen and the window. Once the virtual screen is taken care of, however, the window can be rapidly updated with **Wwrtcells**.

```
/*-------------------------------------------------------------------
    VSwrite - write string
-----------------------------------------------------------------*/
void VSwrite(vsnum, vrow1, vcol1, ncols, str, att)
int vsnum;                          /* virtual screen */
int vrow1;                          /* starting row */
int vcol1;                          /* starting column */
int ncols;                          /* number of columns to write */
char *str;                          /* string */
int att;                            /* attribute */
{
    VSCREEN *vs;
    CELL *cellp;
    int i;
    BOOLEAN pad;

    if (vsnum == BADVSCREEN)
        return;
    vs = vscreen[vsnum];
    if (vrow1 < 0 || vrow1 > vs->vrow2 || vcol1 < 0 || vcol1 > vs->vcol2)
        return;
    pad = ncols != GIANT;
    if (vcol1 + ncols > vs->vcol2 + 1)
        ncols = vs->vcol2 - vcol1 + 1;
    for (i = 0; i < ncols && str[i] != '\0'; i++) {
        cellp = &vs->ca[vrow1][vcol1 + i];
        cellp->chr = str[i];
        cellp->att = (char)att;
    }
    if (pad && i < ncols)
        repcell(&vs->ca[vrow1][vcol1 + i], ' ', att, ncols - i);
    else
        ncols = i;
    if (vcol1 < vs->vwincol1) {
        ncols -= vs->vwincol1 - vcol1;
        vcol1 = vs->vwincol1;
    }
    Wwrtcells(vs->winnum, vrow1 - vs->vwinrow1, vcol1 - vs->vwincol1,
      &vs->ca[vrow1][vcol1], ncols);
}
```

We clip the **ncols** argument to the boundary of the virtual screen. Then we use a **for** loop to transfer the characters one by one into **CELL**s, stopping when **ncols** characters have been transferred or when we hit the null byte. If the row has to be padded, **repcell** handles it for us. Now we have to write the window. We may have updated the virtual screen starting with a part to the left of the window. In this case we reduce **ncols** appropriately and reset the starting column, **vcol1**, to the starting column of the window. The actual update takes just a single call to **Wwrtcells**.

VSfill uses a similar strategy. For each row to be filled, we'll use **repcell** to update the virtual screen and then call **Wwrtcells** to update the window. Alternatively, we could update the window with just one call, to **Wfill**, but using **Wwrtcells** is probably slightly faster.

```
/*------------------------------------------------------------------
    VSfill - fill rectangle
-------------------------------------------------------------------*/
void VSfill(vsnum, vrectp, chr, att)
int vsnum;                                /* virtual screen */
RECT *vrectp;                             /* rectangle */
char chr;                                 /* fill character */
int att;                                  /* fill attribute */
{
    VSCREEN *vs;
    RECT vrect;
    int vr, wcol1, wcol2;

    if (vsnum == BADVSCREEN)
        return;
    vs = vscreen[vsnum];
    if (!intersect(vrectp, vs->vrow2, vs->vcol2, &vrect))
        return;
    for (vr = vrect.r1; vr <= vrect.r2; vr++) {
        repcell(&vs->ca[vr][vrect.cl], chr, att, RWIDTH(&vrect));
        wcol1 = MAX(0, vrect.cl - vs->vwincol1);
        wcol2 = vrect.c2 - vs->vwincol1;
        Wwrtcells(vs->winnum, vr - vs->vwinrow1, wcol1,
            &vs->ca[vr][vrect.cl], wcol2 - wcol1 + 1);
    }
}
```

Again, as in **VSwrite**, we may have started filling to the left of the window, so we are careful to make sure that **wcol1** isn't negative. Note that in the call to **Wwrtcells**, the column subscript of the **CELL** array is **vrect.cl**. Technically this may not be right, because **wcol1** may be to the right of that point. However, we're *filling*, after all, so every column gets the same treatment, and it doesn't matter where we start, provided we stay within the virtual screen rectangle that got filled. It's also possible that the rectangle on the virtual screen started *above* the window. We didn't bother checking for that, because **Wwrtcells** will return without doing anything if its row argument is negative. The part of the virtual screen rectangle to the right and below the window is also handled naturally by the clipping action of **Wwrtcells**.

Panning a window relative to the virtual screen requires several steps:

1. The window's location relative to the virtual screen has to be changed. For horizontal moves, member **vwinrow1** of the **VSCREEN** structure has to be increased or decreased; for vertical moves, member **vwincol1** has to be adjusted.

2. If the current cursor location is outside of the new window position, the cursor row or column has to be changed appropriately.

3. The contents of the window have to be updated, because the window now shows a different part of the virtual screen. We could redraw the entire window from the **CELL** array but it's worthwhile sliding as much of the old contents into position as we can with **Wslide**. We slide in the opposite direction of the move. This can be done only if the distance

moved is small enough so that there is some overlap between the old and new contents. After sliding what we can, we redraw the rest of the window by calling **redraw** (shown earlier in this section).

Here's the code for **VSpan**. It's a fairly long function because each of the four directions has to be treated separately.

```
/*-------------------------------------------------------------------
     VSpan - move window relative to virtual screen
----------------------------------------------------------------*/
void VSpan(wnum, dir, dist)
int wnum;                             /* window */
int dir;                              /* direction */
int dist;                             /* distance */
{
    VSCREEN *vs;
    RECT srect, wrect;

    vs = vscreen[VSgetvsnum(wnum)];
    Wgetphys(wnum, &srect, FALSE);
    RASG(&wrect, 0, 0, RHEIGHT(&srect) - 1, RWIDTH(&srect) - 1);
    switch (dir) {
    case DIR_UP:
        if ((dist = MIN(dist, vs->vwinrow1)) <= 0)
            return;
        vs->vwinrow1 -= dist;
        vs->vcurrow = MIN(vs->vcurrow, vs->vwinrow1 + wrect.r2);
        if (Wslide(wnum, &wrect, DIR_DOWN, dist))
            wrect.r2 = dist - 1;
        break;
    case DIR_DOWN:
        if ((dist = MIN(dist, vs->vrow2 - wrect.r2 - vs->vwinrow1)) <= 0)
            return;
        vs->vwinrow1 += dist;
        vs->vcurrow = MAX(vs->vcurrow, vs->vwinrow1);
        if (Wslide(wnum, &wrect, DIR_UP, dist))
            wrect.r1 = wrect.r2 + 1 - dist;
        break;
    case DIR_RIGHT:
        if ((dist = MIN(dist, vs->vcol2 - wrect.c2 - vs->vwincol1)) <= 0)
            return;
        vs->vwincol1 += dist;
        vs->vcurcol = MAX(vs->vcurcol, vs->vwincol1);
        if (Wslide(wnum, &wrect, DIR_LEFT, dist))
            wrect.c1 = wrect.c2 + 1 - dist;
        break;
    case DIR_LEFT:
        if ((dist = MIN(dist, vs->vwincol1)) <= 0)
            return;
        vs->vwincol1 -= dist;
        vs->vcurcol = MIN(vs->vcurcol, vs->vwincol1 + RWIDTH(&srect) - 1);
        if (Wslide(wnum, &wrect, DIR_RIGHT, dist))
            wrect.c2 = dist - 1;
    }
    redraw(wnum, &wrect);
    VSsetcur(wtable[wnum], GIANT, GIANT);
}
```

Let's look at what this function does when the move is downward. You should then be able to figure out the other three directions easily. First we want to describe the size of the window in terms of a rectangle relative to it. This makes the subsequent arithmetic on row and column numbers a little simpler. **Wgetphys** gives a rectangle relative to the physical screen, and the **RASG** macro calculates the window-relative rectangle and stores its coordinates in **wrect**. In the **DIR_DOWN** case, if the distance to be moved is greater than the distance from the bottom edge of the window (**wrect.r2 + vs->vsinrow**1) to the bottom edge of the virtual screen (**vs->vrow2**), we reduce it accordingly. If the window is already as far down as it will go, we just return. Then we increment the window's location (**vs->vwinrow**1) by that distance. If the cursor's row is now above the window, we change it to the first row of the window so it will remain visible. Now we try to slide the old contents of the window upward by an amount equal to the distance moved. This amount may be more than the height of the window, but **Wslide** will just return if there's nothing to slide. If **Wslide** is effective (recall that the window module is not required to implement **Wslide**), we relocate the first row of the window-relative rectangle by the distance moved. This defines the rectangle that has to be redrawn by the call to **redraw**, at the end of the **switch** statement. Finally, a call to **VSsetcur** cements the possibly new cursor location. A value of **GIANT** for row and column numbers means that they should be left as they are, but we still have to call **Wsetcur**, which **VSsetcur** does for us.

Now let's look at **VSsetcur**. Its job is easy if the new location is within the window because then it only has to translate the cursor coordinates to window-relative coordinates and make a call to **Wsetcur**. However, if the cursor is to be moved to a location outside of the window, the window has to be moved. This is an important feature. It's what makes virtual screens scroll automatically behind their window as the cursor is moved about by the application or by the user.

If possible, we want to use **VSpan** to move the window because it can slide most of the window's contents (with a call to **Wslide**) rather than redraw it. Remember that **VSsetcur** will often be called to reposition the cursor to a row or column just out of the window. This must be very fast or else the screen editor, spreadsheet, or whatever, will appear to scroll sluggishly, a defect that users pick up on quickly. However, **VSpan** can only be called if the cursor is out of bounds only horizontally or only vertically, since the window can be moved in only one direction at a time. So we break the cases down like this:

1. If the new cursor location is within the window, leave the window alone.

2. If the cursor's row is OK, but its column is too far to the left or right, pan the window to the left or right with **VSpan**. Move it as little as possible, so that the cursor will lie along the left or right edge of the window.

3. Similarly, if the column is OK, but not the row, pan the window up or down.

4. Both the row and column are off. Relocate the window and redraw it completely. Place the window so that the cursor is approximately centered in the window. We could have done this by calling **VSpan** twice (like a chess knight), but that would entail so much computation that redrawing is probably faster. After all, we do have everything we need in the **CELL** array.

After ensuring that the cursor is inside the window, we calculate its window-relative coordinates and call **Wsetcur**. Here's the code:

```
/*-----------------------------------------------------------------
    VSsetcur - set cursor position relative to virtual screen
-----------------------------------------------------------------*/
void VSsetcur(vsnum, vrow, vcol)
int vsnum;                              /* virtual screen */
int vrow;                               /* row */
int vcol;                               /* column */
{
    VSCREEN *vs;
    RECT srect, wrect;
    int wrow, wcol;

    if (vsnum == BADVSCREEN)
        return;
    vs = vscreen[vsnum];
    if (vrow == GIANT)
        vrow = vs->vcurrow;
    if (vcol == GIANT)
        vcol = vs->vcurcol;
    if (vrow < 0 || vrow > vs->vrow2 || vcol < 0 || vcol > vs->vcol2)
        return;
    vs->vcurrow = vrow;
    vs->vcurcol = vcol;
    Wgetphys(vs->winnum, &srect, FALSE);
    if (RHEIGHT(&srect) <= 0 || RWIDTH(&srect) <= 0)
        return;
    if (vrow >= vs->vwinrow1 && vrow < vs->vwinrow1 + RHEIGHT(&srect)) {
        if (vcol < vs->vwincol1)
            VSpan(vs->winnum, DIR_LEFT, vs->vwincol1 - vcol);
        else if (vcol >= vs->vwincol1 + RWIDTH(&srect))
            VSpan(vs->winnum, DIR_RIGHT,
                vcol - (vs->vwincol1 + RWIDTH(&srect)) + 1);
    }
    else if (vcol >= vs->vwincol1 && vcol < vs->vwincol1 + RWIDTH(&srect)) {
        if (vrow < vs->vwinrow1)
            VSpan(vs->winnum, DIR_UP, vs->vwinrow1 - vrow);
        else if (vrow >= vs->vwinrow1 + RHEIGHT(&srect))
            VSpan(vs->winnum, DIR_DOWN,
                vrow - (vs->vwinrow1 + RHEIGHT(&srect)) + 1);
    }
    else {
        vs->vwinrow1 = MAX(0, vrow - RHEIGHT(&srect) / 2);
        vs->vwincol1 = MAX(0, vcol - RWIDTH(&srect) / 2);
        RASG(&wrect, 0, 0, RHEIGHT(&srect), RWIDTH(&srect));
        redraw(vs->winnum, &wrect);
    }
```

```
        wrow = vrow - vs->vwinrow1;
        wcol = vcol - vs->vwincol1;
        Wsetcur(vs->winnum, wrow, wcol);
}
```

The situation in which the cursor is already within the window, so no moving is necessary, is detected in the **else** clause just before the **VSpan** in the direction **DIR_RIGHT**.

The last window function is **VSslide**. This is more complex than **VSpan** because it changes not only the contents of the virtual screen, but the window, too, if the slid rectangle is currently visible. Sliding the virtual screen is exactly like sliding the physical screen in the memory-mapped implementation of the physical screen module (Sec. 3.7.2) because both use the same **CELL** array structure. The window is then updated by calling **Wslide** for part of it, which may or may not be effective, and then redrawing the rest of it. This is the same strategy used in **VSpan**. We'll first show the code for **VSslide** and then make a few comments to help you understand what's going on. As with **VSpan**, each of the four directions is treated separately.

```
/*------------------------------------------------------------------ ------------------
      VSslide - slide rectangle (always succeeds)
---------------------------------------------------------------------*/
void VSslide(vsnum, vrectp, dir, dist)
int vsnum;                              /* virtual screen */
RECT *vrectp;                           /* rectangle */
int dir;                                /* direction */
int dist;                               /* distance */
{
    VSCREEN *vs;
    RECT vrect, srect, wrect;
    int vr, vr1, vr2, vc1, vc2;
    CELL *tmp;

    if (vsnum == BADVSCREEN)
        return;
    vs = vscreen[vsnum];
    if (!intersect(vrectp, vs->vrow2, vs->vcol2, &vrect) || dist <= 0)
        return;
    Wgetphys(vs->winnum, &srect, FALSE);
    switch (dir) {
    case DIR_UP:
        vrect.r1 = MAX(vrect.r1, dist);
        if (vrect.c1 == 0 && vrect.c2 == vs->vcol2) {
            for (vr = vrect.r1; vr <= vrect.r2; vr++) {
                tmp = vs->ca[vr - dist];
                vs->ca[vr - dist] = vs->ca[vr];
                vs->ca[vr] = tmp; /* contents have no significance */
            }
        }
        else
            for (vr = vrect.r1; vr <= vrect.r2; vr++)
                movmem((char *)&vs->ca[vr][vrect.c1],
                    (char *)&vs->ca[vr - dist][vrect.c1],
                        sizeof(CELL) * RWIDTH(&vrect));
        RASG(&wrect, vrect.r1 - vs->vwinrow1, vrect.c1 - vs->vwincol1,
            vrect.r2 - vs->vwinrow1, vrect.c2 - vs->vwincol1);
        if (Wslide(vs->winnum, &wrect, DIR_UP, dist))
            vr1 = MAX(vs->vwinrow1 + RHEIGHT(&srect), vrect.r1) - dist;
```

```
            else
                vr1 = vrect.r1 - dist;
            wrect.r1 = vr1 - vs->vwinrow1;
            wrect.r2 = vrect.r2 - dist - vs->vwinrow1;
            break;
        case DIR_DOWN:
            vrect.r2 = MIN(vrect.r2, vs->vrow2 - dist);
            if (vrect.cl == 0 && vrect.c2 == vs->vcol2) {
                for (vr = vrect.r2; vr >= vrect.r1; vr--) {
                    tmp = vs->ca[vr + dist];
                    vs->ca[vr + dist] = vs->ca[vr];
                    vs->ca[vr] = tmp;
                }
            }
            else
                for (vr = vrect.r2; vr >= vrect.r1; vr--)
                    movmem((char *)&vs->ca[vr][vrect.cl],
                        (char *)&vs->ca[vr + dist][vrect.cl],
                            sizeof(CELL) * (vrect.c2 - vrect.cl + 1));
            RASG(&wrect, vrect.r1 - vs->vwinrow1, vrect.cl - vs->vwincoll,
                vrect.r2 - vs->vwinrow1, vrect.c2 - vs->vwincoll);
            if (Wslide(vs->winnum, &wrect, DIR_DOWN, dist))
                vr2 = MIN(vs->vwinrow1 - 1, vrect.r2) + dist;
            else
                vr2 = vrect.r2 + dist;
            wrect.r1 = vrect.r1 + dist - vs->vwinrow1;
            wrect.r2 = vr2 - vs->vwinrow1;
            break;
        case DIR_LEFT:
            vrect.cl = MAX(vrect.cl, dist);
            for (vr = vrect.r1; vr <= vrect.r2; vr++)
                movmem((char *)&vs->ca[vr][vrect.cl],
                    (char *)&vs->ca[vr][vrect.cl - dist],
                        sizeof(CELL) * (vrect.c2 - vrect.cl + 1));
            RASG(&wrect, vrect.r1 - vs->vwinrow1, vrect.cl - vs->vwincoll,
                vrect.r2 - vs->vwinrow1, vrect.c2 - vs->vwincoll);
            if (Wslide(vs->winnum, &wrect, DIR_LEFT, dist))
                vcl = MAX(vs->vwincoll + RWIDTH(&srect), vrect.cl) - dist;
            else
                vcl = vrect.cl - dist;
            wrect.cl = vcl - vs->vwincoll;
            wrect.c2 = vrect.c2 - dist - vs->vwincoll;
            break;
        case DIR_RIGHT:
            vrect.c2 = MIN(vrect.c2, vs->vcol2 - dist);
            for (vr = vrect.r1; vr <= vrect.r2; vr++)
                movmem((char *)&vs->ca[vr][vrect.cl],
                    (char *)&vs->ca[vr][vrect.cl + dist],
                        sizeof(CELL) * (vrect.c2 - vrect.cl + 1));
            RASG(&wrect, vrect.r1 - vs->vwinrow1, vrect.cl - vs->vwincoll,
                vrect.r2 - vs->vwinrow1, vrect.c2 - vs->vwincoll);
            if (Wslide(vs->winnum, &wrect, DIR_RIGHT, dist))
                vc2 = MIN(vs->vwincoll - 1, vrect.c2) + dist;
            else
                vc2 = vrect.c2 + dist;
            wrect.cl = vrect.cl + dist - vs->vwincoll;
            wrect.c2 = vc2 - vs->vwincoll;
        }
        redraw(vs->winnum, &wrect);
    }
```

If there's no intersection with the rectangle to be slid and the virtual screen, or if the distance is negative, we just return. In these cases the call to **VSslide** is superfluous, but presumably it was easier for the caller to let

VSslide figure that out. We get the physical screen rectangle corresponding to the window with **Wgetphys**, which we'll use later to calculate the height and width of the window. We'll review the **DIR_UP** case in detail; you're on your own for the other three cases, but they should be fathomable.

If the distance above the rectangle is less than the distance to slide it, we increase the first row number appropriately, so that the slide will take it exactly to row 0. Then we distinguish between two situations:

1. *The rectangle covers the full width of the virtual screen.* We can just interchange rows, without moving anything except pointers. Recall from our discussion of **VSnew**, earlier in this section, that the **CELL** array actually is made up of a vector of row pointers that each point to a row of **CELL**s. We must *interchange* row pointers, not just assign a pointer to its new location, or else we might lose a row or end up with two pointers that both point to the same row.

2. *The rectangle is narrower than the virtual screen.* We have to move the *contents* of the partial rows up one by one, using the function **movmem** (see Sec. 2.8). We leave the row pointers alone.

In neither case do we care about the contents of the part vacated by the rectangle that we slid. This correlates with the semantics of sliding in the physical screen and window modules. Once the virtual screen rectangle has been slid into position, it's time to update the window. As with **VSpan**, we could simply redraw the entire window, but it's worthwhile to try to slide a rectangle within the window, if possible. This rectangle is not the same as the virtual screen rectangle—it's given instead by the intersection of the window and the virtual screen rectangle. The **RASG** macro calculates this intersection. As you go through the arithmetic, remember that we want a window-relative rectangle, not a virtual-screen-relative one. Now we try to slide it with **Wslide**. If this works, we reduce the rectangle to the part that was not slid; if it doesn't work, we leave the rectangle alone. Anyway the rectangle that results now has to be redrawn. But the coordinates first have to be translated again so that they are virtual-screen-relative, which is what **redraw** uses. This call is at the end of the **switch** statement, since all four directions use it.

7.6. Summary

This chapter followed the same pattern as the previous one. We first defined virtual screens, which can be larger than the physical screen. Each is viewed through a window. The window pans automatically across the virtual screen as the cursor is moved, or it can be panned explicitly with the function

VSpan. Clipping to the window boundary was handled for us by the window module, and redrawing was automated by keeping track of everything written to the virtual screen. Hence, users of the virtual screen interface need not supply their own redrawing function.

We redid the screen module of the editor of Chapter 5 yet again, this time to use virtual screens. The screen looks the same as the window version of Chapter 6, but the implementation is a little smaller because virtual screens are easier to program for than are windows. A big advantage of the virtual screen version is that it automatically scrolls sideways, so it can edit lines much wider than the physical screen.

If we were to continue upwards with further abstractions, we would use virtual screens to implement alert boxes, drop-down menus, textual prompt boxes, and so on. There's no room left to do that in this book, but Appendix C explains how you can get source code that shows you how it's done.

APPENDIX A

IBM PC BIOS Access Functions

This Appendix contains the source code for the IBM PC Basic I/O System (BIOS) interface, which is used in Chapters 3 and 4. A few functions are included here that aren't used in the programs in this book.

This code works with Lattice C and Microsoft C. To use it with other MS-DOS C compilers, you'll probably have to change the way registers are passed to and received from the BIOS interrupts. The BIOS functions themselves, of course, will remain the same.

One function, **BKavail**, can't be programmed in C with the Microsoft compiler because its **int86** interface function doesn't return the zero flag. I haven't shown the rather trivial assembly language version that substitutes, but it's included with the source code described in Appendix C.

```
#include <dos.h>
#include "display.h"

/*
    Interface to IBM PC BIOS.  Not all functions or features are implemented.
*/

/*
    Video
*/
```

```
#define INT_VIDEO      0x10
#define F_SETMODE      0
#define F_SETCTYPE     1
#define F_SETCPOS      2
#define F_RDCPOS       3
#define F_RDPPOS       4
#define F_SELPAGE      5
#define F_SCLUP        6
#define F_SCLDN        7
#define F_RDAC         8
#define F_WTAC         9
#define F_WTC          10
#define F_SETCLR       11
#define F_WTDOT        12
#define F_RDDOT        13
#define F_WTTTY        14
#define F_CURSTE       15
#define F_WTSTR        19


/*
    Equipment determination
*/
#define INT_EQUIP      0x11
#define MASK_NPRT      3
#define SHFT_NPRT      14
#define MASK_NCOM      7
#define SHFT_NCOM      9
#define MASK_NFLP      3
#define SHFT_NFLP      6
#define MASK_VDEO      3
#define SHFT_VDEO      4
#define MASK_MATH      1
#define SHFT_MATH      1


/*
    Keyboard
*/
#define INT_KBD        0x16
#define F_READ         0
#define F_AVAIL        1
#define F_STATUS       2


/*---------------------------------------------------------------------
    BEequip - determine equipment
              Arguments aren't used if NULL.
---------------------------------------------------------------------*/
void BEequip(nprtp, ncomp, nflpp, ncolp, monop, mathp)
int *nprtp;                             /* number of printer ports */
int *ncomp;                             /* number of serial ports */
int *nflpp;                             /* number of floppy drives */
int *ncolp;                             /* number of display columns */
BOOLEAN *monop;                         /* monochrome (vs. color) display? */
BOOLEAN *mathp;                         /* math coprocessor? */
{
    union REGS inr, outr;

    int86(INT_EQUIP, &inr, &outr);
    if (nprtp != NULL)
        *nprtp = (outr.x.ax >> SHFT_NPRT) & MASK_NPRT;
    if (ncomp != NULL)
        *ncomp = (outr.x.ax >> SHFT_NCOM) & MASK_NCOM;
    if (nflpp != NULL)
        *nflpp = ((outr.x.ax >> SHFT_NFLP) & MASK_NFLP) + 1;
```

```
        switch ((outr.x.ax >> SHFT_VDEO) & MASK_VDEO) {
        case 1:
            if (ncolp != NULL)
                *ncolp = 40;
            if (monop != NULL)
                *monop = FALSE;
            break;
        case 2:
            if (ncolp != NULL)
                *ncolp = 80;
            if (monop != NULL)
                *monop = FALSE;
            break;
        case 3:
            if (ncolp != NULL)
                *ncolp = 80;
            if (monop != NULL)
                *monop = TRUE;
        }
        if (mathp != NULL)
            *mathp = (BOOLEAN)((outr.x.ax >> SHFT_MATH) & MASK_MATH);
    }


/*-------------------------------------------------------------------------
    BVsetmode - set video mode
        CGA modes:
            0    40 x 25 BW
            1    40 x 25 color
            2    80 x 25 BW
            3    80 x 25 color
            4    320 x 200 color
            5    320 x 200 BW
            6    640 x 200 BW
        MDA mode:
            7    80 x 25
        (EGA card defines more)
-------------------------------------------------------------------------*/
void BVsetmode(mode)
int mode;                                    /* mode */
{
    union REGS inr, outr;

    inr.h.ah = F_SETMODE;
    inr.h.al = (unsigned char)mode;
    int86(INT_VIDEO, &inr, &outr);
}

/*-------------------------------------------------------------------------
    BVgetstate - get current video state
                 Arguments aren't used if NULL.
-------------------------------------------------------------------------*/
void BVgetstate(modep, numcolsp, pagep)
int *modep;                                  /* returned mode */
int *numcolsp;                               /* returned number of columns */
int *pagep;                                  /* returned page */
{
    union REGS inr, outr;

    inr.h.ah = F_CURSTE;
    int86(INT_VIDEO, &inr, &outr);
    if (modep != NULL)
        *modep = outr.h.al;
    if (numcolsp != NULL)
        *numcolsp = outr.h.ah;
```

```
    if (pagep != NULL)
        *pagep = outr.h.bh;
}


/*------------------------------------------------------------------
    BVsetctype - set cursor type
-------------------------------------------------------------------*/
void BVsetctype(startline, endline)
int startline;                          /* starting scan line */
int endline;                            /* ending scan line */
{
    union REGS inr, outr;

    inr.h.ah = F_SETCTYPE;
    inr.h.ch = (unsigned char)startline;
    inr.h.cl = (unsigned char)endline;
    int86(INT_VIDEO, &inr, &outr);
}


/*------------------------------------------------------------------
    BVsetcpos - set cursor position
-------------------------------------------------------------------*/
void BVsetcpos(row, col)
int row;                                /* row */
int col;                                /* column */
{
    union REGS inr, outr;

    inr.h.ah = F_SETCPOS;
    inr.h.dh = (unsigned char)row;
    inr.h.dl = (unsigned char)col;
    inr.h.bh = 0;
    int86(INT_VIDEO, &inr, &outr);
}


/*------------------------------------------------------------------
    BVrdcpos - read cursor position
-------------------------------------------------------------------*/
void BVrdcpos(rowp, colp, startlinep, endlinep)
int *rowp;                              /* row */
int *colp;                              /* column */
int *startlinep;                        /* starting scan line */
int *endlinep;                          /* ending scan line */
{
    union REGS inr, outr;
    BOOLEAN mono;

    inr.h.ah = F_RDCPOS;
    inr.h.bh = 0;
    int86(INT_VIDEO, &inr, &outr);
    *rowp = outr.h.dh;
    *colp = outr.h.dl;
    *startlinep = outr.h.ch;
    *endlinep = outr.h.cl;
    /* bug in BIOS - cursor scan lines sometimes reported wrong */
    if (*startlinep == 6 && *endlinep == 7) {
        BEequip(NULL, NULL, NULL, NULL, &mono, NULL);
        if (mono) {
            *startlinep = 11;
            *endlinep = 12;
        }
    }
}
```

```
/*-------------------------------------------------------------------
      BVselpage - select active display page
--------------------------------------------------------------------*/
void BVselpage(page)
int page;                                    /* page number */
{
    union REGS inr, outr;

    inr.h.ah = F_SELPAGE;
    inr.h.al = (unsigned char)page;
    int86(INT_VIDEO, &inr, &outr);
}

/*----------------------------------- -------------------------------
      BVsclup - scroll up
--------------------------------------------------------------------*/
void BVsclup(amt, row1, col1, row2, col2)
int amt;                                      /* number of rows to scroll */
int row1;                                     /* top row */
int col1;                                     /* left column */
int row2;                                     /* bottom row */
int col2;                                     /* right column */
{
    union REGS inr, outr;

    inr.h.ah = F_SCLUP;
    inr.h.al = (unsigned char)amt;
    inr.h.ch = (unsigned char)row1;
    inr.h.cl = (unsigned char)col1;
    inr.h.dh = (unsigned char)row2;
    inr.h.dl = (unsigned char)col2;
    inr.h.bh = A_NORM;
    int86(INT_VIDEO, &inr, &outr);
}

/*-------------------------------------------------------------------
      BVscldn - scroll down
--------------------------------------------------------------------*/
void BVscldn(amt, row1, col1, row2, col2)
int amt;                                      /* number of rows to scroll */
int row1;                                     /* top row */
int col1;                                     /* left column */
int row2;                                     /* bottom row */
int col2;                                     /* right column */
{
    union REGS inr, outr;

    inr.h.ah = F_SCLDN;
    inr.h.al = (unsigned char)amt;
    inr.h.ch = (unsigned char)row1;
    inr.h.cl = (unsigned char)col1;
    inr.h.dh = (unsigned char)row2;
    inr.h.dl = (unsigned char)col2;
    inr.h.bh = A_NORM;
    int86(INT_VIDEO, &inr, &outr);
}

/*-------------------------------------------------------------------
      BVwtac - write attribute and character
--------------------------------------------------------------------*/
void BVwtac(amt, chr, att)
int amt;                                      /* number of characters to write */
char chr;                                     /* character to write */
int att;                                      /* attribute */
{
    union REGS inr, outr;
```

```
        inr.h.ah = F_WTAC;
        inr.h.al = (unsigned char)chr;
        inr.h.bh = 0;
        inr.h.bl = (unsigned char)att;
        inr.x.cx = (unsigned)amt;
        int86(INT_VIDEO, &inr, &outr);
    }

/*------------------------------------------------------------------
    BVsetbdr - set color border
--------------------------------------------------------------------*/
void BVsetbdr(att)
int att;                                /* attribute */
{
    union REGS inr, outr;

    inr.h.ah = F_SETCLR;
    inr.h.bh = 0;
    inr.h.bl = (unsigned char)att;
    int86(INT_VIDEO, &inr, &outr);
}

/*------------------------------------------------------------------
    BVwttty - write teletype
--------------------------------------------------------------------*/
void BVwttty(chr)
char chr;                               /* character to write */
{
    union REGS inr, outr;

    inr.h.ah = F_WTTTY;
    inr.h.al = (unsigned char)chr;
    inr.h.bl = A_NORM;
    int86(INT_VIDEO, &inr, &outr);
}

/*------------------------------------------------------------------
    BKread - read keyboard character and scan code
    RETURN: Character read.
--------------------------------------------------------------------*/
int BKread(scanp)
int *scanp;                             /* scan code */
{
    union REGS inr, outr;

    inr.h.ah = F_READ;
    int86(INT_KBD, &inr, &outr);
    if (outr.h.ah == 55 || outr.h.ah == 74 || outr.h.ah == 78)
        outr.h.al = 0; /* make numeric pad *, -, and +
                          available as function keys */
    *scanp = outr.h.ah;
    return((int)outr.h.al);
}

#ifdef LATTICE
/*------------------------------------------------------------------
    BKavail - determine if keyboard character is available
    RETURN: Is it?
--------------------------------------------------------------------*/
BOOLEAN BKavail()
{
    union REGS inr, outr;

    inr.h.ah = F_AVAIL;
    return((BOOLEAN)((int86(INT_KBD, &inr, &outr) & 0x40) == 0));
                                        /* testing zero flag */
}
```

```
#else
/*
    Microsoft C's int86() doesn't return the flags -- use assembler routine
    instead.
*/
#endif

/*------------------------------------------------------------------
    BKstatus - get keyboard shift status
    RETURN: Status bits:
                    0:   right shift
                    1:   left shift
                    2:   control
                    3:   alt
                    4:   scroll lock
                    5:   num lock
                    6:   caps lock
                    7:   ins
------------------------------------------------------------------*/
int BKstatus()
{
    union REGS inr, outr;

    inr.h.ah = F_STATUS;
    int86(INT_KBD, &inr, &outr);
    return((int)outr.h.al);
}
```

APPENDIX B

IBM PC Screen Access Functions

This Appendix contains Intel 8086 assembly language code for several functions referenced in Chapter 3: **wrtscrn**, **wrtstr**, and **wrtcell**. There's also a function to read the screen, **rdscrn**, which isn't referenced in the main text.

These functions interface with Lattice C and Microsoft C, using the large model only. The techniques used, however, are compiler-independent, and the changes for other C compilers are fairly straightforward.

File **wrtscrn.asm**:

```
; This file contains functions to copy all or part of a 4000-byte screen
; buffer to or from display memory, without snow.
;
; If speedy flag is 1, copy is done as fast as possible. This may produce
; snow on a color monitor. By default, the flag is 0.
;
; This routine uses the BIOS video mode to automatically distinguish
; between monochrome and color controllers.
;
; Set the constant SLOWMONO to 1 if you want to slow down the display so
; you can test the responsiveness of your display algorithms (the AT runs
; so fast it may hide inefficiencies that show up on a slower computer).
;
; Usage:
;
;     extern int speedy;
;
```

```
;     /*-------------------------------------------------------------
;          wrtscrn - update IBM PC display memory
;     --------------------------------------------------------------*/
;     void wrtscrn(srcptr, start, nwords)
;     char *srcptr;              /* pointer to 4000-byte screen buffer */
;     int start;                 /* offset into buffer, display memory */
;     int nwords;                /* number of WORDS to write */
;
;     /*-------------------------------------------------------------
;          rdscrn - read display memory (always reads whole screen)
;     --------------------------------------------------------------*/
;     void rdscrn(dstptr)
;     char *dstptr;              /* pointer to 4000-byte screen buffer */
;
; For LARGE model only.
;
; This routine (especially the color part) is based on code written by
; Augie Hansen of Omniware.
;
; The only difference between wrtscrn and rdscrn is how the source and
; destination pointers are set up for the move instructions.  The flag
; "reading" is set to 1 by rdscrn and then set back to 0.
;

ifdef LATTICE
include LM8086.MAC
endif

SLOWMONO equ    0
SRC_PTR  equ    6
START    equ    10
NWORDS   equ    12
MONODSP  equ    0b000h              ; monochrome display memory
COLRDSP  equ    0b800h              ; color display memory
VSTAT    equ    3dah                ; video (CRT) status register
HRTRCE   equ    1                   ; horizontal retrace bit mask
VRTRCE   equ    8                   ; vertical retrace bit mask
         IF     SLOWMONO
WRDCNT1 equ 2
WRDCNT2 equ 2
         ELSE
WRDCNT1 equ     240                 ; no. of words to copy during vert. retrace
WRDCNT2 equ     94                  ; no. of words to copy during horz. retrace
         ENDIF

ifdef LATTICE
        dseg
        public  speedy
speedy  dw      0                   ; 1 => don't wait for retrace
endif
ifdef MICROSOFT
DGROUP  group   _DATA
_DATA   segment word public 'DATA'
        assume  ds:DGROUP
        public  _speedy
_speedy dw      0                   ; 1 => don't wait for retrace
endif
reading dw      0                   ; 1 => rdscrn (as opposed to wrtscrn)
dspmem  dw      0                   ; display memory segment address
ifdef LATTICE
        endds
endif
ifdef MICROSOFT
_DATA   ends
endif
```

```
        ifdef   LATTICE
                pseg
                public  wrtscrn, rdscrn
wrtscrn proc    far
        endif
        ifdef   MICROSOFT
WRTSCRN_TEXT segment byte public 'CODE'
                assume  cs:WRTSCRN_TEXT
                public  _wrtscrn, _rdscrn
_wrtscrn proc   far
        endif
                push    bp
                mov     bp,sp
                push    si
                push    di
                push    ds
                push    es
                pushf

; Set up display memory address first time only.

                cmp     dspmem,0        ; first time through?
                jne     gotdsp          ; no - already got address
                mov     ah,0fh          ; get current video mode fcn
                int     10h             ; go to BIOS video services
                cmp     al,7            ; monochrome?
                je      mono            ; yes
                mov     dspmem,COLRDSP  ; color display
                jmp     gotdsp
mono:
                mov     dspmem,MONODSP  ; monochrome display

; Here on every call.

gotdsp:
                cmp     dspmem,MONODSP  ; monochrome?
                jne     color           ; no
                mov     dx,1            ; yes - update must always be speedy
                IF      SLOWMONO
                mov     dx,0            ; color algorithm, but without retrace waits
                ENDIF
                jmp     movsetup
color:
        ifdef   LATTICE
                mov     dx,speedy       ; follow caller's wishes
        endif
        ifdef   MICROSOFT
                mov     dx,_speedy      ; follow caller's wishes
        endif
movsetup:
                cld                     ; set up for auto increment
                cmp     reading,1       ; are we reading?
                je      read            ; yes - reverse the directions
                mov     es,dspmem       ; dest. pointer into es and di
                mov     di,[bp + START] ; offset it by start arg
                lds     si,dword ptr ss:[bp + SRC_PTR] ; source pointer into ds, si
                add     si,[bp + START] ; offset it by start arg
                mov     bx,[bp + NWORDS]; set up count
                jmp     speedck
read:
                mov     ds,dspmem       ; source pointer into ds and si
                mov     si,0
                les     di,dword ptr ss:[bp+SRC_PTR] ; dest. pointer into es and di
                mov     bx,2000         ; set up count
```

```
; If speedy update, update screen with a single move.

speedck:
        cmp     dx,0            ; speedy?
        je      copy_blk        ; no - do it a little at a time

; Move data all at once.

        mov     cx,bx           ; get count
        rep movsw               ; move a block of char/attr words
        jmp     done            ; that's all!

; Move data slowly, only during horizontal and vertical retrace periods.
; The buffer is copied to the display memory in blocks.  Each block
; is copied in two parts.  First, a chunk of words (character and
; attribute) is copied during the vertical retrace period, and then
; individual words are copied during the horizontal retrace periods
; of the normal screen update period.

copy_blk:
        mov     cx,WRDCNT1      ; number of words to copy
        cmp     bx,cx           ; are fewer than that remaining?
        jge     decr1           ; no - move that much
        mov     cx,bx           ; yes - use smaller count
decr1:
        sub     bx,cx           ; reduce count of remaining words
        mov     dx,VSTAT        ; c/g adapter status register
wait_v_refresh:
        IF      SLOWMONO
        jmp     move1
        ENDIF
        in      al,dx           ; read status
        test    al,VRTRCE       ; test vertical retrace bit
        jnz     wait_v_refresh  ; loop until in a refresh period
wait_v_retrace:
        in      al,dx           ; read status
        test    al,VRTRCE       ; test vertical retrace bit
        jz      wait_v_retrace  ; loop until retrace starts

move1:
        rep movsw               ; move a block of char/attr words

; Check if all words have been moved

        cmp     bx,0            ; are we done?
        je      done            ; yes, we are

; Copy single bytes during horizontal retrace periods.

        mov     cx,WRDCNT2      ; number of words to copy
        cmp     bx,cx           ; are fewer than that remaining?
        jge     decr2           ; no - move that much
        mov     cx,bx           ; yes - use smaller count
decr2:
        sub     bx,cx           ; reduce count of remaining words
        shl     cx,1            ; we're actually moving bytes, not words
        mov     dx,VSTAT        ; read c/g adapter status register
wait_h_refresh:
        IF      SLOWMONO
        jmp     move2
        ENDIF
```

```
              in       al,dx
              test     al,HRTRCE     ; test horizontal retrace bit
              jnz      wait_h_refresh ; loop until not in a retrace period
              cli                    ; can't tolerate an interrupt here
      wait_h_retrace:
              in       al,dx
              test     al,HRTRCE     ; test horizontal retrace bit
              jz       wait_h_retrace ; loop until retrace starts
      move2:
              movsb                  ; copy a single byte!
              sti
              loop     wait_h_refresh
              IF       SLOWMONO
              mov      cx,500        ; delay a while
      goofoff:
              dec      cx
              cmp      cx,0
              jne      goofoff
              ENDIF

      ; Check if all words have been moved

              cmp      bx,0          ; are we done?
              jne      short copy_blk ; no - do it again
      ; Clean up and return to caller.

      done:
              popf                   ; restore flags...
              pop      es            ; ...and registers
              pop      ds
              cld
              pop      di
              pop      si
              pop      bp
              mov      reading,0     ; set flag for writing
              ret

      ifdef LATTICE
      wrtscrn endp
      endif
      ifdef MICROSOFT
      _wrtscrn endp
      endif

      ; rdscrn enters here

      ifdef LATTICE
      rdscrn  proc     far
      endif
      ifdef MICROSOFT
      _rdscrn proc     far
      endif
              mov      reading,1     ; set up for reading
      ifdef LATTICE
              jmp      wrtscrn       ; now be like wrtscrn
      rdscrn  endp
      endif
      ifdef MICROSOFT
              jmp      _wrtscrn      ; now be like wrtscrn
      _rdscrn endp
      endif
```

```
ifdef LATTICE
        endps
endif
ifdef MICROSOFT
WRTSCRN_TEXT ends
endif
        end
```

File **wrtcell.asm**:

```
;   /*-------------------------------------------------------------------
;       wrtstr - write string
;       -------------------------------------------------------------*/
;   void wrtstr(row, col, str, ncols, att)
;   int row;                                 /* starting row */
;   int col;                                 /* starting column */
;   char *str;                               /* string to write */
;   int ncols;                               /* number of columns to write */
;   int att;                                 /* attribute */
;
;   /*-------------------------------------------------------------------
;       wrtcell - write vector of CELLs
;       -------------------------------------------------------------*/
;   void wrtcell(row, col, cellptr, ncols)
;   int row;                                 /* starting row */
;   int col;                                 /* starting column */
;   CELL *cellptr;                           /* vector to write */
;   int ncols;                               /* number of columns to write */
;
; For LARGE model only.

ifdef LATTICE
include LM8086.MAC
endif

row     equ     6                   ; stack offset of row arg
col     equ     8                   ; col arg
cellptr equ     10                  ; cellptr arg (4 bytes)
str     equ     10                  ; str arg (4 bytes)
ncols   equ     14                  ; ncols arg
att     equ     16                  ; att arg

ifdef LATTICE
        dseg
endif
ifdef MICROSOFT
DGROUP  group   _DATA
_DATA   segment word public 'DATA'
        assume  ds:DGROUP
endif

ifdef LATTICE
        endds
endif
ifdef MICROSOFT
_DATA   ends
endif

 ifdef LATTICE
        pseg
```

```
            public  wrtcell, wrtstr
wrtcell proc    far
endif
ifdef MICROSOFT
WRTCELL_TEXT segment byte public 'CODE'
        assume cs:WRTCELL_TEXT
        public  _wrtcell, _wrtstr
_wrtcell proc   far
endif
        push    bp
        mov     bp,sp
        push    si
        push    di

;   Get arguments.

        mov     dh,[bp + row]        ; dh = row
        mov     dl,[bp + col]        ; dl = col
        mov     di,[bp + ncols]      ; di = ncols
        les     si,dword ptr ss:[bp + cellptr]  ; es, si = cellptr

;   Set up invariant parameters.

        sub     bh,bh                ; active page is zero
        mov     cx,1                 ; character count is one

;   Test for remaining characters.

next:
        cmp     di,0
        je      done                 ; done when di == 0

;   Output one character.

        mov     ah,2                 ; set cursor position
        int     10h                  ; video interrupt
        mov     al,es:[si]           ; get character from cell
        mov     bl,es:[si+1]         ; get attribute
        mov     ah,9                 ; write attr/char
        int     10h                  ; video interrupt

;   Increment for next iteration.

        dec     di
        inc     si
        inc     si
        inc     dl
        jmp     next

;   Here when all done.

done:
        cld
        pop     di
        pop     si
        pop     bp
        ret

ifdef LATTICE
wrtcell endp
endif
```

```
        ifdef MICROSOFT
        _wrtcell endp
        endif

        ifdef LATTICE
        wrtstr proc     far
        endif
        ifdef MICROSOFT
        _wrtstr proc    far
        endif
                push    bp
                mov     bp,sp
                push    si
                push    di

;   Get arguments.

                mov     dh,[bp + row]        ; dh = row
                mov     dl,[bp + col]        ; dl = col
                mov     di,[bp + ncols]      ; di = ncols
                mov     bl,[bp + att]        ; bl = att
                les     si,dword ptr ss:[bp + str]  ; es, si = str

;   Set up invariant parameters.

                sub     bh,bh                ; active page is zero
                mov     cx,1                 ; character count is one

;   Test for remaining characters.

        next2:
                cmp     di,0
                je      done2                ; done when di == 0

;   Output one character.

                mov     ah,2                 ; set cursor position
                int     10h                  ; video interrupt
                mov     al,es:[si]           ; get character from cell
                mov     ah,9                 ; write attr/char
                int     10h                  ; video interrupt

;   Increment for next iteration.

                dec     di
                inc     si
                inc     dl
                jmp     next2

;   Here when all done.

        done2:
                cld
                pop     di
                pop     si
                pop     bp
                ret

        ifdef LATTICE
        wrtstr endp
        endif
        ifdef MICROSOFT
        _wrtstr endp
        endif


        ifdef LATTICE
                endps
```

```
endif
ifdef MICROSOFT
WRTCELL_TEXT ends
endif
        end
```

APPENDIX C

Contents of Source Files

This Appendix lists the contents of the source files that contain the major display and keyboard modules. Files containing example programs are not listed. Only external functions, macros, constants, variables, and types in each file are enumerated; static functions and variables are omitted.

All source files, including the example programs, are available in computer-readable form (about 9000 lines of code). A user interface toolkit that uses virtual screens and keyboards is also available. For ordering information, write to:

> Advanced Programming Institute, Ltd.
> Box 17665
> Boulder, CO 80308

C.1. Display Utilities Module (Chap. 2)

File display.h:

> Typedef **BOOLEAN**; constants **TRUE** and **FALSE**
> Macros **MIN** and **MAX**

Constants **DIR_UP**, **DIR_DOWN**, etc.
Typedefs **CELL** and **RECT**
Constant **GIANT**; variable **GIANT_RECT**
Macros **RWIDTH**, **RHEIGHT**, **RASG**, and **RCPY**
Constants **C_UL**, **C_UR**, etc.
Constants **A_NORM**, **A_INVERSE**, etc.

File dsputil.h:

Declarations for **dsputil.c**

File dsputil.c:

Function **enclosing**—rectangle enclosing 2 rectangles
Function **intersect**—intersection between 2 rectangles
Function **strrep**—build string from repeated character
Function **strtok**—get next token (UNIX compatible)
Function **xmalloc**—allocate zeroed memory; terminate on error

C.2. Portability Module (Chap. 2)

File port.h:

Constants **OLDC**, **UNIX**, and **OLDTTY**
Declarations for **port.c**

File port.c:

Function **cget**—get a character from keyboard
Function **cready**—see if keyboard character is ready, without returning it
Function **movmem**—move block of memory
Function **repmem**—replicate values through memory
Function **setmem**—set memory to character value
Function **setraw**—put terminal into raw mode
Function **syserr**—print system-call error-message and terminate
Function **unsetraw**—restore terminal flags

C.3. IBM PC BIOS Interface Module (Chap. 3 and Appendix A)

File bios.c:

Function **BEequip**—determine equipment
Function **BKavail**—determine if keyboard character is available
Function **BKread**—read keyboard character and scan code
Function **BKstatus**—get keyboard shift status
Function **BVgetstate**—get current video state
Function **BVrdcpos**—read cursor position
Function **BVscldn**—scroll down
Function **BVsclup**—scroll up
Function **BVselpage**—select active display page
Function **BVsetbdr**—set color border
Function **BVsetcpos**—set cursor position
Function **BVsetctype**—set cursor type
Function **BVsetmode**—set video mode
Function **BVwtac**—write attribute and character
Function **BVwttty**—write teletype

File bkavail.asm:

Function **BKavail,** Microsoft version

C.4. IBM PC Screen Access Module (Chap. 3 and Appendix B)

File wrtscrn.asm:

Function **rdscrn**—read display memory
Function **wrtscrn**—update IBM PC display memory

File wrtcell.asm:

Function **wrtcell**—write vector of **CELL**s
Function **wrtstr**—write string

C.5. Physical Screen Module (Chap. 3)

File pscreen.h:

Declarations for **ps_z19.c, ps_termc.c**, etc.

File ps_z19.c:

Function **PSbeep**—sound bell
Function **PSbegin**—initialize display
Function **PSend**—terminate display
Function **PSfill**—fill a rectangle
Function **PSheight**—get height of physical screen
Function **PSsetcur**—set cursor position
Function **PSshowcur**—turn cursor on or off
Function **PSslide**—slide a rectangle
Function **PSsynch**—bring screen up to date
Function **PSwidth**—get width of physical screen
Function **PSwrite**—write string
Function **PSwrtcells**—write vector of **CELLs**

File ps_termc.c:

Same functions as **ps_z19.c**

File ps_curse.c:

Same functions as **ps_z19.c**

File ps_bios.c:

Same functions as **ps_z19.c**

File ps_mm.c:

Same functions as **ps_z19.c**

C.6. Keyboard Module (Chap. 4)

File **keycode.h**:

Constants **K_UP**, **K_HOME**, etc.

File **keyboard.h**:

Declarations for **keyboard.c**

File **keyboard.c**:

Function **Kbegin**—initialize keyboard
Function **Kend**—terminate keyboard
Function **Kget**—get keyboard code
Function **Kready**—check if keyboard code is ready
Function **Ksynch**—update display if keyboard isn't ready

File **kc_real.c**:

Function **keycode**—get key code

File **kc_gnrc.c**:

Same function as **kc_real.c**

File **kc_ibmpc.c**:

Same function as **kc_real.c**

File **kc_table.c**:

Same function as **kc_real.c**

C.7. Screen Editor Modules (Chap. 5)

File **edit.h**:

Constants **HIGHASCII**, **MAXBUF**, and **MAXLINE**
Declaration for **edit.c**

File edit.c:

Function **EMtext**—get text corresponding to row

File edio.h:

Declarations for **edio.c**

File edio.c:

Function **EIOreadf**—read file into buffer
Function **EIOwritef**—write buffer to file

File edtext.h:

Declarations for **edtext.c**

File edtext.c:

Function **ETappend**—append new line of text to end of buffer
Function **ETbegin**—initialize text buffers
Function **ETchanged**—determine if buffer has changed since last write
Function **ETclear**—clear out buffer completely
Function **ETdelchar**—delete character from line
Function **ETdelline**—delete line of text from buffer memory
Function **ETend**—terminate text buffers
Function **ETinschar**—insert character into line
Function **ETinsline**—insert fresh line into buffer memory
Function **ETlen**—get length of line
Function **ETnumlines**—get number of lines in buffer
Function **ETreplace**—replace line of text with new text
Function **ETtext**—get line of text
Function **ETunchanged**—turn off buffer's **changed** flag

File edscr.h:

Declarations for **edscr.c**

File edscr.c (includes physical screen, window, and virtual screen implementations):

Function **ESbegin**—initialize screen module

Function **ESclear**—clear text area

Function **ESdelchar**—delete character from row of text

Function **ESdelrow**—delete row from text area

Function **ESend**—terminate screen module

Function **ESheight**—get height of area where editor can show text

Function **EShelpfinish**—clear help display and restore screen

Function **EShelpstart**—prepare screen for help display

Function **EShelpwrite**—write one line of help text

Function **ESinschar**—insert character into row of text

Function **ESinsrow**—insert blank row into text area

Function **ESmsg**—display short message

Function **ESmsg2**—display message, concatenating two strings

Function **ESprompt**—prompt user to type in response

Function **ESscrldown**—scroll text area down one row

Function **ESscrlup**—scroll text area up one row

Function **ESsetcur**—set cursor position

Function **ESshowall**—show all rows that are visible

Function **ESshowcur**—turn cursor on or off

Function **ESshowrow**—show text for row, starting at specified column

Function **ESswitch**—switch to buffer

Function **ESview**—toggle between big and small windows

Function **ESwidth**—get width of area where editor can show text

C.8. Window Module (Chap. 6)

File **window.h**:

Constant **MAXWIND**

Constants **F_UNFRAMED**, **F_AUTO**, etc.

Declarations for **window.c**

File **window.c**:

Function **Wbegin**—initialize window module

Function **Wdispose**—eliminate window

Function **Wend**—terminate window module

Function **Wfill**—fill rectangle
Function **Wgetphys**—get window's physical size
Function **Wgettop**—get top window
Function **Whide**—hide window
Function **Wiszoomed**—determine if window is zoomed
Function **Wnew**—create new window
Function **Wsetcur**—set cursor position
Function **Wsetfrm**—set window's frame appearance
Function **Wsetphys**—set window's physical size
Function **Wshowcur**—turn cursor on or off
Function **Wshuffle**—force next window to top
Function **Wslide**—slide rectangle
Function **Wtop**—force window to top
Function **Wunzoom**—restore window to former size
Function **Wwrite**—write string
Function **Wwrtcells**—write vector of **CELL**s
Function **Wzoom**—make window full screen

C.9. Virtual Screen Module (Chap. 7)

File vscreen.h:

Declarations for **vscreen.c**

File vscreen.c:

Function **VSbegin**—initialize virtual screen module
Function **VSdispose**—eliminate virtual screen and window
Function **VSend**—terminate virtual screen module
Function **VSfill**—fill rectangle
Function **VSgetcur**—get cursor position relative to virtual screen
Function **VSgetsize**—get size of virtual screen
Function **VSgetvsnum**—get window's virtual screen number
Function **VSgetwloc**—get window's location relative to virtual screen
Function **VSgetwnum**—get virtual screen's window number
Function **VSnew**—create virtual screen

Function **VSpan**—move window relative to virtual screen
Function **VSsetcur**—set cursor position relative to virtual screen
Function **VSshowcur**—turn cursor on or off
Function **VSslide**—slide rectangle (always succeeds)
Function **VSwrite**—write string

BIBLIOGRAPHY

[ARN] Arnold, Ken. *Screen Updating and Cursor Movement Optimization: A Library Package*. Electrical Engineering and Computer Sciences Department, University of California at Berkeley. ND. Usually reprinted and included in documentation that accompanies a UNIX system.

[ART85] Artwick, Bruce A. *Microcomputer Displays, Graphics, and Animation*. Englewood Cliffs, NJ: Prentice-Hall, 1985. Also published as *Applied Concepts in Microcomputer Graphics*.

[CGI85] *Computer Graphics Virtual Device Interface*. Document X3H3/85–47, X3 Secretariat. CBEMA, 311 First St., NW, Suite 500, Wash., D. C. 20001, 1985.

[DUN86] Duncan, Ray. *Advanced MS–DOS*. Redmond, WA: Microsoft Press, 1986.

[HAN86] Hansen, Augie. "Instant Screens." *PC Tech Journal*. Vol. 4, No. 6, June 1986, pp. 96–107.

[HOP83] Hopgood, F, R, A.; Duce, D. A.; Gallop, J. R.; and Sutcliffe, D. C. *Introduction to the Graphical Kernel System (GKS)*. London: Academic Press, 1983.

[IBM84] *Technical Reference, Personal Computer AT (1502494)*. IBM Corp., 1984. (The Technical Reference for the PC or the PCjr will do as well. The assembly language listing of the BIOS is the important part.)

[KER78] Kernighan, Brian W., and Ritchie, Dennis M. *The C Programming Language*. Englewood Cliffs, NJ: Prentice-Hall, 1978.

[LAT86] Lattice C Compiler, Lattice, Inc., Box 3072, Glen Ellyn, IL 60138.

[MIC86] Microsoft C Compiler, Microsoft Corporation, 16011 NE 36th Way, Redmond, WA 98073.

[NEW79]   Newman, William M., and Sproull, Robert F. *Principles of Interactive Computer Graphics, Second Edition.* New York: McGraw-Hill Book Company, 1979.

[NOR85]   Norton, Peter. *The Peter Norton Programmer's Guide to the IBM PC.* Bellevue, WA: Microsoft Press, 1985.

[PIK83]   Pike, Rob. "Graphics in Overlapping Bitmap Layers." *ACM Transactions on Graphics.* Vol. 2, No. 2, April 1983, pp. 135–160.

[ROC85]   Rochkind, Marc J. *Advanced UNIX Programming.* Englewood Cliffs, NJ: Prentice-Hall, 1985.

Index

Announcing. . . .

The Annual Prentice Hall Professional/Technical/Reference Catalog: Books For Computer Scientists, Computer/Electrical Engineers and Electronic Technicians

- Prentice Hall, the leading publisher of Professional/Technical/Reference books in the world, is pleased to make its vast selection of titles in computer science, computer/electrical engineering and electronic technology more accessible to all professionals in these fields through the publication of this new catalog!

- If your business or research depends on timely, state-of-the-art information, The Annual Prentice Hall Professional/Technical/Reference Catalog: Books For Computer Scientists, Computer/Electrical Engineers and Electronic Technicians was designed especially for you! Titles appearing in this catalog will be grouped according to interest areas. Each entry will include: title, author, author affiliations, title description, table of contents, title code, page count and copyright year.

- In addition, this catalog will also include advertisements of new products and services from other companies in key high tech areas.

SPECIAL OFFER!

- Order your copy of The Annual Prentice Hall Professional/Technical/Reference Catalog: Books For Computer Scientists, Computer/Electrical Engineers and Electronic Technicians for only $2.00 and receive $5.00 off the purchase of your first book from this catalog. In addition, this catalog entitles you to special discounts on Prentice Hall titles in computer science, computer/electrical engineering and electronic technology.

Please send me _____ copies of The Annual Prentice Hall Professional/Technical/Reference Catalog (title code: 62280–3)

SAVE!

If payment accompanies order, plus your state's sales tax where applicable, Prentice Hall pays postage and handling charges. Same return privilege refund guaranteed. Please do not mail cash.

- ☐ PAYMENT ENCLOSED—shipping and handling to be paid by publisher (please include your state's tax where applicable).
- ☐ BILL ME for The Annual Prentice Hall Professional/Technical/Reference Catalog (with small charge for shipping and handling).

Mail your order to: Prentice Hall, Book Distribution Center,
Route 59 at Brook Hill Drive,
West Nyack, N.Y. 10994

Name _____

Address _____

City _____ State _____ Zip _____

I prefer to charge my ☐ Visa   ☐ MasterCard

Card Number _____ Expiration Date _____

Signature _____

Offer not valid outside the United States.

Dept. 1

D-PPTR-CS(9)